A Hitchhiker's Journey Through Climat
MW01416487

A Hitchhiker's Journey Through Climate Change

All you need to know about climate change,

but were afraid to learn and laugh at.

Terigi Ciccone

With Jay Lehr, Ph.D.

Copyright © 2020
All Rights Reserved

ISBN: 9798637194773

Dedication

This book is written for the youth of Generation Z and the Millennials and the parents and grandparents who love their children and grandchildren and want them to have a glorious future.

We are going on a freelance journey through the rough and tumble landscape of climate change, and I will be your companion and your guide. So, please join me on this adventure as we discover many cool and exciting climate science facts. We'll also have some fun along the way, so bring your notebook and crayons, and you too will come away with a good measure of my optimism about our planet, our climate, and our future.

With love in my heart, this book is dedicated to my Generation Z son Nemmo and Millennial partner Rachel.

Acknowledgment

To the many knowledgeable scientists who did and continue to do the heavy scientific lifting in this exciting and emerging field of climate science.

Contents

About the Author

Terigi Ciccone, President Info Alliance Consulting, Engineer, Artist, Author, loves reading and travel, naturalist. Dedicated father to three loving children and three grandchildren, loving husband, lousy golfer.

Teri has over 45 years of experience in gas turbine technologies for aviation, power generation, oil and gas industries, and ship propulsion.

A career-focused on international co-production, co-development, international licensing, and joint venture startups. He also had resident tenure in Belfort France for the co-design, build, and test of the world's largest-ever 100-MW gas turbine for power generation. He also headed up the co-design, prototype manufacture, and testing of the industrial 3-MW gas turbine In Florence, Italy. Teri was also responsible for Italian production and deliveries of turbines and compressors for the first ever Russia to Europe gas pipeline.

Teri has a BS and MS in engineering from Northeastern University, graduate from General Electric's 3-year Manufacturing Management and Technical Marketing Programs. Obtained Middlesex College US government contract certification and graduated from various courses at GE Executive Development Center, and received various Managerial, and Innovation awards.

Born in Italy and, and at the age of 9, immigrated to the USA in 1956.

PREFACE

Where are we?

Climatically speaking, the Earth is in a perfect place. We're in the Goldilocks zone! Not too hot - not too cold, not too wet, not too dry. The increased CO2 of the past few decades gave us a vast greening of the Earth by the equivalent of half the size of Australia. The elevated CO2 has been a blessing for all life on Earth, providing free fertilizer for jungles, forests, and prairies. But the increased CO2 continues to be especially beneficial for the poorest people in Africa, South America, and Asia who reap abundant agricultural yields, reducing famine and malnutrition.

A greener planet also makes for a cooler world because plants will absorb more of the sun's heat to manufacture more sugars. This then reduces the amount of solar heat to be absorbed and stored by the land, seas, and air. For the past several decades, we have been in a moderate warming period, and that's been very good for humanity and all the other bio-life on earth. But then, almost twenty years ago, this temperature increase stopped. Scientists are investigating to determine if we're in a short pause or if it's the start of a new global cooling cycle.

Socially speaking, humanity has never been in a better place, and many persons share my view. In his April 19, 2019 commentary on the anniversary of Earth Day, economist Nickolas Loris published his optimism, "On Earth Day; Gloomy Predictions Haven't Come to Pass." Loris not only reminds us about the many doomsday predictions that never materialized, but he also shares with us the ecological and humanitarian achievements of these past fifty years.

The hidden history of climate change. Unfortunately, people don't realize how good humanity has had it for the past century or more. Every day they are barraged by headlines on the twenty-four-hour news cycles, a flood here, a hurricane there, a drought, volcanoes, tidal waves, etc. No wonder so many people are left feeling empty and worry so much. We're told that global warming is coming, and the seas will rise so much that coastline cities like New York and Miami will be flooded and destroyed by hurricanes. But fearmongering is nothing new and moves in cycles. The scientifically unsophisticated public is taken advantage of by opportunistic politicians, greedy climate industry, attention-seeking "elites," nobility and redemption groveling "do-gooders."

But in the earth's past, we had a few better periods like 2,000 years ago, when during the Roman Warm Period, the climate was warmer than it is today. Even in places like Scotland, grapes were planted and harvested. Then, a thousand years ago, the weather was again warm enough for the Vikings to settle in Greenland and prosper for several hundred years before the climate went cold again. There were also several frigid periods causing grave results, like the freezing period that destroyed the Vikings settlements in Greenland. One particularly awful period was called the Maunder Minimum that started about 1645 and lasted until 1715. The global temperatures were about one to one and a half degrees Centigrade cooler than this modern, warm period. Farming growing seasons were shortened by more than a month, leading to widespread famine in the northern temperate zones.

Where is the truth? Get ready because we're going on a journey of discovery with Curious Clair. We are going on a freelance journey through the rough and tumble landscape of climate change. We will look only at facts, evidence, and data. I may sneak in an opinion or two, but it will be clearly labeled. We'll also avoid the simplistic traps and seductions offered by Team A or Team B or Team-Uninformed. We will see where reason, science, logic, common sense, and a confident sense of humor leads us. I will warn you when (and if) science gets a little complicated and will help you by giving the Cliff Notes Summary until you grasp the meaning. At times we will find truth in all the wrong places, like with Mark Twain, Socrates, and Curious George. At other times we will try and dig deeper into the rubbish bin of history and retrieve knowledge from the false promises of prior good intentions.

Please come join us on our journey! This book is written for parents and grandparents who love their children and grandchildren and want them to have a glorious future. It will also benefit Gen-Z, Millennials, Gen-X, and maybe even a few of my fellow Baby Boomers that still harbor a youthful optimism that the coming tomorrows will be ever Healthier, Brighter, and Sunnier for all humanity. The science and economics are accessible and understandable once the polemics are removed. We will also explore why we are misled by the press, the media, politicians, teachers, the climate change industry, etc. For this reason, we plan to adapt this book for grade school children next year.

There's a lot at stake, hundreds of billions of dollars have already been spent on CO2 research and industry. But now, trillions and tens of trillions of dollars are being discussed, and evermore powerful interest groups are lining up to get front row seating from the public trough.

No fear! Come and share my optimism. Since I have completed my journey, I would love to be your guide. On this journey, we will confidently get a complete understanding of the science of climate change. That knowledge will remove all angsts and vitriol and unite us in our shared goal of living in a healthier and cleaner planet, rotating in vibrant weather and climate systems. Bring your notebook, your crayons, and a curious mind, and don't forget to pack your sense of humor and a pinch of self-deprecation.

Here's the program we will follow. In the introduction, we will begin by building the foundational knowledge base. We will need that to start and then complete the climate change journey. We will show and use scientific charts to explain the concepts. Meanwhile, we'll use simple language and good humor wherever we can. We'll explore only facts and data and avoid speculating on motives and feelings. We'll discuss the need for intellectual curiosity, the need for critical thinking, and especially the importance of scientific reading. Here's the outline:

In Chapters 1-5, we'll present the fundamental questions on climate change, and provide answers that are supported by data. Here's a quick heads up, outputs from computer models are not data.

In Chapter 6, we stick our toe in the controversial waters dealing with the concept of human-made CO2, the origins of the UN-IPCC and the 97-percent consensus, skeptics /deniers, and political observations.

Chapters 7 and 8 focus on the ethics, education, social, and political impacts of climate change.

In chapter 9, we pull out our climate change science, data, facts, and charts, to find out what the real climate scientists have in their forecast. Then we'll double-check them against time-tested forecasting specialists and watch them wield their unique tools. Here we also answer the critical climate change "inconvenient question:" "Mommy! Why did you tell me the Bogeyman was real and that he's coming in 12-years?"

Field Guide: Like Charles Darwin, we will document the facts and data we discover during our journey and package it as Field Guide. The Field Guide, which is a detailed summary of the complete journey, will surely be a fascinating adventure for you. If time is short and you feel that you already have a good grasp of all sides of this subject, feel free to cut to the Cliff Notes version, which comprises of the Field Guide.

ANNEX A, Climate change fun facts, is my favorite part of the book. We present some examples of forecasts that went spectacularly wrong and added some images just because they're a ton of fun.

ANNEX B, The supplemental charts. Throughout the book, we insert many charts and graphs in a convenient small format to keep the text flowing smoothly. However, some charts need to be seen in greater detail, and here we present them in full-page format.

Now let's read the book!

And have lots of smart-fun!

Introduction

Rated G - Family, Pets & Friends You Must Keep

Before we start our climate change journey, let's first take a moment to assess where we are on this subject. We are a global crossroads, within our planet, our country, our states, our towns, our churches, and even our families. Many close friends have replaced each other with newly forged allies at arms. The tune of alarm and panic has been imposed on most of us by self-serving politicians, captains of industry, agenda-driven press/media, and self-righteous do-gooders. But as dramatized in the figure,[1] the first victims of this climate change, social wars have been our sons and daughters. Our millennial and Gen-Z sons, daughters, and grandchildren have been the cannon fodder of our climate change conflicts.

We, the much-confounded and much-deceived general public, are left with two terrifying prospects. First, to try and figure out what's going on here and where did we go so wrong? Second, what knowledge and what advice can we give to these parents and grandparents who want to make things right and prevent any future damages. Of particular concern are the millennials who are now or will soon become parents themselves. Even more importantly, how can we keep this malaise from spreading beyond Gen-Z?

Fear not, it can be done. You've bought this book, which is the first big step. However important this first step may seem; it is still not enough. You now must commit to reading the whole book, think, and reflect on what you are reading. To reward and encourage you to read it, I will make the subject as interesting and as simple as possible, OK? To sort this out and let you have some fun along the way, I would like you to take this entrance exam and see if we can agree on these six simple points:

1. Can we agree that there are more than a billion people in the world today who live on the knife-edge of starvation, sickness, and deprivation with little hope for tomorrow?
   Yes No
2. Can we agree that most of these people will die from the poor conditions suffered within their developing countries rather than from climate change today, or over the next decade? Yes No

3. Can we agree that almost two billion humans have been provided with little or no electricity to improve their conditions? Yes No

4. Can we agree that we, in the developed world, have a moral obligation to do these people no harm, and not profit from them? More importantly, we must try and help them improve their lives today? Yes No

5. When faced with a significant problem, should we solve it with our brains and develop an informed solution based on the best available data, and pursue it with an open mind? Yes No

6. Can we agree that being precise with questions we ask and the answers we proffer, is essential? Yes No

Now, let's tally-up your score and see what recommendations we offer:

Score	Recommendation No. 1	Recommendation No. 2
6/6	Read only Intro & Chap 1-5, 9	Apply for early sainthood
5/6	Read Intro, Chap 1-6, 9	Eat more veggies
4/6	Spend more time in reality	Attend church/temple regularly
3/6	Become a used car salesman	Read a self-help book
2/6	Don't forget the medication	Seek professional help
1/6	Return book to the shelf	Run before they catch you
0/6	Check for a heartbeat	N/A

1. THE JOURNEY:
Where are we going?

We're [2] going on a freelance journey through the rough and tumble landscape of climate change. Like Curious Clair, [3] we will look only at facts, evidence, and data. I may sneak in an opinion or two, but it will be clearly labeled. We'll also avoid the traps and seductions offered by Team A or Team B and see where reason, science, logic, common sense, and a caring heart leads us. I will warn you when (and if) science gets a little complicated. In such cases, I may simply offer you the Cliff Notes summary and let you proceed. But, if you want to check out the details, there are plenty of endnotes that will take you to the source.

Let's define the challenges and try to understand how we ended up getting where we are today. In the distant 1960s, there was an emerging concern about the pollution of the air, land, and seas. There were a few environmental zealots, like me, but no climate zealots or climate change end-of-the-world prophets. This *esprit de mond* united itself under the flag of the United Nations, and we all danced and sang the tunes of "the Age of Aquarius" in perfect harmony and held hands across the globe. But in the early 70s came the shock of the "OPEC oil embargo." This decision to stop exporting oil to the United States brought the world's economy and spirit to its knees.

The OPEC oil embargo started two fierce races; first to advance technologies to find more oil and gas and extract more of it from each well. The second was to decide what energy was going to replace the "limited" oil and gas in the next several decades. Was it to be high tech coal or nuclear or some combination of the two? In an attempt to get a "political advantage," the nuclear advocates were the first to raise the "danger" of coal-produced CO_2/pollution and global warming. The environmentalists quickly conflated CO_2 with air and environmental pollution and jumped on this theme. They were soon joined by politicians, academia, and the media as they saw it as a new resource. More money and higher taxes for the politicians, more research grants for industry and academia, more hardware to design/build/sell by companies. To ignite and reinforce these goals, the press/media spread misinformation and concealed many truths. They also fabricated many tear-jerking stories about the polar bears starving and our environment laid to waste.

Then, out of nowhere, other scientists started warning us that we were at the doorstep of a new ice age, meaning that ice will soon cover the surface of the Earth, and the temperature will drop down drastically. This report took center stage for a few years. Many newspapers, T.V. news, and magazines, like "Time," joined the rush to "save mankind." International teams formed to analyze the limits of the planet's capabilities, how many people world survive the ice, how much food production would we lose? Had the Earth's population exceeded its capacity for food, raw materials, and clean water? [4] We were whiplashed only a few years later by the claxons of CO2-fueled global climate change, alarming us into a warming hysteria.

The alarm bells went off in 1979 with the Three Mile Island nuclear mishap. This incident was used to fuel the hysteria to mobilize resources and save Mater Gaia. Gaia is Latin for "Mother Earth goddess," and we had to rescue her from the evils of technology and human greed. The global solution was to have the United Nations take control of the environment and climate change, resulting in the formation of the IPCC (Intergovernmental Panel on Climate Change.) The IPCC started as a scientifically chartered group of international scientists. However, by 1988, it turned away from science to the world of politics and big money. The primary issue was that the IPCC was not chartered to find either the causes or the degree of global warming. Instead, their sole purpose was to identify human activities that caused CO2 induced global warming and how to fix it on a worldwide scale.

Until the late 1980s, the field of climate science was mostly ignored by the greater scientific community. But suddenly, it became the *cause célèbre* as the U.S. government research funds increased from a few million dollars a year to billions and then tens of billions a year. Many scientists and universities jumped on the global warming gravy train. Even those scientists who were initially skeptical of the human-made CO2 started to rethink their careers and financial aspirations. As the decades passed, many world-class scientists, such as Dr. Curry and Dr. Lindzen, who had worked with the IPCC, began to question their direction and motives. These scientists became concerned with the "data" that was used or not used. They were most concerned with how the IPCC's data was coupled with alarming projections of global warming disasters, creating the great divide we have today.

So here we are today; we have Team A and Team B. Team A got off to a fast start, championing the IPCC and following the path of least resistance and maximum funding. Their "consensus" is that the warming of the Earth is caused by anthropogenic (human-made) CO2 that is driving the greenhouse heating effect. The elegance and marketing advantages were brilliant. It gave the uninformed public a simple one-cause villain and one "easily understandable" fix: humankind must reduce CO2 production activities at all costs.

Team B eased into a much different direction, following the classical, rigorous scientific method described in paragraph I.5 below. Slowly at first, but eventually, more and more of Team A members were moving to Team B. Team B set off to search out the root cause of the temperature changes using the best available research methods, minds, and instruments. The problem was and continues to be that Team B is made up mostly by nerdy older scholars. The subject is complex and provides no quick solution that's easily understood by the general public.

Team B made little effort to find a friendlier way to deliver their findings and solutions. Worst, many said that the climate problem did not exist, and was blasted for "blasphemy" by Team A. Team B's approach was ridiculed, their members were called "deniers" and "skeptics," and campaigns were launched to damage their careers and livelihood. But Team B's message lacked the drama of alarm bells and world-class spokesmen like Al Gore, Hollywood actors like Leonardo DiCaprio, TV networks, newspapers, and the politicians. Sadly, this problem persists, and Team A, to this day, continues to enjoy about 90 percent of the ever-growing pot of government research dollars.

Our Journey: But we are going on a journey of discovery with Curious Clair. We'll pack our lunch and see where science, data, reason, and common sense takes us. We will see how some facts and figures of Team A may supplement some assertions offered by Team B and vice versa. On this journey, we will confidently get a complete understanding of the science, remove the angst and vitriol and hopefully unite us all in our shared goal of living in a healthier planet rotating in robust weather and climate systems.

We'll start by answering meaningful, straightforward questions that have been avoided and obscured for too long. We will respond to these questions with answers that are scientifically correct and presented in ordinary everyday language that's understood by the general public and high school students. Please pay close attention and take lots of notes as there will be a mid-term exam along the way. We'll be informative in a way that's socially acceptable, intellectually stimulating, and just plain fun. For your comfort and entertainment, this book is divided into several levels with appropriate ratings:

We start the journey by understanding the role of science in our society, where I will share my eternal optimism and why. Then follows a brief discussion on the approach we will take and point out the importance of asking clear, simple, straightforward questions that need more than a simple "yes" or "no" response. What we attempt to know is, where did the temperature change, and to what extent did it change from a given or stated date to the next, i.e., from date A to date B. Furthermore, we strive to find out the direction in which the temperature changed, its causes and outcomes. Then we'll quickly move on to why we need the Rules of The Game and conclude with the difference between Scientific Reading Vs. Passive Reading and touch upon ethics and data integrity.

CHAPTERS 1-5:
THE FUNDAMENTAL QUESTIONS

Rated P.G.: In these Chapters, we'll discuss the fundamental questions on climate change. We'll go over the solar system, the sun, how much energy it gives off, how much of it reaches us, and see what that energy does to the land and seas and air. We'll look at the role of CO2 and the greenhouse effect, where it comes from, and why it's so essential. We will check our opinions, preconceptions, and sharp objects at the door and try to review as many facts and data as we can. We'll have plenty of pictures and diagrams and lots of reference notes connecting you to various books, articles, and websites. There you can get even more detailed information and see better displays. We also give all the appropriate credits to the people who did and continue to do the heavy scientific lifting.

CHAPTER 6: CONTROVERSIAL DISCUSSIONS

Rated-Adults Only: Here, we will tackle some of the more controversial subjects, but again based solely on the scientific levels as is best understood today. We will steer clear of questioning motives and modes of behavior and will avoid all vitriol. But for safety and good manners, please make sure that everybody checks all weapons at the door and, most importantly, like Mark Twain, strap on your sense of irony and humor.

CHAPTER 7: ETHICS, SOCIAL, EDUCATION, AND POLITICAL OBSERVATIONS

Rated-Beware: Meaning NO bumper sticker mentality; NO Sloganeering; NO snowflaking and NO safe spaces. Here we put everything on the table regarding social, economic, educational, ethical, moral, and political observations. We'll focus on how we are impacted by the consequences of climate change policies, politics, and endless and senseless debates.

CHAPTER 8: HISTORY OF CLIMATEGATE AND THE HISTORY OF THE UN/IPCC

Rated-Dramamine Required: It's a-rocking' and rolling' rollercoaster ride. We take a forensic look at the history of climate change, and the origins and checkered history of the United Nations' Intergovernmental Panel on Climate Change (UN/IPCC) and the questionable actions and ethics of NOAA.

CHAPTER 9: CLIMATE FORECAST

Rated-Time to Get Real: Here, we present the climate forecast for the next fifty to seventy years. We throw away the security blanket and give you a simple list of facts and data and welcome you to the sunshine of science and truth. We highlight some new and exciting scientific developments and see how a once-scientific wasteland has become a significant source of discoveries and scientific adventures.

FIELD GUIDE

Rated-Safe Harbor and Working Harbor: All's well that ends well, and it will. But to be sure that whatever happens, we need to keep our wits, our sense of humor, and a little bit of self-deprecation. We'll look back and reflect on our journey. But unlike Bilbo Baggins, we're not going to sit back and write a travelogue, or vanity blogs, or tweets. Instead, we'll explore how we can summarize our findings and understandings. That way, we can share our knowledge and contribute to shaping and reshaping public policy for the benefit of humankind.

ANNEX A: CLIMATE CHANGE FUN

Rated Funny Bone Required. Here we present the top ten most significant climate alarmist predictions that went spectacularly wrong. We'll also indulge in relooking at Famous Predictions on Climate Change, more fun facts, and a great selection of climate change cartoons.

ANNEX B: SUPPLEMENTAL CHARTS

Throughout the book, we have inserted many charts and graphs in a more convenient smaller format to keep the text flowing smoothly. However, some diagrams may need to be seen in greater detail. For this reason, these specific charts are designated with an asterisk (i.e., Fig I.1.1*), and will have a full-page view of those charts in this Annex B.

Let's Go!
Bring your noteboo k, crayons, and a curious mind.[5]

2. OVERVIEW, WHERE ARE WE?

Climatically speaking, the Earth is in a perfect place.[6] We're in the Goldilocks zone! Not too hot, not too cold, not too wet, not too dry. We have satellite evidence of a vast "greening" of the Earth by the equivalent of half the size of Australia[7] in the past several decades. That means more vegetation and smaller deserts. In the Earth's past, we had seen a few better periods like 2,000 years ago during the Roman Warm Period. The climate was warmer than it is today, and grapes were planted and harvested in Scotland. A thousand years later, it was warm enough for the Vikings to settle in Greenland and prosper for several hundred years before the climate went cold again. Most often, however, the

Earth has been in far worst places.

In the four billion years the Earth has been around, there have been thousands of climatic ups and downs. During these ages, the Earth experienced many ice ages, including one that froze the planet into what's known as "Snowball Earth." There have also been many warmer ages, including a period when tropical forests and alligators extended to the north polar regions and south to Antarctica.[8] This Arctic biological activity resulted in the coal, natural gas, and petroleum we find today in the extreme areas. The last ice age ended about 11,500 years ago.[9] Today, and in the previous 9,000 years, we've been in an "interglacial warm period," meaning in the next several thousand years, the glaciers will likely return.

Socially speaking, humanity has never been in a better place, and many persons share my view. In his April 19, 2019 commentary on the anniversary of Earth Day, economist Nickolas Loris published his optimism, "On Earth Day; Gloomy Predictions Haven't Come to Pass [10]. Loris not only reminds us about the many doomsday predictions that never came, but he also shares with us the many ecological and humanitarian achievements of these past fifty years."

But too many people don't realize how good humanity has had it for the past century or more. Daily they are barraged by headlines on the twenty-four-hour news cycles, a flood here, a hurricane there, droughts, volcanoes, tidal waves, etc. No wonder so many people feel empty and worry so much. We're told that global warming is coming, and the seas will rise so much that coastline cities like New York and Miami will be flooded and destroyed by hurricanes. But fearmongering is nothing new and moves in cycles. The scientifically unsophisticated public is taken advantage of by opportunistic politicians, attention-seeking "elites," nobility/redemption "do-gooders," etc.

Over a century ago, we had the drumbeat of "devil rum" that marched us to Prohibition. We had the witch trials in Salem, and later the burning of Joan of Arc in France where thousands of heretics were accused and executed for climate witchcraft. In the 1960s, a group of well-intended *savants* met in Rome, Italy, and began a dramatic campaign to "educate us" on how humankind had reached the limit of the planet's resources. Dozens of books were written, and movies made to dramatize and scare us like *Soylent Green*, *Planet of the Apes*, and *Dune*. Then came the headlines in the mid-1970s that a new ice age was here, and a decade later, we were snapped into global warming, supposedly.

But here is the evidence that proves that the Earth has never been in a better place. Two hundred years ago, less than one billion people were living on planet Earth. Today we have over seven billion. People are living a longer, healthier, and happier life. Each year hundreds of millions of people escape the wrenching hunger and poverty in underdeveloped and developing countries. Hundreds of millions of people are getting cleaner air, cleaner water, and more nutritious and healthier food. Our young people today have a very good life and prospects for an even brighter future.[11]

Yes, we have a long way to go, but let's get some joy from the progress we've made so far and continue to make for humanity worldwide. That happened because of affordable, reliable, and abundant fossil-fueled energy that allowed more food production, cleaner water, medical attention, and education. We are living longer and with a life span rising by more than twenty years in just the past half-century alone. And who has been the biggest beneficiaries of this progress? Yup, it's the poor! Look 2,000 years ago; the wealthy had it all; big houses, plenty of food, clean clothes, etc. And they had it because their slaves and servants did the backbreaking work. These people were mostly treated as beasts of burden and given only the barest essentials to keep them alive so they could drudge and endure the next day. By contrast, today, the poorest in the USA and other industrialized countries have it better than the lords and emperors who lived about 2,000 years ago.

This happened because we harnessed the power and energy of fossil fuels. Unfortunately, the accompanying figure[12] reminds us that once we have grasped a belief, it's hard to let go. It's hard to let go unless and until you examine the data with a capable and open mind. If you can't or won't analyze data with an open mind, then you can't let go of old ideas, and you end up living in a world of dogma instead of knowledge.

Today one man driving a tractor can produce more food than a thousand slaves did a mere 150 years ago, that too at a much lower cost. As so clearly stated by Alex Epstein in his bestseller *The Moral Case for Fossil Fuels*, the poor are the biggest winners from affordable and reliable fossil fuels. These same fossil fuels have and will continue to increase their wealth. In a few decades, the poor, especially in Africa, will be able to afford the scrubbers, filtration, and sewage equipment to clean up their environment. The reason we made these monumental strides is because of the burst in science, technology, and industry in the past 100-200 years with the light bulb, steel, machinery, affordable fuels, and other materials.

These wonders were made possible because of education, especially in the hard sciences; physics, chemistry, mechanics, mathematics, etc. Dogma, by contrast, has always led to deprivation. But these hard sciences have become very specialized, "nerdier" and increased the gap between the scientists and the general public. Our educational, social, and political institutions need to fill this gap. But too often, opportunists seek to exploit this gap for their own material gains and social status.

3. APPROACH:

Have fun and learn cool stuff along the way

A long time ago, on a soccer field far, far away, I learned how to make successful and fun soccer teams for boys and girls. This helped infuse a bond between the kids, created good team harmony, and built lasting values. I did this by using an old teaching process that my middle school basketball coach taught me. "Coach," he said, "don't try to teach." As we get into the questions in Chapter 1, don't think of this as a science book, but more as a cookbook. Consider each issue as a recipe where I'll provide the ingredients and directions. Then you offer time and attention to make sure you understand the problem, prepare it, and cook it up.

<u>List of ingredients:</u>

- First, read my proffered response a couple of times if necessary.
- Challenge my response, whether you agree with it or not.
    - o Use data, not what you heard from somebody or the media.
    - o Test this with your own real-world experience and measure it against what you see around you.
    - o Read and listen to all materials as a true "skeptic."
    - o Contextualize data. What was it like a hundred years ago? How many people died from it? Do I trust the source, and what's their track record?
- Avoid sources that present their "facts" in general terms, large fonts and bright colors and with no data.
- Avoid sources that use conspiratorial, dramatic, or world-ending language.
- If the article seems more likely to be legitimate, read it, but do so as a scientific skeptic, not with religious fervor.

- But if this looks like too much work, take my word for it and have a pickle.
- As a last resort, email me—I'm here just for you!

So, come along and let's have some fun learning what we can along the way. And if you want to hold on to what you believe, who knows, someday you might read this book a second time.

4. TEAM PLAY:

And He said, "Let there be team A and B."

Now and again, we forget that the all-knowing, loving, and caring God, is not only the best engineer in the universe but also has a pretty good sense of humor. Could Saturday Night Live writers come up with a script for a platypus or quantum mechanics and quarks? So, about half-past His day of rest, He said to Himself, "Self, looky here how much fun those people are having down there playing climate change football. Let me see if I can stir the pot a bit, they can call it "evolution." I have lots of good people down there—I'll divide them up into two teams.[13] While they slept, He went to Team A and breathed into their left ear so that they would think first with their heart and later with their brains. On to Team B, again the same ear thing and they would think first with their minds and then with their hearts. Voila! It was done, and it was good. Maybe?

What's the difference between them? The difference is that they think in a different sequence. Let me "splain this to you, Lucy." Here you are, a caveman hunting for a meal, then right in front of you jumps a saber-toothed tiger,[14] also looking for a meal. But you can't decide if it's a fight or flight, and you don't have the time to think about which to choose. Your brain automatically fires up the flux capacitor, and in three seconds, you scramble up the nearest tree and climb as high and as fast as you can. Once you see that Tiggy can't climb, you turn off the flux thing and slow down to reflect, "Wow. What just happened? Did I do the right thing, or could I have done something better?" See, now you're trying to solve a problem if it comes up again.

Credit;ttps://www.neurosciencemarketing.com/blog/articles/inner-caveman.htm

Several moons later, a stroke of genius comes to you. "I'll tie this sharp pointy rock to the end of this stick, so next time Tiggy comes along, I'll stick this rock and pole in him instead of just running away. I can cook him up for dinner after I invent fire."

If instead of thinking fast with your heart, you had thought slowly with your brain, trying to solve that problem in the best way at the worst possible time, you would have been the meal. But instead, here you are safe in your cave and start high fiving yourself for having solved the tiger problem. So anytime in the future in any similar case, you would run as fast as you can and climb up the closest tree. But wait. Maybe the next time it's a cheetah, who can run and climb more swiftly than you. Or maybe there's no tree, in which case you are a walking Happy Meal looking for a customer.

Or take another example: You have a musical show to put on stage. Who do you want on the stage? A spontaneous-thinking artist who knows how to "touch the heart" and light up the audience, or a methodically-thinking, analytical engineer? Silly question, yes? But would you hire this creative, socially attuned guy to design and build the theater or run the box office? No way, Jose! Most of us can do both ways of thinking, but unfortunately, very few can do this dual-action thinking at a high level. Maybe Team A, instead of trying to get all the kudos from the A tribe, should talk things over with the methodical-thinking engineer from Team B. Maybe together, they can arrive at a solution that has the best chance of working for the most people for most of the time. Later, we'll enlist some additional help in understanding the role of science in society from Mark Twain and his friend, the dung Beetle.

5. RULES OF THE GAME

Ethics, Science, and Definitions

A motto used by NASA, "In God we trust; all others must bring data."[15] So, if we use the same conceptual NASA motto, we need some rules of the game. For example, like a touchdown is six points, or if the ball is caught before it hits the ground, the batter is out.[16] But before we get into the specific rules, we need some definitions that we will use extensively in reading this book. Let's first highlight some recent setbacks we have experienced in our scientific Process and culture. The following two articles should speak for themselves. The reader is encouraged to go online and read entire articles, take them in context, compare them with their experience, and piece it together with the following definitions.

1. Science, Society, and Culture: "Democracy's Plight" is the title of an editorial, written by Rush Holt and published in the February 1, 2019 edition of the journal *Science*.[17] It's a very timely piece about data integrity and scientific authenticity coming under more and more scrutiny and doubts. Holt elegantly reminds us that we should not take liberty or free speech for granted.

One particular quote [18] is notable: "Observers speak of truth decay, dismissal of expertise, and neglect of evidence. Collectively, these are problems of enormous importance because they threaten democracy itself." In the battle of public opinion, opinions are too many, while facts and data are ignored too often. The public press, politicians, and Hollywood celebrities are overloading the airwaves with ever-increasing protests, sloganeering, indoctrinations, and fearmongering. All done based on lots of "good intentions" and very little data. In his concluding recommendation, Mr. Holt states,

TWO WOLVES AND A SHEEP VOTING ON WHAT'S FOR DINNER

"The scientific community should undertake a major initiative—enlisting business, industry, and cultural and political leaders—to communicate that evidence-based thinking, which is available and not just to scientists. Because the public largely regards science as successful and beneficial, they may be more interested in why and how it works."

2. "The Road to Bad Science[19] is Paved with Obedience and Secrecy." The article goes on to say, "The skeptics who had doubted Anvers's claims all along may now feel vindicated, but this is not the time to celebrate. Instead, the discipline of cardiovascular stem cell biology is now undergoing a process of soul-searching. How was it possible that some of the most widely read and cited papers were based on heavily flawed observations and assumptions? Why did it take more than a decade for scientists to finally accept that the near-magical regenerative power of the heart turned out to be a pipe dream?"

The sad conclusions are that our peer review process is severely flawed. *"Peer reviews only involve a 'review,' i.e., a general evaluation of major strengths and flaws, and peer reviewers do not see the original raw data nor are they provided with the resources to replicate the studies and confirm the integrity of the submitted results. Peer reviewers rely on the honor system."* As we go forward in our journey, please vigilantly keep in mind these two articles. The unfortunate part is that they are not isolated cases, instead in too many cases, they become mere tools of self-serving interests.

3. Definitions: For your amusement and entertainment, below, I have divided the definitions into two fully functional rational groups. The first group, JTFM, is for the Nerdy Readers, and you'll make full use of these definitions as we make progress into Chapters 1 and 2. The second group, GBS, is for busy, social people who spend more time on social media, watch T.V., have demanding families and careers, take care of children and dogs, etc..

The JTFM- Group: Just the Facts, Ma'am

Science is the pursuit of understanding and explaining the elements of the universe around us.

Data are facts, figures, relationships, etc. that are obtained by measurements, mathematics, and experiments used to support or to challenge a theory, scientific law, or scientific consensus.

Theory is a structured idea of a possible explanation of a natural process that is not as of yet substantiated by data.

Law is an explanation of a natural object or process, for example, Newton's law of gravity.

Shelf life: A period during which a law remains valid. An idea, theory, or concept may remain valid for thousands of years, such as the Pythagorean Theorem. Alternatively, it may last only a few days or until somebody comes up with a better explanation and proves it with experiments, data, mathematics, etc. For example, Einstein showed that Newtonian gravity was a good approximation but not as accurate as his relativistic model. But then it's only a matter of time before someone will come up with a new law and we'll shelf Mr. Einstein.

Skeptic: A skeptic is a real scientist. It's any person or any group who challenges a scientific law, theory, idea, or consensus, and does so with data. Soon after Einstein published his theory of relativity, he received a letter from Germany signed by 100 top scientists refuting his argument. Einstein's brandishing reply was, "If I were wrong, one signature would have been sufficient."

Scientific Method is a 6-step disciplined procedure.

- Ask a question,
- Do background research,
- Construct a hypothesis,
- Test hypothesis by experiment(s), or calculations,
- Analyze the data and conclude a Theory,
- Share all results, tests, data, calculations, etc. for skeptical review.

The GBS Group: Got to Believe Something

Belief [20] is the acceptance of an idea or concept that we firmly hold onto in the absence of data. Beliefs are right and proper in church and esoteric debates but have no role in science.

Opinions refer to how we show preferences, like who we vote for, T.V. programs we watch, or the church we go to or not. Opinions can play a limited role in science, where it might help us choose between funding experiment A and not experiment B to validate the Theory of X.

An Activist [21] is any person whose aggressive behavior is shaped by his beliefs and adherence to dogma.

A consensus [22] is a group of people who share the same beliefs or opinions, like the dress code at the country club. It has zero scientific value or authenticity, whereas, in science, one person can disprove a million better educated and better-credentialed peers.

Denier[23] is any person or group who fails to adhere or conform to the Consensus.

Dogma[24] is a belief so profound that it replaces religion.

Socially Responsible [25] is a euphemism for persons seeking to acquire wealth, nobility, or moral superiority at someone else's expense.

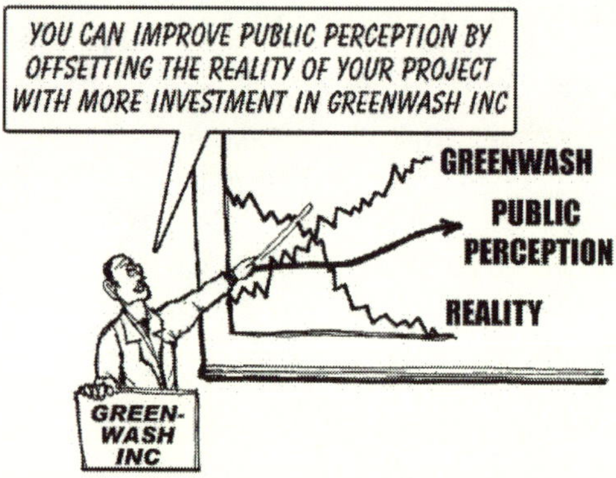

6. SCIENTIFIC AND CASUAL READING

Let's jump to this particular endnote, [26] open the website, and together let's read it as real scientists, which means skeptical readers:

- Look at the website address. Our first impression is it's NASA, which seems like it's a reliable source of data from the U.S. Government.

- The colossal headline screams "Climate Change, How Do We Know?" and then we see a big graph showing that the CO2 has almost doubled from an average of about 220 in the last 400,000 years. Nowhere does it tell where is the evidence that links a cause-effect relationship between CO2 to a measurable temperature increase.

- On the graph, we have two highlighted statements: "1950 Level" showing a 310-ppm level, and a second labeled "Current Level" at about 410 ppm. What is not said here is more telling than what is said. Before 1956 all measurements were based on the unreliable or questionable ice core data. Then starting in 1956, direct measurements started using very accurate instruments.

- There is no mention of the fact that that the most significant part of the CO2 rise has come from the sun-warmed oceans.[27]

- But the subliminal impact—let's call it "information staging"—really looks frightening, and to the casual reader, it sounds reasonable. After all, it's NASA and NOAA.

- Then it makes a statement that "Most of these climate changes are attributed to tiny variations in Earth's orbit that changes the amount of solar energy our planet receives." This refers to the effects of the Milankovitch cycles and is a true statement. But again, with no context and the use of the words "very small variations," along with the use of a tiny font, trivializes these killer cycles.

- Then makes a highlighted sub-headline: "Scientific evidence for warming of the climate system is unequivocal" and credits the IPCC for this statement. Another true statement that everybody knows that the Earth has been warming since the end of the little ice age in the 18th century and the modern warming of 1978-1998.[28]

- It then proceeds to make several true statements about the increasing temperature, rising seas, melting Arctic sea ice, etc. But none is quantified or tied back to their graph of CO2.

- But off to the right is a dramatic text box stating that 97 percent of the scientists agree that in the last hundred years, most of this increase is "most likely due to man-made activity." But NASA provides no data to support, quantify it, or contextualize the statement. Worse yet, this statement directly contradicts the comment about the Milankovitch cycles, which is written in tiny font sizes. Still, the staged CO2 message is given a vast and colorful center stage.

- This is a dramatic example of "staged information," where a few truths are presented, then some half-truths are stretched, then show a bold statement about the 97 percent consensus. (Go back above and re-read the definition of "consensus.") There's no mention that the more significant part of the increased CO2 comes from the warming of the oceans, which it says is caused by the orbital changes of the

Milankovitch or solar cycles. As a result, the author succeeds in misleading the ordinary person and giving the media the sensational headlines, it craves.

- In Chapter 6, we get into the details and derivation of the 97 percent consensus and the involvement of NASA/NOAA in the "Climategate" mess. Here NASA/NOAA was forced by a British investigation to reveal how NASA/NOAA changed the U.S. temperature history to make it match the rise in CO2—thereby allowing NASA/NOAA and the IPCC to say that the increase in CO2 was indeed responsible for the temperature increase.

~ 1 ~

THE BASIC QUESTIONS

Rated G - Family, Pets & Friends You Must Keep

QUESTION 1: *WHAT IS THE WEATHER, CLIMATE, AND WHAT IS A CLIMATOLOGIST?* [29]

Weather[30] is the temperature, the humidity, rain, and the misty winds on our face, the frost on the eyebrows that you experience today, or will experience next week, next month, and next year. Weather is a short-term thing, just like my attention span. Secondly, the weather is always experienced locally and greatly influenced by your local conditions, like topology (mountains or valleys), latitude (tropics or the state of Maine), coastlines, or deep canyons. For example, if it's snowing in your backyard in Portland, Maine, it's probably hot and sunny in Sarasota, Florida. Or maybe it's raining in Kansas City and freezing in Moscow. Weather is also regional like it's always hot and humid in the tropics at sea level or where there's little difference between winter and summer temperatures. Although on the equator, Mount Kilimanjaro has five distinctive weather zones as you climb from the bottom of the dry and hot savannas to the snowy 20,000-foot top. On the contrary, in Antarctica, there is a considerable temperature difference between winter and summer temperatures of about 100° F, even if the temperature never goes above the freezing point.

We will be using the terms "Global Weather" and "Global Climate" repeatedly. But note that there is no such thing as "Global Weather." Global weather has never happened and never will. That's like saying that the average family in the USA has 2.56 children: it's a useful tool for a broader understanding of weather cycles and trends, but not a reflection of reality.

Climate, on the other hand, is what you experienced in the disco 1970s or will experience in the next twenty or thirty or a hundred or thousand years. Some scientists may say ten years is the minimum crossing point; others will

say fifteen or more. In any case, climate happens over a long time. During this time, we may experience a little change, but that change is so small and insignificant that our bodies do not even notice it. However, over the decades, that slight difference may have a significant impact on the flora and fauna and human conditions. With climate, many scientists are more interested in the trends rather than the actual values of the parameters (temperature, precipitation, humidity, etc.) The climate can also be considered as being either local or regional or global and at any level over a long time. Over the last 30 or 40 years, vast amounts of money have been spent trying to come up with an estimate of the "global climate" and how it may change over time. A lot of progress was made in its measurements and modeling, but more work still needs to be done. Much more accuracy is required before we can use them to make multi-billion or multi-trillion Dollar policy decisions.

What's a climatologist?31 Curious Claire is not a meteorologist, nor a weather-person; she is a climatologist, a person who studies the climate. It all sounds so simple, but in reality, it's much more than that. Here I am writing a book on climate change, so am I a climatologist too? Well, I have two engineering degrees and have worked with turbines, generators, oil drilling platforms, jet engines, and a bunch of combustion stuff for half a century. I've been an avid reader of science journals and have even poked around with relativity and quantum mechanics. But no! I am neither a scientist or a climatologist, nor am I pretending to be one.

Furthermore, I'm here not to present my scientific theories, my test results, or any original work. But since I am good at science and have a technical and mathematical background, so I can understand and appreciate the extraordinary work done by real climate scientists and real climatologists. My role is merely to focus on the fantastic tasks done by many brilliant intellectuals and then summarize, arrange, and present it in a manner that is easily digestible by the public, high school students, non-technical college students, and especially by parents and grandparents of grade school children.

It's noted and appreciated that climatologists must have two skill sets. First is a broad knowledge of many different fields of science, including meteorology, economics, physics, geology, chemistry, math, oceanography, fluid dynamics, hydraulics, engineering, atmospheric science, and especially computer science and modeling. Secondly, they must also have specific credentials in one or more of the above disciplines. That's why it's essential to have a scientific group with members from different scientific backgrounds, working together on climate science. A Ph.D. is a must to enter the door. The reason is that many tests involve different academic disciplines, sophisticated instruments, and tools for designing, developing, using, and interpreting with many different climate tests, theories, and especially proxies that are used for the various measurements.

QUESTION 2: *HOW DO WE MEASURE WEATHER AND CLIMATE CHANGE?*

Claire[32] explains to her visiting family about the importance of accuracy in temperature measurements, which is perhaps the most critical weather and climate indicator. It's the most measured, studied, and discussed element. We can use an old alcohol or mercury thermometer to measure it, which we'll discuss in detail later in the chapter. Other weather measurements include wind speeds and directions that we measure with an anemometer. Barometric Pressure is the weight of a column of air in the sky, from your body to outer space, pushing down on everybody and everything on Earth. It is measured in PSI (Pound per Square Inch) by using a barometer. Different barometric pressures in different regions of the Earth cause winds. These winds will combine and blend with other winds to establish weather fronts and movements and are used to predict weather fronts and forecasts. Other instruments include the hygrometer, which is used to measure the amount of water vapor in the air, or humidity. This tells us how dry it is in Arizona or how sticky it feels in Florida. But it also becomes vital in cloud formation, which we'll discuss in the later chapters and is an essential factor in the discussions on climate models, the greenhouse effect, and climate change. With the help of a rain gauge, we measure the amount of rainfall over a month or weeks or years. It can be as simple as a cylindrical bucket and a ruler to see how deep the water is.

There is also another class of machinery called "weather vehicles."[33] These devices carry weather instruments that will take various weather measurements. Satellites are used more and more to carry a variety of tools, like Radar, especially Doppler, which can see the size, density, and motion of the clouds. This technology has dramatically increased the ability to forecast unfailingly for several days in advance. There are also "remote sensing systems deployed and stationary on land and especially the mobile ones roaming the oceans to see what's happening on and below the surface. We also continue using old fashion Weather balloons as an inexpensive and reasonably reliable way to send various weather instruments into the air, to measure temperatures, pressure, water vapors, etc.

Now, a bit more detailed discussion on the satellites, and why and how they became so crucial in weather and climate systems studies: Weather satellites started in the late 1970s and continue to carry ever more sophisticated instruments taking more accurate, reliable, and continuous readings. Satellites can carry devices and take measurements that can't be done from the Earth, sea, or balloon-based systems. They can be sent to specific orbital spots and remain fixed over the area of interest and can take thousands of readings per day and so can record changes and trends. Satellites can also be deployed in orbits to sweep and cover large global areas over specified paths around the earth. They can be used to measure the Earth's cloud cover and the energy of the sun reaching the Earth's upper atmospheres. They can take radar measurements to see if the seas are rising or falling with accuracies and reliabilities that were never possible with the more common tidal gages. Lastly, they can be deployed into outer space to gather data on what's going on with the sun, other planets/moons, and galactic cosmic rays.

On earth satellites, when programmed with sophisticated computer algorithms, and instruments can also take measurements to see:

- The Arctic and the Antarctic ice mass coverage, its thickness and identify whether it's growing or shrinking, and at what rates.
- Measure directions and speeds of ocean currents.
- Detect how the oceans mix and redistribute heat around the seas and back into the air.
- Measure how much of the sun's energy reaches the Earth's outer atmosphere.
- The amount of the sun's energy reflected in outer space by the clouds and by the air. The amount of this reflection is called the "Albedo Effect." For example, in the tropics, where there are a lot of large and dense clouds, the albedo maybe 35 percent. Meaning 35 percent of the sun's rays never reach the ground or the oceans but are instead reflected outer space.
- It can also measure the amount of sunlight reflected up to the sky by ice and snow, by the land, and seas.
- Measure how much of the sun's energy is absorbed by the ground, the biosystem, and the oceans.
- Satellite born instruments can measure the snow cover in Nebraska to estimate crop yields that farmers will use to devise alternate crop planting options.
- Obtain more data more accurately and other dynamic systems, as discussed in the following chapters.

Scientists also continue to develop and build ever more exotic land-based, sea-based, or satellite-based modern devices that can detect and measure many non-Earth factors that influence our weather and climate. For example, they can tell us how many cosmic rays are bombarding the Earth from deep space or measure the strength of the sun's magnetic fields and solar winds. They help determine if the oceans are rising and by how much. Or if the CO2 is being released from the warming oceans into the air and at what rates. Some of these satellites born instruments can also tell us what's happening on, in, and around the sun. They can also show us if there are any changes in temperatures on other planets like Mars or Saturn and how the storms are whirling in Jupiter's atmosphere.

These measurements may help us distinguish climate changes that are unique to Earth or that are common with our sister planets. Many reputable and distinguished scientists have measured recent temperature increases on the moon, Mars, and Jupiter that appear to be in line with some of the temperature increases on Earth. This may substantiate claims that human activities are not the only source of climate change on Earth.

QUESTION 3: *HOW ACCURATE ARE OUR WEATHER AND CLIMATE MEASUREMENTS?*

The accuracy[34] and integrity of weather and climate measurements have always been a concern. But until recent decades, it was generally ignored because we did not have the means to know and control them very well. These errors and omissions were not as consequential as they are now. A hundred or even fifty years ago, our major weather concerns were more limited to local weather reports in Boston or Cleveland. But now, when we have a flight from NYC to LAX, we need to know more detailed and reliable weather information, like is it snowing in St. Louis where we have a layover? Or, the farmer in Nebraska who needs to know the spring wheat production forecast in Ukraine. He

needs the best possible information so he can better estimate the number of acres of winter wheat he should plant for today's global markets.
We especially need better and more reliable information to make the dramatic, expensive, and consequential social policy decisions on what actions we should consider preparing for the coming and continuing climate changes. For these and countless other reasons, we rely on scientists to obtain and process diligently ever more expansive and consequential weather and climate data. While scientists, engineers, and software programmers know about the importance and the need for this data accuracy, the general public is not remotely aware of its significance or of how challenging these tasks can be. But more importantly, the costs and consequences of poor decisions made because of unreliable data or accurate data incorrectly interpreted.

When we are looking at very long term climate data, we may have to use multiple proxies, which adds an extra layer of complexities, costs, and sources of error. For example, one of the most commonly used proxies is the ancient temperature or CO2 levels from ice core samples. Also, for the last few hundred years, tree ring data was a primary source of annual temperatures. But since the past half-century, direct atmospheric readings are being used, which are incredibly accurate and reliable.

Therefore, as we look at figure 1.3.2, we see CO2 shoot up like a rocket starting in the mid-1950s. We know that in the mid-1950, we stopped using proxies to measure the atmospheric CO2 content and started using direct readings from the Mauna Loa weather station in Hawaii. So, we need to ask ourselves, was this dramatic increase in CO2 real, or could it be partially skewed by the change in the measurement process? Or in the early 1960s, we stopped using tree ring data where we could, when certain discrepancies were found during the period

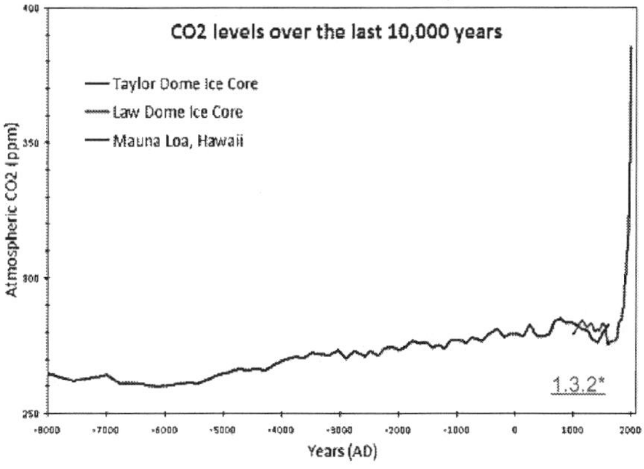

when we had both tree ring and thermometer records. We cannot merely take such changes in measurements in a vacuum but must now leave some room for doubt.
For example, look at figure 1.3.2,[35] which shows the CO_2 content of the Antarctic ice sheets that are thousands of years old. Before the mid-1950s, the CO_2 estimates were calculated based on the CO_2 gas content in the ice cores. The CO_2 levels measured in this fashion never seemed to get much over 280 ppm over a ten thousand year period. Now note that starting about 6,000-years ago we see a small but steady increase as we look from left to right. And the growth seems at a reasonable constant rate until the mid-1990s. Here the classical assumption is that the CO_2 and the temperatures were both going up, and we'll cover their relationship later.

But recently scientist are also looking at the slope going down if we stand in the 1950s and look right to left. Doing so raises the question, is CO_2 getting squeezed out from the glaciers by its enormous weight as it ages and perhaps also in combination with CO_2 being chemically sequestered out, and in what proportions? Then starting the mid-1950s, we see a very substantial and fast rise in CO_2 levels, and we see the now-familiar CO_2 hockey sticks. Did the CO_2 shoot up that fast, or was part of the anomaly caused by the change in measurement methods?

How would the average person know? Was this dramatic change ever explained in a clear, understandable way to the average citizen? For now, let's refer to the subject in a more general term as "data integrity," and we'll come back to this in later chapters to see the challenges it poses. Here is another simple example. If we wanted to measure the temperature in the Boston area 200 years ago, we might have taken say, twenty thermometers to twenty different locations. We would have made some general decisions about putting a few along the coast and the rest in various spots in the city and countryside—mostly on farms. We may have only put one or two in the mountains or forests because these stations needed to be manned, and data recorded several times a day. Then, maybe once or twice each day or week or month, they might have been consolidated, obtaining an average "Boston temperature" for October 1820. How would we compare that to the Boston weather of October 1920 or 2020 to see if it's been increasing or not? Well, it poses quite a challenge:

- Over the last one hundred years, some trees might have grown around the thermometer, while in 1918, the thermometers might have been in full sun all day long. Now what?
- Some instruments had to be moved for some reason, like a major highway construction; how did that affect the temperature readings?
- Some instruments might have gradually gone out of calibration for months or even years before they were repaired or replaced. What do we do with the suspect data during the questionable period? Ignore it? Guess what it could have or should have been?
- When the instruments were replaced, how were they replaced? Some variables include the same height from the ground, the same protecting box, mercury replaced by alcohol thermometer or thermocouples, etc.
- How about a weather station that was next to a dirt road until it was covered by cement in 1926 and by tar in 1963? Later, to be reconfigured back to a dirt road when the area became a nature park in 2004?
- How would we compare, contrast, and integrate those temperatures[36] with temperatures leading up to 2020? Very different and very challenging:
  - Instruments that were once in a pasture are now near airport runways and jet exhausts! Another place at the end of the airport near a brick or glass building.
  - Another one was near a shady, sandy road that's now an asphalt parking lot.
  - Another went from a barn side to a skyscraper rooftop.
- Thermocouples have replaced many thermometers; how were the readings "stitched together"?
- Other weather stations were just abandoned because of the high costs of maintaining them or were replaced by a remote thermocouple, telemetry, or not even replaced.

1.3.3

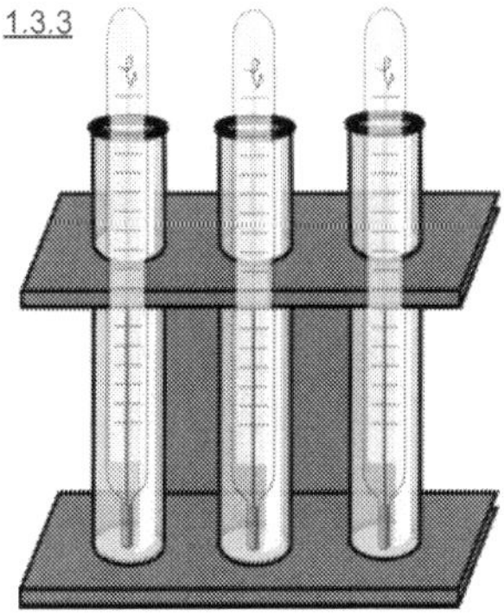

- How to reconcile[37] the effect of the pollution of the 1940-1990s with the pristine skies of the 1800s when clouds play such an important role?
- And the cloud cover of 1819 was probably quite different from today as a result of the increasing levels of "aerosols," which play such a vital role in cloud formation, the "greenhouse" and

"Albedo" effects.

In recent decades, and especially since the satellite period, hundreds of Earth-based weather stations were abandoned for a variety of reasons, including cost and data reliability. Over the past several decades, NASA and NOAA have been trying to "normalize" current and historical recorded land-based and sea-based weather records. Note in the below figure[38] where we see two sets of precisely the same data! The blue line represents the actual land-based temperatures from 1,218 stations in the US at the time the readings were taken. Compare that to the red line, which represents these very same temperature records but after they were "normalized" by NOAA.

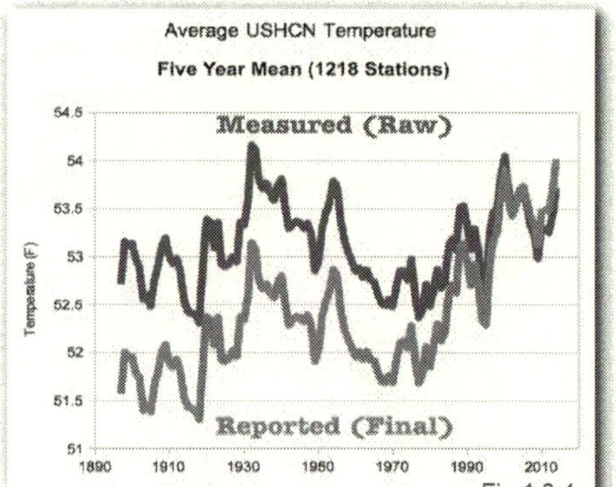

Fig 1.3.4

"Normalization" has a clear and justifiable scientific and practical basis. But many scientists say that the process is susceptible to errors of assumptions or execution. Some scientists, like Dr. Easterbrook, claim that these historical records were purposely manipulated. Accusations have been made that these temperatures were skewed to fit the current narrative of CO2 induced global climate change. The historical blue line data has been changed at least four times over the past few decades, and now in its final form, the red line shows a more dramatic, steeper temperature rise since the 1980s and lowered the temperatures in the previous decades! These days, when we are asked to make multi-trillion-dollar decisions based on the question, "did the temperature increase by 0.2 or 0.4^0 C over the last century?" Issues such as these have become extremely serious and consequential.

QUESTION 4: *IS CLIMATE CHANGE REAL?*

Yes, is the accurate and straightforward answer, because the vast majority of people might be thinking, "Well, yes, it rained last week and may snow next week." But it's a poor question to ask because at best, it lacks context or perspective. At its worst, it's a set up for a confrontation. Also, this question violates the code we laid out in the introduction of our hitchhiker's journey of not asking questions that can be answered by a simple yes or no. So, if we are asked that question, we need to reframe it to give it context and perspective. For example, we might respond by asking, "by climate change, do you mean a change that could impact our children or grandchildren years from now, or are you asking if it may be a rainy April this year?" Most people know that in the past, there were ice ages and wooly mammoths, and if they saw the movie "The Grapes of Wrath," they also know how hot it was in the 1930s and how many lives were destroyed by that heat. Now, having reframed the question, let's address it first in historical terms and then draw some inference for what's ahead for us.

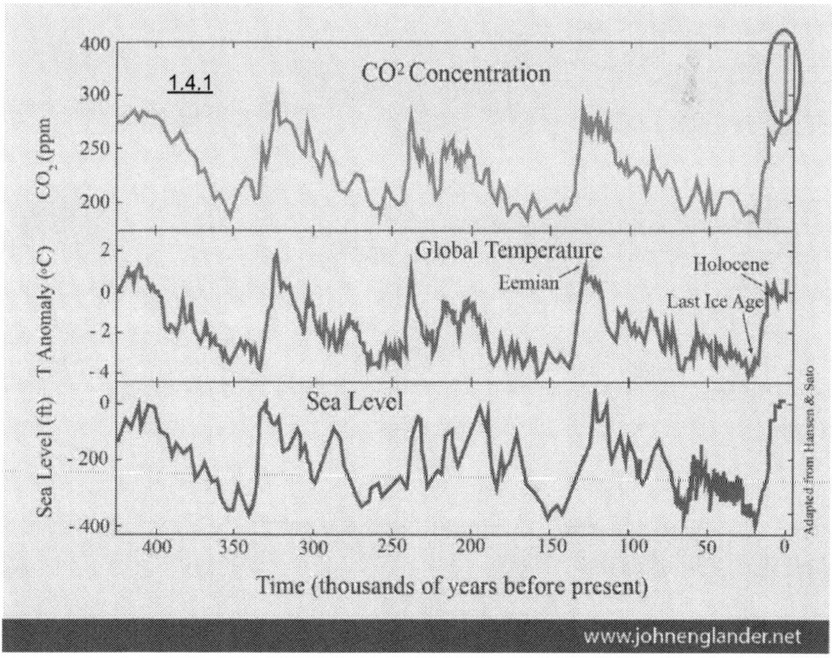

Figure 1.4.1*[39] shows both weather and climate are constantly changing; they have always been changing and will continue to change.
There are many and complex causes of this climate change. Some of these causes may be very dramatic while others not so much. To get started, let's divide these causes of climate change "drivers" into five distinct groups.

<u>The first group</u> is related to the planetary orbit of the Earth around the sun, and we all know this takes about a year. We know that when the sun is shining brightly in the northern hemisphere in July, we feel warm. But in winters, when the same sun is shining equally bright, it doesn't feel as warm. So, we might ask, what's causing the difference? Let's take a quick look.

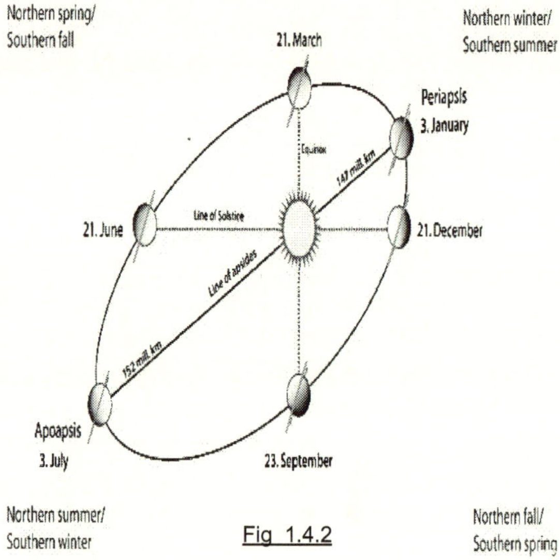

<u>Fig 1.4.2</u>

One reason for this seasonal heat difference is the change in the distance between the Earth and the sun as the year progresses. In grade school, we were taught that the Earth is about 150 million kilometers away and goes around the sun in about 365 days. But the 150 million kilometers is an average for the year. This distance is changing every day and every second throughout the year. As seen in figure 1.4.2, *[40] the gap between the Earth and the sun varies throughout the year from a maximum distance of about 152 million kilometers to a minimum of about 147 million kilometers. This changing distance is what gives us the four seasons; spring, summer, fall, and winter. This happens because the orbit of the earth is not round; instead, it's an ellipse or egg-shape. Also, the Earth is not at the center of the oval, but off to one side, as shown in the drawing.

Now you have a good understanding of the shape of the Earth's orbit around the sun and the position of the sun relative to the Earth's orbit. Good, but now I must tell you that the shape of this orbit changes a little bit each year. After thousands of years, the Earth's orbit becomes more and more round, more like a meatball and less like an egg. Then slowly, it will keep on changing and will again become more egg-shaped until it reaches the maximum egg shape or "ovality." A complete cycle, from maximum to minimum ovality and back to maximum ovality, takes more than 100,000 years.

How significant is this change in the solar orbit? Presently the sun is about ninety-three million miles away, but slowly this distance will increase to a maximum of 120 million miles, almost 30% farther away. It's like when you're sitting around a campfire nine feet away, and then you move back to twelve feet away. You know it's going to feel colder at twelve feet than nine feet. Then the sun slowly starts moving closer until the Earth orbit is nearly round, and then the distance is only eighty-three million miles away. That's like going from a perfect nine feet from the fire to seven feet, and you're going to feel a lot warmer, maybe even too hot. So yes, this changing of the shape of the solar orbit will change the distance between the Earth and the sun and will cause significant climate change. Most scientists say it's what caused the last five ice ages (Fig. 1.4.1) that seem to occur about every 100,000 years. But not to worry, we are many thousands of years away from that problem.

The second group is caused by the change in the tilt of the Earth relative to the sun. This "axial tilt" presently is about 23.70^0 (Fig. 1.4.3). *[41] But again, things are always changing. In the northern hemisphere, the Earth will slowly tilt more and more towards the sun. Then it slowly starts leaning back away from the sun. 40,000 years later, it will return nearly to where it is today. This tilt can go to as much as 24.50^0 and as little as about 22.70^0. This change in angle determines how much more or how much less of the sun's heat reaches the northern hemisphere and vice versa for the southern hemisphere. The result of the tilt is significant because it makes the difference between winter and summer and spring and fall, and everything in between. Let's go back to our campfire example and park our butt on a log and look at figure 1.4.2 again. At the lower left, you see "3 July," and your immediate reaction is, "Wait, this can't be right! July is when the Earth is farthest from the sun! How can it be the warmest, at least in the northern half of the planet?" And to make matters more confusing, you look at the top right-hand corner and see "3 January," which you know in the north is the coldest, but here you are at the point closest to the sun. How can this be?

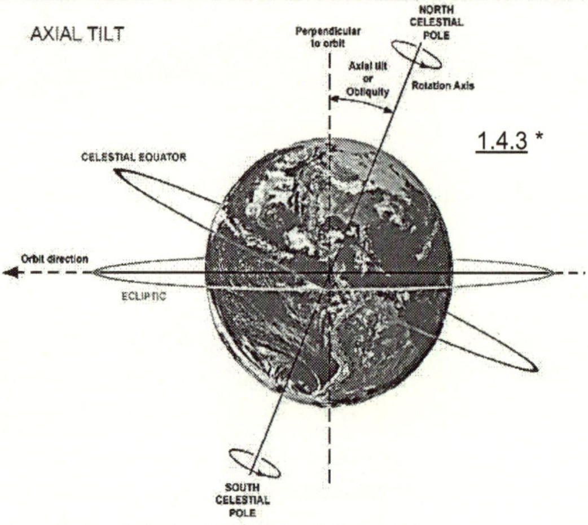

1.4.3 *

Source : http://upload.wikimedia.org/wikipedia/commons/6/61/AxialTiltObliquity.png

Here's what is going on. First, look at figure 1.4.2, the small picture of Earth at the "3 July" position, and notice the little vertical orange line going through the planet. You can see it better in figure 1.4.3, where it's called the North/South "Celestial pole." In the north, in July this line is tilted towards the sun and see the southern hemisphere is tilted maximum away from the sun. Now let's go back to the campfire, stand up very straight ten feet away, and assume the fire is on a pedestal at the same height as your tummy (your belt is your equator). Now feel the heat on your tummy; it's warm. But as you go up and down your body, it feels colder on your head and feet, right? Now, step back one foot, hold on to two of your most trusted friends and lean your upper body towards the fire twenty-five degrees and slide your legs back away one foot back and tilt by the same twenty-five degrees. Now, what do you feel? Your head is going to feel much warmer than it did before you tipped—your tummy just about the same. It then gets colder as you go down and is the coldest at your feet. Your upper body just went from spring to summer, and your lower body went from fall to winter. Of course, the exact opposite will happen if you tilt the top of your body from vertical back away from the fire.

So, in July, this forward tilt gives the northern hemisphere more heat than it loses by being a little farther away from the sun. But the total heat coming towards the Earth is a bit more in January and lower in July because the sun is not in the middle of the orbit. The exact opposite will occur in July when, on the whole, the planet is a little farther from the sun. Finally, because of this tilt, we in the northern hemisphere get summer in July when we are farthest away, and winter comes when the Earth is closest to the sun. That's a perfect thing for all of the Earth; otherwise, it would be unbearably hot during the northern summers and even colder during the northern winters. Another example of the Earth's Goldilocks zone.

The sun and Earth have a few other cycles that make additional changes in the relative distance and orientation of the planet relative to the sun. These impact the amount of energy that Earth receives from the sun and where there's more heat, i.e., northern versus the southern hemisphere. These include two types of "precession" and one called "Solar Wobble." Their effects are much smaller than the above orbit and tilt and are beyond the scope of this chapter.

The third and fourth source of climate change: Some changes in the Earth's climate and weather are caused by changes within the sun itself. The sun undergoes very complicated and powerful magnetic cycles from high magnetic activity to low magnetic activity. From Earth, it's easy to tell the difference because when the magnetic activity is high, we see lots of sunspots. When we see few or sometimes no sunspots, we know the sun is in the low activity period. Ever since Galileo got his first telescope for his birthday, scientists have been carefully counting the number of sunspots for hundreds of years. Over time, improvements in telescopes and now satellites, we are currently doing an excellent job of getting an accurate count every day, and the data is freely provided to all.

The change in the sun's magnetic activity causes two changes in the Earth's weather and climate. One is Total Solar Irradiance (TSI), and the other is the change in Galactic Cosmic Rays (GCR). We'll get into those details and impact later. For now, we'll summarize it as follows:

- Regarding TSI, there is an increase in the TSI arriving on Earth during the more active sun periods and less in low activity cycles. But the total energy increase or decrease seems too small to explain any apparent change in the global climate. There are some indications that the composition of the TSI also changes, i.e., less ultraviolet (UV) and possibly more infra-red (IR) during low activity. That may make a more significant difference individually than in total. For example, the vast amount of UV is absorbed by the atmosphere, and only a tiny amount makes it to the land and seas. So, a reduction in UV does not have an immediate impact on the energy that reaches us here on the ground and the sea.

- On the other hand, IR is not absorbed by the air, and nearly all reaches the land and oceans. Thus, it keeps heating the ground and oceans even in times of low solar activities. Scientists must do a much more in-depth analysis to reach a more comprehensive TSI/global climate change cause and effect relationship.
- Global Cosmic Rays (GCR) are much better understood today than a mere five years ago, which appears to be much more consequential to climate change than TSI variation. The effects of GCR has recently been solidly coupled with the solar magnetic activity. During periods of high activity, the sun produces mighty solar winds and magnetic fields that block many of the GCR from reaching the Earth. During periods of low solar magnetic activity, the solar winds and magnetic fields are weaker and more GCRs penetrate the Earth's atmosphere, lands, and oceans.
- Many of these GCRs that enter the atmosphere will collide with the atmospheric gasses and aerosols and create "cloud seeds." In areas with an abundance of water vapor in the air, the increased number of these cloud seeds will cause more, bigger, and denser clouds during low activity periods. This increased cloud cover and cloud mass will create more rain and prevent more sunshine from reaching Earth. The net result is that the planet is colder and wetter in areas of lots of water vapor. But in areas with little water vapor in the air, there will be even less cloud formation causing more sunshine, resulting in the usually hot and dry regions to become warmer and drier.

<u>The fifth group:</u> Lastly, and independently of the above four factors, a portion of the Earth's climate change is caused by the greenhouse gasses that are contained in the Earth's atmosphere. As seen in 1.4.1 above, we note that there has been a steady rise in the amount of CO2 in the Earth's atmosphere within the last century, and CO2 is one of the known greenhouse gasses. Many scientists have attributed the recent temperature increase primarily due to this CO2 increase. Other reputable scientists contend that perhaps the CO2 increase might be contributing to some

increased warming. In any case, it's hard to tell if the human-made portion of the CO2 is enough to make a noticeable difference. This is at the core of many debates and is discussed in depth below and later chapters.

<u>Other heat sources:</u> Two other sources of heat are contained within the planet. One is the heat generated by the decomposition and fermentation of biomatter (i.e., rotting leaves). The other is the heat generated within the Earth's internal nuclear-powered furnace. These last two are generally treated as constants and not discussed much when dealing with climate change. But they both are considered as limited options for replacing a small portion of the electricity generated by fossil and nuclear fuels.

To summarize, this is what we know: whether we are all doing something or nothing at all, whether we are burning coal or firing up the nukes or getting 100 percent of our energy from renewables or not. We will continue to experience climate change, and the vast majority is out of the control of humankind.

QUESTION 5: *What the Heat?*

1.5.1

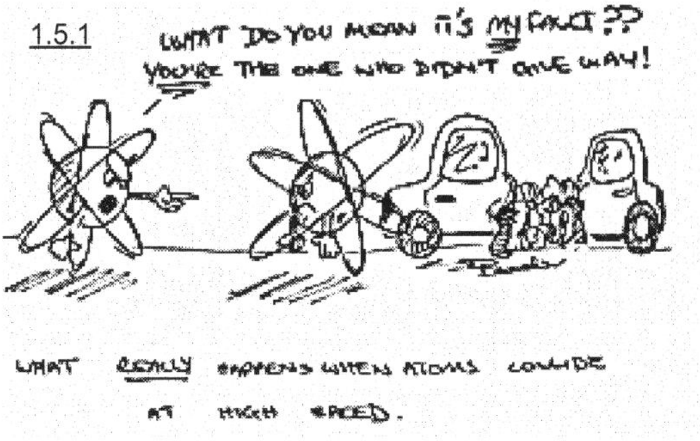

<u>Brace up because</u> this is going to be a mouthful! Heat is the random or "Brownian Motion" of atoms, molecules, and other subatomic particles in a system. A system may be a glass of water or a cloud or the planet Earth and everything else in the universe. Temperature is how we measure the energy of this motion. We measure it in degrees Fahrenheit, Celsius, Kelvin, or electrically with millivolts or spectral

wavelengths and even in more exotic ways. So, if we put more energy into a system, say, like heating a pot of water, the motion and speed of the atoms in the water increases, as does the energy of the molecules colliding at higher speeds. Faster speeds mean more collisions and more powerful collisions. Similarly, the same thing is happening with the container, and the stove rack and things start heating (Fig. 1.5.2).[42]

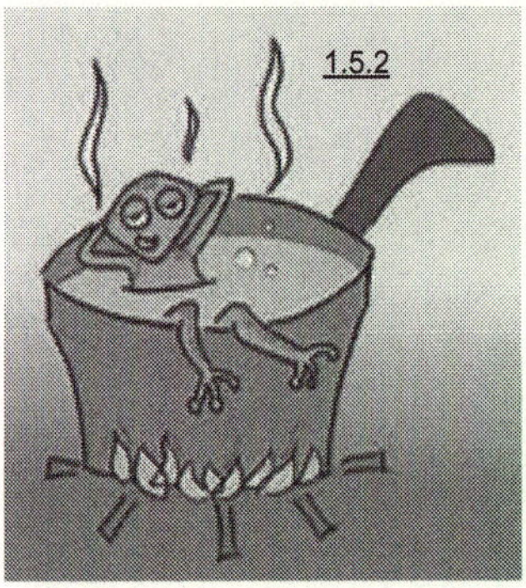

Conversely, if we chill the same pot, the motions of those same atoms and molecules slow down, and the temperature goes down. If we chill the system, say, a beaker of water to almost absolute zero (-273^0 C), nearly all that motion stops and weird things start to happen, like super electrical conductivity and other bizarre quantum stuff. But as of today, we don't know how to chill something to absolute zero, and we'll continue to focus on weather and climate. Now comes the question, how does heat move? How do we get heat from one thing to another? Like from the sun to the Earth or from the flame to the pot as pictured in 1.5.2?[43] The answer is there are three ways heat moves from hot to cold. The cold never goes to the heat.

<u>Convection</u> is what you experience when holding your hands over a bonfire, where the hotter air near the flame rises to the cooler air and warms your cold hands.

<u>Conduction</u> is like warming your hands by wrapping them around a hot cup of coffee.

<u>Radiation</u> happens when I put my hands beside the bonfire, and the infrared portion of the light waves travels from the flame to my hands by electromagnetic waves. Sometimes we get one or more of these methods working at the same time.

Now let's take a look at the water in the pot and see what happens when we put water at 20^0 C on a burner and turn on the heat. We look at the thermometer, and the red line starts going up. The question is, how high will it go? We keep watching it and see that when it gets to 90^0 C, it stops. What happened? Why did it not continue to keep going up until all the water is boiled off into steam? Now suppose the temperature in the kitchen and every object in the room is at 15^0 C. When we put water in the pot at 20^0 C, it immediately starts to cool down, because everything in the kitchen is at 15^0 C. The 20^0 C pot and water starts radiating, convecting, conducting some of its heat to the cooler 15^0 C stuff in the room. The heat from the warmer pot and water moves to the other cooler things in the room, because nature does not like any temperature imbalance.

So, when we start the flame, it starts to heat the water, but it also starts heating everything around it. Not all of the heat goes from the flame to the water. Some of the heat goes to the pot, some of the heat from the flame, pot, and water goes to the air, you, the walls, etc. Moreover, if we turn on a fan and blow the warm air away from the container, it will accelerate this heat transfer to the surrounding stuff. Perhaps with the fan on, the water temperature in the container can only get to 70^0 C., But we can get it back up to 90^0 C or more if we turn up the flame.

We can also flip this heat/motion thing on its head.[44] For example, if you take a big hammer and smash it on an anvil hard, then put your hand on the anvil or the hammer; you will feel it has turned hot. Or if you smash it with a little hammer, then it only heats up a bit. So we can change heat (thermal energy) to kinetic energy (energy of motion) and back the other way. This is called a "reversible reaction."

Now comes the fun part. Energy will always move in one direction and never the other way around (high to low, hot to cold, fast to slow). We use this phenomenon in thousands of different ways every day without even knowing it. Engineers and scientists call this the "second law of thermodynamics." If I put an ice cube on top of a hot pan, the heat from the pan moves to the ice cube by one or more of the three means described above until the temperature difference is eliminated.
Similarly, in this case, the heat from the pan warms up the ice cube until it melts and keeps heating it until the water turns to steam and vaporizes. With all the water gone, the stove continues to heat all the other stuff in the

kitchen until a new higher temperature equilibrium is reached. In weather and climate, this is a fundamental concept, as it explains many things. It describes how the sun warms the air, sea, and land during the day and why and how it cools at night. It also helps to explain how the oceans store heat and how that heat is redistributed around the planet in a vain effort to eliminate all heat and energy differences. Another thing it explains is how that heat is distributed around the globe in a futile attempt to reduce all heat and energy differences.

QUESTION 6: *SOURCES OF HEAT?*

The Earth itself.[45] There is a considerable scientific debate on how much or how significant this heat is. In a July 19, 2011 article in *Physics World*,[46] a group of scientists estimated this internal heat to be approximately 50 percent of the total heat that is radiated from the Earth into outer space. Others consider that figure at only a few percentages. The debate will likely continue for a long time because it is challenging, if not impossible, even to estimate. With today's technology to estimate the Earth's core temperatures, many assumptions need to be made. Also, what remains a significant unknown is how much of this core heat is generated by the radioactive decay of Uranium and Thorium, versus how much is from the primordial energy, left from the formation of the Earth.[47]

Eons ago, kinetic energy from the asteroids and meteors smashing to the Earth (remember the hammer hitting the anvil?) imparted a lot of energy into the Earth's core. We do know that this internal heat (nuclear plus residual) accounts for the molten core that generates the Earth's magnetic field and helps protect us from some of the sun's UV rays, solar cosmic rays, and solar winds. It's also the same energy that moves the tectonic plates around the planet and occasionally results in volcanic eruptions, earthquakes, and tsunamis. It is also the source of the geothermal power used in countries like Greenland and Iceland to make electricity and entertains us as we watch "Old Faithful" periodically explode at Yellowstone National Park. For climate change purposes, we can't control this internal heat, which we can't even measure. Therefore, we'll treat it as a constant and "ignore it" until better data becomes available.

Other heat sources can include natural sources, like a forest fire or human-made sources such as the agricultural industry and cooking fish. In addition to heat, these natural and human-made activities also produce CO2 and other gasses and compounds like methane, which further contribute to global warming, as discussed later.[48]

Human-made heat comes in two flavors. The first is the direct sources, like the chemical discharge of combustion power plants, or cars, trucks, and waste heat from electrical power plants. Then there is indirect "heating" by the retention and storing of heat when we produce CO2, which then contributes to the greenhouse effect. Note that CO2 does not provide any heat by itself, but it does help the Earth retain some heat by preventing it from escaping to outer space too quickly. This is the greenhouse effect, and acts as a blanket around the Earth, and enables all life on earth. By the greenhouse effect, the sun's energy is first absorbed by the air, land, and oceans and stored during the day. Then later at night, it keeps the Earth system warmer by preventing some of that heat from quickly escaping back to space at night. Much more on this in the later chapters.

~ 2 ~

INTERMEDIATE QUESTIONS

Rated GGF – Family and Good Friends

QUESTION 7: *HOW DOES THE SUN'S ENERGY GET TO THE EARTH?*

The Earth system[49] is made up of its land, seas, and atmosphere, where about 95% of the energy comes from the sun in the form of radiation by way of electromagnetic waves.[50] Only a minuscule amount comes from the solar mass ejections and solar winds. Second, only a tiny, tiny amount of energy released from the sun is directed towards the Earth. The rest shoots off in all directions into outer space, with some going to our sister planets and moons and the vast majority wandering in space for billions of years. Only a part of the energy directed at the Earth reaches its system because of the Earth's energy shields. The Earth's shield systems include two significant guards; the Earth's magnetic field, and the second is the clouds[51] and air (Fig 2.7.1.*[52]) So, let's examine each of these systems in detail.

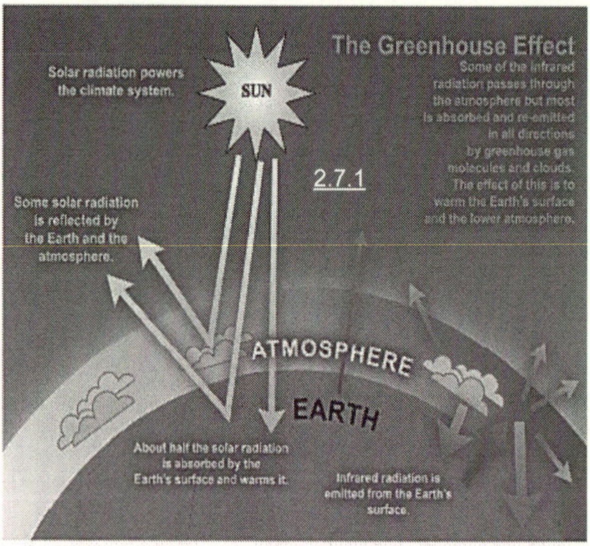
The Greenhouse Effect
Solar radiation powers the climate system.
SUN
Some of the infrared radiation passes through the atmosphere but most is absorbed and re-emitted in all directions by greenhouse gas molecules and clouds. The effect of this is to warm the Earth's surface and the lower atmosphere.
2.7.1
Some solar radiation is reflected by the Earth and the atmosphere.
ATMOSPHERE
EARTH
About half the solar radiation is absorbed by the Earth's surface and warms it.
Infrared radiation is emitted from the Earth's surface.

Clouds: On a typical day, clouds reflect about 20-30 percent of the suns' energy rays into outer space. But the actual values at any one place will vary depending on where you are on Earth. In one area, it can be a little over 3 percent, like in a high-altitude desert in Arizona. In another place, it can be 30 percent or more in the lower level and more humid zones, like in Florida. Some rays that reach the ground are also reflected or bounced back into space by the ocean, snow, ice, cars, and even by kids playing with mirrors. The rest is absorbed by the Earth's bio-system, land, sea, and air. Clouds are a critical factor in the Earth's energy cycle and balance. Clouds are groups of tiny water droplets (not a gas), and not all clouds are the same. Some clouds are high and wispy and offer little shielding and absorption, while in the lower altitudes, the denser and thicker clouds, those that have a white top layer and darker bottoms, do the most reflecting and absorption.

Figure 2.7.2 [53] is a representation of this cloud cycle. It forms clouds when unmeasurably small seeds [54] occur via natural and human-made processes like dust and gasses that float up into the air. When they reach certain levels, depending on the altitude, and the pressure, temperatures, humidity, etc., the atmospheric water content, called "water vapor," or what we experience as "humidity," starts grouping and sticking and condensing around these seeds in a process called "nucleation." They continue to group and grow until tiny water droplets form. These water droplets continue to grow and cluster until they are big enough, and then it starts to rain or snow. The size of the cloud then decreases, and the cycle begins again. More about

the importance of clouds later, when we get into the IPCC climate modeling.

Earth's magnetic field: The Earth has a powerful magnetic field that deflects away from the Earth many charged particles from the sun's solar wind,[55] solar mass ejections, and the solar cosmic rays and some galactic cosmic rays. In fig 2.7.3, we see a representation of the solar-charged particles streaming towards Earth at very high speeds. Some of these particles have no electric or magnetic charge, so they go right through the magnetic shield. But the Earth's magnetic field redirects a substantial number of the charged particles and guides many of them to the north and south poles, where we can see them in the northern sky at night as the aurora borealis and in the south as the aurora australis. [56]

It's important to note that there's no such thing as a north pole location because the magnetic north pole keeps moving around by hundreds of miles. In the last few years, new research seems to indicate that galactic cosmic rays may be a much more significant driver of weather and climate change than previously thought.[57] I will discuss magnetic fields and cosmic rays in the subsequent questions below.

QUESTION 8: *HOW MUCH SOLAR ENERGY REACHES THE GROUND?*

The sun sends the vast majority of its power towards the planet by light, or more precisely by electromagnetic waves. TSI is how we measure the amount of energy received from the sun by the Earth's uppermost part of the atmosphere (edge of space). In simplified terms, we measure not just the light we see but all the other invisible lights, like infrared and ultraviolet, that we can't see. We measure this TSI in watts hitting an imaginary perpendicular flat mirror that's a one-meter square located over the equator at the very edge of space. This baseline TSI measures about 1,361 watts per square meter (or 1,361 W/M^2 = 1.361 KW/M^2) in one second. Over an hour, it would accumulate enough power to run a 100-watt bulb for about thirteen hours. This amount will also vary depending on the Earth's relative position towards the sun, as described above in the Milankovitch cycle. Once we adjust for the light that's reflected into space and averaged over the planet with all geometrical factors, time of day, latitudes, etc.,[58] the baseline average energy arriving on Earth, at the edge of space, is about 341 W/M^2. Now from that, we have to subtract about 100 watts by the energy reflected up by the air, oceans and land and clouds, leaving us with 240 Watts. We then subtract 77 about watts for the energy absorbed by the atmosphere and clouds, and we have a net of 163 W/M^2 as the net "global energy average" arriving on the lands and the oceans.

But the actual amount of power that reaches the rooftop of your house depends on many specific local factors. For example, your elevation above sea level, how far your home is north or south of the equator, the amount of cloud cover in your area, the humidity of the air, and the time of day (noon or dawn). Lastly, if you want to go green and convert that TSI to electricity, we need to know how your roof panels are oriented towards the sun and the conversion efficiency of the solar panels you would install. We'll get into these details later on, but for now, let's say that the average TSI at your home solar panel is estimated at 150 W/M^2. Now, if we assume an 80 percent efficiency factor for the solar panel, that would translate to about 120 W/M.[2] This means that less than nine percent of the 1,361 W/M^2 (120 / 1,361 = 8.8 %) benchmarks energy can be put to practical work on your home in the form of electricity. This is the reason that climatologists call sunlight a very "diluted," or a watered-down source of power.

We need to do many more studies on TSI because when the sun is less active, TSI is reduced. But this does not mean that the same amount reduces all of the different kinds of electromagnetic wave energies. Second, not all electromagnetic waves carry the same level of energy. Here's an illustrative example, let's assume we have a stampede of wild animals rushing from the sun to the Earth. We have some elephants and lions, a lot of camels, a few horses, hundreds of cute bunnies, and thousands of fireflies. We end up with an energy density curve, as shown in figure 2.8.1.[59] Here we see the mighty elephant (blue line,) in the 480-610 nanometers (nm) range, which is the visible light, blue. On the right side, we have the camels, aka the shortest of the invisible infrared waves in the 600 nm range. Then we have several horses to the right, and we conclude with thousands of fireflies above the 2,000 nm range.

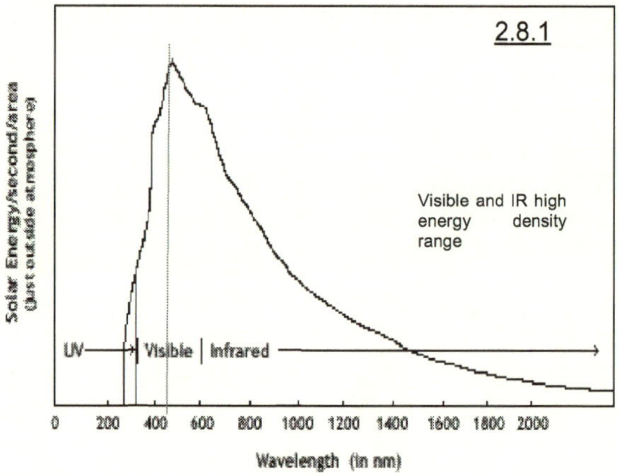

To the immediate left of the visible band, we have the ultraviolet range. Notice that it's not as powerful as the visible light or the shortest bands of the infrared. Data tells us that during periods of low solar magnetic activity, the UV portion of the TSI will decrease much more than the visible and infrared wavelengths. This is significant because we know that nearly 100 percent of the UV is absorbed by air, and only a tiny amount reaches the land and oceans. Whereas the vast majority of the visible and IR goes right through the air and heats the soil and oceans. It is also this visible and short wave IR portion that has the highest energy density, and that's the part that's absorbed by the land and seas. For example, UV might carry about 100 W/M^2 of energy compared to the visible red light that brings 2,000 $W/M.^2$ Making visible light about twenty times more potent than the UV. So, during a period of low solar activity, we might expect the air to cool faster while the oceans and land will cool at a much-much slower pace.

But to paraphrase Dr. Judith Curry, there are still so many unknowns; we are barely scratching the surface of our knowledge of climate change. Climate science is far, far from "settled." For example, we see that plants are more sensitive to decreased UV, even if the total change in TSI is not reduced very much. What's the connecting mechanism? Is it some bands of UV, and if so-which bands and by how much acting on what? The decreased UV also demonstrates another dramatic example of the drastic decrease in the temperature of our atmosphere. And we have ample evidence of that going on for over the last decade.[60] More details in later chapters.

QUESTION 9: *DOES THE SUN'S ENERGY LEVEL CHANGE?*

The sun is a hot, wild, boiling and roiling thermal, and magnetic jungle that is in constant turmoil. Not only does the TSI of the sun change,[61] but other changes also occur. Satellite images of the sun taken with x-rays, UV rays, or different spectrum wavelength, show many dramatic changes occurring in the sun, on the sun, and around the sun in its eleven-year magnetic cycle. One of the most dramatic events is that during these eleven-year magnetic cycles, the sun temporarily loses its magnetic polar field and then flips where the North magnetic Pole becomes the South Pole and vice versa. If we look at figure 2.9.1,[62] we will notice that this flip occurs at the very end of each cycle. For example, at the end of, say, cycle 22 as it transitions into cycle 23. This flip signals the start of a new cycle. During the more active parts of the cycle, we see a dramatic increase in the number of sunspots, and near them, we see these high towering bright magnetic field arches, some even bigger than a pile of Earth.

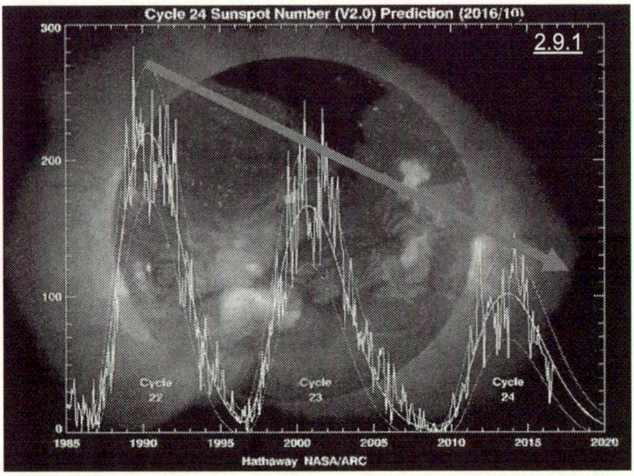

During the high activity periods, like the tips of cycles 22, 23, and 24, as seen in figure I.9.1,[63] we see over 200 sunspots in cycle 22, and a little less in 23, and a whole less in period 24. We also see an increase in the sun's temperature on the surface, the corona, and the interior change by millions of degrees Celsius. We can also measure that coronal mass ejections are less frequent and less potent during periods of low activity periods and increase as the magnetic activity level rises. The amount of energy that reaches the top of the Earth's atmosphere, TSI, fluctuates by about 0.1 percent throughout the eleven-year cycle, as shown in figure 2.9.2.[64]

Researchers once considered the amount of energy arriving from the sun as the "solar constant." They have discovered that the sun's luminosity and other energy ejections can also change over long-time scales. During the low solar activity, the sun produces almost the same level of visible and infrared, but reduced production of the other light waves, like x-rays and UV rays that are typically absorbed by the air. But also note that not all solar cycles are created equal. Looking at the blue line, we see a trend in decreased solar activities in the past three cycles. What does that mean for us on earth? What do we expect the next cycle to continue down, stay the same, or go up? And what does

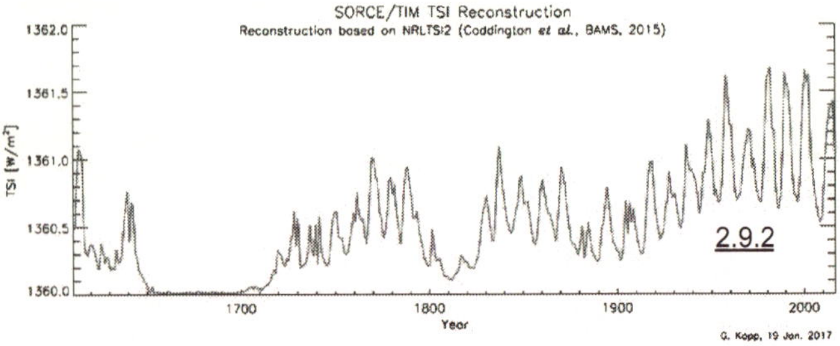

that mean to us earthlings? Maybe a peek at figure 2.9.2 may give us a preview of things to come.

Here we see that the sun experience a sizable shift in TSI over a much longer time. For example, during the seventy years called the "Maunder Minimum," the sun had few or zero sunspots. Many scientists theorize this period of low TSI helped drive the Little Ice Age, 1620-1740 when the Earth cooled by more than 1^0 C. However, it's also known that the sun has increased its luminosity [65] by about 30 percent over its four billion-year lifespan. The recently launched satellite Glory carries an instrument called the Total Irradiance Monitor (TIM). Scientists expect that it will help maintain the long-term TSI record. This record is critical for scientists who are trying to determine if longer-term solar cycles exist and how they might affect the Earth.[66]

Maunder minimum

QUESTION 10: *GLOBAL WARMING OR CONTINUING GLOBAL CLIMATE CHANGE?*

Great question and of importance to all of us. So, let's make sure we give this matter all the attention it deserves and put it into proper context. For starters, we'll use the more appropriate wording and say yes, global climate change is real. It is and has always been here. It was here a million years ago and will be here next Tuesday and millions of Tuesdays from now. But let's get very specific and start by quantifying what the climate has been doing in the last century and a half: The IPCC and the consensus group want us to focus mostly on the period 1940 to 2000. This is the period on which media, press, and the "consensus group" like to focus our attention.

Undoubtedly there has been a temperature increase of about half a degree Celsius during this period, but for now, let's get back to the basics again: The weather is short term while the climate is long-term. So, let's look at a more extended period and go back 150 years.

1860 to 2000, as see here, we see in figure 2.10.1,[67] which is vital since this is also the period where we have recorded instrument records and "proxy" records. First, we notice an overall increase of about 0.7° C and topping out in 1998. We also note from this chart by Dr. Easterbrook from his US Senate testimony that there also appears to be five distinctive periods of about twenty-thirty years each, corresponding to the average twenty-two-year complete solar magnetic cycle. Two of these cycles are "cooling," where the trend was down, and three where the directions were up.

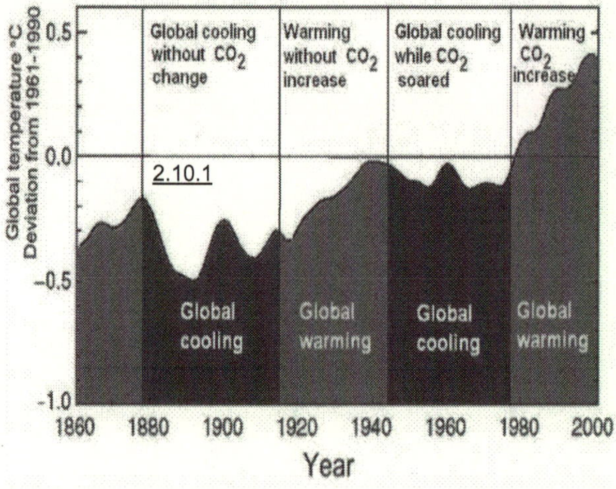

Not shown in this graph is cycle 24, 1999-2019, which is the third cycle down. So, from 1860 to 2019, we see three cycles up and three cycles down and with an overall trend up by less than half a degree Celsius in the last 150 years.

Next, we want to focus in greater detail on figure 2.10.2. And I choose this period because here we have both the land/sea-based data and the satellite data. Here we note the details showing that a significant drop followed the peak temperature in 1998-1999. This indicates that there has been a considerable temperature decrease

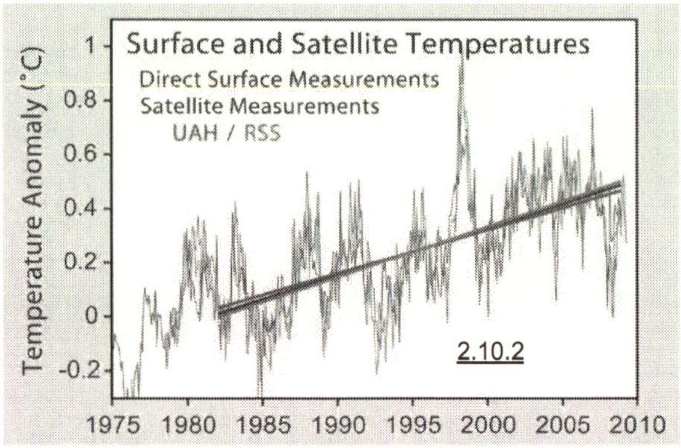

after 1999, as measured by the more reliable-accurate satellite data. Some consensus scientists are calling this cooling period a "pause" in the inescapable CO2-induced global temperature rise. It may be—let's keep exploring!

Now the big picture of the last 10,000 years. This is the earth's temperature history since the end of the last ice age, called the Holocene." This is the period of the rise in human civilization, agriculture, and recorded history, figure 2.10.3. [68] Let's see if we can put the past 150 years into a clearer perspective. Now we get a very different impression! On the left side of the chart, coming out of the last ice age 10,500 years ago, we see the Holocene warming ending about 7,000-years ago (red arrow). But then we also note that the global temperatures have been in a general decline for the last 3,500 years (see the green arrow trend.) For example, there have been five warming cycles in the past 3,500 years, and the much-advertised global warming of 1978-1999 has been the weakest warming period in 9,000 years. When looked at it from this perspective, the warm period of the end of the 20th century does not seem all that menacing from a "global warming" perspective. We are also left to speculate what cataclysmic event (s) took place 9,000 to 6,000-years ago that caused such wild temperature swings?

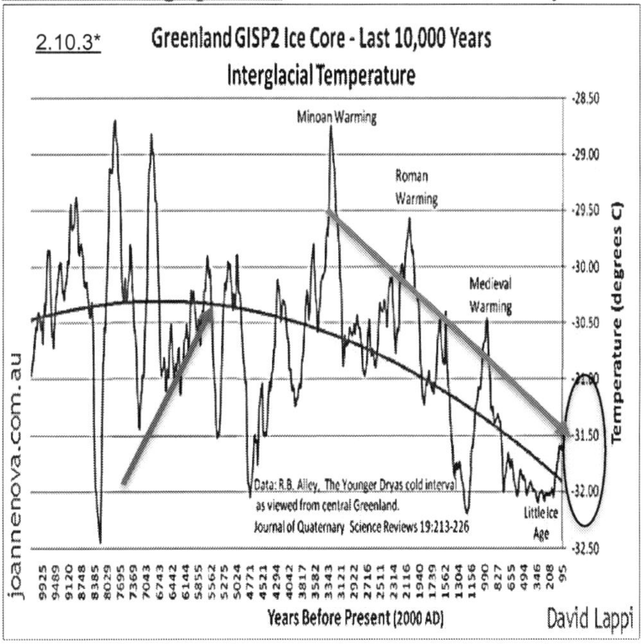

This chart seems more menacing from a "global cooling" perspective. Based on what we see on this chart, we see less concern for global warming, unless there has been something unique going on in the past fifty years, which defies physics and that we have not seen or understood yet. File this information, and let's keep exploring on our journey.

The critical question that we face is where is this temperature going in the next ten, fifty, a hundred, or five hundred years or more? And that's the reason we are taking this journey. But I'm already feeling a little better, at least for now.

QUESTION 11: *DO FOSSIL FUELS CAUSE POLLUTION AND DESTROY THE ENVIRONMENT?*

Yes, but only if you don't care about the environment or if you can't afford the technology to clean up the byproducts of the combustion, then there will be a mess. In 1970 I took my first business trip to Youngstown, Ohio. It was my first exposure to the real world of coal used for making steel and electricity. On my first night there, I was sleeping in a motel when my companion started banging on my door, "you got to see this! The river's on fire!" Yep, we looked out of the window, and the night was lit up, and the flames were flowing down the river. It was an oil and coal dust slick on the Cuyahoga River, polluted from decades of industrial waste that had caught fire near the Republic Steel mill, causing millions of dollars in damage to cars and railroad bridges.

To my horror, I found out that it wasn't even the first time [69] this river had caught fire. In the morning, as we drove to the steel plant, we saw the dust, dirt, and fly ash covering everything—streets, houses, cars, people—and a gray haze hung in the morning air. It was sad, but not hopeless. A few years later, I tried to join the newly formed Sierra Club of Boston, New York, and was working in the power generation industry trying to figure out how to burn coal cleanly. There were many competing options: electrostatic precipitators, filters of various media, scrubbers, Lurgi gasification plants, fluidized beds, etc.

The good news is that today's modern and retrofitted power plants have reduced many of the pollutants by 90 percent or more and the environmentally harmful SO_2 by 98 percent. Figure 2.11.2[70] is a feel-good chart published by the EPA to show how much progress we have made. This, however, does not mean that environmental problems have been solved. We are far from it! But it's good for the body and soul to take some satisfaction from the significant progress that has been made and continues to be made as it further motivates us to try even more in the years ahead.

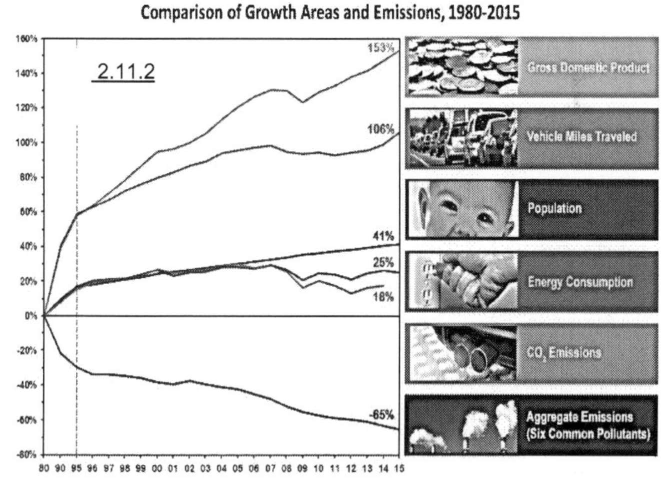

New areas of environmental challenges that are being tackled by the EPA now include diesel trucks on the roads and naval ship emissions, aircraft, and air qualities in the cities. Meanwhile, in Figure 2.11.3,[71] courtesy of

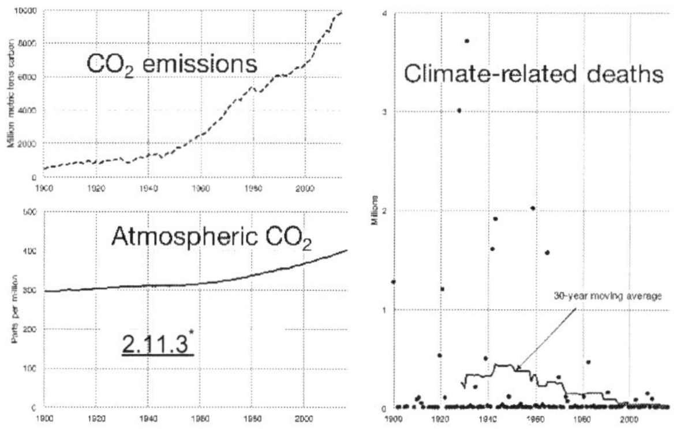

the Center for Industrial Progress and the book by Alex Epstein, "*The Moral Case for Fossil Fuels,*"[72] we see a substantial and fast decline in climate-related deaths. During this same time, there has been a significant increase in total atmospheric CO2, both from human-made emissions and naturally produced CO2.

However, as of today, there is no economically viable technology to capture CO2 even if we wanted to. As previously stated, CO2 is not a pollutant, and its role in damaging the environment is disputed. The issue here is that many partisans have sought to confuse and blur the difference between pollution and claims of CO2-induced global warming. Again, CO2 is not a pollutant; it's a gas that is essential for all life on Earth since it's the necessary component of the carbon cycle on this planet that allowed life to come into existence and vital for maintaining it.

We must reorient our educational and community discussions to stop vilifying CO2 and learn the vital role it plays on the Earth's ecological, biological and economic systems. We'll discuss this later in the book. But to summarize, all life on Earth, all plants, all phytoplankton, all living creatures, tall grasses and flowers, and trees, and you and I depend on an abundance of CO2 for our wellbeing and our lives.

QUESTION 12: *WHAT ARE RENEWABLE AND NONRENEWABLE SOURCES OF POWER?*

Before we get more into climate change and CO2 and how much increase or decrease is acceptable, let's get a sound understanding of what this is all about. It's about energy, the energy we use every day without ever thinking about it. The energy that makes our lives sustainable and the power we, in the affluent developed world, use and take for granted. Now, to keep it brief and to the point, we will only discuss electrical power—how we make it, how to make it clean and affordable, how we use it, and how we try to store it. Imagine for ten seconds what your life would be like without electrical power. We'll get into the moral, humanistic, and ethical needs for it later on. But for now, let's get a basic understanding of how we make electricity.

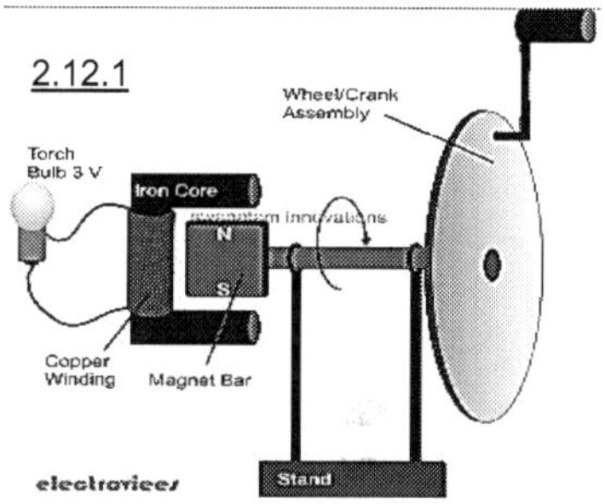

How we make electricity is a very simple process. Looking at our sophisticated design in figure 2.12.1,[73] we have three pieces in our electricity-producing machinery. One is the rotor, where on one side is a magnet, and on the other side, a handle for me to spin. The second part is the stator; it's the part that does not move at all. It includes iron core field straps (black horseshoe) wrapped with lots of wires (dark red), casing structures, and bearings, softly connecting the rotor to the stator by metal brushes. The third piece is a source of power; that would be my hand turning the crank. And voila! I crank the handle, and it lights the bulb, or power the washing machine, or charges the batteries for our eco-friendly electric cars.

Now we're not making any energy here. All we are doing is changing one form of energy, the mechanical energy provided by the hand, to the electromagnetic energy of electricity coming out of the two wires. The more mechanical power (measured in, horsepower) we put in, the more electrical power we produce (measured in watts) we get out. Second, this device produces only electricity—no pollution, no emissions, no noise, no heat, no smoke, no nothing else.

We can replace my hand with a foot pedal, a windmill, a gasoline engine, or a nuclear-powered steam turbine or whatever. Now let's look at the various sources of mechanical power we can use to turn this rotor and get the electricity we need. There are countless options, but they all fall into one of these five groups: chemical energy, nuclear energy, mechanical energy, stored energy, or photovoltaic energy. Along the way, we will discuss which of these sources are renewable or nonrenewable and which are or aren't eco-friendly. Moreover, we'll also get some comparative perspective on their reliability, affordability, availability, and safety.

Chemical: The simplest example of chemical power is the act of combining oxygen and carbon in what we call burning, oxidation, or combustion. Burning occurs at the molecular level, where we get oxygen and combine it with carbon. From the air, we get oxygen while we get carbon from wood, or hydrocarbons (coal, oil, or natural gas). In extraordinary applications, we can also combine oxygen and hydrogen, where the byproduct of that burning is only water. But since hydrogen is costly to make and very dangerous to handle, store, and transport, it's reserved only for exceptional applications.

Today most of this "burning" occurs in advanced technology engines like a combined cycle, gas-fired plant, or fluidized coal plant. These plants first get mechanical power from oil or gas-fired turbine (like a jet engine). Once that is done, we take the hot exhaust gas and use it to make steam to run a steam turbine. Then use both to drive a generator, replacing my hand in the above figure (that's getting exhausted). For home emergency backup electricity, we can buy a small unit comprising a lawnmower engine to run a small generator. Today, coal, oil, and natural gas are burned in very high-technology combustors to get the mechanical and heat energy to power the turbines. They provide the power needed to spin the generators and produce the electricity we need. They are also used to back up intermittent and unreliable solar or wind turbines.

<u>Advantages of these chemical/fossil systems are:</u>

- The fuels are obtainable from nearly all places on the planet.
- There is an abundant supply which, thanks to technology, keeps growing and is being produced at ever lower costs.
- Power plants have low-cost installations and maintenance.
- They require a tiny piece of land and can be located close to major population centers, thereby increasing efficiencies and lowering costs for us consumers.
- They are very reliable and make electricity safe and affordable.
- Except under the most extreme conditions, they are available 24/7/365, rain or shine, winter storms, or blistering summer heat.
- They are also used to back up the less reliable or intermittently available power sources such as solar or wind or hydro.
- Technological advancements in the last thirty years have made it possible to reduce nearly all the pollutants.

<u>Disadvantages include:</u>

- Fossil-fuels are nonrenewable, and maybe in five or eight or ten centuries, we will eventually run out of them.

- Compared to solar and wind, fuel costs are higher.
- We must renovate old power plants to clean up pollution and make them more fuel-efficient.

Other considerations:
- Produces atmospheric CO2; is this good or bad, or just unknown today? The jury is still out.

Nuclear: Nuclear energy is generated at the atomic level in a process we call "fission," meaning we take a big, unstable, and heavy atom like uranium 235 and break it apart into U233, plus other elements, compounds, and stuff. In this breaking-up process, tremendous heat is released, which is then modulated and controlled to make steam for the turbines to power the generators to produce electricity.

Major advantages include:
- It's the cheapest, most reliable, and the safest way of making electricity.
- Nuclear produces no pollution, and thermal pollution is about the same as fossil plants.
- Nonrenewable fuels, but who cares? It can make more fuel than it uses.[74]

Disadvantages of uranium-nuclear:
- Psychological and media-induced phobias and trauma.
- Long-term storage issues of radioactive wastes (spent fuel rods).
- Expensive licensing process because of irrational and media-induced fearmongering.

Other considerations:
- Thorium reactors will solve the long-term spent fuel storage issues that we have with uranium if we can muster the national will to go there.

Mechanical energy: Mechanical energy already exists in nature, such as redirecting naturally occurring energy into a form more useful to us. Examples of this energy include wind turbines, water turbines, tidal turbines, and river flow-submerged turbines.

Major advantages:

- No cost of fuel
- No pollution
- Low-cost maintenance

Major disadvantages:

- May require extensive use of land and reconfiguration of the ecologies in adjacent areas. But these sources often entails destroying a river and building a lake by flooding a valley to gather the necessary water to drive the hydro-turbines.
- Location is critical to catch natural wind positions, sunny spots, or high mountain lakes and rivers.
- In most locations, it needs hundreds of miles of transmission lines, increasing costs and burdens of local environments.
- Requires extensive use of energy and materials to build the installations.
- Wind turbines and solar are not reliable, and even waterpower/hydro may need a backup fossil power plant.
- They kill many birds, bats, fish, and other animals.
- River turbines are not reliable in the low-water flows that occur in the summer.

Stored Energy: We can save energy in a variety of ways. We can store electrical energy into batteries for cell phones or electric cars, but not enough to power air conditioners in Arizona or heat a home in Minnesota. We can store energy potential in what's called "Pumped Hydro." That's where we use electrical energy that we don't immediately need to pump water up the side of a mountain to fill reservoirs at the top that can later make electricity when the hydro turbines need it. This excess electricity can also pump air into the ground in areas known to have salt domes (huge caves deep underground) and then extract it later to drive air turbines. So, the stored energy is neither "clean" nor "free." It takes one of the other four energy sources to make it viable, along with the costs to generate and store it, not to mention wasted and inefficient energy. If you're driving a Tesla, your car is powered by coal, nuclear, or gas/oil plants.

Major advantages:

- Puts excess power to limited work.

Major disadvantages:

- Very inefficient, as it uses more power to charge batteries, push the water uphill, or compress air into the ground than it ever gets back when used to make electricity. It's a net negative energy source with limited usage.
- High-capacity batteries are unstable and will occasionally burn or explode.
- High investment costs and other ecological disadvantages.

Photovoltaic: This is where we use the wizardry of quantum mechanics and trick photos to convert sunshine into electricity in a relatively cheap way and without any mechanical, chemical, or nuclear forces. The problem with this, as we saw above, is that sunlight is a much-diluted energy source. Massive amounts of solar arrays are needed to power ten light bulbs. The industry is diligently working to dope or cook-up complex materials and collectors that will make the photocells more efficient. And, if there are some significant breakthroughs, it might become more economically viable than it is today.

Major advantages:

- Zero pollutants, zero CO2.
- It needs no fuels other than sunshine, wind, or water.
- Low power generation costs when it's available.

Major disadvantages:

- Not reliable; it works only when the sun is shining.
- Not efficient as we move away from the equator to the densely populated northern hemisphere.
- Needs backup power from chemical or nuclear electrical plants.
- It requires extensive use of land.
- After twenty to twenty-five years, the solar panels need to be discarded that may pose serious environmental risks.

What are renewable energy sources? Indeed, the solar, wind, and hydro are "renewable," and most are "free" fuels. Fossil fuels are nonrenewable, as it will take millions of years to replace them. Uranium-nuclear fuels are nonrenewable, but who cares? Breeder reactors can make more fuel than they use. Thorium nuclear reactors as free-renewable because the energy source material, thorium, is unlimited and almost as cheap as aluminum. Wood is renewable but impractical because of the low fuel density, pollution, and cost of transportation.

~ 3 ~

ADVANCED QUESTIONS

Rating FF – Family and Friends

QUESTION 13: *WHAT WIND & SOLAR AND ONE-OFF COUNTRIES AND THEIR EXPERIENCE*

13.1 Background. Why is wind power and solar power, not making significant gains in providing a substantial amount of clean, renewable electricity? For example, the USA has been at about eight percent wind and two percent solar for more than a decade; why is it not growing? To answer these questions, we need a better understanding of some fundamental elements, requirements, and limitations of the electrical generation business.

The big picture; it's all about the "Grid." The grid is the electrical industry term used to describe all of the hardware and software needed by the utility company to take fuel, like coal or sunlight and convert it into electricity. Then distribute that electricity by way of wires, transformers, sub-stations, etc. to all of its customers. That includes all equipment, software, personnel, and training. It needs a professional organization to ensure meeting all of the requirements. These requirements include safety to the environment, protection from malfunctions, security to customers, and safety for the community. For example, PG&E (Pacific Gas and Electric), a major California utility, is in bankrupt proceedings. They were held liable for billions of dollars because a few wires were damaged and started significant fires in California. Customers and regulatory agencies are extraordinarily demanding and unforgiving.

We'll keep it simple and use the following example: Let's assume we are a local electric utility in Smallville, USA. It's a city of 50,000 families and another 25,000 families in the surrounding farms, along with small factories, professional offices, shops, a hospital, bakeries, etc. One thing they all have in common is the need for reliable and affordable electricity and a clean and eco-friendly environment. Over the years, Smallville set up a modern grid to assure a 99.98 percent reliability. Their calculations show that to guarantee the 99.98 percent availability, they need at least a 75 percent excess capability; of which 25 percent must be in the "spinning reserve mode," another 25 percent must be in the "peaking mode," and 25 percent in the "back-up mode." Let's study each of these thoroughly.

Spinning Reserve. If some malfunctions happen at any time and shut down a generating plant, a back-up plant needs to kick-in and pick up 100 percent of the lost power in seconds. If it's a few seconds too late, the electrical demand will overwhelm the grid, causing a "brown-out," or worse, a "blackout." It's as if all the customers of a bank show up at the same time, demanding to take out all their money immediately, and it's a disaster.

The only way to ensure that this blackout doesn't happen is to have a back-up fossil power plant already running at about 90-95 percent of rated power. The problem, however, is that when operating in this spinning reserve mode, this back-up plant is still burning almost 90 percent of the fuel they would burn in a full-power manner. But in this spinning reserve mode, the back-up plants do not produce any electricity. However, they still produce the same levels of CO2 and pollution, burning almost the same amount of fuel as they would if there was no solar or wind plant. Now the good news with the fossil plants is that they can back each other up. But because of their limited availability and lack of reliability, sun and wind plants cannot back up any plants. As a result, electrical industries are wasting capital, fuel, and operating costs. More importantly, because of this spinning reserve requirement, a solar plant may only end up reducing the carbon footprint by a few percent at best. This discovery came as a total shock! How is it that no one ever told us? We've stumbled on a real-life mystery with real consequences, what do we do?

Peak mode: This is the extra electrical power that's needed twice a day, typically for two to three hours each. First is the morning peak demand, from six to nine AM to cook breakfast, get ready to go to school and work. The other high demand period is usually from about five to seven PM. That's when the extra power is needed to cook dinner, fire up the AC or central heat, etc. But solar plants can't fill either of these peak demands.

That's because solar produces electricity near mid-day when it's needed the least.

In contrast, a wind plant, especially near the oceans, or on a platform on the sea, might be put to work a few hours in the morning or evenings. But, in all cases, it still needs the spinning reserve fossil-fuel back-up plant running at about 90 percent of rated power, 100 percent of the time. Again, it seems we have stumbled across another significant unknown. Who knew this, and why did nobody tell us?

Back-up Reserve: These power plants are like a spare tire in the trunk of a car; they sit there until called to duty. But unlike the spinning reserve, these reserves don't need to be up and on-line in seconds. So, they only operate when they are started up, typically for scheduled maintenance on other plants. Depending on the type of plant, it may take several hours or more for them to come online, and then they may run for days, weeks, or a year non-stop. Moreover, they may or may not need one of the above fossil fuel backup plants. But to have a 200-300 Million dollar plant just sitting there, doing nothing most of the time is going to be very expensive. But this is understandable. It's like paying the insurance company to make sure the bank doesn't run out of money and crash.

To sum up, grids are required to have near-perfect reliability because a brownout or blackout is unacceptable. It would cost millions of dollars in damaged grid equipment and lost revenues, millions of dollars in damages to customers' equipment and products, and lost services to the public. It will impact their customers' everyday lives. It will possibly cost lives at hospitals and nursing homes and to the elderly in their own homes. So, solar and wind plants have some pressing challenges:

- Solar and wind plants need 100 percent support by fossil fuel plants, 100 percent of the time. Thus, duplicating the power generation capital costs, and operating costs with little/no apparent reduction in CO2, or pollutants or cost of fuel.
- When the fossil backups are running in the spin reserve mode, it means they are not operating in their optimum design efficiency. As a result, they produce more pollutants and possibly more CO2 than they would if they were working at 100 percent capability.

- Solar and wind require extensive use of land. In some cases, 200 times more land. We'll get into further details in later discussions.
- They are more susceptible to security concerns because they are located in remote areas and spread over thousands of acres.

<u>From my March-2019 blog:</u>

Background info, what is the contribution of wind and solar energy in combatting global climate change?[75]

Global-scale, in 3017, Solar and wind accounted for less than 3% of global electricity consumption.

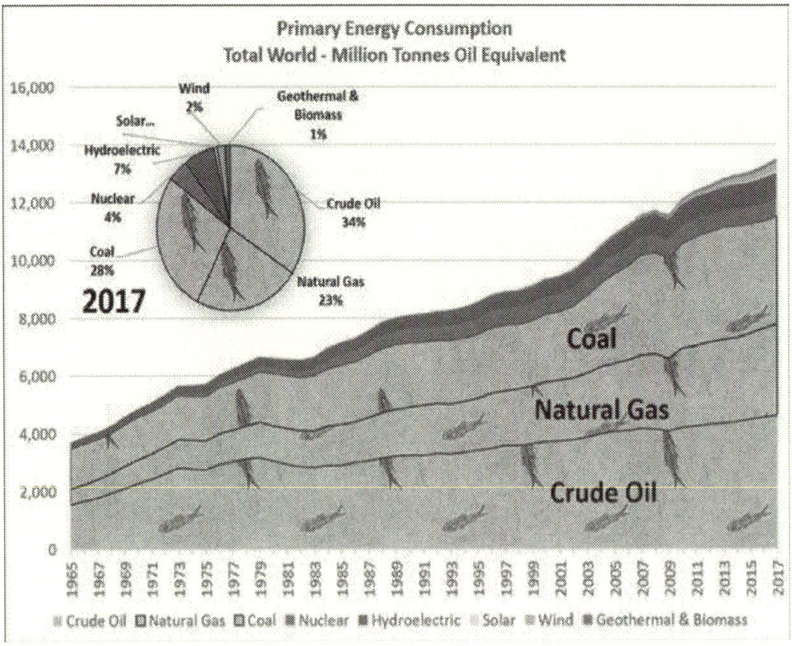

Are they even maintaining their small share? Note also that these renewables are having trouble keeping their relative percentage, because of the continuing increases in other, "non-renewable" sources.

13.2 Experience in one-off countries. We're now taking our journey overseas and see what those people are doing to control this perceived climate change problem. Come, let's take a guided tour and see the real-life experiences of countries that made the bold decision to go all-in, all-green.

Germany is the number one producer of wind and solar electrical power in the world on a per capita basis. In 2004 Germany launched an aggressive plan to replace many of their coal and nuclear plants with wind and solar.[76] By 2018 Germany had an installed electrical base of about 210 gigawatts. Of that, 28 percent was wind power, 26 percent solar, and the remaining 46 percent by their old fossil fuels, nuclear, and a little hydro. At least that is the "adjusted" nameplate rating of the power capability of these plants when operating under the best conditions. However, we find out that their real results are startlingly different. But why is that so? Well, while these solar and wind plants can produce 46 percent of Germany's needs, in actuality, they only produce about 12 percent of the nation's total electrical output. So again, we stumble across another mystery. Again, who knew this and why were we not informed about this crucial fact? Who knew that the world's most prosperous and industrialized country couldn't even produce enough electricity to meet the needs of its own people and industry?

To relieve this national shortage, Germany has been importing vast amounts of electrical power, mostly from France, and are paying through the roof. In 2018 the average cost of electricity in Germany was about 30 Euro cents per kilowatt-hour. By contrast, in the USA, the same power costs are about 12 Dollar cents per kilowatt-hour.[77] At today's exchange rate of $1.14, the average German person or company pays more than three times for his electricity than his USA counterpart. The reason for this huge disparity is that in the USA, the combined capability (in operation and construction) of wind and solar is only 10 percent versus 84 percent in Germany.

German public reaction: Let's look at some of the consequences of this German policy decision to move to a near-zero CO2 electrical system:

- As early as 2013, the problems of their electrical generating choices started going public. An article published in the German publication, Dissident,[78] leads off with a startling headline; "Green Energy Bust in Germany; Can an energy system move off carbon-based fuels and nuclear energy at the same time? Will Boisvert argues that the German

Energiewende shows why not?" The article then goes into many details, including this startling admission: "Unfortunately, the nameplate capacity trumpeted in the media is a drastically misleading measure of the electricity added to the grid. *While wind and solar nameplate capacity represented 84 percent of Germany's average electric power generation of 70.4 GW, it ultimately generated only 11.9 percent of total electricity* (up from 11.2 percent in 2011). There are simple *reasons for that discrepancy: night, clouds, and calm. The output of wind and solar generators varies wildly with the weather and the time of day; during most hours, they produce a small fraction of their nameplate power—or nothing at all."*

- Germany is the world's largest importer of electrical power. Most of it comes from France that is bought by Germany at a premium price! In an article [79] published by Clean Energy Wire, May 2, 2018, the headline reads: "French export of cheap nuclear power to Germany could surge." Essentially the German industry, economy, and standard of living did not crash because France was there to bail them out but at a price, of course.
- On top of that, the German wind turbines also have the reputation of killing hundreds of large birds, and thousands of small birds and bats[80] every year by the 52,000 installed turbines. As a result, the big E-Environmentalists are up in arms over these killings!
- Back to Germany's problems, which are not getting any better. In the past several years, Germany had to launch a major program to rebuild dozens of fossil-fueled plants on an accelerated basis. Germany signed a massive contract with Russia[81] to build a natural gas pipeline from Siberia to fuel their baseload electrical demand and to back up its unreliable wind and solar plants. In an article on cnbc.com, on July 11, 2018, Tom DiChristopher writes, *"Behind Nord Stream 2: The Russia-to-Germany gas pipeline that fueled Trump's anger at NATO meeting...."*
    - Germany may be forced to cancel this pipeline, further aggravating their electrical shortages.
    - That would leave Germany to pay billions of dollars in cancellation costs for the pipes, compressions, and the transmission equipment. They may also have to cut back or postpone some planned new fossil plants, scramble and pay premium prices for an alternate

fossil-fuel solution. On top of that, they will continue to have shortages for decades.

- o Their already expensive electrical costs may likely double or quadruple in the next few years and still have an electrical shortage with no improvements to their environments.
- o Germany's GDP growth rate for 2019 was 0.12 percent.[82] By contrast, the USA was 2.2%, with the high cost of energy dragging the German economy.[83]

Here is Germany's electrical industry at the end of 2019:

			annual	annual	production		
source	GW-Hrs.	@ adjusted factor	cap TW	% Capacity	TW	% TW	% capacity
bio	8.2	1	502.8	3.9%	44.8	7.7%	8.9%
hydro	4.8	1	294.3	2.3%	18.8	3.2%	6.4%
solar	48.8	1	2,992.4	23.2%	46.7	8.1%	1.6%
wind-off	7.5	1	459.9	3.6%	24.6	4.2%	5.3%
wind	53.2	1	3,262.2	25.3%	101.8	17.6%	3.1%
oil/misc.	4.4	1	269.8	2.1%	5.9	1.0%	2.2%
NG	29.9	1	1,833.5	14.2%	91.3	15.7%	5.0%
coal-all	43.9	1	2,691.9	20.9%	170.9	29.5%	6.3%
Nuke.	9.5	1	582.5	4.5%	75.2	13.0%	12.9%
total	210.2	1	12,889.5	100.0%	580	100.0%	4.5%
tot-renew	122.5	1	7,511.7	58.3%	236.7	40.8%	3.2%
balance	87.7	1	5,377.8	41.7%	343.3	59.2%	6.4%

Nuke: has an installed/planned capacity of 9.5 GW-Hrs., and at 100% planned utilization could generate 582.5 TW in 2019, to produce 4.5% of Germany's needs. In actuality, it produced 75.2 TW or 13% of Germany's entire 2019 power. While only utilizing 12.9% of its generating capacity. Said in another way, Germany can generate 100% of its needs using only nuclear (75.2/12.9%=583TW) if it was allowed to produce it at near 100% of its existing capacity.

Wind: has an installed/planned capacity of 60.7 (7.5+53.2) GW-Hrs., and at 100% planned utilization could generate 3,722.1 (3262.2+459.9) TW in 2019, to produce 21.8% of Germany's needs. In actuality, it produced 126.4 TW (101.8+24.6) or 21.4 % of Germany's entire 2019 power. While only utilizing 8.4% (5.3+3.1) of its generating capacity. Said, in another way, Germany has the installed capacity to generate almost 259 % of its needs using only wind (126.4/8.4% = 1,504 TW). But in actuality, it produced 126.4 TW with and installed capacity of 1,504, giving it a capacity factor of 8.4%. This means that wind power is producing electricity 8.4% of the time or averaging about 2.02 hours/day.

Solar: has an installed/planned capacity of 48.8 GW-Hrs, and at 100% planned utilization could generate 2,992TW in 2019, to produce 4.5% of Germany's needs. In actuality, only 1.6% of its total generating equipment was productively utilized in 2019."

Other unique countries that are advertised and applauded for their renewable, clean, and green energy generation:

Albania, Iceland, and Paraguay obtain nearly all their electricity from renewable sources (Albania and Paraguay 100 percent from hydroelectricity, Iceland 72 percent hydro, and 28 percent geothermal). Norway gets almost all its power from renewable sources (97 percent from hydropower). These countries all have a similar profile; few people, lots of land, lots of mountains, and lots of rain.

"Onl... ...ngs are infinite; the universe and human stupidity."
Albert Einstein
3.13.1

Sweden has a funny but sad story that needs to be told. Sweden gets 54 percent of its electricity from hydro and biomass. As with Albania, Iceland, and Paraguay, Sweden has lots of lands, mountains, water, and a small population. They launched a vast wind program a decade ago, which is proving to be problematic in their challenging environment. In their northern latitudes, solar was out of the question. Wind also has some issues (Fig. 3.13.1.[84]). This photo is from the front cover from a recent article from the online service, "whattsupwiththat.com." Here we see an amusing picture of a Swedish helicopter trying to de-ice a wind turbine like an airport tanker truck de-icing an airplane. Only the windmill is about four to five times bigger than a Boeing 747's. But a helicopter can only carry maybe 10-20 percent of what a truck can. So, by the time they've finished one or two-blades, they need to start all over again. Now imagine a wind farm with hundreds of these turbines. This picture is worth thousands of words and a few giggles. But it's not funny for Sweden.

Sweden and the other Nordic Countries also have several different challenges. They include the prohibitive costs of building wind farms in the wild and stormy North Sea and the little sunshine they get in their northern latitudes. Like Germany, Sweden is also experiencing significant electrical shortages, especially in its more populated and industrialized southern regions.

Japan. For decades Japan relied on nuclear power, producing 75 percent or more of its electricity. Then, after the Chernobyl and Fukushima disasters and the resulting political pressures from environmental groups, they did a fast turnaround and made substantial investments in wind power. But now, after a decade of electrical shortages, Japan also had to pivot on its electrical strategy. Like Germany, Japan also started to re-build fossil fuel plants and reloading some of their older nuclear plants. Hopefully, this allows Japan to fill their electrical shortage gap until they can decide what to do in the long run.

California. Figure 3.13.2[85] is a photo of the largest solar farm in the USA that just went online. It's an incredible 500 MW (megawatt) plant providing a much-advertised power for 160,000 homes. It requires 9.5 square miles of farmland or 6,080 acres. The article,[86] however, did not mention and never showed any

3.13.2

photos of the fossil plant(s) needed to provide the necessary backup power. And yes, California has the highest cost of electricity in the USA.

13.3 Summary: Grids are required to have near-perfect reliability because a brownout or blackout is unacceptable. It would cost millions of dollars in damaged grid equipment and millions more in lost revenues. The utility may even be held liable for millions of dollars in damages to customers' equipment, lost products, and lost services, and significantly impact their customers' lives. It may even cost lives, loss of life at hospitals, nursing homes, and the elderly in their own homes. So, solar and wind plants have some pressing challenges:

- Solar and wind need 100 percent backup by fossil fuel plants, 100 percent of the time. Thereby duplicating the power generating cost of capital, fuel, and operation. And, with no measurable reduction in CO2, pollutants or cost of fuel.
- When the fossil backups are running in the spinning reserve mode, which is at less than 100 percent of rated power, they are not efficient. That means they produce more pollutants and more CO2 than they would if they were working at 100 percent capability.
- Solar and wind require extensive use of land. In some cases, 200 times more land for the same generating capacity. We'll get into further details in later discussions.
- They are more susceptible to security concerns because they are located in remote areas and spread over thousands of acres.

Table 3.13.1 ESTIMAE UK LCOE for projects starting in 2015, £/MWh Table 59

Power generating technology		Base	Backup	Total
Wind	Onshore	62	60	122
	Offshore	102	60	162
Solar	Large scale PV (Photovoltaic)	80	60	140
Nuclear	PWR (Pressurized Water reactor)	93	0	93
Biomass		87	0	87
Natural Gas	Combined cycle gas turbine	66	0	66
	Combined cycle gas turbine Plus carbon capture & storage	110	0	110
Coal	Advanced Supercritical Coal with Oxy-comb. CCS	134	0	134
Coal	Integrated gasification With Oxy-combo. CCS	148	0	148

Source; https://en.wikipedia.org/wiki/Cost_of_electricity_by_source#7s8d6f87

13.4 Comparative estimates. Provided in 3.13.1[87] is comparative power generation costs in the United Kingdom for projects begun in 2015.

- Note 1: For wind & and solar backup, an estimate of 90 percent of a combined cycle, a natural-gas-fired gas turbine is used.
- In the UK, the Department for Business, Energy, and Industrial Strategy (BEIS) publishes regular estimates of the costs of electricity from different generation sources. Following is a summary on the views of both the Department of Energy and Climate Change (DECC.)
- LCOE (Levelized Cost of Electricity.)

QUESTION 14: *IS CLIMATE CHANGE REAL AND WHAT'S CAUSING IT?*

14.1 Background. The press, media, scientists, industry, academics, and politicians have been beating three drums in a crescendo over the last thirty years:

- The first drum claims that human-made CO2 caused and continues to escalate the dangers of climate change.
- Forbes magazine and many press and media raise the alarm on climate change-induced volcanic eruptions.[88]
- The second claims that human-made CO2 climate change will cause planetary-scale disasters resulting in countless deaths for humanity and possibly all life on earth.
- Lastly, we are told we have only ten to twelve years to prevent it by stopping all production of human-made CO2.

Author's perspective. The past twenty-five to thirty years does not seem to have added clarity or movement towards any useful resolutions. Instead, the venom and vitriol are only getting louder and shriller, and the "science" that backs up the CO2 claim keeps getting less and less specific. There's more to these questions than science and math. Otherwise, we would have settled the matter with the first thirteen questions we already answered. Yes, we will provide additional scientific facts and rationale to reinforce these 13 thirteen answers as we journey forward into the remaining items. But obviously, there's more going on that we need to disclose and be aware of. Otherwise, how else could we explain the fact that we have so many divergent interests, so powerfully aligned and advocated, if this was simply a scientific problem?

As an engineer, I would first tackle this fundamental question; what's the common denominator that aligns these different entities like the press, industry leaders, academics, and politicians? I would submit that they all have three things in common:

1. Money.
2. Power.
3. Social status.

With that on the table, we now resist the temptation of jumping on these emotionally charged baits and proceed with the underlying science, economics, and social behaviors. But rest assured, we will come back to address these three "social drivers" once we build our solid scientific base of knowledge. For now, we will do what any sound scientist or engineer is supposed to do—whip out the scientific method, continue to ask ever more penetrating questions, investigate facts and processes, do some experiments, and come up with our theories. Then we will make a comparison to see how these factors match up. Finally, we'll use the scientific process and basic economics to define the optimum "pro-human" solutions without resorting to endless hype, fear-mongering, and end-of-the- earth diatribes.
Deal?
Good!

Back to science. Let's start this scientific method by taking a look at the word "change" in the above question. The first question is, change from what, and change to what? And let's not forget how much change of this is needed to get how much change of that. Lastly, what is the cost of those changes, and will those resulting changes be good, bad, or only nothing? Of course, good or bad must always be defined to mean good or bad for humankind as a priority.

To answer these questions, let's start by looking at figure 3.14.1[89] and see what climate has been doing for the last 1,000 years. The first thing we notice is lots of changes. Some changes are very warm, lasting a long time. While some are a little colder, lasting a short time, others are much colder and lasting a long time. Finally, some are small changes and lasting a short time. To summarize, we'd have to say that <u>climate change is not unusual, it's normal!</u>

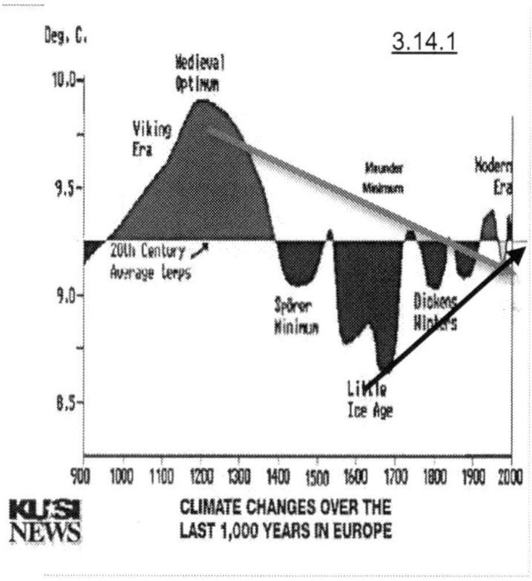

<u>Change is normal!</u> But wait, how about the degree of the change? Is that abnormal? The charts show us that Medieval Warming lasted about 400 years and was much warmer than our much fretted Modern Era. Next, we notice that in the past 800-900 years, the Earth has been substantially colder than during the Modern Era, especially the Little Ice Age. The last thing we highlight on this chart is that for the last 1,000 years, the overall trend appears to be down (green arrow), meaning it's getting colder. But if we look at the direction over the last 400 years (black indicator), it is up, meaning it's getting warmer. Does this mean we are on a long-term decline, and the Modern Era is a blip in the trend, or are we on a new long-term upward trend, as the Viking warm period? We have a lot more work to do before we can answer this question. But there are four things we can categorically state at this point:

- History repeatedly tells us, in no uncertain terms, that warm periods have been good for humanity. Populations increased. Civilizations and cultures flourished. We all experienced less turmoil and more peace and prosperity. By contrast, cold periods saw conflicts, wars, starvations, pestilence, and misery.
- Climate is changing, has always changed, and will continue to change, no matter what humankind is thinking of doing, is or is not doing.

- We need to move forward and learn a lot more before we panic into simplistic, expensive, and futile solutions.
- As a self-proclaimed student of history, a naturalist, and pro-human, I fear the cold, not warming.

14.2 Causes of climate change. Now, let us start by restating the obvious; it's all about the sun, Baby!

The sun. For the next thousands of years, the sun will be the primary driver of weather, climate, and climate change. The sun provides the Earth with more than 95 percent of the energy that arrives at the planet. The remaining 5 percent is made by the natural Earth cycles, forces, and some minuscule amount by human-made activities. But there's another fact that's hardly ever mentioned in press and media. Those are the dramatic and cyclic changes that the sun goes through every 11 -years and other more extended periods. Let's state the fact as clearly and succinctly as possible. During the next several thousand years, 95 percent or more of climate change will occur because of what the sun is doing or not doing.

In recent decades we discovered that the sun is not as stable as we once thought it was. Instead, we now see the sun going through powerful "solar cycles" that directly and indirectly contribute to the Earth's climate. Another undeniable fact that's hardly ever mentioned is that the sun also warms the other planets and moons. During this most recent warming cycle, we had the science and instrumentation to see comparable warmings on our sister planets and even our moon. One article published in "The Washington Times," May 31, 2016,[90] discussed the research conducted using the NASA Mars Reconnaissance Orbiter that allowed an unprecedented examination of the warming trends on Mars.

14.3 The second cause of climate change, which determines how much solar energy arrives from the sun to the Earth, is the Milankovitch astronomical cycles. These cycles change the positions and the distance of the planet from the sun as they interact among and between each other and the other planets. We'll get into the detail on the science and the whys, when's, and how's later. But first, let's present a more graphic description of the weather because that's what we experience each day. This will help us lay the scientific basis that will follow in later chapters. After all, what is climate other than the trends of weather over a long period?

Leading causes of the weather. "It's too hot. It's too cold. I'm tired of the rain. I wish this spring would last forever. Don't worry; there's plenty of snow at the top of the mountain." This is the weather. We talk, complain, and think about it, but nobody can do anything about it. No-bo-dy-can-do-nothing-about-it! Capish?

However, with the help of modern science, like satellites, Doppler radar, telemetry, etc., we are getting pretty good at predicting how the weather is most likely to change over the next several days. In Florida and Hawaii, it's so easy; we don't even need weather persons. At other locations, say, near tall mountains or along the coastlines, predicting the weather is harder, and forecasts are less reliable. In this section, we will discuss in descriptive detail (no math, I promise) the significant elements and forces that cause weather changes.

Wind.[91] Here's a mouthful! The wind is the movement of the air[92] as a result of the temperature differences and atmospheric pressure differences from one part of the world to another. Those differences are caused by the sun heating the Earth in one area and not the other. This is true at all levels, as the sun is shining on one part while on the other side, it's night. It also happens at the regional level, where part of the land that's heated is a mountain, and another part is a valley. At the local level, like along the coast, the Earth is warmed faster than the ocean, or if half of the sky is cloudy and half is not. Warm air is lighter than cold air, so it goes up the sky, and then the colder air rushes in to fill the void created by the warm air that went up to the sky. Remember, nature doesn't like imbalances of any kind.

Near a warm and sunny beach in the early afternoon, we usually get a gentle, cooling breeze coming in from the ocean. This happens because the air over the land warms faster than the air over the water. As the warmer air rises, the colder air that's over the ocean rushes in to fill the void. Then, as the atmosphere cools the warmer air, it comes back down and completes the cycle, as seen in figure 3.14.2.[93] But at night, the process generally reverses because the water is now warmer than the land. But at other locations and circumstances, it can be a wild ride, like a jet stream. Jet streams are fast-moving rivers of air at the boundaries of massive weather fronts. Here one is hot and the other cold. They flow west to east in the opposite direction in response to the sun's warming rotation from east to west. At the jet stream core, which is about ten to fifteen kilometers high, the airspeeds can reach several hundreds of miles per hour and move in serpentine paths over continents. The fast-moving core winds drag the adjacent air, forming a velocity gradient. The wind speeds are very -very fast near the center and keep slowing down and down until it reaches near-zero speeds, some hundreds of Kilometers away. Naturally, if mountains or tall buildings get in the way, the wind changes directions and speed in many turbulent and unpredictable ways.

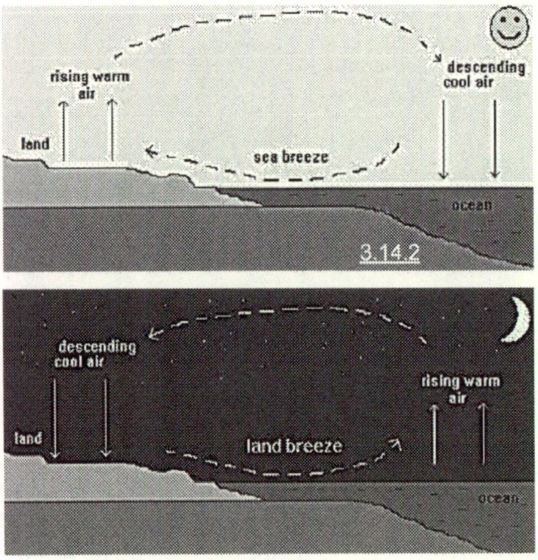

Bottle on left was sealed at 14,000 feet, and was crushed by the increased atmospheric pressure at 9,000 and then down 1,000 feet .

Barometric pressure is the weight of the volume of air on top of you. At sunrise, if you are at the beach at sea level, and the temperature is 15° C, there's a column of air on top of you going all the way up into outer space. The weight of that air is pressing down on you with a force of about 14.7 PSI (pounds per square inch) of your body. If you then go to the rooftop restaurant for brunch at 250 feet high, the pressure on you decreases from 14.7 to 14.3 PSI. Meanwhile, your friend, who is mountain climbing at 2,400 feet, the pressure on him is only about 10.9 PSI. Now the heaviest or densest air is at sea level. As we go up, it progressively gets less and less dense until it gets near outer space, where it's about zero PSI. So, going from sea level too, say, ten feet up reduces the pressure more than if you're at 250 feet up and go up to 260 feet. Figure 3.14.3[94] summarizes it very nicely.

The relationship between atmospheric pressure and temperature. Now your brunch is finished, and you go back down to the beach, and the sun has been warming it up for about five hours. Now It's the hottest time of the day, that's when the sun is directly overhead, about noon. Now you might say, "But wait. Why does it usually feel warmer an hour or two after the sun's apex has already passed us?" That's because an hour after the apex, you're getting a little less energy from the sun on your head. But the Earth you are standing on has already been heated by the sun, and some of that stored heat in the ground starts radiating and convecting up to you. You are now heated on the top by the sun and from the bottom by the warm ground.

WARNING -Warning - Fans of the Indianapolis Colts; you may want to skip the rest of this discussion. New England Patriots fans take copious notes.

Let's say its noon in Indianapolis, and the footballs are brought to the field for practice and then for play. The balls came out of a toasty locker room at 75° (Fahrenheit), and the footballs and the air inside the footballs are also at 75° F, and the PSI is 13.0. But on the playing field, it's a chilly 25° F. The footballs and the air inside starts to cool down until it reaches 25° F. The question is – what happens to the balls? The simple answer is that the pressure in the balls decreases to 11 PSI. The refs, who flunked thermodynamics 101, take the balls back in the locker room. By the time they decide how to measure them, get the instruments, and take the first readings, all the balls have warmed up a bit. The first ball is measured, and the pressure is 11.8 PSI. They scratch their heads for a while, and about half-hour later, they measure the remaining balls. However, because they all have warmed up a bit more, the pressure is now up to about 12.1 to 12.8 PSI.

What does this tell us about thermodynamics? Well, that maybe if the referees had measured all of the balls on the field, they would have found about 11 PSI in all the footballs. And if they had taken all of them back inside and let then warm up again to 75° F (maybe an hour later), they might all have been at about 13 PSI.

So, what have we learned? We learned that low temperatures deflate footballs the way Tom Brady likes them. Hot temperatures overinflate footballs the way that Aaron Rogers loves them. But neither Roger Goodell nor Tom Brady can repeal the laws of thermodynamics. Meanwhile, Bill Belichick keeps working on it.

<u>Barometric pressure and specific volume.</u> Now, let's put together these three pieces (pressure, temperature, and volume) together and see what that does to generate wind. If we decrease the air temperature, the air density will increase while the volume will decrease. Alternatively, if we reduce the pressure, the air volume will increase, and temperature will rise. So, we will need to specify two of these variables to see what it does to the third. But, you may ask, if hot air rises, why is it colder at the top of the

mountain than at the base? The answer is that on top of the mountain, the air is less dense because of the lower barometric pressure. Another example of this relationship is that at sea level, water boils and turns to steam at 100° C. But if you are at the top of Mount Kilimanjaro at 20,000 feet, it will start boiling at 81°C. Or if you're below sea level, like in parts of Death Valley California, the boiling point is about 102° C.

<u>14.4 The weather machine.</u> So, here we have laid out our model weather machine, presented in our sophisticated illustration figure 3.14.4.[95]

- Here we have the sun as the engine, providing nearly 100 percent of the power to drive it, which we'll call "temperature."
- We have the transmission, as the way, the heat from the sun is distributed geographically in one part of the world and not in the other. It's like a transmission that sends different speeds to each wheel, resulting in erratic motion. We'll call this "specific volume."
- We then have barometric pressure, which regulates how much air enters the engine.

3.14.4

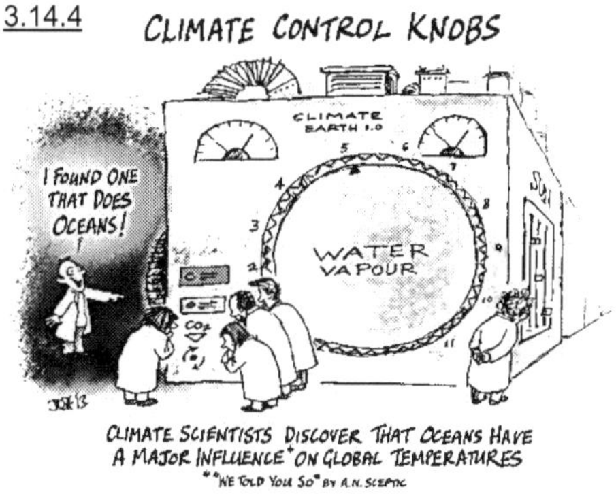
CLIMATE CONTROL KNOBS
CLIMATE EARTH 1.0
I FOUND ONE THAT DOES OCEANS!
WATER VAPOUR
CLIMATE SCIENTISTS DISCOVER THAT OCEANS HAVE A MAJOR INFLUENCE* ON GLOBAL TEMPERATURES
* "WE TOLD YOU SO" BY A.N. SCEPTIC

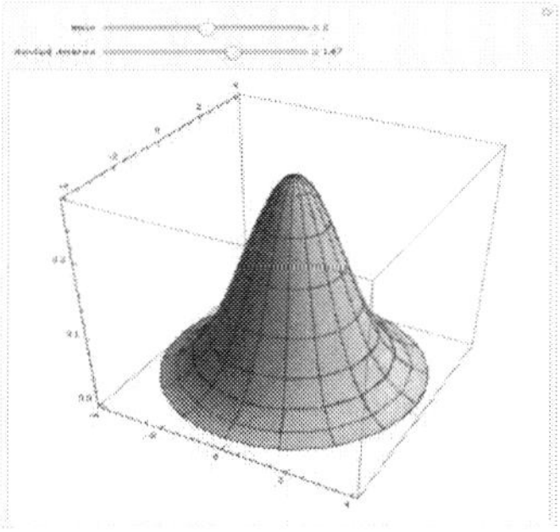

This drawing by Unknown Author is licensed under CC BY-NC

3.14.5

<u>How the Earth receives the sun's energy.</u> Let's turn on the engine and see what happens. We have sunlight arriving on the planet and spreading out like a three-dimensional bell curve, see figure 3.14.5. The top-center of the bell is precisely on the equator, and it's at the highest point on the bell. That means that the energy density there is the maximum. At the bottom of the bell are the north and south polar regions. The amount of energy received from the sun is less, and it's now spread over a vastly larger area.

For example, take Quinto, Ecuador (00 North and 00 South), at noon, when the sun is directly overhead, Quinto gets the most heat density. Now Chicago is directly north of Quinto, and it's also noon in Chicago, and it's also the hottest time of the day. But Chicago is 54.6 degrees north of Quinto, that's more than halfway between Quinto and the north pole, so it's a whole lot colder in Chicago. Meanwhile, Medan, a city in Indonesia, is also on the equator, but precisely on the opposite side of the world, and its midnight there, the coldest part of the day.

But as we have so often stated, nature does not like any energy imbalance, on Earth, or anyplace in the universe. Thus, in hotter areas, the air rises to the upper atmosphere, and the colder, denser air moves into the bottom to fill the void. We first discussed in Question 5, how the heat difference also sets up differences in barometric pressures. These differences in temperature and pressures push and pull the air around to try to eliminate these temperature and pressure differences. The air is the medium used by the Earth to redistribute this heat and pressure imbalance, which we call "wind."

On Earth, where we have land, oceans, and air are all set in motion to eliminate these temperatures and pressure imbalance. It does so in the atmosphere primarily by the wind. In the seas by water movements like the Gulf Stream in the Atlantic and the Pacific with the "Pacific Oscillator" and "El Niño Nino/La Niña." On land, it does it primarily by radiation, convection mostly to the air. On the Earth, some of this heat is also conducted deeper into the ground, which is essential for plants to grow. It warms up and dries out the soil in the spring, allowing plant roots to grow. Some of the heat in the warmed Earth is radiated and convected back up into the air, creating vertical wind streams that help gliders fly around without engines.

But along the way, the winds have to overcome many obstacles posed by obstructions like mountain ranges and narrow canyons, plus human-made buildings and cars, trucks, planes, and wind turbines. In rare cases, it can also be caused independently of the effects of the sun. For example, the low temperatures mass of the Antarctic ice will always be much colder than the sea and air temperatures of the southern temperate regions. Thus, like the jet stream in the north forms, it forms a planetary sub-weather system, which we call a "polar vortex."

Temperature and localized differences. Another significant temperature difference is between the air in the valleys and that at the top of the mountains. In figure 3.14.5a,[96] we see snows on top of Mount Kilimanjaro, in Africa. Now, Mt Kilimanjaro, like Quinto, is also on the equator, but the temperature over there is radically different. As previously discussed, the higher you go, the colder it gets. Mount Kilimanjaro is so high and massive that it creates its sub-weather system. The top of the mountain is cold enough to snow and accumulate it. The low pressure there is so high it sucks up much of the available water vapor and air from miles around. This rising air and water vapor condense, becoming clouds. Then it precipitates on the colder side of the mountain in the form of rain or snow, depending on the temperature and pressure differences.

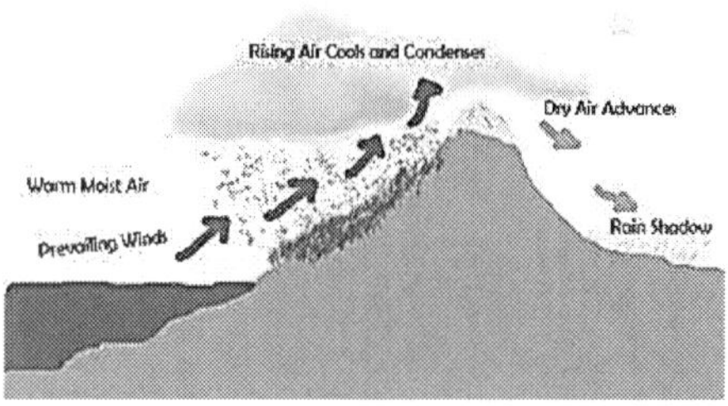

So, when it's 29° F and snowing on top of Kilimanjaro, the snow accumulates, but down in the valley, it may be 80° F. As a result, the hot air from the valley starts rushing up the mountain. When it reaches near the top, some of the snow melts in the air, and it rains. But some of the snow does something strange. Because of the low boiling point previously discussed, the snow heats so rapidly that it sublimates into water vapor. Meaning, the snow is melting so fast that it doesn't even bother to first liquefy into the water. Instead, it goes straight to water vapor. So as the cold airstrips and condenses the water vapor as it's sucked up the mountain, it's condensed in the colder mountainside. There it rains or snows, but the other, warmer side of the mountain, is an arid wasteland. Ecologically speaking, the weather system is in a dynamic balance, but the people, animals, and vegetation on the wrong side of the mountain are screwed. A balanced ecosystem is not necessarily a "good" system.

An even more prominent example of this extreme temperature and pressure difference and its cycle is in the tropical Pacific Ocean. Here this similar upward rush of air from the western Pacific Ocean to the sky is so fast that it is the primary driver of the now familiar and periodic El Niño. In the process, it creates its temporary atmospheric system, which is the air/water equivalent to that of Kilimanjaro. Then, after some years, the process reverses, causing the cooling cycle, which we call La Niña. This cycle was only recently discovered, and we still have a lot to learn about it.[97]

The waters. Above, we discussed the boundaries between land and air, and land and oceans, and how that affects weather changes. Now let's start by comparing the properties of water and water vapor and see how they affect the weather. Also, let's keep in mind that 20-30 percent of the sun's energy never reaches the land or the oceans. Some are reflected in outer space by the air, and the atmosphere and clouds absorb and some of it.

More than 70 percent of the Earth's surface is covered and filled with water, accounting for about 96 percent[98] of all of Earth's water. The rest of the 4 percent exists as water vapor in the air; flowing in rivers; stored in lakes; in icecaps and glaciers; in the ground as soil moisture; and in aquifers and wells. A small fraction is even stored in you and your dog and the grasses and the trees. How water heats up, cools down, loses, and redistributes the sun's heat is very different from how the land and air do it. Water, primarily in the oceans, receives the sun's rays. Before the rays penetrate the surface water, a significant amount is reflected by the water back through the air, where some are stored in the air and clouds, which we call "the greenhouse effect." The seas absorb the rest of the sun's rays and heat. But water absorbs the sun's energy-heat, mostly from the infrared rays (IR) and the visible wavelengths, and it does so much more slowly than land. The oceans can absorb and store four times more heat than the air. The heated water on top expands, which makes it less dense than the colder water. As a result, the warmer waters keep rising to the top layers; whereas, the more frigid, denser waters sink and keep sinking to the bottom. At the very depths, these colder waters remain there for centuries or even many millennia.

The warmer waters generally stay within 100-200 meters from the ocean top, and the temperatures keep reducing as we go deeper and deeper. These top 100 meters of warmer waters may move at about one or two miles per hour and may take a decade or more to redistribute and mix with adjacent cooler waters. But they are still generally limited to this top 100-200 meters.

The coldest of the cold waters are at the deepest parts of the ocean; the mixing speeds down there may be less than one inch per century. The tiny amount of warmer water that mixes with the colder waters below is generally limited to conduction. The warmer top layers in the seas are also the reason that ocean ice, icebergs, and coastal glaciers will continue to melt around the waterline, even when the air temperature is below the freezing point.

This warmer water phenomenon also explains why so much fog is over the oceans, as it continues to evaporate up and then condense as it comes into contact with the colder air on top. The different water temperatures of the oceans redistribute locally and over the planet at very different rates. The best-known example of this temperature redistribution is the Gulf Stream of the Atlantic Ocean. Seen in 3.14.6,[99] the flow speeds of the top layers of the Gulf Stream can reach a breakneck pace of about five miles per hour. But it gets slower and slower as we go deeper and deeper. All told, it takes about 500 years for these top layers of water to complete the full Gulf Stream cycle.

Water fun facts:

- Water is the only substance that is capable of reversing density direction as a function of temperature. What does this mean? Like all other substances, water shrinks and gets denser as it gets colder. But unlike different materials, when water reaches about 2° C, the direction changes. As it gets colder and colder, it starts to expand and the volume increases. That's why we see ice on top of the waters and not at the bottom, and that's why we see the tips of icebergs float in atop the seas. Those icebergs are about 10 percent less dense than the water they float on, then why 90 percent is below the water level. "So, what?" you might ask. The "so what" is enormous! The most dominant factor is that if the ice formed and fell to the bottom of the oceans, there would be no fish in the world. And if you believe the expanded definition of Darwin, these "fish" would not have been there to crawl on land and become reptiles, dinosaurs, birds, monkeys, and you and me. Fish lay their eggs on the bottoms, so if it's an ice bed—no fish.

- Conversely, if the warm water did not rise and stayed at the top 200 meters or so, it may not have been possible for phytoplankton to grow and prosper. Trees, plants, and grasses only produce about 30 percent of the planet's oxygen, whereas the planktons and other marine vegetation produce 70 percent of the Earth's oxygen. No plankton means no fish, and no plankton means too little oxygen for birds, animals, and you and me.
- Planktons and marine vegetation sustain life on Earth in other ways. In oceans, they are the feedstock for the aquatic food chain. They are the vital elements that recycle the major part of CO^2 by producing sugars and releasing oxygen to the atmosphere and water. All that work and contribution to the life cycle occurs mostly in the warmer waters of the top 100-300 meters. Below that, these lifeforms are less and less productive until it gets to near-zero deeper down.
- Also, warmer water holds less dissolved gasses than colder water, and the colder it gets, the more it absorbs. We see this in our everyday experience, like when we open a warm bottle of soda, then repeat it with a cold soda. When we open a warm pop, it outgasses more CO2 very quickly and sprays the soda on our face. Conversely, when we open a chilled soda, we get little or no out-spray. The same thing happens in the ocean. As the waters warm and expands (as discussed above) and rises to the top, it also releases some of the dissolved gasses it held when it was colder, thus providing benefits for the planet and us.
  - For example, a fish like a trout or arctic char that needs more oxygen than a carp is more likely to live in the colder waters and the carp in the warmer waters. This temperature difference rewards the more adventurous fish who braved the move to the colder waters with more oxygen and more plankton and more food sources. This adaptation/movement also kept the warmer waters from overpopulating.
  - It is also a fact that much more sea life, including planktons, are found in the colder waters than the warmer waters of the tropical regions. That's because the colder northern waters are opaquer than the crystal-clear waters of the Caribbean, which have far fewer planktons and fish life.

- This change in water temperatures allows the Earth to modulate the amounts of gasses in the air vs. in the water. The oceans will release more CO^2 to the air to support the growing biomass that comes with warmer periods. Conversely, when it gets colder, the oceans reabsorb the CO^2 because plant life has slowed down, and it saves the excess $CO2^2$ for when it cyclically warms back up.

Land. Now let's look at the ground. Land includes our lawn, farmland and mountains, you, the seals in the north and penguins in the south pole, the grasslands in Argentina, mountains of Peru, and the trees in Canada. Land heats very differently than water and air. Ground reflects very little of the sun rays to outer space. That's one reason why land heats up faster than water. Most of the heating of land and oceans is by visible light, IR, and some long-wave UV. On the beach, infrared is why you feel warm, and your skin burns, and UV is why you get sun blisters. Land absorbs heat very quickly but does not store heat as long as the oceans do, losing it just as fast. On land, the energy keeps getting absorbed until night comes. Then the warmer ground starts losing the heat back to the cooler air, mostly by radiation and a little by convection. This radiation keeps going up through the atmosphere during the night (second law of thermodynamics again). When these rays reach the sky and clouds, some are absorbed (greenhouse effect), and some of the radiation goes directly into outer space.

Next, we find that not all land is created equal. Some materials, like asphalt, rocks, bricks, cement, buildings, and streets, absorb more heat and faster and retain it longer than grasslands, wetlands, and trees. This ability to retain heat is a contributor to weather and climate change in the form we call the "urbanization effect." This urbanization effect can add as much as two or three degrees celsius in major urban areas compared to farmlands just a few miles away. Las Vegas is probably the best example of this urbanization effect. So, if you are a weatherman or a climatologist, this means that you must be very careful where you put your earth-based thermometers to make sure you don't create wrong temperature profiles or trends.

Air. The air is a fluid mixture of many different gasses and many different aerosols, dust, and water vapor. Primary gasses include 78 percent nitrogen, 21 percent oxygen, and 0.04 percent carbon dioxide (CO^2). These gasses do not include the water vapors and aerosols that help make up clouds. The water content in clouds can be minimal, as the wispy clouds at higher elevations. But in lower elevations, clouds are much more massive and may weigh up to 500 metric tons per cubic kilometer of air. Cloud properties are challenging to measure, quantify, and model, so for now, we'll ignore them. But they do play a significant role in climate and weather change as we'll discuss later. One of the major criticisms of the UN/IPCC climate models is that they don't take global cloud distributions, size, and densities sufficiently into account.

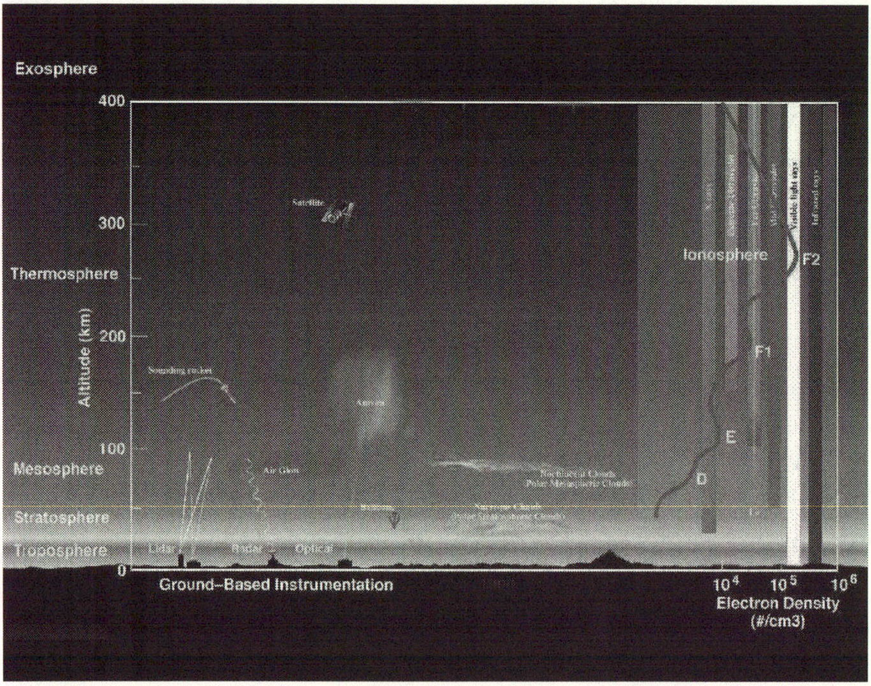

As seen in Fig. 3.14.7[100] There are five layers of the atmosphere going from sea level up to more than 600 kilometers. These layers are very fluid and will change in different ways depending on what's pushing or pulling them, like the sun's heat, solar winds, pressure and temperature differences, etc. The exosphere is the highest layer at over 600 km. The air is thin and made mostly of hydrogen and helium, and it gradually fades into the vacuum of outer space. Next is the thermosphere, which is the hottest part of the air at about 1,500° C. This heat is caused by charged particles from the sun (solar winds) and deep space cosmic rays colliding with the atmospheric gasses and where we see them as the aurora borealis in the north polar regions and in the south as the aurora australis. Here the air is still thin enough for space shuttles and the international space stations to best operate. Next, the mesosphere that starts at about 85 km high and the top of the mesosphere is the coldest part with a temperature of approximately minus -900° C. Here also is where most of the meteors burn up. The stratosphere is next at 50 km up and has a lot of ozone, which heats the atmosphere while absorbing the sun's harmful UV rays, and because the air is still very thin, it's where most jets like to fly. The troposphere is the layer above the Earth, where most of the clouds are located and where most of the weather actions occur.

Figure 3.14.7 also shows us where the various forms of the sun's energies are absorbed. On the extreme right, we see that one hundred percent of the visible and IR (long-waves) blast through the clouds and atmosphere and is absorbed by the land and seas, whereas all other short-wave forms of light are absorbed by the air and clouds at various altitudes. So, at the top of a mountain, you will need more sunscreen protection than at Miami Beach.

3.14.8

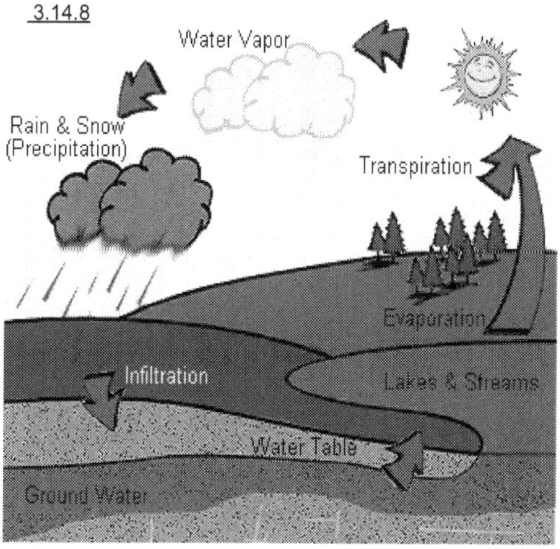

Water vapor. As seen in 3.14.8,[101] water vapor plays a crucial role in the Earth's water cycle and is an absolute necessity in the Earth's ability to sustain all life. In the simplest of terms, the sun heats the waters and forms water vapors that rise into the air. At some altitudes, temperatures and barometric pressures, some of these tiny water vapor elements will meet up with an aerosol particle. The aerosol may be a dust particle from a volcano, farmland, industrial pollutant, a car, jet or whatever and become the seed around which the water vapor starts to condense and stick. We see an example of this in the sky as long cloud streaks behind a high-flying jet. Those white streaks are not smoke, and they are not pollution. They are clouds forming around the aerosols released by the jet engines and the water vapor sticking on them.

As more and more water vapors stick, these seeds grow bigger and bigger, and more and more of these seeds accumulate water vapor until a cloud form. This natural process is called “nucleation.” The clouds keep getting bigger and bigger as more and more of these droplets are created. The cloud also becomes more substantial and massive as each of these condensed water vapor droplets keeps getting bigger and heavier. At some point, when enough of them are big enough, it starts to rain or snow. As the rain droplets fall down the sky towards Earth, if it's warm enough, they will hit the ground as rain. If it's a little bit cooler, it may come down like hail, or if it’s icy, it will be snow. This water then spreads across the land and seas. The plant life absorbs some, and some end up in rivers and lakes and seas and oceans, and the cycle starts again.

Now a quick word on aerosols. The press and popular media will generally use the word “aerosols” in a negative context, often confusing and conflating it with CO2 and pollution. But only a tiny portion of these aerosols are bad for humanity and the environment. These are sulfur (SO_x) and nitrogen (NO_x) compounds, which are produced by volcanic activity and burning fossil fuels. The good news is that today we have the technologies and wealth to eliminate/prevent nearly all of these human-made pollutants. But there’s nothing we can do about the volcanic sources.

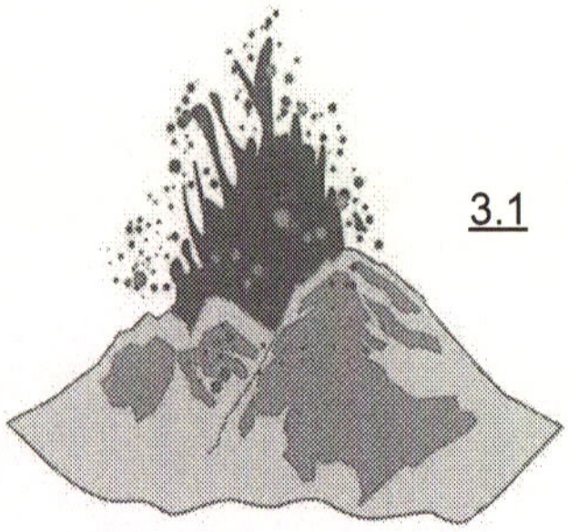

3.1

14.5 Volcanic eruptions[102] usually play no role in climate change but may play a significant role in weather change. In the above-described water cycle, volcanic eruptions play a substantial role in weather change because it provides the cloud seeding aerosols. In addition to contributing to the increased cloud formation, dust and pollution gasses will form a barrier that shields the sun's rays and will cool the Earth. But all bets are off when, in sporadic instances, there are several significant eruptions over a few years. A significant eruption or explosion is where millions of tons of these gasses and micro dust particles are spewed into the atmosphere. There, they cause disruptive weather consequences. One concern is that these dust clouds reduce the number of the sun's rays reaching the Earth.

When there's a massive eruption, these clouds can cover vast areas and can last for months, causing the air and land to cool, thus destroying a year's worth of agriculture in the affected areas. Lastly, we also have a reduction in the UV light that reaches the plants, allowing more mold and fungus to grow, further reducing agricultural production. This UV light reduction also causes an increase in the spoiling of the food that's already been produced, leading to more food shortages.

<u>The year without a summer.</u> One such exception was in 1816, also known as the "Year Without a Summer," when in New England alone, more than 1,300 deaths were directly caused. Most of these deaths resulted from starvation attributed to agricultural failures. But perhaps just as many deaths were caused by the poorly preserved food stocks that were spoiled by bacteria and molds that were not killed by the disinfecting UV light from the sun. This eruption occurred on Mount Tambura in Indonesia, and was a super-eruption, ejecting billions of tons of dust, gasses, and aerosols into the atmosphere. This eruption significantly reduced the amount of the sun's energy from reaching the Earth, causing the average global temperature to decrease by 0.7–1.3° F. This eruption followed on the heels of another massive explosion of Mount Mayon in 1814 in the Philippines. Thus, we had the infamous multiyear temperature decline.

In later discussions, we will present in greater detail how a new and better understanding of the tidal effects of the moon, sun, and planetary cycles, possibly combined with cosmic rays, may give us the foreknowledge to help us predict when one of these catastrophic eruptions is likely to occur.

Earthquakes and new volcanoes,[103]

Earthquakes do not cause either global weather or climate change. However, we will discuss them briefly here because recent scientific studies indicate a possible connection between the planetary cycles, sun cycles, and cosmic rays. Cosmic rays impact weather and climate change and are also likely to impact earthquakes. New volcanoes may also cause localized disruptions as new land is formed, like the Hawaiian Islands. And because they have impacts on global weather and ocean levels, we will discuss them later in context with the solar cycle and galactic cosmic rays.

14.6 Earth's latitudes,

Fig 3.14.11 [104] Regarding both weather and climate, where you live matters, and it can matter a lot! If you live in the tropical areas, close to the equator, it's where the sun's rays more directly reach the planet. As a result, it's hot and generally humid. That's far different than the colder temperate zones, and as you move away from the equator, north or south. The further you go, the colder it gets, and really cold as you go closer to the north and south poles.

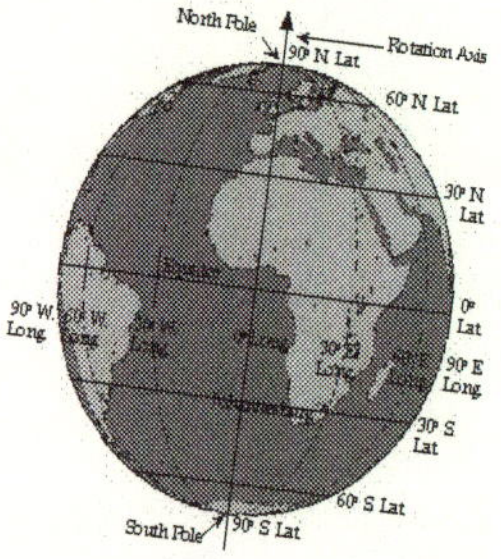

3.14.11

14.7 Earth's thermal blanket.[105] The greenhouse effect is hugely beneficial for the Earth. It's the blanket that keeps us in the Goldilocks zone by preventing more heat from escaping at night than it gets from the sun during the daylight hours. Ninety-five percent of this greenhouse effect is due to the water vapor content in the air. The other five percent is caused by the so-called "greenhouse gasses," where CO2 is the second-largest contributor, and methane is the third, and other gasses fill in the balance.

QUESTION 15: *WHAT IS THE "GREENHOUSE EFFECT"?*

<u>15.1 The importance of the Greenhouse effect</u> cannot be understated. Scientists contend that, without the greenhouse effect, the global Earth temperature would be about 30° C colder than it is today. That's a huge deal! Without it, we would be looking at a global temperature at about -15° C instead of the + 15° C that we enjoy today. Without it, our beautiful little blue-green planet would be trapped in a super ice age and look more like a dirty, lifeless snowball. The greenhouse effect is a straightforward and essential natural mechanism. It helps regulate the Earth's temperature, making it more stable and able to sustain life.

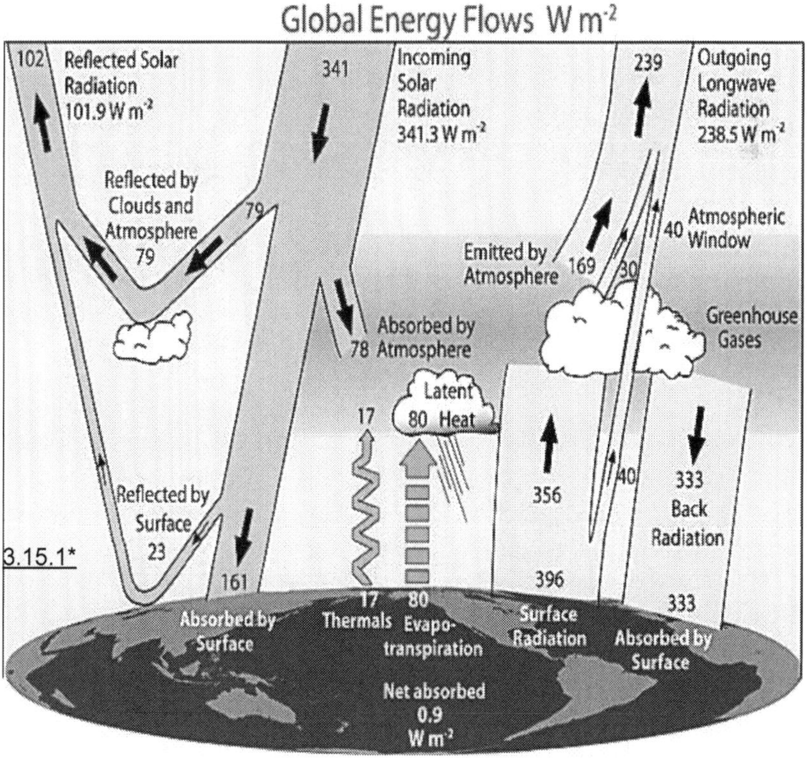

3.15.1*

Heat input. The effect of the greenhouse gasses starts with the sun's yellow rays coming to Earth, as seen in 3.15.1[106] and warming the planet during the daylight hours with a mean global TSI of about 341W/M^2. Some of the energy that approaches the Earth is reflected in outer space by the clouds and air, and smaller amounts by the Earth's ice cover and oceans and land. The part that reaches the Earth's system is about 70-75 percent, where three things start to happen to these sun's rays. The first part is used to power the planet's needs, like plants that need the sunshine for photosynthesis and animals to breathe and keep warm. Humans also get clean energy with solar electricity, and farmers to grow their crops and beach lovers to get a great tan. The second part is stored in the warm air we enjoy and warm oceans and seas when we swim in summer on Cape Cod and year-round in Florida

Radiation output.[107] If too much heat goes straight back to outer space, it will cause a big problem, which we see in high altitude deserts. There, during the day, the Earth gets very hot, very quickly. The air is quite thin, and there are few clouds, so more of the sun's rays get through and heat the soil. But, all that stored energy in the Earth and rocks is quickly radiated and convected back towards the air at night. This rapid loss of heat causes the desert nights to get very cold very fast. The result is that these regions have large temperature swings between night and day and is one of the reasons why there are few species of plants and animals that can live in these conditions.

15.2 Regulating mechanism. This mechanism allows the planet to manage how much and how little and how fast the stored energy is allowed to escape back into space. On the far right, we see some energy is also re-radiated back to Earth "back radiation." So, the land and oceans have two sources of heat, some directly from the sun and some from the atmosphere. In the blue-green arrow, we see "evaporation-transpiration," which is the heat from water evaporating into water vapor and the vegetation-respiration. One hundred percent of this heat "latent heat" is absorbed by the atmosphere. With the brown arrow, we see "thermals" this is heat from warm air rising, and the cold air filling the void left by the rising warm air and is also totally absorbed by the air. This warmed air cools down and is eventually radiated into outer space. But fear not because the portion that escapes into space is replaced by the heat absorbed from the incoming sun's energy, "absorbed by the atmosphere."

Now comes the question, how does the atmosphere store this heat? The vast majority is stored by the water vapor in the atmosphere, and the remainder is stored by the greenhouse gases (GHG), where CO2 is the most significant contributor, along with methane, Sox, etc.

Look at the tan-colored arrow, "surface radiation." Some of this heat goes directly into outer space, and some are absorbed by the atmosphere into the greenhouse effect. This is the heat coming off the land and oceans. The tan upward ray lifts the excess heat back into the atmosphere and from there eventually radiates back a portion into outer space. But not all of it escapes, as some of this heat is retained by the air and by clouds for a short time. This temperature regulating system forms the "blanket" that keeps us in the comfy Goldilocks zone.

Balanced system. However, if more heat is trapped and stored for too long in the air, the clouds, land, and oceans and not enough radiate into outer space, it would not be a good thing. If this keeps going too long, it will mean each new morning would start out being a little warmer (or colder) than the day before, and so on. After some time, it would keep getting warmer and warmer (or cooler and cooler) and cause significant changes in all plant and animal life. We see a dramatic example of this on Venus, where CO2 makes up nearly 97 percent of the atmosphere compared to .04 percent on Earth. Even here on Earth, in the far distant past, at times, it got so warm that the oceans rose to alarming levels, there was little ice on the surface, and tropical plants and animals thrived even in the polar regions. At other times it lost too much heat too fast, and we had many ice ages. These days, many scientists sound the alarm about global warming, not enough heat escaping fast enough. The cause of this imbalance, meaning more energy coming to Earth than is radiated back into space, is caused

3.15.2

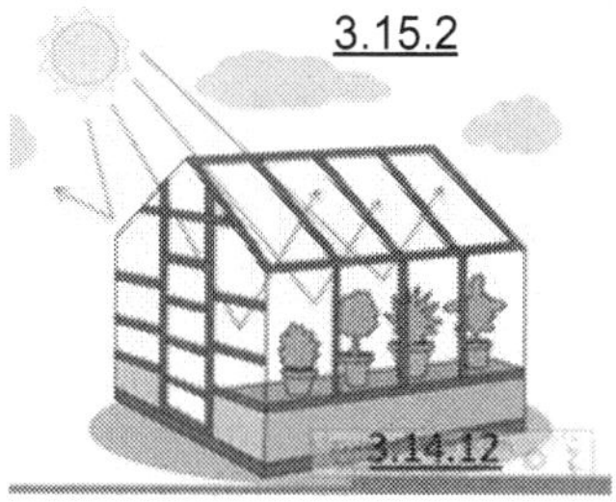

primarily by water vapor and a small amount by the greenhouse gasses trapped in the air and clouds.

15.3 Let's summarize[108] this chapter! Energy comes the Earth from the sun, and some of it is immediately reflected space by the air, clouds, and surface, and some temporarily stored by the atmosphere. Secondly, what we call weather is nothing more and nothing less than the Earth's air, land, and oceans attempting to eliminate the temperatures and pressure imbalances caused by the sun heating one part of the planet and not the other. These imbalances are imposed on Earth by the asymmetrical heating caused by the sun. Then, the weather is how the Earth responds to these forces imposed on the planet by the ever-changing dynamics of what happens within the sun and the relative position of the sun concerning the Earth. Weather patterns over 15 years or more are what we call "climate."

~ 4 ~

GENIUS QUESTIONS

Rated AUS—Are You Sure?

QUESTION 16: *WHAT ARE THE GREENHOUSE GASES, AND WHAT'S UP WITH CO2?*

Background: Greenhouse gases are natural atmospheric gases, plus other gaseous compounds and stuff we call "aerosols," along with dust floating around in the air. Greenhouse gases are both natural and human-made. Collectively, these gases, and with the overwhelming help of water vapor and clouds, absorb the sun's heat during the day. At night, the air and the tops of the clouds radiate some of this heat back to outer space. However, some warmth, stored by the land and oceans during the day, is radiated back to the air and clouds during nighttime. So, while the clouds and air are cooling from the top, they keep getting warm from the bottom for some time, until they reach a new equilibrium. This mechanism, which slows down the rate of cooling of the air and clouds, is called the "greenhouse effect," and plays a crucial role in stabilizing the rate at which the Earth cools at night.

The greenhouse gases include:

- Water vapor: technically, it's not a gas, as it's a vaporous form of water, but it accounts for about ninety-five percent of the total greenhouse effect.
- CO2 is next on the list, accounting for about 3.5 percent of the global greenhouse effect.
- Methane is next[109] , and it's the singularly most potent greenhouse gas, about eighty-six times more productive than CO2. But because there's so little of it, it accounts for about 1 percent of the greenhouse effect. Also noteworthy is that the methane volume in the atmosphere has been

steadily increasing in the last 200 years, nearly doubling. Today it accounts for about 1.8 ppm or about 0.4 percent of CO2 that's at 415 ppm.

- The remaining greenhouse gases include[110] nitrous oxides, sulfur dioxides, and fluorinated gases and account for the residual greenhouse effect.

Now let's look at the critical questions. How much is this cooling rate slowed down by the greenhouse effect? Too slow a release of heat leads to global warming. Too fast, and you have global cooling. So, let's get a bit into the details.

CO2 in the last 150 years. Coinciding with the industrial revolution, the CO2 atmospheric content has risen steadily by more than 40 percent. That is an undisputed fact, but that's where the agreement ends. The claim by the "consensus" scientists is that this increase is all human-made and is the singular cause of their predicted global warming. When we ask these consensus scientists about the naturally occurring CO2, the question is generally ignored.

CO2 balance sheet. Many equally accredited scientists claim that most of the CO2 increase came from natural sources, such as the increased bioactivity and especially by the warming of the oceans. More about this later, but let's get into the CO2 math. Below in Table 4.16.1 is an estimate of the annual CO2 global budget in gigatons of CO2 per year. The data source is the IPCC: figure 7.3 AR4. Like any good accountant, on the left, we list the causes that produce the CO2 and how many gigatons each source provides per year. On the right side, we have CO2 consumers and how much they consume each year.

Table 4.16.1[111] CO2 Production	Gigaton/yr.		CO2 Consumption	Gigaton/yr.
Animal & microbe decomposition	220		Land/plant absorption	450
Vegetation respiration	220		Oceans	338
Ocean release	332			
Sub Total Natural CO2	772		Subtotal	788
Human-made	29			
Total production	**801**		**Total consumption**	**788**
% human-made CO2 (29/801)	3.6 %		Imbalance (801-788)- % (13/801)	13 1.6 %
Human-caused CO2 global imbalance	NA		(3.6% X 1.6 %)	0.06 %

A quick summary of the table reveals some startling facts:

- Note that the natural production of CO2, at 772 gigatons, is less than the annual natural consumption of 778 gigatons. So, nature is eating up 0.3 percent more CO2 than nature is producing (788–772). This tells us two important things; First, the amount of CO2 in the air is not static but changes from year to year depending on natural cycle exchanges. The second thing it tells us is that the imbalance is less than 0.3 percent, which is well within the error margin of the estimate. However, if this production shortfall were to last for many years, it would lead to CO2 starvation of plants, which is discussed in detail later on.
- Human-made CO2 accounts for about 3.6 percent of the total yearly production of CO2. But when combined with the consumption, the human-made contribution to the imbalance is a trivial amount, only 0.008 gigatons or 0.06 percent. Again, well within the error margin of the estimate
- How accurate are these estimates? If we assume that these percentages are within a 5 percent error margin, we will have to conclude that these human-made CO2 contributions are statistically insignificant at the 95 percent level of confidence. Or said differently, we are 95 percent confident that the human-made portion of the CO2 is trivial. Even if we were to double the already increased CO2 from 400 ppm to 800 ppm, it would still be insignificant or unmeasurably small as far as global warming is concerned. We'll get into these details in the following

chapters. But perhaps more noticeable is that we have and are looking at an increase in CO2 consumption.

- Increased consumption of CO2 implies that if more CO2 is available, it will stimulate more plant and plankton growth, resulting in a "Greener Planet." And that is what has happened in the past few decades as confirmed by NASA, April 26, 2016.[112] This article shows an increased leafing [1] over the last 35 years, equal to two times the area of the United States. Secondly, it states that the increased CO2 levels are responsible for at least 70 percent of this leafing increase.
- Secondly, NASA satellite data estimates that the planet has been "greening" over the last few decades by the equivalent of half the landmass of Australia. When combined with a comparable increase in the ocean phytoplankton, it also means a more productive ocean life.
- Now we have to question the validity of the data. Even if we assume that we are about 95 percent correct, we will need to repeat these calculations for many years to be sure this was not a one-off event. Secondly, we also need to see and analyze the trends, and from that, raise more and better questions to get more accurate answers.
- Recent measurements indicate that CO2 has increased from about 280 to over 415 ppm. But if the human-made portion is about 3.6 percent, then the human-made increase is only about 5 ppm out of a total increase of 135 ppm (415-280) x 0.036 = 5 ppm.

If total CO2 has increased by about 135 ppm (415-280 = 135), and humanity is responsible for about five ppm, this begs the big question that nobody is asking: *What forces and factors produced the other 130 ppm?* Here again, we are faced with another mystery. Missing vital facts keep popping up and stacking up, but where are the answers? Is this merely sloppy or incompetent reporting, or is it purposely withheld?

Let's recap: Thus far, we have established a few fundamental facts that are worth restating. And let's start with a paper by Dr. Nabil H. Swedan in

[1] "Increased leafing" means plants are growing bigger, faster and more robust. "Increased Greening" means more land covered by vegetation.

2019, titled; "*On the carbon cycle and its interactions with the biosphere*" First published in the Russian Journal of Earth Sciences. The paper, "*... reveals that interactions between the carbon cycle and the biosphere may be calculated using traditional thermodynamic equations.*"

"Presently, anthropogenic activities have changed the natural carbon cycle and climate parameters, which have direct effects at the societal, industrial, and economical levels ..."

DANGER - TECH NERDS ONLY!
All others go to 4.16.1. Do not pass GO; do not collect $200.

Let's take a look at table 2 and table 4 below from the referenced paper:[113]

- *"The [*warming*] period 18,470–13,800 Before Present (BP) followed the last Glacial Maximum, characterized by severe cold and dry climate [Van der Hammen, 1974]. Cold surface temperature, reduced carbon dioxide content in the atmosphere, glaciers cover of land, and decrease of water availability; all are unfavorable for life ..."*
- *Conversely, the cooling period between 112,320–106,500 BP reveals contraction in the size of the green matter. Plants contributed heat to surface warming, and simultaneously their mass increased. This is evident from the decreases in the content of carbon dioxide in the atmosphere,*
- *"The calculated Net annual percent Greening of the surface is 0.08 percent, line 6 of Table 4. [FAO, 2016a] records reveal surface greening of 0.03 percent annually and [Zaichun Zhu et al., 2016] observed annual surface greening of 0.44 percent. The calculated Net annual percent Greening falls well within the observed range..."*
- *"Therefore, a comparison of most of the computed and relevant climate parameters for the objectives of this work with climate models cannot be made at this time."*

Author's Note:

- In table 2 below, we see that during the warming period (18, 470-13,800 Before Present, BP), the plant growth was spurred by the warming temperatures (+6 ° C), the increasing CO2 (0.012) and the greening of the Earth. The paper states the relationship of the greening of the planet (0.03 percent) compared to the cooling period (112,320-106,500 BP) of (-4.5° C) that showed a decrease of greening and an increase in desertification.

- In Table 4 below, we see the same pattern on the global climate of the past few decades. While CO2 continues to rise throughout the period, we see that the benefit of this increase in CO2 is driving a surge in CO2 consumption and greening.
- In the detailed calculations, Dr. Swedan asserts that the greening of the Earth also contributes to a cooler planet. As the increasing biomass absorbs more sunlight for photosynthesis, it reduces the heat to be absorbed by the Earth.
- One crucial point that the tables do not show is that, with the increasing supply of CO2, there also comes an increase in the CO2 consumption by plants.
  As shown in Table 4.16.1 above, we see that perhaps we need to emphasize, not so much the available supply of CO2, but rather the net imbalance (supply – consumption). There we see that the human-made CO2 contribution of the excess supply is a mere 0.06 percent of the total CO2 available amount.

Unfortunately, what tables 2 and 4 do not show is that: With the increasing supply of CO2 there also comes an increase in the CO2 consumption by plants:

- *Total CO2 increase = 135 PPM (415-280)*
- *manmade CO2 accounts for only 5 ppm (135 X 3.6 percent)*
- *Where did the other 130 ppm come from?*

Warming period Cooling period)

Table 2	Period Description ((BP)	18,470–13,800	112,320–106,500
	Surface temperature change, ∘C	6.0	-4.5
1	Climate transformation duration, years	4670	5820
2	The average concentration of carbon dioxide, ppm	235.00	250.00
3	Average annual change in carbon dioxide, ppm	0.012	−0.006
4	Annual percent Greening of the surface	0.003	−0.001
5	Annual percent Deforestation of the surface	0.000	0.000
6	Net annual percent Greening of the surface	0.003	−0.001

Table 4	Period Description	1993–1998	2000–2005	2005–2010	2010–2015
1	Climate transformation duration, years	5	5	5	5
2	Average concentration of carbon dioxide, ppm	361.63	374.52	384.74	395.23
3	Average annual change in carbon dioxide, ppm	1.920	2.050	2.020	2.190
4	Annual percent Greening of the surface	0.265	0.274	0.263	0.277
5	Annual percent Deforestation of the surface	0.224	0.215	0.187	0.195
6	Net annual percent Greening of the surface	0.041	0.059	0.076	0.081

The Big question that the climate scientists are trying to understand and deal with is, where is this extra 130 ppm of CO2 coming from?

A significant portion is coming from the oceans. In 4.16.1,[114] we see a basic scientific chart of the absorption (or solubility) rate of CO_2 in ocean water. It tells us that as the water gets warmer, it can dissolve or hold less CO_2. All gasses are soluble in water, and while each gas has its individual absorption curve, all show the same relationships.

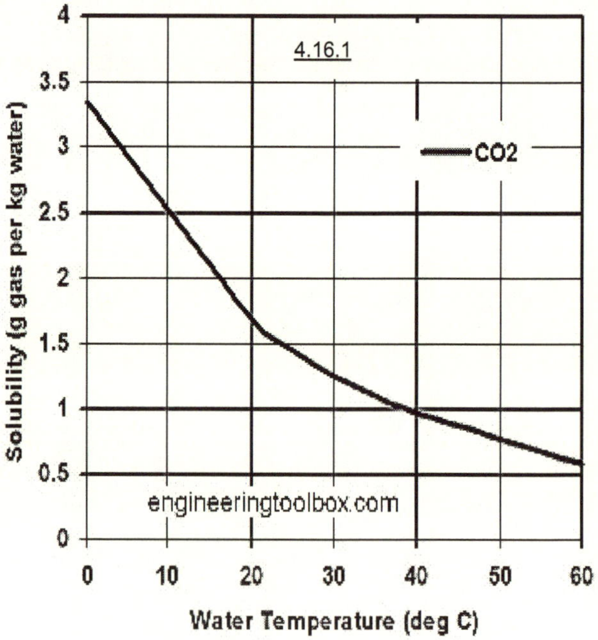

Please note that this absorption rate is even more potent at the lower temperatures. For example, if the ocean temperature in a zone near the Antarctic is 5° C, water can hold three grams of CO_2 per kilo of water. But if the water warms to 10° C, it will release 0.5 grams of CO_2 per kilogram of water. The result is that about 16 percent more CO_2 is released from the ocean to the atmosphere by this 5° C temperature increase. But if we go to Florida, where the water is about 30° C, and we raise it by the same 5° C, only about 4 percent more CO_2 is released. We all know this from our daily experience when we open a bottle

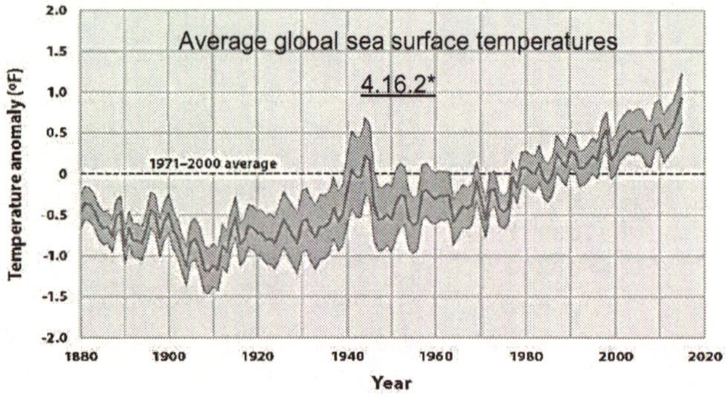

of Coke that's at room temperature. First, we get the big fizz-gush in our face, which is CO2 escaping. Then if we leave it on the kitchen counter for thirty minutes, it goes flat, meaning that nearly all the CO2 has escaped from the liquid to the air in the room.

The second piece: We know that in the past one hundred years, the ocean surface temperatures have warmed up by about 2° F, as shown in 4.16.2.[115] It's easy to see how these warming oceans have released countless gigaton of CO2 into the air each year, in just the past thirty-forty years.

The next critical question: what are the ocean temperatures doing in the deeper parts? The simple answer is that we don't know.

In 4.16.2,[116] the temperature changes are generally limited to the top 100-300 meters. Secondly, "The average global sea surface temperatures" are not just the temperatures of the water, but also includes the temperatures of the air, immediately above the waters. These temperatures are measured by ships and buoys worldwide.[117] The data shown in the graph came from the National Oceanic and Atmospheric Administration (NOAA) Global Historical Climatology Network (GHCN) and International Comprehensive Ocean-Atmosphere Data Set (ICOADS).

But we don't know much about what's happening in the deeper and deepest parts of the ocean. We understand that these colder waters at the bottom hold far more CO2 than the surface waters, as shown in 4.16.1. Therefore, even a tiny increase in the temperatures of these deeper waters might be a source of the unexplained rise in CO2. And this would all happen without us knowing anything about it. Blane Perun published an article on his website, "TheSea."[118] There he tells us that about 90 percent of all volcanic activities on Earth occur at the bottom of the oceans, close to the tectonic boundaries. There, vast amounts of CO2 might "*be released without any detectable increase in the ocean's surface temperatures*."

We'll address this underwater tectonic activity in detail in questions 18 and 19 below. There we will also make a connection between the sun's magnetic activity levels, cosmic rays, and the Earth's volcanic and tectonic activities.

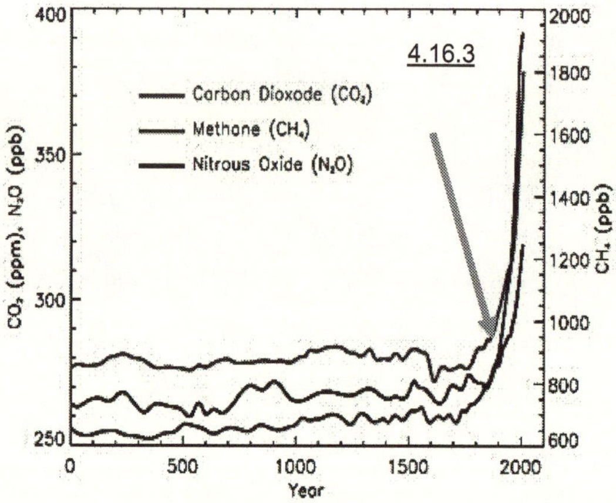

And other greenhouse gases? Have they also increased with the rise in surface ocean temperature? Yes, as we find the answer demonstrated in 4.16.3,[119] where we see an increase in all the greenhouse gases from 1750 up to today. Some went up more and some less because each gas has its peculiar solubility property curve based on its individual chemical and physical properties. But for now, we'd have to consider the proposition that humankind is the only major cause of the dramatic rise in CO2 with some suspicion.

Additional observations: There is a necessary clarification we need to add to this chart, and please look at the location of the blue arrow in 4.16.3, then look below at 4.16.3a,[120] where we track the corresponding temperatures. Before 1958, the composition of atmospheric CO2 was determined by the amount of CO2 trapped in glacial ice. But, after 1958, all subsequent CO2 readings were directly measured in the atmosphere at Mauna Loa station in Hawaii. How were these radically different measurements stitched together? Perhaps we can glean some insight by looking at the contemporaneous temperature record. Here we note how the temperature estimates went from various proxies to tree ring and then to actual thermometer temperatures. However, this became quite the controversy, dubbed "climate-gate" with accusations of data fudging by climate scientists. A summary of the issues and methods is provided by this article in Newsweek,[121] raising into question the reliability of tree-ring data. That raises some very significant potential sources of errors and possible abuse, as discussed in subsequent chapters. With this as a backdrop, some climate scientists are also raising questions on the data accuracies and reliabilities of ice core CO2 records and is the subject of emerging and intense debates.

In Questions 18 and 19 below, we explore the relationship between earthquakes and volcanoes and the eleven-year solar cycles,[122] which might

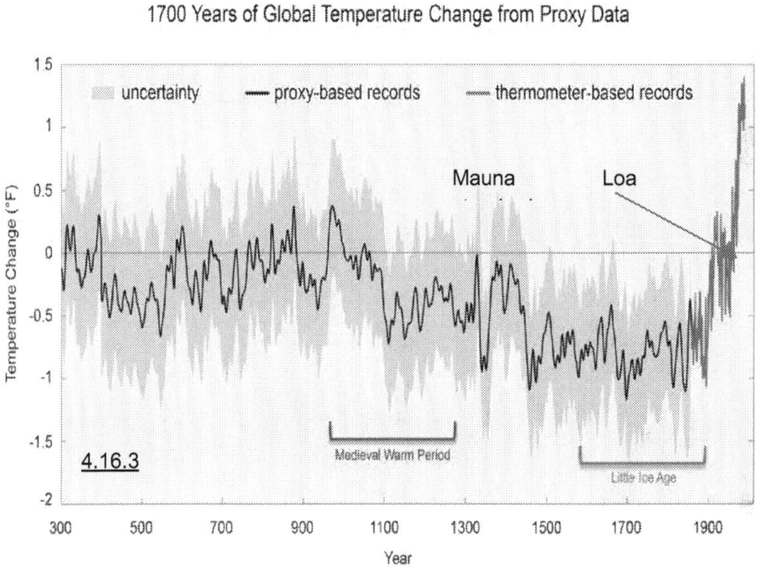

help to explain increased underwater volcanic and earthquake activities.[123] These deep-water tectonic would undoubtedly increase deep-water temperatures and release vast amounts of all gases without us being aware of it.

If we are entering a cooling period, as some scientists are predicting, the oceans may continue to produce more CO2 for some years to come even as the planet cools. The good news is that the additional quantities of atmospheric CO2 will help maintain a more robust photosynthesis process and stabilize agricultural production for some additional years. Lastly, once the oceans start cooling, it will begin to suck back some CO2 from the atmosphere, but hopefully not too much and not too fast.

In chapter 6, we'll discuss in greater detail the role and controversy surrounding the sources of CO2, its role in global climate changes, and the consequences and benefits of the increasing CO2 levels. Alarmist scientists say[124] that CO2 may also have the ability to increase or magnify the power of the water vapor to absorb and retain more energy heat and for longer. They have built about one hundred and seventeen computer models and have run them to simulate this apparent amplifying effect. Recent NASA experiments seem to support some minor elements of this theory. Other equally accredited scientists say even if it does, it's so small that it's meaningless. In other words, it's like adding one more flee at the end of the tail that will alter a dog's behavior. To date, however, there is no data to back up this positive amplification feedback loop. But, one thing that we can all agree on is that the temperature of the air, water, and the volume of CO2 in the last 150 years have increased. And the increase has been for plants, animals, and humans around the world.

QUESTION 17: *IS THERE A RELATIONSHIP BETWEEN GLOBAL TEMPERATURE AND OCEAN LEVELS?*

Alarms of rising oceans were raised and continue to shriek at extraordinary levels. High profile politicians, actors, authors, and "climate activists" warn us regularly that the massive ice sheets in the Antarctic, and the Arctic, are melting. They remind us that in a matter of decades, oceans will rise to the point where they will destroy many coastal cities, and the process would become "irreversible." The IPCC and the media have speculated and prophesied that by 2100, we would have ocean levels increase by five to ten feet or more. Graphic photoshopped pictures of New York skyscrapers are embellishing book covers, showing buildings flooded to several floors high. Miami is shown vanishing under the sea, and Disney World will soon follow. The "consensus" team emphatically asserts that human-caused CO2 is responsible for global warming and the melting of the polar ice, that's causing the ocean levels to rise. Press, media, TV, and politicians continue to dramatize this narrative, scaring the uninformed public. Of particular concern is targeting this fear-mongering, especially to our impressionable young children in schools. Why? To gain support for their plan, which is what?

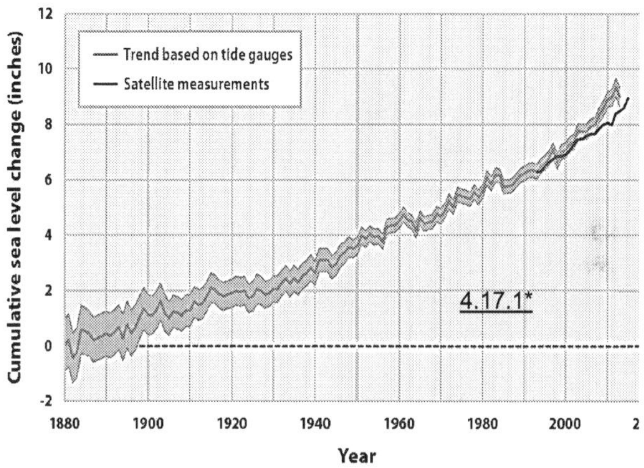

Shut off the alarms. But let's get back to science and examine the fundamental data and facts to see where this journey takes us. Looking at 4.17.1,[125] we immediately notice that in the last 140 years, the oceans have risen by a total of about seven inches, averaging about one to two millimeters per year. Let's put that in perspective: that's equal to an annual increase of about the thickness of a few of these pages. The rise is trivial.

Now compare 4.17.1 to 4.16.2 discussed above and see the very close correlation between the rise in ocean level with the increase in known ocean surface temperatures. Following the scientific method, let's now look at the physical properties of water. In 4.17.2,[126] we see that the volume of water increases with a rise in temperature. This data proves that sea level has risen at about the same rate that the oceans have been warming.

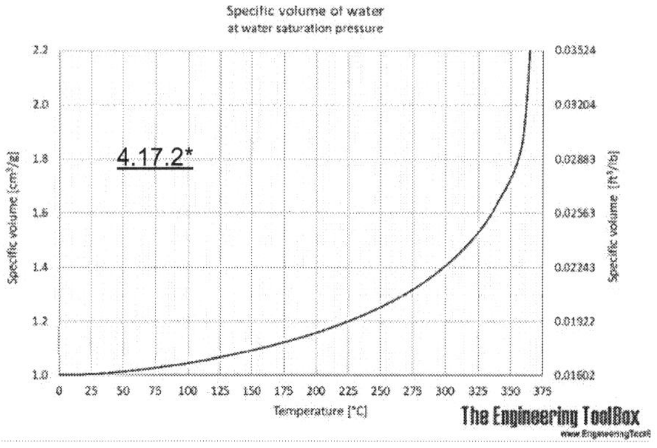

The assertion that the melting polar ice is the cause of the ocean level rise [I] is contradicted by the scientific community and even the UN/IPCC. In the detailed section of their Fifth assessment report, the IPCC states: "Water volume rises with temperature because of thermal expansion—another primary driver of sea-level rise."

From[127] 1971 to 2010 is 0.4 to 0.8 millimeters per year, with an estimated confidence level of 90 to 100 percent [Rhein et al., 2013]. This corresponds to a warming rate of about 0.015 degrees C per decade in the upper 700 meters of the oceans between 1971 and 2010. The difference between the above thermal expansion of the IPCC and the Skeptic scientists differs based on the amount and not the concept. These differing positions are understandable because estimating the many parameters involved is not an exact science. There are too many unknowns, and scientists have to make many challenging assumptions and estimates. These assumptions include the bulk of the Earth's water, its temperatures, its densities, the influence of the many ocean bottom volcanic and tectonic events, to name a few. The margin of errors in these assumptions could result in wild discrepancies.

Melting floating ice can't add to ocean levels. Let's look at 4.17.3[128] and discuss some additional physical and chemical properties of ice and water and answer some other basic questions.

- Can melting sea ice, like in the much-discussed north polar region, cause ocean levels to rise? "Not so much" is the simple answer. We all know from grade school and watching the movie *Titanic* that about 90 percent of an iceberg, or any floating ice, is below the waterline while 10 percent is above the water. This happens because when water is chilled and starts to freeze, it expands, so ice is about 10 percent less dense than the water that made it up. And the opposite happens when the ice melts back into the water; it shrinks by the same 10 percent. So, when sea ice melts, the 10 percent that was floating above the water combines with the 90 percent under the water, occupying the same original water volume.

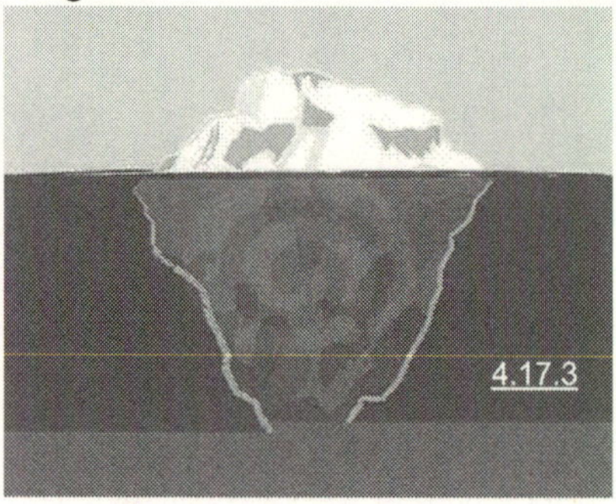

- What about the melting of the land glaciers? The Antarctic[129] contains about 90 percent of the world's ice mass and is the 800-pound gorilla in the room, so let's start with that. About 44 percent of that Antarctic ice is in the ice shelves (it's floating at the coastal edges), mostly in the western regions on the Pacific Ocean. More than 50 percent of the

Antarctic sheet is land-based and can be several miles thick. Historical data confirms that there are zero days per year where the temperature is above freezing, and then for only a few hours per day and only along the coast. Consequentially little or no continental Antarctic ice ever reaches the oceans. During bright and sunny days, a small amount of surface of the continental and shoreline ice is destroyed by infrared rays from the sun. But this ice does not melt into the water; rather, it sublimates directly into water vapor.

- Sublimation means that the ice goes directly from the solid to the gaseous phase (water vapor), without ever going through the liquid phase.[130] When the sublimated water vapor reaches the cold Antarctic air, the vast majority of it quickly turns to snow and falls back on the glacier. The winds blow only a tiny amount over the Antarctic ocean. Nearly zero goes into the oceans as water.
- Coastal Antarctic ice, dramatized with films, photos, and articles in newspapers, press, and the TV showing large ice sheets tumbling into the ocean, did contribute to sea rise. The vast majority of coastal ice breaking off occurs in the north-western part of the Antarctic. These dramatic falling cliffs are not caused by global warming air, melting it (recall from above, it hardly ever gets above freezing in Antarctica) even on the coasts. Instead, the melting is occurring at the water level by the warmed Pacific Ocean. Here the water splashes and melts and gouges caverns in the ice, forming large ice shelves or overhangs. This process continues until the weight of the overhang is big enough to cause the overhung ice to break and tumble off, and that's when we get the sensational pictures and footages. Recall, however, that 90 percent of this coastal ice is under the water and is not subjected to the relatively warmer top layer nor subjected to the violent splashing. So yes, some of this ice will melt into the oceans and will cause some water level rise, but the volume is still unmeasurably small. One last quick fun fact: glaciers don't grow on the coastal edge. Instead, they flow there like a river from the inland ice sheets, pushed by the weight of the central ice mass. Yes, ice flows like water; but very slowly, which is also an indicator that the central ice mass is growing, which the satellite data confirms.

NASA[131] published a study on October 30, 2015, saying that Antarctica is accumulating ice at a rate of about 112 billion tons per year. It has already replaced all the ice that melted in the previous several decades. Another NASA study reports an increase in the rate of Antarctic snow accumulation. Currently, enough continental ice is accumulating to outweigh the losses caused by its shrinking coastal glaciers. Credits: Jay Zwally, Journal of Glaciology.[132]

Yes, there was substantial glacial melting in Greenland, Alaska, and other northern hemisphere locations, which added some waters to the oceans during the warming of the past several decades. However, these glaciers tend to melt and then increase in about twenty-year cycles, depending on the local conditions.[133] A number of these glaciers are now growing at a significant rate, like the famed Jakobshavn glacier in Greenland.[134] A world scorecard is kept that shows which glaciers are melting, and which are growing. But the long-term batting average seems to be about 50 percent. A recent article in *USA Today* from March 26, 2019, states, "... Natural cyclical cooling of North Atlantic waters likely caused the glacier to reverse course", said study lead author Ala Khazendar, a NASA glaciologist on the Oceans Melting Greenland (OMG). This news was widely reported in the press, including the Associated Press (March 29, 2019) and NBC News.[135]

Another side effect briefly discussed above is that when water gets warmer, it expands, and when it gets colder, it contracts. We are now going to get into some detail about why water is so fascinating. Water is the only substance that does a remarkable thing; when the temperature starts getting lower, close to 4° C, it stops contracting and starts to expand in the form of ice. In <u>4.17.2</u> above, we see that at 0° C, one kg of water occupies one cubic liter of volume, but at 70° C, it occupies 1.02 liters of water. That's about a 2 percent increase in size. That increase may not appear to be very much for a significant increase in temperature swing of 70° C. But when we are dealing with unmeasurable trillions of gigatons of ocean waters, even a 0.25° C increase in temperature will result in a rise in ocean waters, even with little or no polar/glacial ice melting.

<u>Besides water temperature</u>, other factors need to be accounted for when we say the ocean level is rising or falling. At the local level, the ocean can appear to "increase" or "decrease" due to changes on the land, along with other unique factors in the surrounding areas that have nothing to do with water temperature or polar ice melting. These are caused by land settling,

such as we see in downtown Boston, where the landfill of 150 years ago[136] keeps on settling — thus giving the appearance that the ocean is rising when, in fact, it's the local land that's sinking. The second source of complexity is caused by erosion of soil by wind and sea, which can give the appearance that the ocean is rising, like in the Carolinas coastline. Or an even more dramatic event, like Monomoy Island near Cape Cod, where at times the island disappears, giving the impression that the ocean is "seen" rising. But then it will reemerge some decades later, looking like the sea dropped.[137] Locally, it may appear that the sea is rising, but nothing is happening except that sand is pushed around by wind and sea currents and children playing with their little red shovels.

At the local level, there's also the sedimentation[138] effect. For example, the sand and soil of the Mississippi valley are continuously eroding and are carried into the streams, then rivers, the Mississippi, and finally to the Gulf of Mexico. Locally, it can be dramatic, like in New Orleans. Here the Mississippi River deposits about 200 million tons of earth, dirt, and rocks per year from the continental USA into the nearby Gulf of Mexico.

Another significant factor is the movement of the Earth's tectonic plates. The Earth's crust floats on top of molten lava and is about eighteen miles thick. But the crust is not a solid piece. It's made up of "plates," which keep floating and moving around. Where, for example, two plates meet, like at the infamous San Andreas fault line, unpleasant things start to happen. One, they meet head-on, like in India-Nepal-China, where the tectonic plate of the Indian subcontinent crashes into the massive Asian continent. There it meets incredible resistance and Voila! Mount Everest and K2, and the other mountains and countryside around keep growing about half an inch per year. Much of that land build-up is coming from the retreating shorelines of the Indian subcontinent, thus lowering the ocean level. This will result in a net loss of submerged land in the ocean, and it will appear as the ocean level is decreasing.[139] Earthquakes, volcanoes, and tsunamis also contribute to this continuing rearrangement of the land, and oceans respond and adjust accordingly.

One last item is "the spring back effect." During the last ice age, parts of North America, Europe, and Asia were covered by ice as much as one mile thick or more. It sucked so much water out of the oceans that it created a land bridge from Asia to North America. The weight of this massive ice crushed and compressed the Earth for tens of thousands of years. But, like a spring, the land is still recovering from the disappearance of the glacial mass and slowly expanding and springing back up. While scientists try to figure out if the seas are rising or falling, one or two millimeters per year, they have to sort out for all of these factors. Besides, they also have to contend with the fact that tidal gauges also get banged around by novice boat captains like me. Fortunately, more reliable satellite data of the last forty years confirms this rise of about one to two millimeters per year before any of these complex adjustments are made. The journal *Nature*, January 2019,[140] did an excellent job in discussing these adjustments in detail.

QUESTION 18: *IS THERE A RELATIONSHIP BETWEEN CLIMATE CHANGE AND VOLCANIC ACTIVITIES?*

This is like asking if there's a relationship between ice cream sales and shark attacks. But watch out! It's a trick question with a straightforward, non-causative answer. The immediate and correct answer is yes, there's a near-perfect one-to-one correlation between ice cream sales and shark attacks. But it's not because sharks like to bite people who eat ice cream. It's because on a hot, sunny day, more people go to the beach and more people go into the water, and more people buy ice cream.

So, while the two have absolutely nothing to do with each other, they are both driven by the same forcing function, which, in this case, is the hot weather. In this example, we see the difference between what scientists call "causation" apart from "correlation." So, it seems with volcanoes and climate change. One may cause the other, but no. Instead, both are driven by a natural force, which is the increased bombardment of the Earth by galactic cosmic rays during periods of low solar activities.

In a recent peer-reviewed paper, "Explosive volcanic eruptions triggered by cosmic rays: Volcano as a bubble chamber," Dr. Toshikazu Ebisuzaki found a cause-and-effect relationship between galactic cosmic rays and volcanic eruptions in silica-rich volcanoes.[141] The team examined the timing of eruptive events from four volcanoes in Japan over the past 306 years. They found all of the volcanic events occurred during periods of low solar magnetic activities.

Dr. Henrik Svensmark[142] is a physicist and professor in the Division of Solar System Physics at the Danish National Space Institute in Copenhagen. He is known for his theory of the effects[143] of galactic cosmic ray (GCR) on cloud formation as a cause of climate change. His approach was confirmed in his laboratory and at CERN[144] using cloud chamber nucleation experiments. Followers of this theory are investigating the cause-and-effect link between the Earth's interior with the increase in GCR that enters the Earth system during times of reduced solar activities. His approach was also supported by the work of Prof. Valentina Zharkova on how solar activity levels strengthen or weaken the solar magnetic fields and solar winds. During high solar activity periods, this effect stretches out to all the planets and reduces the number of cosmic rays. Consequently, far more high energy galactic cosmic rays reach the worlds at times of low solar activity.

QUESTION 19: *IS THERE A RELATIONSHIP BETWEEN CLIMATE CHANGE AND EARTHQUAKES?*

A few years ago, this question would have been lightheartedly dismissed with some reference to the *National Inquirer*. But recently, there have been several developments that are making a strong case for a connection between very high energy GCR penetrating the Earth's shields and the silica-rich magma in volcanoes and the Earth's crust. We touched on these briefly in Question 18 above but chose to keep them separate to distinguish between a connection based solely on cosmic rays and other possibilities dealing with the moons, sun, and planetary tidal forces acting on the Earth.

Galactic Cosmic Rays: Please read the above developments concerning earthquakes and replace volcanoes," with "earthquakes," you will have the same answer. Recently a publication titled "Do Cosmic Rays Trigger Earthquakes, Volcanic Eruptions?" *July 2, 2018*; by John O'Sullivan,[145] provides a summary of recent developments from the Oppenheimer Ranch Project (ORP):[146]

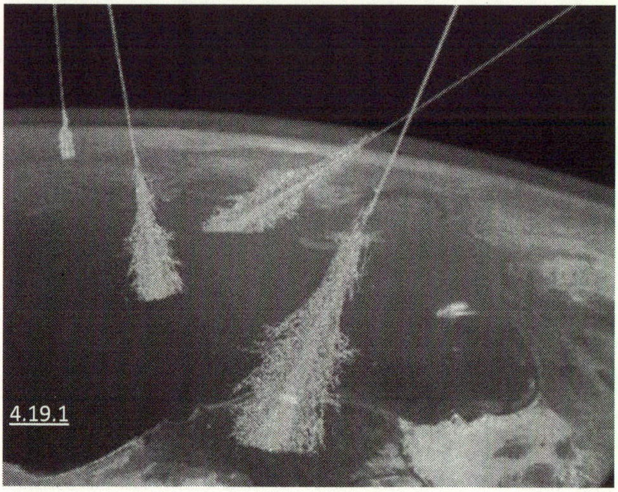

- First, a cause-and-effect relationship between high energy cosmic rays and volcanic eruptions and earthquakes appears undeniable. Figure 4.19.1[147] shows four cosmic rays setting off a reaction shower in the Earth's atmosphere.
- Also, recent studies in China and Florida have independently found a strong relationship between low solar activity,[148] especially with very few sunspots over a long time, and the most significant earthquakes and volcanic eruptions.

In either case, we don't yet know how galactic cosmic rays are connected with low solar activity. Do they act independently, or does one provide the trigger that sets off the explosive energy produced by the other? Also, a January 11, 2019 article in the journal Nature, includes information about how fast and how much the north magnetic pole of the Earth has been moving around in the past few years. This movement indicates that the molten nickel-iron magma sea is moving and twisting around and beneath the Earth mantle. This magma motion is putting stresses and strains on the tectonic plates that float on it, becoming a primary source of earthquakes.

Tug-of-war: "Can Astronomical Tidal Forces Trigger[149] Earthquakes?" is the title of an article by Robin Wylie published on April 29, 2015, in the Scientific American. The report states, "The idea that celestial bodies can cause earthquakes is one of the oldest theories in science. In 1687 Newton's universal law of gravitation revealed ocean tides are caused by the attraction of the sun and moon. And in the 1700s, scientists started to wonder if these same distant bodies might also affect geologic faults. This idea flourished in the 19th century. The French seismologist Alexis Perrey spent decades searching for a link between earthquakes and the phases of the moon." The Scientific American, published in 1855, had an article on his work. Even Charles Darwin mused on the subject (page 259).

Later studies suggested a link between oceanic tides and some earthquake activity, but proof that the gravitational tug of the moon and sun can set[150] off tremors remained elusive. But, over the last few years, scientists have been developing a possible unifying theory that the gravitational tides of certain individual planets may be the stimulus for the now-familiar eleven-year solar magnetic cycle.

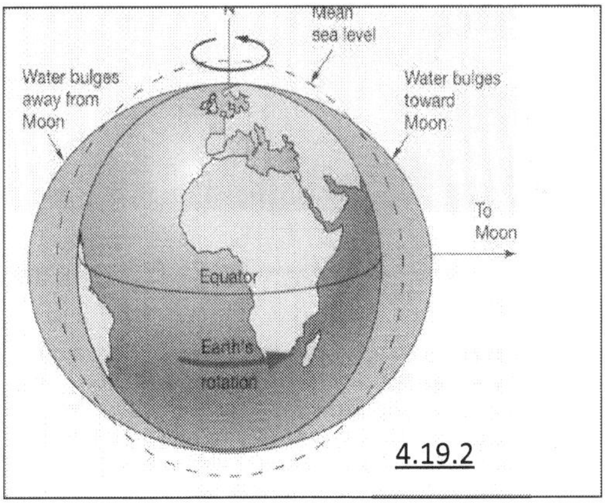

4.19.2

For now, looking at 4.19.2,[151] we'll say if this interaction of planetary tidal forces is strong enough that it can slosh around the solar plasma, there is no way the Earth can escape from the same gravitational effects. As such, with the molten core of our world sloshing around a bit more, it's understandable how that would at least contribute to earthquakes. And all of these actions and interactions seem to coincide with a weakened solar magnetic field and weakened solar winds, making the Earth more susceptible to increased GCR flux.

QUESTION 20: *WHAT IS MEANT BY THE*

"EARTH'S ENERGY BUDGET"?

> Author's observation: Think for a moment about the incredible science, engineering and computer programming involved in doing this task of measuring TSI at the edge of space. It's amazing, we truly are in the golden age of climate science. I recall in high school, how scientists were praised and revered as we were preparing to land on the moon and in the breakthroughs of DNA research. How things have changed! Did the scientists bring this upon themselves, or have our societal values shifted greatly and in a sad direction?

Background: The Earth's energy budget is like your checking account; we measure what comes in and what goes out. When we balance it, every week, or every year, if the balance is not a zero - Huston, we have a problem. However, here we are not balancing dollars but TSI, total solar irradiance. In the previous sections, we discussed that the measured TSI arriving from the sun to the Earth in the form of electromagnetic waves, at the edge of space is about 1,361 W/M^2. But that's at the equator, on a flat surface and at the extreme limits of the Earth's atmosphere. Then, as we move north or south from the equator, it gradually decreases and approaches zero at the poles.[152]

Now, this may come as a shock, but the Earth is not flat like a pizza. In fact, it is round, like a meatball. If we look at 4.20.1,[153] we see the proximity of the sun to the equator, where the sun's rays meet on the globe at point b, we see a small circular area. But at point a, near the North Pole, we see the same amount of light spread over a much larger area. We might be inclined to say, "Aha!" Light arriving at the poles is spread over a much larger area. So, the number of rays coming from the sun, called "solar flux," has to be about half or a third less at the poles than on the equator. Close, but no cigar! Remember, we are are talking about an area and not just a line. Recall from Chapter 3, a better

4.20.1

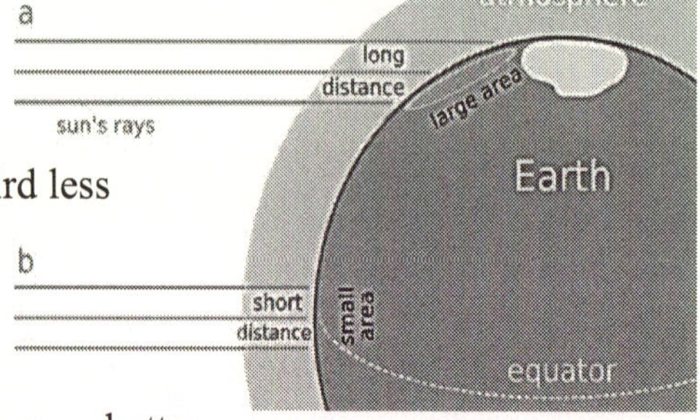

representation of the sun's traveling energy density arriving on Earth looks more like 3.14.4. Go back and check it out.

In 4.20.2,[154] we see the dramatic decline in the energy density arriving at different parts of the Earth, depending on how close you are from the equator. Graphed here are the daily average energy densities. For simplicity, ignore the measurements on the left axis, as it is in Jules/m^2 rather than the more familiar W/m^2, but the shape of the curves is the same on either scale. As a comparison base looks at 45^0 latitudes, that's about Chicago. But at 20° North, there are no cities or even significant towns, and virtually near-zero energy arriving there for 2-3 months of the year. Compare this to the equatorial regions which have near-zero variation in energy from winter to summer.

4.20.2

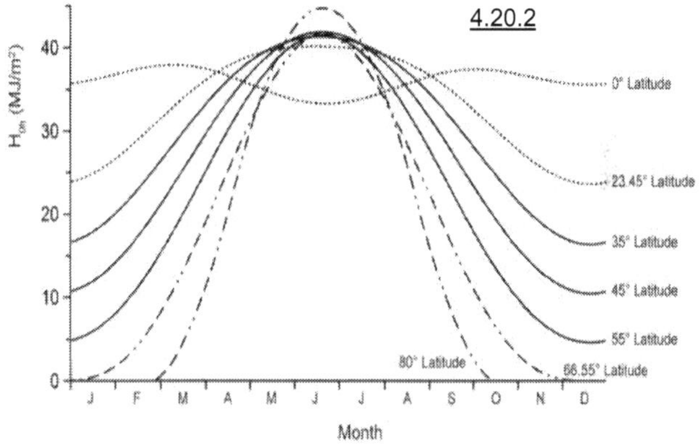

In addition to the monthly changes in energy density arriving at the Earth, we also have the variations as the day progresses from sun-up to sundown and through the night to dawn. Looking at 4.20.3,[155] we see that at sunrise, the energy level is near zero, then slowly building up and reaching the maximum (for each latitude), then descending to near zero again at sunset. This energy density distribution is traveling east to west at about 1,000 miles/hour. Once we do all the math, with pie and squaring and

4.20.3

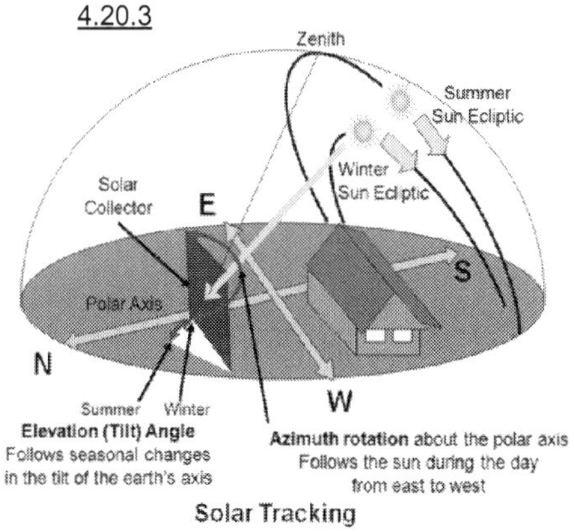

stuff, we find that the average global TSI flux for the planet goes from 1,361 W/M^2 at the equator at the edge of space to a global average about 341 watts per square meter at the edge of the Earth's atmosphere. That's enough power to light three 100-watt bulbs in the kitchen and one 40-watt lamp in the fridge. That's the starting point of our Earth energy budget.

But first, let's restate the obvious about this statistic we call global average TSI. Global TSI is meaningless in discussing the weather, and the long term weather trends we call climate change. Those work only at the worldwide level, where the temperature differences put in motion the air and the waters in a futile effort to eliminate the temperature differences discussed above. But how does this 341 global average TSI change over time tell us what climate changes in the future might be? Should we budget for more shorts and swim-suits, or start building greenhouses to grow food undercover to stay alive. Let's relook at 4.20.4,[156] where I want to draw your attention to how sensitive the Earth system appears to be in only a slight change in TSI. Point a, with a TSI of 1,360, is only one TSI less than the period b that preceded, and that followed a. But point a is the Maunder minimum, 70 years of cold, and starvation around the world.

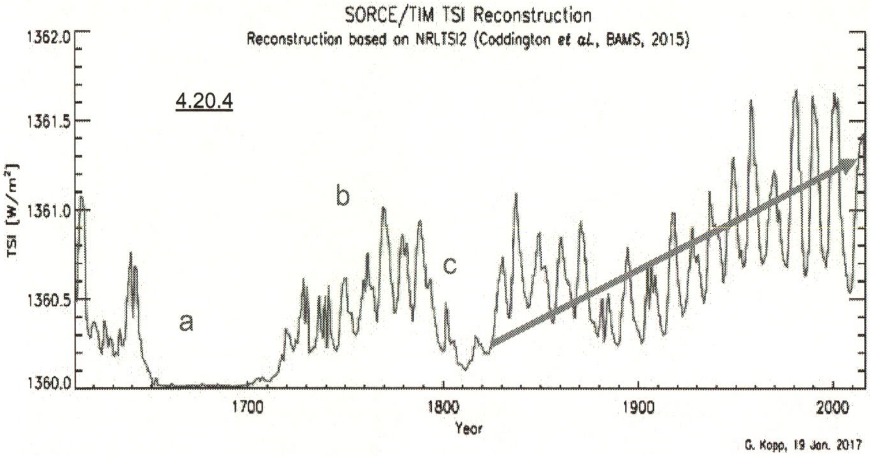

Similarly, point c is the Daulton Minimum, again characterized by an extended cooling period. Still, thankfully it was not as severe and did not last as long as the Maunder period. By contrast, we see point b where we see a comfortable, warm period which resumed again after the Maunder period. Secondly, with the blue arrow, we note the near-perfect correlation between a one TSI increase (an increase of only 0.07 percent) and the corresponding global temperature increase of one degree C from 1840 to today. As the song goes, "little things, mean – a – lot."

Earth's energy budget: OK, now let's look at 4.20.5[157] from a paper titled "Principal Uncertainties in Climate Models," where we see all the inputs and outputs of our planet's energy, AKA the TSI budget. It would be

4.20.5*

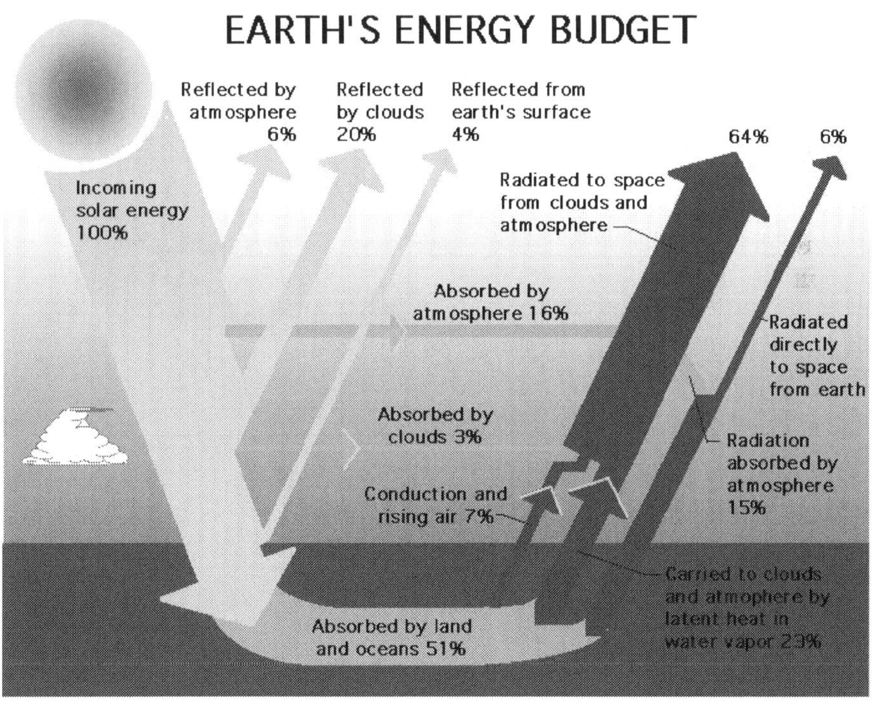

great if we can end the cycle with a perfect zero because if the end number is positive, say +0.1° C, it means that tomorrow's solar heating period will start +0.1° C warmer than yesterday. If we did this for ten days or ten years in a row, we would have a runaway global warming. And the same thing would also happen if we had a deficit of -0.1° C. We would soon have a runaway global cooling. But our diagram here shows us we are in balance; 100 percent in and 100 percent out.

Now let's take a closer look, and let's start with the sun. Here we have our average global TSI at 341 W/m^2 or 100 percent of the sun's energy arriving at the Earth's atmosphere. The first thing that happens is that 6 percent of that energy is bounced back to outer space by the air, so we are left with 94 percent. Then another 20 percent is bounced back into space by the tops of the clouds, so 94 -20 = 74 percent. Then 4 percent is reflected by the Earth, ice/snow, and seas, and we are down to 70 percent. From that, 16 percent is absorbed by the air, and 3 percent by clouds. That leaves 51 percent, which is absorbed by the land and seas, and all the plants and animals, and we now have 100 percent in the input side.

Now let's look at the output side, where we see 64 percent radiated back up from the clouds and the atmosphere and lands and oceans. Another 6 percent is emitted back to space directly by the Earth and another 23 percent back to the atmosphere by water vapor and another 7 percent by the Earth's conduction and convection. Are we in thermal balance? Does the heat input into the Earth equal the heat radiated away from the Earth? Let's do the math. (-64 -6 -23 -7) = -100 percent. So, the system is in balance. Now, let's say that for a few days there are 1 percent more clouds. No problem. So, the Earth receives and absorbs 1 percent less heat, then at night radiates 1 percent less heat back to space, so it's still in the balance. But not so fast—let's take a closer look at the red 6 percent first. This is the only absorbed energy radiated directly into outer space, no stops along the way. The remaining 64 percent hangs around for a while in the air and clouds (the greenhouse effect) and eventually and slowly radiates it back to space during the night and chilly mornings.

The "consensus view" is a two-fold CO2 induced effect, and the first one is the increase in the quantity of CO2 in the atmosphere. Let's assume CO2 increases the total energy absorbed by the air and cloud by, say, from 64 percent to 64.001 percent. Then supposedly, the higher CO2 content in the air and clouds will somehow change the very nature of water vapor or trigger it in some fashion so that the entire 64.001 percent now cools more slowly and hangs around a bit longer. They call this mechanism "radiative forcing." Bottom line—there is no debate about the increase in total CO2 and the resultant small increase in air and cloud temperature retention. The discussion and controversy, however, is about this "radiative forcing." Is it real or not, and if so, by how much? Tens of billions of dollars have already been spent trying to find and validate this concept.[158] But thus far, it's only an interesting idea with no supporting evidence or data.

How to manage this energy budget? This is where the hard work begins. We have to address the hard questions as well as the funky and absurd questions. For decades, for centuries, people have been saying, "Everybody talks about the weather, but nobody does anything about it." So, let's ease into it. Are you an optimist, a fatalist, a control freak, or a combination of these? Let's start this question on the input side.

How to mitigate global warming on the input side?

- Milankovitch cycle — *Do nothing*. This cycle will continue to affect the distance, position, orientation, and movement of the Earth relative to the sun. They occur over 20,000 and 40,000, and 100,000, and 400,000-year cycles. It happens at the astronomical levels and is powered by the gravitational interactions among the sun, moon, the dominant and nearby planets, and the giant planets. So, while we can send satellites to measure stuff, there's no way we can change any of it.
- Solar cycles — *Do Nothing.* No way, Jose. The sun is too far, too big, too hot, and totally beyond any conceivable reach by humanity.
- Heat Absorption — *Yes-we-can.* If global warming is happening, there are a few things, both easy and economical, that we can do to reduce the amount of heat that's absorbed by the Earth. Below are the most useful, practicable, and indisputable ways to decrease the heat absorbed by the land:
  - Plant trillions of trees, bushes, millions of acres of grasslands. This will increase the amount of CO2 absorbed by the plants and reduce the heat available to warm the ground.
  - Coat all the roads and parking lots with white-reflective paint, so more of the sun's heat is reflected into space. Thus, less energy will radiate at night back up into the air and clouds, thereby reducing the greenhouse effect.
  - Mandate that all new roofs use highly reflective coatings and paint all buildings white.
  - Mandate that all new constructions use reflective nano-coatings with greater reflective properties on all windows and glass panes in skyscrapers, buildings, cars, trucks, and trains.

- Mandate that everybody wears a four-foot-wide, tin-foiled sombreros and mylar reflective ponchos.

- What about the greenhouse effects– *Yes, in a limited way?* Reduce emissions of methane and CO2 by increased use of solar and wind power? Well, not so much. We've seen they need fossil fuel backup plants and CO2 emissions don't decrease. A viable "insurance policy" might be needed to build thousands of nuclear plants. That would give us the safest, cheapest, and cleanest energy and end the CO2 debate. Yes? No? Maybe?
- Lastly, we might push the state-of-the-art for battery technology, but it's costly and dangerous. Large batteries tend to be unstable, as the battery fire issues occasionally remind us of the Teslas where we have today, especially after a crash.[159] At other times there have been incidents without an accident.[160] But there's an issue with big lithium batteries that generally make them unstable and dangerous.[161]
- Darwin approach– Adapt to what you can't control.

How to mitigate for global cooling: If Zharkova, Svensmark, Easterbrook, etc. are correct that there is something close to a grand minimum solar starting with cycle 25 and continuing into 26 and hopefully not into 27, then we should:

- See the Darwin approach, adapt, or perish.
- Start building millions of square miles of greenhouses to grow food under shelter to mitigate starvation for people. We should get confirmation of this cooling in the next 3-5 years.
- Build thousands of square miles of food preservation and storage facilities at the first signs of a confirmed approaching Dalton type of Minimum.
- Start building hundreds of coal and nuclear power plants ASAP to heat our homes, buildings, greenhouses, barns, etc.

~ 5 ~

SUM AND SUMMARY

Rated PG – Proud Grownups

QUESTION 21: *HOW BIG IS THE CLIMATE CHANGE INDUSTRY*

It's tough to put a number on this cost because it's like an octopus with thousands of tentacles in many academic, industrial, political, and governmental institutions. So, let's start by looking at how the interests of these entities are financially aligned and see if there's a reinforcing mechanism that's stimulating the ever-bigger budgets. Since it's a circular relationship, we could start with any of them, so let's arbitrarily start with academia.

Let's take a trip to Small Town USA and see what's going on.

Academia:[162] In this group, we have universities where professors, or professor wannabes, have a vital interest in getting as many research grant dollars as possible and publish as many papers as they can. Their careers, livelihood, and social status depend on it. As the old saying goes, "*Publish or perish.*"[163] Their annual income may substantially rely on this by as much as 20-50 percent. This incentive may be the difference between belonging to the country club or not, or if their next car is a Chevy or Mercedes. It also means whether or not they get tenure or an offer from MIT or Harvard. Here's where the government steps in and puts its elbow on the scale because the US Government is the primary source of the vast amounts of research dollars awarded each year. It also means that government employees need to be hired to review the grant applications, critique them, request changes, and negotiate the dollar amounts. And if one scientist needs a hundred hours to prepare the grant request, it may take 500 or more hours for the bureaucrats to do their thing. And of course, the most prominent projects need the best people. What ends up happening is that it provides incentives for the bureaucrats to please their bosses and support their political goals.

If the political goal is to advance the case for the human-made CO2 agenda for whatever reason, the funds will overwhelmingly go in that direction. Private industry may also weigh their influence in the process because they may see downstream governmental regulations that will favor (or harm) their industries. Their lobbyists come out in full force, along with their advertising dollars, much to the benefit of the media and their talking heads. As more and more funds are allocated to support the desired premise, more and more funding requests are submitted and granted. Then, more bureaucrats need to be hired to process the grants, leading to more papers published that support the premise. This activity allows the press/media to report on the "growing number" of scientific papers published supporting the politically popular proposition. Now please refrain from asking silly questions like what about the science, where does that come into play?

In actuality, these papers may or may not have any tangible scientific values. But the sheer increased volume of published articles is exploited to give gravity and urgency, thereby reinforcing the desired premise. How can the average person sort all of this out? Bottom line: following the "consensus" is beneficial for universities, good for professors, good for government bureaucrats, useful for politicians and commerce in general. Probably not so much for the average person, who has to pay for those grants via taxes, downstream regulations, and fees while receiving zero benefits. We'll do a deep dive on this in Chapter 7.5, titled "Fraud and University Grants."

Industry:[164] If Smallville needs more electrical power, it could build a single fossil-fueled combined with a gas-fired cycle plant. It requires about twenty acres of land and about a total of one hundred and fifty million dollars.

But if politicians and academics want to push for a "green-renewable" wind solution, the electrical utility companies will offer their full support! Why? Because it aligns with their interests. If a wind plant also costs one hundred and fifty million dollars, this windmill will need an identical backup fossil power plant. So, the industry gets a total sale from Smallville of three hundred million dollars and twice as much profit. The oil and gas industry is also fully supported. Why? Because the backup fossil plant will still burn about 90-95 percent of the same fuel as it would burn if there were no wind farms. So, the oil company gets great press for supporting the "green" plant. The existence and costs of the backup plant, extra land, fossil fuel burn, and no significant reduction in CO2 are never mentioned or shown by the compliant media/press. Imagine the electrical utility company, which spends twice as much on the plant, and still doesn't save much fuel. What does it get? It passes on the higher electrical costs to the consumer, and now has a more extensive billing base to which it adds its healthy profit percentage.

Politicians:[165] Politicians can tell their constituencies as to how they were able to bring in planet-saving green technologies to their communities. They also show their constituents how they muscled the greedy utility by reducing their "unconscionable" request for a rate increase by 25 percent. In reality, the rate increase requested may have been ten cents per kilowatt-hour but settled for seven and a half cents. So, everybody loves them and reelect them, maybe even promote some from Congress to the US Senate. Not so bad. To this political group, we also have to add the local schoolteachers, chamber of commerce, and local businesses

who want to shine and be seen as sponsors of this planet-saving green revolution.

Mr. and Mrs. Consumer:[166] At first glance, the project sounds pretty good to the average persons, the tax-payers. After all, they get green planet-saving technology, and the politician cut the rate by 25 percent (note the slight change in the words). But this euphoria comes to a quick halt when the consumer gets the electric bill, which has gone up by twenty dollars a month! Then, six months later, the consumer receives another note saying his electric rate will again increase by another ten dollars a month. Again, a year later, our consumer will probably be hit by an additional seven dollar bill per month. Within a two or three year period, Mr. and Mrs. Consumer are paying thirty-seven dollars extra per month, for their electricity. How did this happen?

If they're a family of four, with a yearly income of forty-thousand dollars, they just take a "pay cut" of about four hundred and fifty dollars per year. Now for families in the top ten percent income bracket, this extra electricity cost may not even be noticeable. For the top 15-percent, maybe it's a minor inconvenience. But the level of financial pain goes higher and higher as the income levels go lower and lower. In many instances, it will get to the point that hard choices will need to be made, like heating the home or rationing medications or food.

What about commerce,[167] like owners of the local supermarkets, dry cleaners, shoemakers, barbershop, gas station, etc. who also have to bear their price increase? How are they going to make up for that expense? Are they going to increase their prices to offset their increased electricity bill? Maybe yes, but perhaps they have no choice and must absorb the cost. Now this will bring another round of cost increase to our Mr. and Mrs. Consumer household by another four to five hundred dollars a year.

On top of that, Mr./Mrs. consumers will also have their income taxes go up by another $100-200 a year to pay for the university research grants, additional bureaucrats who need to be hired, and the green tax incentives given to the utility. This means that his "pay-cut" is now reaching over a thousand dollars per year. Worse yet, what benefit did he, his family, or anybody in this community get from this "planet-saving" adventure? The sad answer is nothing, and it's the same for his 50,000 neighbors. They were all impoverished by this CO2 myth. On top of that, they got no reduction in CO2, no decrease in pollutants, their countryside is scarred by these ugly windmills that are killing hundreds, maybe thousands, of birds per year.

Let's look at the report card[168] and see who the winners and who the losers are of this green planet-saving initiative.

- The winners are the politicians, academics, government bureaucrats, and the wealthy who own industries, etc. Here's an excerpt from an interesting article from U.S. News & World Report; by Nancy Pfotenhauer, May 12, 2014. The title is *"Big Wind's Bogus Subsidies. Giving tax credits to the wind energy industry is a waste of time and money."* The article goes on to say, "*Despite being famous for touting the idea that the rich don't pay their fair share of taxes, investor Warren Buffet seems to be perfectly fine with receiving tax breaks for making investments in Big Wind.*"[169] Buffet then says, "*I will do anything that is covered by the law to reduce Berkshire's tax rate.*" Adding, "*For example, on wind energy, we get a tax credit if we build a lot of wind farms. That's the only reason to build them. They don't make sense without the tax credit.*"
- The losers are the average American middle class/taxpaying families as well as the small businesses that can't pass on the increased cost to consumers and may have to cut back on employees or their benefits. Not to mention the working poor who usually work in these small businesses. Will they have to take pay cuts to keep their meager jobs, if not lose them outrightly.

- The community is probably the biggest loser. The taxpaying base is reduced, and services will need to be cut back. Some of the consequences will include:
  - Fewer teachers and bigger classroom sizes, resulting in reduced quality of education.
  - Reduced firefighters, police, street cleaning, parks, charitable organizations, etc.
  - A widening gap between the haves and have nots will also result in heightening social tensions and unrest, further fuelling social conflicts.

The USA climate change research industry: We will not try to estimate the excess costs imposed on the average citizen resulting from the climate change industry. In general, they include restrictive building codes that drive up the construction costs of new housing, new business startups, and the loss of farmlands and grazing pastures required by the solar and wind farms. The subject is so complex and overwhelming that it would need an 800-page book to explain it. So, for now, we'll limit our discussion to the portion that's spent by the U.S. government to support climate change research.

Climate change research has become a massive business since the founding of the U.N.'s IPCC committee in 1988. The General Accounting Office (GAO) data shows that in 1993 two-point four billion dollars were spent on climate research. It then grew steadily to nearly twelve billion dollars by 2014, a significant growth achievement that any hi-tech CEO would be proud of. Also, a supplemental twenty-six billion was added in 2009 by President Obama. Total expenditures for 2020 will likely exceed twenty billion dollars. Let's put this in context and compare it to the single most expensive U.S. public-funded science project to date.[170]
"*Conclusion - After examining the reports and removing double-counting, calculations show that from the Fiscal Year 1993 to FY 2014, total U.S. expenditures on climate change amounted to more than $166 billion in 2012 dollars. By way of comparison, the Congressional Budget Office estimated that the entire Apollo program, operating from 1962 to 1973 with 17 missions—seven of them sending men to the moon and back—cost $170 billion in 2005 dollars, which equals about $200 billion in 2012 dollars if we use the Consumer Price Index to adjust that figure. In 'fighting' climate*

change, the United States government is spending almost as much as it did on all the Apollo missions." [171]

If records were available through 2018, we could probably demonstrate that for climate change, we have already spent double what we did for the entire Apollo Program.

It's also ruefully noted that of these twenty billion dollars per year, about 90 percent is spent on chasing the elusive CO2 related studies, which has been abused. For example, if a researcher at any university wants to survey the life span of the snowy owl, he's not likely to get any government funding. But if the grant request is structured to read "How the snowy owl is impacted by CO2 climate change," it's almost assured it will be granted. By contrast, if a university professor wants to study the impact of the sun's magnetic field on terrestrial climate change, it's likely not to be funded. But if it's changed to "How the sun's magnetic field may increase the terrestrial CO2 cycle", it's much more likely to be approved. Lastly, who benefits from these silly studies? Excellent question with no matching answers. Such are the social, political, and economic norms and pressures of the times. With all this money on the table, we have major universities, private entities, and individuals competing for these research dollars. Over the years, they have divided into two teams.

Here's how they've grouped and what they do. But before we categorize their actions and decision processes, <u>let's look at one sample behavioral driving force:</u>

- Suppose you're thirty years old, in the early stage of your career. You have a young family to raise, feed, and school. You have the payments on your Tesla, your school loans and the monthly dues at the tennis and swim club and the fitness center. You have spent twenty-five years in "socially responsible" schools and institutions and were taught by "socially responsible" teachers and professors. You have gotten tenure or are aspiring for it and have a career to build. What do you do? What choices do you make? Pursue secure funding grants or pursue science in the classical scientific method?
- By contrast, you are a tenured professor, close to retirement, worked at a prestigious university, and are now looking forward to moving to Florida. Your children have completed their education. You paid for it and now pray to God that they make something of their knowledge.

> You have values you want to hold on to and pass on to your grandchildren. What choices do you make?

So, ladies and gentlemen, and everything in between, here are the options available to you. You can join Team A or Team B—no other options are available to you in this polarized world.

Team B: If you are financially, emotionally, and socially secure, you are more likely to join Team B. The position of the Team B scientists is to study all of the natural and human-made factors summarized in the above questions. You are comfortable to point out that while human-made activities can and does contribute to weather and climate change, it's to a much lesser extent than the natural cycles and factors. As such, you want to take the discovery journey and see where truth and data lead you.

The problem is that Team B does not have a centralized organization and does not have a well-funded political lobby. Instead, this team is made up of individuals and a few small independent groups of scientists who lack the resources, money, and organization to drive an effective public relations campaign or gather funding monies as Team A does.

In the USA, Team B gets less than 10 percent of the U.S. government climate research grants. It must rely on the fact that most of their studies are unfunded, performed by unpaid retired professors, or partially funded by small private donations and done much like a second job. Most are done pro-bono, for which they are insulted and condemned by the press, media, the CO2 industry, and politicians.

Team A is supported by the United Nations and the "Consensus" community. It's founded on the notion that human-made activities are the principal drivers of climate change. Besides, almost 98 percent of their efforts are focused on what happens on planet Earth with CO2 and maybe two-percent for its cousin, cow-induced methane. They perform zero studies on any of the natural or cyclic elements and forces. Their studies focus primarily on the consequences of global warming like polar ice melting and how much the global ocean levels will rise, instead of investigating what causes them to grow. They also spend enormous resources on air and water pollution, where it's clear that ocean acidification, volcanoes, and earthquakes may not be the contributing causes or consequences of global warming. Most of their studies are focused on understanding the impact and effects of human-made climate change on humans, animals, and the global environment. How many billions or trillions of dollars will we pay for the cost of the rising ocean? How can we measure it? How do we forecast it? What social, financial, and emotional trauma must we endure? And, what policy adjustments need to be made and actions to be taken to prevent or mitigate their consequences? These studies are not to advance science but to promote "climate terror."

The core goal of Team A is the United Nations' Intergovernmental Panel on Climate Change or IPCC. The IPCC was created in 1988, with the specific mandate "to assess on a comprehensive, objective, open and transparent basis the scientific, technical and socio-economic information relevant to understanding the scientific basis of risk of human-induced climate change, its potential impacts and options for adaptation and mitigation."[172] Please note that their charter only permits them to investigate human-made climate change and not study any climate change cause or impact from nonhuman-made forces. Their charter does not allow them to investigate any of the other natural factors. There are very few scientists working at the IPCC. Their role is primarily administrative—to coordinate the scientific work performed and funded by scientists from the various U.N. member countries.

Team A has the power and prestige that comes with the bales of cash, Hollywood celebrities, famed spokesmen like Obama and Leonardo DiCaprio, and countless prime ministers and worldly luminaries. They hold self-ingratiating TV spectacles like the Oscars or headlined events like the Cannes Film Festival, where attendees travel in their private planes, wearing silk gowns with lots of bling-bling.

The climate change industry in the U.K.[173,174]
Following is an excerpt from an excellent article by Peter Lilley for the U.K. Global Warming Policy Foundation (GWPF). This is the same organization that sponsored the first public presentation by Drs. Valentina Zharkova and Henrik Svensmark. Here we are given a peek into the influence brought on

by politicians and industry groups at the expense of the general public. Peter Lilley has held several important positions under Prime Ministers Margaret Thatcher and John Majors and was one of the only three Members of Parliament to vote against the British Climate Change Act.

THE HELM REVIEW OF ENERGY COSTS*, Lessons to be Learned.*
The dogs that didn't bark,[175]*Sherlock Holmes, was right. The most important clue is often 'the dog that did not bark in the night.' So, when the government published a report showing that its* [176] *policy has wasted the best part of £100 billion and rising, yet the guard dogs of Parliament, the hounds of the Opposition and the mongrels of the media let it pass without so much as a whimper, we have to ask: 'why didn't the dogs bark?' Debate rages about whether it is worth spending £40 billion to leave the EU, or £50 billion on HS2 to shorten journeys to Birmingham by 20 minutes. When Professor Dieter Helm, one of our most respected energy economists, revealed that the government could achieve its target to reduce carbon emissions for a fraction of the £100 billion it has already committed, there was a deafening silence. It is not as if Dieter Helm is a climate skeptic. Far from it. He shares the concerns about global warming enshrined in the Climate Change Act, which requires British governments to reduce emissions of carbon dioxide by 80 percent by 2050. His review was commissioned by the government itself to examine how this target 'can be meeting the power sector at minimum cost and without imposing further costs on the exchequer.'*

By any standards, it is an exemplary study–lucid, logically coherent, original, and devastating in its conclusions. One does not have to accept all its analyses or recommendations to recognize that it is an outstanding contribution to policymaking. Helm sums up why the policy of successive governments has been so unnecessarily costly in a single pithy phrase, which may also explain why his report has met such a comprehensive 'ignored.' Governments, Helm reminds us, are not good at picking winners–unfortunately, losers are good at picking governments. Rather than leaving the market to find the most cost-efficient way of reducing emissions, successive Labor, coalitions, and Conservative ministers have all taken it upon themselves to select and subsidize specific technologies. So, his phrase indicts as either losers or gullible, the whole subsidized renewables industry along with the politicians of all parties and their officials who picked or 'were picked by' them.

No wonder they all combined to consign his review to oblivion, and almost no-one had an interest in sounding the alarm. Moreover, governments have not only subsidized research and development (something which Helm supports) or a pilot plant in each technology. Instead, they have financed a large-scale deployment of immature technologies. And they did so by awarding each technology a price for the electricity it generates high enough to make it profitable, then guaranteeing that price, indexed to inflation, usually for 15 years. The only people who could advise civil servants on the cost required to make each technology profitable were the businesses backing that technology! So, the strategy provided a field day to uncompetitive firms. In Helm's words: 'inevitably– as in most such picking-winners strategies– the results end up being vulnerable to lobbying, to the general detriment of household and industrial customers. It also created a playing field for amateur political and civil service'[177] *enthusiasts for each technology. Amateurism and lobbying combined so that: 'Government started with some of the most expensive technologies first and it could be argued that since then it has at times been exploring even more expensive options. Helm's central proposal is to return decision-making to the discipline of the market, wherever possible.'*[178]

<u>WARNING. Warning, Mr. Robinson. Opinion Alert.</u>

There's a good chance that Team B is more technically correct in their science than Team A because it investigates all of the possible causes and sources of climate change, including human-made factors. Secondly, most of their studies are focused on the cause and effect relationships with little to no reviews speculating on the consequences of climate change. But Team B has significant problems. Team A has many more impactful advantages. The people of Team B tend to be nerdy in what they say and how they say it. They have their language and excellent math skills, which is very hard to understand by the general public. They have gray hair and spectacles and don't look or sound cool. As a result, the general public doesn't know what they say and don't want to hear what they have to say.

The second problem is that Team B players may not even care what the general public thinks because they believe that we are incapable of understanding what they are talking about. And while they may be right in what they say, it does hurt their public relations, their messaging, and their federal funding sources.

We opened this discussion by posing the sub-question, "*And what does it mean for the average family, the community, and the planet?*" We are now in a position to provide a clear and comprehensive answer: [179]

1. For the average American family, it means an increased cost of living, lower quality of life, and a much-widened income gap compared to the well-to-dos!
2. And it's the same for the community, further impoverished by the costs of chasing this mythical CO2 delusion with near-zero benefits!
3. For the planet, it means nothing. Even if CO2 was as harmful as we are told, the much-discussed "green energy chase" results in a near-zero reduction of CO2!

QUESTION 22: THE SAMPLE LINEUP[180]

Who's who on team A & team B?

Team A	Team B
Wallace S. Broecker [181] was born in Chicago, Illinois, in 1931. He holds a Ph.D. (1958) in geology from Columbia University. He is currently Newberry professor of geology in the Department of Earth and Environmental Sciences and the Earth Institute at Columbia University, as well as a research scientist with Columbia's Lamont-Doherty Earth Observatory	**Patrick Michaels** [182] is the director of the Center for the Study of Science at the conservative Cato Institute. Michaels is a regular commentator on climate change issues on Fox News and Forbes and contributes opinion articles to U.S. newspapers. He has written several books critical of climate change science and the risks of rising greenhouse gas emissions.
James E. Hansen [183] [184] was born in Denison, Iowa, in 1941. He holds a master's degree (1965) in astronomy and a Ph.D. (1967) in physics, both from the University of Iowa, where he trained with famed astrophysicist James Van Allen. Having retired in 2013 as Director of the NASA Goddard Institute for Space Studies, where he spent a career spanning some four and a half decades, Hansen is currently an Adjunct Professor at Columbia University and Director of the Program on Climate Science, Awareness and Solutions in Columbia Earth Institute.	**Roy Spencer** [185] is a research scientist at the University of Alabama, Huntsville, and self-describes as a climatologist, author, and former NASA scientist. He has testified at a Minnesota state hearing on the impacts of carbon dioxide. Spencer's position on climate change is: "There's probably a natural reason for global warming. We will look back on it as a gigantic false alarm. The Earth isn't that sensitive to how much CO2 we put into the atmosphere. We need to consider the possibility that more carbon dioxide is better than less."

Phil D. Jones [186] was born in Redhill, England, in 1952. He holds a Ph.D. in hydrology (1977) from the Department of Civil Engineering at the University of Newcastle upon Tyne. Most of his career has been spent with the University of East Anglia's Climatic Research Unit (CRU), which he served as Director from 1998 until 2016. Jones is currently a Professorial Fellow in the School of Environmental Sciences at the University of East Anglia.	**Dr. J Lehr** [187] received the nation's first Ph.D. in Ground Water Hydrology in 1962, following a degree in Geological Engineering from Princeton University. He published 30 books and over 400 journal articles.[188] He is an outspoken proponent of sane environmental regulation and currently the Science Director [189]with the Heartland Institute and President of Environmental Education Enterprises, which advances personal freedom while achieving environmental goals that are mutually inclusive rather than exclusive.
Syukuro Manabe [190] was born in Japan in 1931. He received his Ph.D. in geophysics from [191] the University of Tokyo and joined the U.S. Weather Bureau - Geophysical Fluid Dynamics Laboratory of the National Oceanic and Atmospheric Administration (NOAA). In 2002, he returned to the U.S. as a Visiting Researcher with Princeton University's Program in Atmospheric and Oceanic Sciences. Currently a Senior Meteorologist at Princeton University.	**Dr. Donald Easterbrook** [192] received his BS, MS, and Ph.D. degrees in geology from the University of Washington. He taught for 40 years at Western Washington University, where he has researched ancient and recent global climate change in North America, New Zealand, Argentina, and various other parts of the world. Dr. Easterbrook has come under harsh criticism in response to his revealing how NASA has been "normalizing" many of their initially published land temperature data to be more in line with the IPCC publications.
Michael E. Mann,[193] creator of the "hockey stick," was born in Amherst, Massachusetts, in 1965. After undergraduate and graduate work in physics and geology, he obtained his Ph.D. in geophysics in 1998 from Yale University. Mann is currently a Distinguished Professor of Atmospheric Science with a joint appointment in the	**Dr. Richard S. Lindzen** [194] is an American atmospheric physicist known for his work in the dynamics of the middle atmosphere, atmospheric tides, and ozone photochemistry. He has published more than 200 scientific papers and books. An outspoken climate contrarian and retired Massachusetts Institute of Technology professor, he sent a letter in 2017 to President Donald

Department of Meteorology and Atmospheric Science and the Department of Geosciences at Pennsylvania State University. Director of Penn State's Earth System Science Center.	Trump urging him to pull the United States out of the United Nations' climate change regime because global climate action is "not scientifically justified."
John Francis [195] was born in 1948 in the United Kingdom. He holds a Ph.D. in theoretical physics (1973) from Queen's University Belfast. He is currently Principal Research Fellow, advising the British government's meteorological division (Met Office) on climate change, and is Visiting Professor at the University of Reading.	**Dr. Judith A. Curry**[196] is an American climatologist and former chair of the School of Earth and Atmospheric Sciences at the Georgia Institute of Technology. She was one of the first scientists who switched from Team A to Team B and has since become a significant voice against the narrative advocated by Team A.
Veerabhadran Ramanathan[197] holds a Ph.D. (1974) in planetary atmospheres from the State University of New York at Stony Brook. He is currently Victor C. Alderson Professor of Applied Ocean Sciences and Professor of Atmospheric Sciences at the University of California San Diego, as well as Director of the Center for Atmospheric Sciences at the Scripps Institution of Oceanography there.	**Dr. Wei-Hock "Willie" Soon** was born in Malaysia, has a degree in earth science and solar physic, and is an aerospace engineer who is a part-time externally funded researcher at the Solar and Stellar Physics Division of the Harvard-Smithsonian Center for Astrophysics.[198]

Team A

Team B

QUESTION 23: *WHAT ARE THE NATURAL CLIMATE CYCLES?*

Throughout this book, we will refer to "Natural Cycles." Presented below in table 5.21[199] is a summary of the natural cycles as best as we know today. These are extraterrestrial cycles, meaning the forcing functions originate from sources outside of the planet Earth. We are learning more and more about each of these cycles every day but have barely scraped the surface. But even more complicated is how these cycles combine, interact, and counter each other. Here we may not even know where to start to scratch.

Table 5.21, The astronomical climate change cycles

Cycle-years	Climate cycle	A related and probable cause of climate cycle
9.1	lunar	Moon's orbital cycles
11	Schwabe	Sunspot cycle tied to Jupiter orbit
22	Hale	Sun's magnetic field reversals
61	Yoshimura	Sun's barycenter motion Jupiter/Saturn tidal beat
84-92	Gleissberg	Solar activities related to Uranus orbital period
120	Velasco	Predicts solar minimum 2040
172	Landscheidt	Uranus and Neptune resonance
210-240	De-Vries/Suess	TSI cycle linked vial a 5/2 resonance to Uranus
934	Bond	Angular momentum - a sum of planets and sun
1,470	Dansgaard-Oeschger	Causes unknown, evidence found through Heinrich events
2,300	Hallslatt/Bray	Solar cycle
26,000	Milankovitch	Precession cycle of the earth tilt
41,000	Milankovitch	Obliquity cycle of the earth
100,000	Milankovitch	Eccentricity cycle of the earth's orbit around the sun
32,000,000	Unnamed yet	Suns vertical oscillations
141,000,000	Unnamed yet	Sun's transverse of the Milky Way

Several cycles are terrestrial, meaning the driving functions originate from the Earth, but are how the earth responds to the above external periods. The most common of these are ocean currents that redistribute the heat in the oceans, and the air, and even a bit with lands. Their periods vary but are usually much shorter than the astronomical cycles, with most lasting about a decade or two.

The primary planetary cycles the:

- Artic Oscillator,
- Antarctic Oscillator,
- Atlantic Multidecadal Oscillation (AMO),
- Pacific Decadal Oscillation,
- El Nino Southern Oscillation.

QUESTION 24: LET'S RECAP AND SEE WHAT WE LEARNED SO FAR.

1. In the introduction, we learned the importance of asking open-ended and penetrating questions. We encouraged challenging dialogues to get

clear and objective facts on which we can build our knowledge base. This course will allow us to construct ever more clear and crisp questions and further expand our knowledge and understanding. We also started the journey with no predetermined direction or destination. As we kept asking questions and getting new answers, some led us north for a new series of questions then west for a few more. At times we even needed to backtrack and pursue an approach we had previously ignored.

2. We learned that we on planet Earth are in a beautiful period with a comfortable and stable environment, and it keeps getting better for almost everyone. The population is growing, getting healthier, and living longer. But there were also many periods in the past that were not so good. There were absurdly warm periods when tropical plants and creatures lived in the Arctic and Antarctic regions. There were also many ice ages, but somehow our human ancestors emerged from the last grand ice age with a Darwinian advantage.

3. Sadly, we also earned how, in the middle of all the blessings we have today, we see a rise or a return to the fear and ignorance of the past dark ages. Regrettably, and more ominously, we also started to see a growing divide within the science community. One group of scientists and their supporters believe that a rise in human-made CO2 will be the singular cause of a runaway planet-destroying warming cycle. The other group of scientists says we're merely undergoing another natural warming cycle. Further, they state that we are already back to an extended cooling period, with the prospect that it could soon get even colder, lasting for several decades.

4. We learned the difference between weather as what we experience in the short-term, and climate, which occurs over long periods. With climate, cyclic trends and directions may be more of an interest than the actual amount of the change. We learned how we measure weather, especially temperature, and the difficulties in trying to define what is a "normal" global temperature. We learned about the challenges of how to stitch together old data sets and new ones and, more accurate satellite data. We made great strides in how we measure and study climate and weather using ever more precise instruments like satellites and space

probes, allowing us to take accurate readings of the Earth, sun, and our sister planets.

5. We then learned how the energy of the sun gets to Earth, which is about 95 percent of the total heating the surface receives. How the ground deflects and recycles this solar heat around by winds and ocean currents. We learned how a portion of this heat is retained in the air and clouds for a while, which acts as a blanket to stabilize the climate. Of particular interest, we saw how the Earth stored the sun's energy over many decades in the oceans, and cyclically redistributed throughout the planet like the Atlantic and Pacific oscillators. We also saw how much of the sun's heat was stored over eons on Earth in the form of hydrocarbons (coal, oil, and gas.)

6. We also explored how the amount of the sun's energy production changes over time and in many complex and repetitive cycles. We studied how this solar energy and variations combine and counteract the gravitational forces of the sun, moon, and planets. How these forces keep changing the distance and tilt of the Earth towards the sun, and how that increases or decreases the energy that reaches our planet.

7. We then examined the various ways that are used to produce electricity with chemical and nuclear forces and quantum reactions. We then defined what resources are renewable and which had undesirable byproducts, such as pollution. We took a detailed look at solar power and wind power. We compared their relative advantages and disadvantages. Most importantly, we uncovered a secret that was hidden from us by the CO2 industry. We found out that wind and solar need a fossil fuel power plant, operating close to one-hundred percent. This back-up is needed when the sun is not shining or when the wind is not blowing. We then asked the question of why nuclear was abandoned; when it's demonstrated to be the safest, cheapest, cleanest, and most reliable source of electrical power.

8. Then we explored how energy, especially fossil fuel energy, has lifted humanity from daily back-breaking hardships. We were amazed to see how this energy also lifted the spiritual burdens of raw survival, thereby giving humanity the freedom to pursue more intellectual and spiritual

enrichment. This was no small achievement. For example, Two hundred years ago, it took about 95 percent of the people doing back-breaking work to try feeding 100 percent of the population. Today, thanks to the energy of fossil fuels, one percent of the people can supply 100 percent of the Earth's population. See Mr. Epstein's presentation to Google employees on this footnote.[200] The much-maligned fossil fuels have enriched humanity, especially in the lower social-economic ranks. Thanks to this energy, the ordinary persons today have a higher quality of life than the kings and nobles had from the dawn of history to a mere one hundred years ago.

9. Then we looked at the relationship between global warming and the rising sea levels, and how the Earth stores and redistributes the sun's heat. We discussed the challenges and adjustments that need to be made to measure these changes reliably. But here we found again a great divide between Team A, who's predicting the significant loss of life, the flooding of coastal cities and damage of livable land. In contrast, Team B presents evidence that the seas are rising only a few millimeters per year and offers no adverse ramifications for humanity or our biosphere.

10. We discussed possible correlations between climate, earthquakes, and volcanoes. We found how the volcanic ejections of dust and gasses have a significant weather impact at the local levels by shielding the Earth from the sun's rays and seeding clouds resulting in increased localized rain and cooling.

11. Some of the Team B scientists are pursuing a possibility that volcanic eruptions and earthquakes are tied to a rise in high energy galactic cosmic rays that enter the Earth at periods of low solar activities. There also seems to be mounting evidence suggesting a possible cause and effect relationship between the increased gravitational tidal forces from the moon, sun, and planets. These forces appear to cause the Earth's diameter to stretch and contract, depending on their collective positions relative to the Earth. This stretching may be as much as one kilometer or more at the equator and be a significant cause of earthquakes.

12. Then we took a quick look at the "climate change industry" and financial interests created by climate change and CO2 positions being

advocated by many political, industrial, and academic centers. We provided a listing of the principal persons who make up Team A, which provides us with an alarmist view that the increasing CO2 will lead to a runaway greenhouse warming Earth. Then we looked at their counterparts in Team B who say, "Yes, temperatures have been on a warming trend for the last 150 years and especially from 1978 to 1998. And, yes, CO2 has increased, but this increase is mostly natural and beneficial. They posit that we may be approaching a grand solar minimum and could see a new mini ice age coming in the next several years and are hoping that the increased CO2 will mitigate the consequences of the coming cooling period".

13. We went into detail about what the Earth's heat budget is and that there are comfortable, safe, and economic measures that we can take to mitigate the problems caused by global warming and global cooling.

14. We then looked at why many scientists chose Team A and not Team B and vice versa.

~ 6 ~

CONTROVERSIAL DISCUSSIONS

Rated PG - over 18, plus Adult Supervision from a Lifelong Trusted Friend

1. INTRODUCTION:

In Chapter 6, we get into a few controversial discussions. These topics were selected because of their impact on the national economy and social structure.

- So, we start with Dr. Lindzen and the "Petition Project" organized and sent to President Trump. This provides a critical perspective on the importance of the CO2 debate at the national and international levels.
- We'll examine the facts and fictions of CO2 to see if it's as bad as we are told, or does it provide us with any benefits or something in the middle? We will also explore the origin, derivation, and the meaning of the CO2 "97 % consensus."
- We'll then take a deep dive into Dr. Easterbrook, who likes to call himself "a simple purveyor of data" and the critical role he played at the national levels.
- A discussion about Dr. Willy Soon gives us insight into the question; is there a real CO2 driven "consensus-industrial complex," who are they, and what's in it for them?
- Is nuclear power the ultimate insurance policy for CO2 global warming?
- Let's read about Truth, Mark Twain, and trusted sources: What the heck do they have in common?

- Check out next "what's the green new deal?" and the rewards vs. the consequences of getting this wrong!
- Lastly, we transition to the need to regain the moral high ground.

A small personal example: [201] Earlier this year, over several months, I could access many "skeptic" and "consensus" climate change articles and websites with no trouble. On one website, I found the complete set of charts used by Dr. Easterbrook in his testimony to the U.S. Senate on climate change. I bookmarked the site and made a quick copy for later study. Several weeks later, I returned to the site, and there was a red warning posted: "This site contains multiple viruses." In the following weeks, I shifted focus to other chapters, expecting the site would resolve the issues. But a few weeks later, the website did not even come up. It was gone! But why?

I quickly shot off complaints against the search engine companies! While I received no replies, within a week, all sites were again accessible. But, for the following many weeks, whenever I put Dr. Easterbrook in the search bar (Google, Yahoo, and Bing), what came up? Mostly sites with various attacks[202] against Dr. Easterbrook and persons and organizations associated with him! Most of the attacks focused their malice on his taking part in Dr. Lindzen's petition to President Donald Trump and his climate change testimony to the U.S. Senate.

We start with Dr. Richard Lindzen and see a sample of attacks on him. Lindzen is an American atmospheric physicist known for his work in the dynamics of the middle atmosphere, atmospheric tides, and ozone photochemistry. He has published over 200 scientific papers and books. From 1983 until his retirement in 2013, he was the Alfred P. Sloan Professor of Meteorology at Massachusetts Institute of Technology (MIT). Lindzen was also the lead author of Chapter 7, "Physical Climate Processes and Feedbacks," of the UN/IPCC Third Assessment Report. Later he started to criticize the 97 percent consensus and the IPCC about what he called "climate alarmism." Dr. Lindzen also earned the ire

of the consensus industry for several well-publicized actions.

Dr. Lindzen's first grievous sin was to defect from the IPCC committee, then became a vocal and public Skeptic. Lindzen wrote scathing op-eds in the *Wall Street Journal* on April 12, 2010,[203] and March 4, 2015.[204] His most egregious sin, however, was his initiative to write a letter to President Trump, urging him to take the U.S. out of the Paris Agreement. Then Dr. Lindzen got hundreds of the world's top climatologists to sign it. Among other visible and respected targets was Drs. Roy Spencer, Roger Tallbloke, and Lord Christopher Monckton because they came to his defense. In article 6 below, we give some details of the particularly vicious attacks on Dr. Willie Soon.

<u>The Petition:</u> [205] In the following few pages is a copy of the petition to President Trump, started by Dr. Lindzen and signed by over 300 world-class *climate scientists.*

President Donald Trump
White House
Washington, DC

Dr. Richard Lindzen
February 23, 2017

Dear Mr. President:
Citizens of the USA and America's admirers everywhere support of your campaign promises to place a common-sense focus on international environmental agreements, either enacted or proposed. In just a few weeks, more than 300 eminent scientists and other qualified individuals from around the world have signed the petition below, urging you to withdraw from the ill-advised United Nations Framework Convention on Climate Change (UNFCCC). More are signing on every day.
We petition the American and other governments to change course on an outdated international agreement that targets minor greenhouse gases, primarily Carbon Dioxide, CO2 *for harsh regulation. Since 2009, the US and other governments have undertaken actions with respect to global climate that are not scientifically justified and that already have, and will continue to cause serious social and economic harm—with no environmental benefits. While we support effective, affordable, reasonable, and direct controls on conventional environmental pollutants, carbon dioxide is not a pollutant. To the contrary, there is clear evidence that increased atmospheric carbon dioxide is environmentally helpful to food crops and other plants that nourish all life. It is plant food, not poison.*
Restricting access to fossil fuels has very negative effects upon the wellbeing of people around the world. It condemns over 4 billion people in still underdeveloped countries to continued poverty.

We are now at a crossroads. Candidates Trump and Pence promised not only to keep the US out of a harmful international climate agreement but also to rollback misdirected, pointless government restrictions of CO2 emissions. My fellow scientists support you as you seek to keep your campaign promises.
It is especially important for members of your administrative team to hear from people like the signers of this letter, with the training needed to evaluate climate facts and to offer sound advice. Climate discussions have long been political debates—not scientific discussions—over whether citizens or bureaucrats should control energy, natural resource, and other assets. Rolling back unnecessary regulation helps Americans and can be done in a way to provide the clean air and clean water you promised.

With Respect,
Dr. Richard Lindzen

Professor Emeritus of Atmospheric Sciences
Massachusetts Institute of Technology.

PETITION

Lindzen Attachment
21 pages

February 23, 2017

We urge the United States government, and others, to withdraw from the United Nations Framework Convention on Climate Change (UNFCCC). We support reasonable and cost-effective environmental protection. But carbon dioxide, the target of the UNFCCC is not a pollutant but a major benefit to agriculture and other life on Earth. Observations, since the UNFCCC was written 25 years ago, show that warming from increased atmospheric CO2 will be benign — much less than initial model predictions.

- *ABDUSSAMATOV, Habibullo Ismailovich: (Dr. sci., Phys. and Math. Sciences.); Head of space research of the Sun Sector at the Pulkovo Observatory, head of the project 'the Lunar observatory,' St. Petersburg, Russia.*
- *ADAM, A.I.: (Ph.D.); Retired Geologist/Palynologist/Academic/Public Servant/Industry Professional; publications include papers on palaeoenvironmental studies and a book, New Emperors' Novel Clothes: Climate Change Analyzed*

- *ALEXANDER, Ralph B.: (Ph.D., Physics, University of Oxford); Former Associate Professor, Wayne State University, Detroit, author "Global Warming False Alarm" (2012)*

- **Note–20 additional pages of signatures follow along with the backgrounds and credentials of each scientist.**

Attacks on Lindzen: Here's a quick sample at the attacks against Dr. Lindzen from the "Consensus" industry. Below are websites, and we'll just let the posts speak for themselves. But in case they take them down, we captured the first paragraph or a few lines from each section:

- Washington Post; ANALYSIS/OPINION: By Anthony J. Sadar*, June 10, 2015,* says in part;[206]
  - *"Many knowledgeable skeptics of the man-made climate change hypothesis lament the incessant ad hominem attacks rather than the fruitful debate."*
  - *"Alan Carlin, challenged the Obama administration's faulty climate science, in his new book "Environmentalism Gone Mad."*
  - *"Characterizing formidable opponents as nut jobs, idiots, or shills is a technique for the lowest form of debate and the realm of spin doctors."*

- By Sarah Sloat, Feb. 17, 2016, Filed under NASA & Satellite, source; Inverse.com.[207] Climate Change-Denying MIT Prof. Richard Lindzen Is Suddenly Popular, Still Wrong. Fact-checking the claims of a well-credentialed skeptic.
  - *"Climate change denier" is not a description most atmospheric scientists embrace, but it's one that Richard Lindzen infamously embraces."*
  - Fortunately for Lindzen, he is retired and is financially and emotionally secure and can ignore the slander.
  - But how can a young professor, newly hired, go to build a career and pay the bills while being slandered in the press/TV and his teaching peers?

- *Anthony Watts/March 9, 2017, Lindzen responds to the MIT letter objecting to his petition to withdraw from the UNFCC. Source Marc Murano-Climate Depot.*[208] In this article, we find Lindzen responding to the MIT letter objecting to his initiating the petition to Trump to withdraw from the UNFCC. Read the Full Article:

2. WHAT'S ALL THE FUSS ABOUT CO2? [209]

We will now have a very detailed discussion on this gas, which has gotten so much attention and stirred so much controversy. It's a gas that people around the world have already spent hundreds of billions to study. That stirs up questions like: could we have put that money to more beneficial uses for the good of humanity and clarity of science? In this chapter, we summarize the significant points of contention that have been raised by interested groups and media and put them in context with the many alarmist scenarios. Let's start with the easy questions first.

Is CO2 increasing? The simple answer is yes! But now we focus on the more critical questions; by how much? Where is it coming from? Is it beneficial, or is it harmful to humankind? Is it dangerous to the biosphere? Since coming out of the Little Ice age (1650 - 1720 AD),[210] atmospheric CO2 has grown from about 280 ppm in the 1800s to about 415 ppm today. That is a fact,[211] but it does not provide a scientific answer as to why, and where's it coming from and what's it doing to our environment.

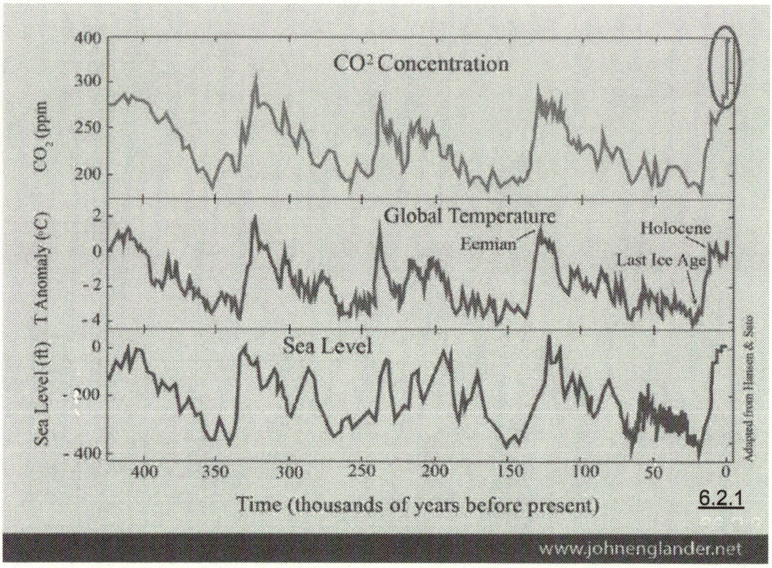

6.2.1

Look at 6.2.1,[212] where we see CO2 levels, global temperatures, and sea levels over the past half-million years. You'll notice CO2 levels have always moved in unison with changes in temperatures and sea levels. What else does the chart tell us? It shows us that there have been five notable ice ages, followed by five warming periods. A complete cycle for these ice ages takes typically a little over 100,000 years. But in all cases, no matter what the change in temperature is doing, we see a corresponding change in the amount of CO2 and a near-identical shift in sea levels. This tells us there is a correlation between global temperature and levels of CO2 in the atmosphere. We also see a similar relationship between global temperature and sea level. Just remember, for now, correlation is not the same as causation.

Where's the CO2 coming from? If we look very carefully at 6.2.2,[213] we see that the CO2 increase always follows, or always comes after a temperature increase. We also notice a decrease in CO2 following a decline in global temperatures. These CO2 changes occur over the years, and sometimes even centuries, and even millennia after the temperature changes.[214] This confirms that the change in CO2 results from a change in temperature and not the cause of the change in temperature. When global warming begins, mostly due to increased solar activity, the air heats first, followed by the land, then much later, the seas warm up. And when the waters finally warm-up, as detailed in chapter 4.17, they release more CO2 into the atmosphere. The next point of interest is that when global warming is increasing, it occurs quite rapidly, and the CO2 increase follows after that (see green indicators). But when global temperature decreases more slowly, then the corresponding decline in CO2 levels will, at times, take thousands of years to match the declining temperatures (dark blue indicators).

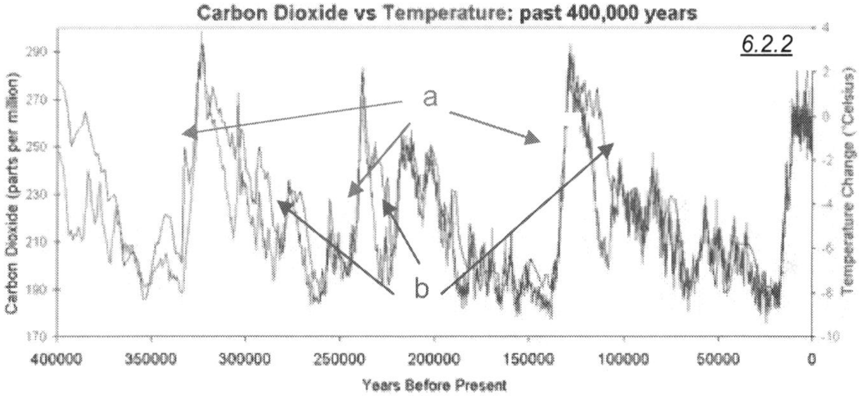

Also, recall from Table 3.15.3 that since 1750, CO2 increased along with all the other greenhouse gases by roughly the same amount. Thus, the more likely explanation is that the warming oceans release CO2 and all the greenhouse gases. Thus, again indicating that increased CO2 results from global warming and not the cause of global warming.

Also, in a paper dated April 21, 2016, "Anthropogenic CO2 warming challenged by 60-year cycle" supports this theory that "atmospheric temperature and ocean temperatures rise first. This is followed by sea-level rise. Then, lastly, the oceans release more CO2. It shows the increased global temperatures at the end of the twentieth century and the subsequent decline starting in 2002." Francois Gervais wrote this article,[215] which was published by *Earth-Science Reviews*. It discusses the relationships between the sixty-year cycle of the North Atlantic Oscillator (NAO) and CO2.

What's the significance of human-made CO2? CO2 is a trace gas currently making up about 0.04 percent of the atmosphere, along with the other greenhouse gases make up a total of 0.055-percent of the atmosphere. This amount of CO2 and the other greenhouse gasses is trivial when compared to 78 percent for nitrogen, 21 percent for oxygen, and water vapor. Second, at any point in time, about 93 percent of the world's total CO2 gas is dissolved in the oceans.[216] Of that, about 40 percent goes in and out of the oceans each year[2]. Let's also recall from the above-referenced articles that: Water vapor causes about 95 percent of all greenhouse warming effects. About 3.5 percent of the greenhouse effect is caused by the world's total CO2, methane about 0.4 percent, natural and human-made the remaining.[217] All of the other greenhouse gases make up the remaining 1.5 percent. From Table 4.16.1, we saw that the human-made portion is about 3.6 percent of the total CO2. The human-made CO2 accounts for approximately 0.06 percent of the overall greenhouse effect of heat imbalance. This exposes the myth that humans are destroying the Earth by producing CO2 by burning fossil fuels.

The second myth: As we saw immediately above, the volume of human-made CO2 is minuscule, and its contribution to global warming is trivial. But they tell us that human-made CO2 will continue to grow at an exponential rate as more and more people turn to more fossil fuels. However, basic science and data show this is not true when we examine the absorption rate of CO2. In figure 6.2.3a, Alex Epstein[218] provides us with a chart from his book, *The Moral Case for Fossil Fuels*. Here, we

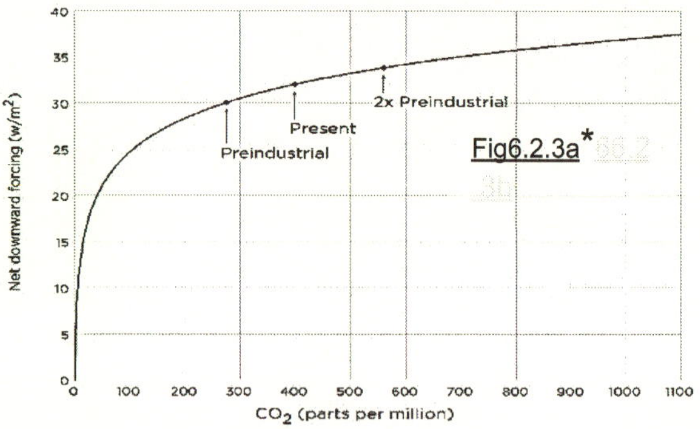

Fig6.2.3a*

[2] Table 4.16.1; (332 / 801)

now expose the second deception of CO2. Although quite simple, this graph requires a little explanation.

- Look at the point labeled "Present." It shows that today, we are at about 415 ppm of CO2. At that rate, CO2 is generating, for lack of a better word, about thirty-two watts per square meter by the greenhouse effect. But look at about a hundred years ago, when CO2 was about 280 ppm. The total CO2 greenhouse effect was producing about thirty watts. By increasing the CO2 by about 45 percent, we have increased the greenhouse heat by only two watts, or about 6 percent.
- Let's recall from previous chapters that average TSI is about 341 watts. Therefore, the total CO2 contribution to TSI is 2/341=0.6 percent. But recall from the Table 4.16.1 that human-made CO2 is approximately 3.6 percent of total CO2. Hence, the human-made CO2 imbalance accounts for 0.02% of the TSI increase (0.6% X 3.6% =0.02%).
- Therefore, 0.02% x 2W=0.00042 watts per meter square has been the energy increase on the planet in the last hundred years because of human-made CO2. Further, that assumes that all the other variables remain the same.
- But now may be an excellent time to paraphrase Dr. Judith Curry: nothing ever remains the same, the climate has too many unknowns.
- Conclusion:
  - The increased heat energy generated in the last one hundred plus years by going from 280 ppm to 415 ppm gave us a 0.06 percent increase in watts or somewhere about 0.0004 watts.
  - Going forward, say we double from the present 400 ppm to 800 ppm, what would that do? It would still be trivial.
  - That's about the equivalent energy increase of lighting one match in Yankee Stadium!

As seen in figure 6.2.3a, the curve saturates out at about 37 watts, so adding more and more CO2 does nothing. It's like painting your house red. After two coats of paint, it will not get any redder, no matter if you put five or fifty more coats of paint on top of the initial two layers.

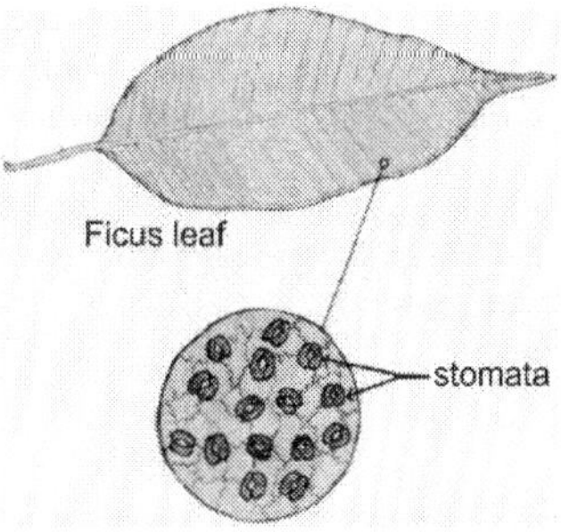

CO2 is essential for all life on Earth! Without CO2,[219] there is no life on Earth! Period, end of the story, and end of everything that matters. No CO2 means no plants, no phytoplankton, no birds, no bees, no dogs or fish, and no you and no me. When CO2 is less than 180 ppm, photosynthesis in plants begins to shut down. At this low level of CO2, 180 ppm, plants do all they can to get as much CO2 food as possible. That means if there is little CO2, plants have to open their leaf pores (called "stomata")[220] more and more to "breathe in/feed on" the low CO2 that's left. But as they open these stomata more, and more water evaporates out of the plant and then it's a race. Does the plant die of not being able to get enough CO2 for photosynthesizing sugars (in essence, starvation)? Or does it die of dehydration—thirst? Water stress test confirms that plants can survive and thrive with 40-70 percent less water in an enriched CO2 environment, whereas in low CO2 conditions, plants wither and die. This has a massive impact on increasing the planets' greening and reducing desertification.

Shut-off the CO2 alarm! Many would have us believe that the increase of CO2 from 280 to 415 ppm in the past century is a cause for alarm. They proclaim it as the cause of the end of life on Earth and intentionally equate it with pollutants like smoke, soot, and carbon monoxide (CO), which is toxic to life. For example, today, we are at 415 ppm, is that the alarming rate they proclaim? By comparison, on the space shuttle, the real alarm to go off at 5,000 ppm. That's ten times what we have on Earth today. On submarines, it alarms at 7,000 ppm. That's twenty times higher. In a crowded movie theater, a reading of 1,700 ppm of CO2 is not unusual, nor is it a danger to anyone.

Fig 6.2.3b

More CO2 is good for you. Figure 6.2.3b[221] is a photo from the *New York Times*

bestseller by Alex Epstein, *The Moral Case for Fossil Fuels.* In this controlled experiment, these four plants are identical species and in age and growing environments.
What's the difference? The size of the trees shows us that CO2 is just not harmful to the environment but very good for humankind and all life. Here we see how much faster and healthier trees grow as we increase the amount of CO2. Alex agrees to the fact that we are adding CO2 to the planet but argues that maybe even more CO2 would be better for the Earth. But then he throws the gauntlet: we showed the many real and tangible benefits of increased levels of CO2. He further challenges the alarmists to show data demonstrating that the CO2 increase has caused any harm! And please don't again confuse and conflate CO2 with pollution or rely on wild speculations about the imminent disasters it will cause.

Patrick Moore,[222] a founding member of Greenpeace and lifelong environmentalist, is struggling to find a path to get the planet to reach 1,000 ppm. That's more than double where we are today. The reader is encouraged to read the article titled[223] "The Global Warming Scam" by Dr. Vincent Gray. My annotations added. The global warming scam is the result of the widespread belief in a new religion, based on the deification of a nebulous entity, "the Environment." Here James G Matkin presents his views and review of the book by Dr. Vincent Gray titled "*The Global Warming Scam and the Climate Change Superscam.*" Here is the opening paragraph: *"When I first developed an opposition to this aberrant pseudo-scientific religion, I was almost a lone voice, both within my community and in the world outside. Now there are many groups of people who have realized the absurdity of the Global Warming theory. Indeed, since the approved technique of assessing such warming shows that it has not been warming for the past 18 years, so they promote Climate Change, instead of global warming."*
Warning![224] This paper is recommended only for tech nerds and those individuals who want to know the details below the headlines! Below are the title page and first elements of the Abstract of the paper. Visit the website at your own risk, and don't forget to bring a gallon of coffee.
THE GLOBAL WARMING SCAM by Vincent Gray Climate Consultant 75 Silverstream Road, Crofton Downs, Wellington 6035, New Zealand Email vinmary.gray@paradise.net.nz (Revised October 2008)

- *"ABSTRACT The Global Warming· Scam has been perpetrated to support the Environmentalist belief that the Earth is being harmed by the emission of greenhouse gases from the combustion of fossil fuels. "*
- *This paper examines the evidence in detail and shows that none of the evidence presented confirms a relationship between emissions of greenhouse gases and any harmful effect on the climate.*

3. HOW DID WE GET THE 97% CONSENSUS? [225]

What's a consensus? Perhaps the better starting question is, does "consensus" have any legitimate role in science today, or did it ever have one? The answer is a definite NO! Let's go back to the Rules of the Game from the Introduction. There we laid out precise definitions: "a consensus has many beneficial roles. For example, in selecting our governors, our presidents, dog catchers, etc. At the county club consensus is how we decide what's the proper dress code. In the winter meetings, the NFL owners reach a consensus that a personal foul is fifteen yards and not ten. But in science, we must follow The Scientific Method that was developed and refined by great scientists like Roger Bacon, Galileo, Francis Bacon, and Rene Descartes. Before *The Scientific Method*, consensus resulted from a Royal Decree by the king or an Infallible Papal Encyclical. Or the judges in Salem, Massachusetts, who declared which persons were to be burned at stake. On remote islands, the chief priests decided which virgin was to be thrown in the volcano to appease the gods. These are all proper samples of a "consensus."

In science, the immediate answer is "absolutely not." This has been the standard code of scientific conduct and ethics since the advent of the scientific method. In other words, it is a gift to us from the age of enlightenment and reason. It was that clarity of thought that allowed one person, Albert Einstein, to demote Newtonian Physics from a law to a suggestion when ultra-precision is not needed. Who knows? Tomorrow one person may downgrade or entirely obliterate Einstein's General Relativity or Special Relativity. And when that happens, it will be a good day for science and humankind. Unfortunately, a bane of humanity has been the many charlatans and opportunists who enter the field with their shortcuts and deceptions.

The derivation of the "97 percent consensus."[226] We'll now describe the mathematical process that was used by the "consensus" to derive the 97 percent.

- Scientific papers were selected that had "Global Climate Change" or "Global Warming" in the Abstract. The population sample 11,944 = 100 percent. The papers were reviewed by employees and selected volunteers for the IPCC.
- Sixty-six percent of the papers surveyed expressed no opinion or did not address the subject.
- Thirty-three percent had a response that there might be some level of AGW, Anthropogenic Global Warming, but did not quantify it or say if it was good or bad or to what degree.
- 0.7 percent rejected the AGW/CO2 concept outright.
- 0.3 percent were uncertain about the cause of climate change.[227]

Total of 100 percent

Courtesy
https://www.clker.com/clipart-10441.html

Here is how the consensus advocates did the calculations:

- 100%- 66% = 34%, total positive respondents.
- 33% said there was some level of human-made global warming.
- 33% divided by 34% = 97%

And that's how the 97 percent consensus was derived. Not precisely a bulletproof process or calculation.

The media chose not to

question the process [228] but continue to use it regularly.[229] Meanwhile, in early 2008, the Oregon Institute of Science and Medicine (OISM) published its Petition Project. Many scientists who rejected the science behind the theory of human-caused global warming were contacted. This was an attempt by OISM to show that far more scientists oppose the CO2 "consensus" than support it. This petition took on particular importance coming soon after the release of the IPCC Fourth Assessment Report. Of particular concern was the Working Group 1 (WG1) report on the "Science and Attribution of Climate Change to Human Civilization."

This petition was signed by 31,487 American scientists, related in some fashion with the environment. Included in this count were 9,029 PhDs. What was the reaction to the petition? Most of the media ignored it. Later a few dismissed and diminished the significance of the 31,487 scientists and never addressed the science or the process they used to arrive at their alarming conclusions. Instead, the survey was attacked by saying there were over 10 million scientists in the USA who agreed with them. Here's their revised consensus calculation:

- Number of skeptic scientists = 31,487.
- Number of consensus scientists = 10,000,000
- 10,000,000–31,487 = 9,968,513
- 9,968,513 / 10,000,000 = 99.7%.
- Their consensus number has increased from 97% to 99.7%.

Sadly, no data of any kind was provided to support who the 10 million scientists were, how they were reached, or how qualified they were. So, the average person needs to go with hope and faith.

4. EASTERBROOK TESTIMONY TO U.S. SENATE [230]

On March 26, 2013, Dr. Easterbrook took part in testimony and Q&A discussion with the U.S. Senate Energy, Environment and Telecommunications Committee on the subject of Climate Change. During his self-introduction, Easterbrook presented his extensive credentials and detailed his fifty-plus years of experience on the subject of climate studies.

He then explained that the U.S. government, universities, and some small private institutions had funded the vast majority of his studies and work. He stated that he never worked for or received funds of any kind from the oil, gas, coal, or any other industry.

Easterbrook felt obligated to make that statement to defend himself against many scurrilous accusations in the media that he is shilling for the fossil-fuel industry. He also stated that he is a lifelong environmentalist and is not associated with any political groups or ideology. His statement was, "I am a simple purveyor of data." In his opening slide, he presented a summary of his discussion list and said that he had a lot of data to back up the facts he would give.

Easterbrook's discussion agenda:[231]

- Global warming ended in 1998; there has been no global warming since 1999.
- Global warming occurred from 1978 to 1998.
    - The Antarctic ice sheets are not melting; instead, they are increasing.
    - There are no ice sheets at the north pole because there is no land there, there's only floating ice.
    - It is floating ice with a standard maximum thickness of about three meters, much of which cyclically melts during the summer.
- Sea levels have been rising at a constant rate[232] of about seven inches per century, not the twenty feet often reported in popular media.
- Snowfall is not below average; it's normal and slightly above normal in the last five years.
- CO2 cannot cause global warming because there's too little of it.
- Storms are not more frequent than usual.
- The oceans are not turning more acidic.
- Oceans are not acidic at all, with a global PH value of 8.2, and it's not changing.
- Some localized lowering of the PH may occur in isolated places. But those are caused by local pollution or local geological changes.

<u>Notable questions</u> asked or points made: Figure <u>6.4.1</u>[233] shows the temperatures of the Earth for the preceding 10,000 years, as[234] we came out of the last Ice Age. On this chart, we're presented with the following:

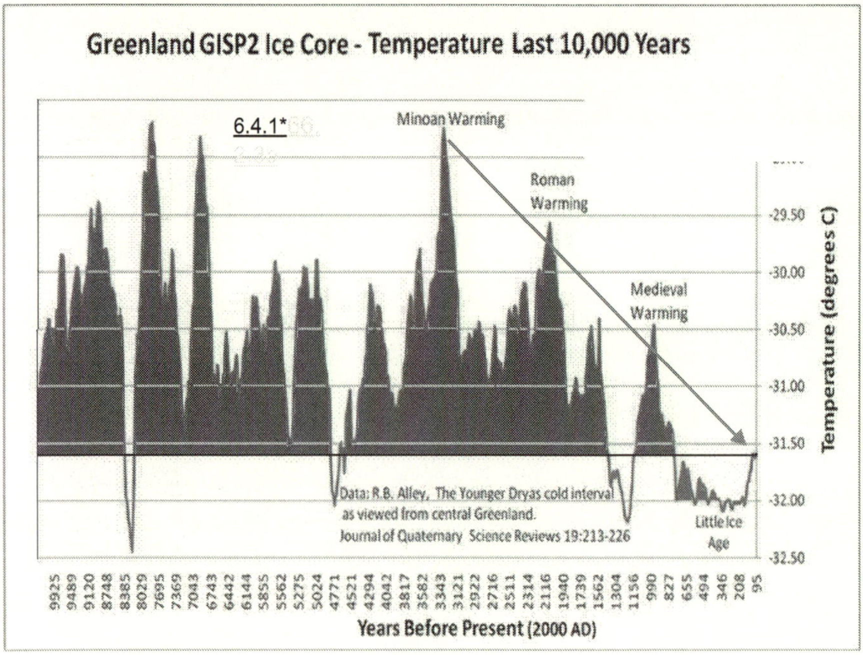

- Over the previous 10,000 years, the Earth warmed up, averaging about 1.5° C warmer than the current Modern Warming.
- The average temperatures of the past 10,000 years have been warmer than today for over 90 percent of the time.
- Since about 3500 BC, we have completed five notable warm peaks. But the trending global temperatures have been on a decline to where we are today (blue arrow).
- This modern, warm period today comes after the Little Ice Age of the 1640-1720 period.

The IPCC and NOAA made repeated claims that our present-day temperatures are hotter than ever before.

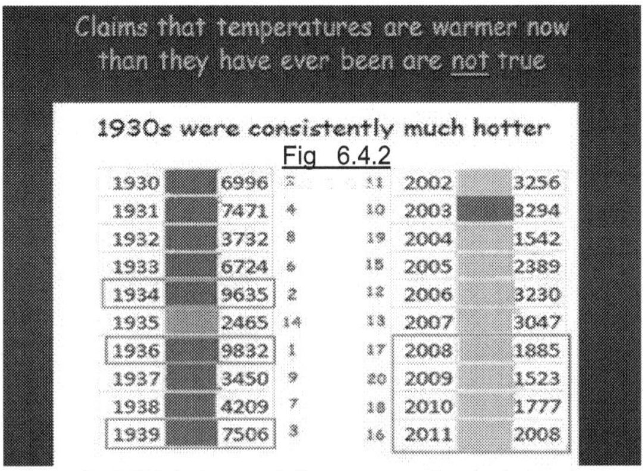

But that's contradicted by historical records over the last 10,000 years, as seen in figure 6.4.1. That's also true over the last century, where we see that 84 percent of the top temperature records were set during the 1930s. But only 14 percent were recorded in the latter part of the 20th century, as seen in 6.4.2.[235] The source of this data is NOAA, and these are the original data sets recorded at the time they were taken; i.e., before NOAA and the GRU unit of East Anglia University, UK made any "adjustments." How and why were these adjustments made, and what was the focus of the Climate Gate scandal, and court proceedings are covered in detail below.

The IPCC and consensus community claim that droughts have become more frequent and more severe. However, data does not support such assertions. As readily seen in figure 6.4.3,[236] we note that both the frequency and intensity appear of droughts have become less severe and less frequent.

Dr. Easterbrook discussed at length the many questionable actions taken by NOAA in the last few decades to "normalize" the historical ground-based temperature data, which is discussed in greater detail below. The purpose of restating a quick summary here is to show the extent and gravity of these "adjustments" done to historical temperatures. The critical questions remain, for instance, why was it done at all? How did they do it, and

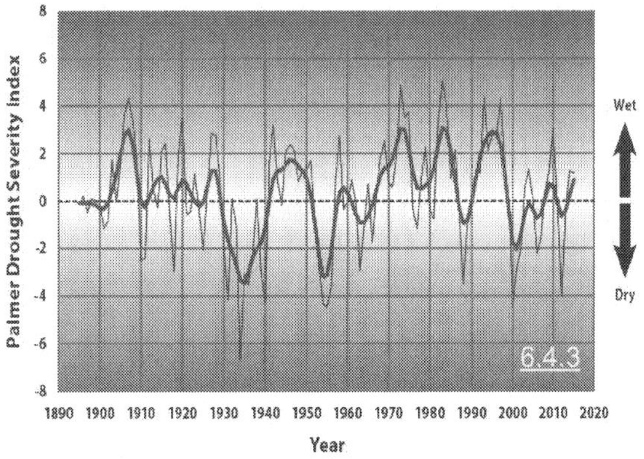

why are they continuing to perpetuate this fudging of historical temperature data?

Fudged data display. We start with the second question and see what resulted from these changes. Let's look at figure 6.4.4,[237]

- The blue line is the record of the original, unchanged historical temperatures.
- The orange line on the chart was made after they made their fourth adjustments of the original data.

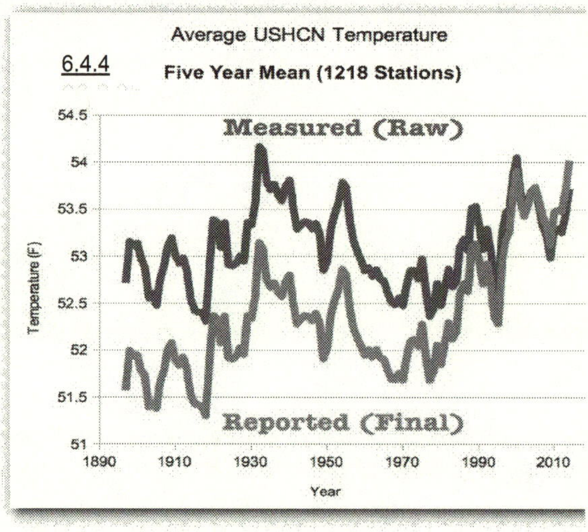

- Two things stand out immediately. Notice how before 1995, the temperatures have all been lowered. None went up, not even one year. Next, we see that the temperatures after 1995 have all gone up in a slight accelerating rate. We also note that the high temperatures of 1930 and 1960 were substantially lowered. This allowed the IPCC/NOAA to claim that the turn of the twenty-first-century temperatures was the highest ever. Plus, it now shows that the fudged temperature acceleration from the late 1970s over the past three decades was made to match the CO2 increase.
- Now that we graphically see the resultant changes, the answer is obvious. The adjustments were made to support the narrative that in the last forty years, global warming is accelerating out of control. It also supports their second claim that it's hotter now than ever before. Many will recall the famous book by John Steinbeck, "The Grapes of Wrath." The book and the movie dramatically present the hunger and misery caused by the extremely high temperatures of the late 1930s, as documented by the original untampered data, see the blue line. In contrast, the orange line is a manufactured deception.

In 6.4.5,[238] we see a different graph of the original climate data. By original is meant the actual temperatures that were recorded concurrently with the weather reading. It means the temperatures

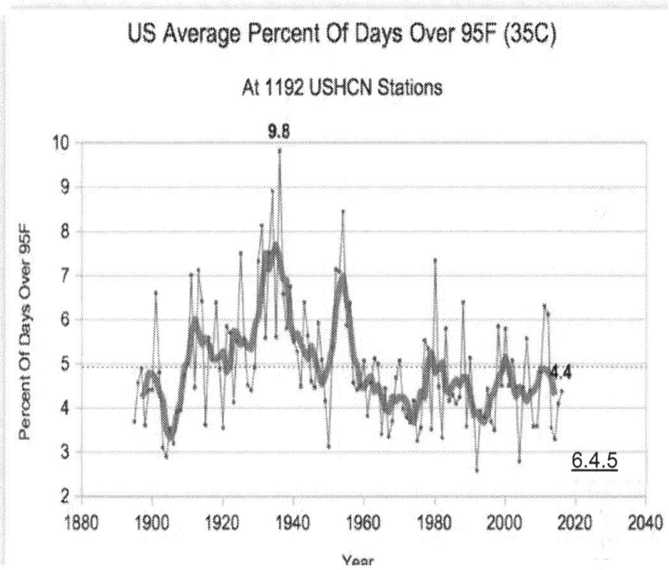

6.4.5

are shown before NOAA/NASA made any adjustments of any kind. It shows the high temperatures recorded in the 1930s. Especially troublesome is the NOAA land-based temperature data and how they were obtained. Better still, how they were "normalized," or as some would say, "fudged." Evidence was found that the codes used to program their models to generate these "adjustments" were made to match the observed trends of the CO2 increase. For example, the GRU sent emails asking NOAA to alter the data to show lower temperatures in the 1930s, higher temperatures to blur the Dalton Minimum, and higher temperatures post 1995 AD, etc.

Although many manipulated versions of this U S Senate testimony are on YouTube and elsewhere online, the link to the complete and original video of the March 26, 2013 testimony is provided at this endnote.[239] Moreover, I strongly recommend you to read the book or see the movie "The Grapes of Wrath."

The saddest part of the presentation was that it surprised no one on the committee. No detailed questions followed.

5. "CLIMATEGATE."

Is NOAA still cooking the historical temperature books? "Climategate" refers to a series of hacked emails and documents that show "evidence" that the Global Research Unit (GRU) of the University of East Anglia (UEA) had done two unscientific and unethical things. That was the basis of the scandal. They, with the help of NASA/NOAA, were "altering" the global temperature data to support the IPCC conclusion that global warming over the preceding one hundred years was caused by human-made CO2. The GRU had a staff of about sixteen climate scientists and researchers who were acting as the central focus unit in England on the IPCC climate change effort. The 5,000 emails and documents that were leaked or hacked spanned over thirteen years before they were exposed.

The first evidence of the leak, which occurred in November 2009, involved an initial batch of 1,079 emails and seventy-two documents as "evidence" of a scandal. It included many prominent scientists who were pushing the human-made CO2 warming theory. If that could be proven, it would mean that such a scandal would be one of the greatest frauds in the history of science. The leaks, emails, and documents suggested:

- A conspiracy to exaggerate data that supports the premise that warming is caused by human-made CO2.
- Possibly illegal destruction of embarrassing information, emails, data.
- An organized resistance against the "skeptic" or "denier" scientists who refuted the IPCC claim.
- A series of personal and professional attacks were coordinated and launched against climate scientists that disagreed with their CO2 story.

GRU/NOAA climate normalizing process

- Adding fuel to these speculations was the stonewalling of their data and methodologies and in resisting all the claims being made under UK laws. These UK laws are the equivalent of the Freedom of Information Act in the USA.

The UK Government launched an official inquiry to investigate the scandal led by Sir Muir Russell into the Climategate affair. Thousands of additional emails were found revealing a systematic policy and practice of how to identify, mock, and destroy the real climate scientists that they labeled "Climate Skeptics" or "Climate Deniers." They published their names, where they worked, where they lived, what schools their children attended, among other details. And, as if that was not enough, they started fabricating rumors and published them as op-eds in major newspapers and websites around the world. These reputable scientists were falsely accused of representing big oil or coal mine owners and various polluters of the planet. These skeptics were also charged with not revealing the sources of their funding. In the end, all of the CRU/UEA and NASA/NOAA data manipulators were cleared of criminal charges of fraud and personal attacks on the "skeptics." But a cloud of suspicion was cast that these many inappropriate actions were swept under the rug for political expediencies. Unfortunately, the general public has a short attention span, and the anthropogenic/CO2 industry has a tenacious long-term game plan. To this day, their actions continue to be ignored by a servile media.

Evidence. Presented in the referenced endnote[240] is an interesting article published in the British daily newspaper *The Guardian*. It shows how the very people involved in the scandal reacted favorably to this "investigation." In this endnote from Newsmax had the headline "*Stats Tampering Puts NOAA in Hot Water*"[241] by Larry Bell; Monday, 01 February 2016, saying in part, *"NOAA's adjustments to previous ocean temperatures between 1998 and 2012 made recent global temperature changes appear more than twice warmer than the original records showed. This was accomplished by throwing out global-coverage satellite-sensed sea surface measurements taken since the late 1970s — the best data available — and upwardly adjusting spotty and unreliable hit-and-miss temperature readings taken from ocean-going vessels which present well-recognized problems."* Read the entire Newsmax article. [242]

"Surface temperature records: policy-driven deception?" By Joseph D'Aleo. The below figures are samples from his report, and the complete, detailed 209-page paper published on Aug 10, 2010, is found on this endnote[243] There is also a shorter and more reader-friendly 52-page summary available here that D'Aleo wrote with A Watts. [244]

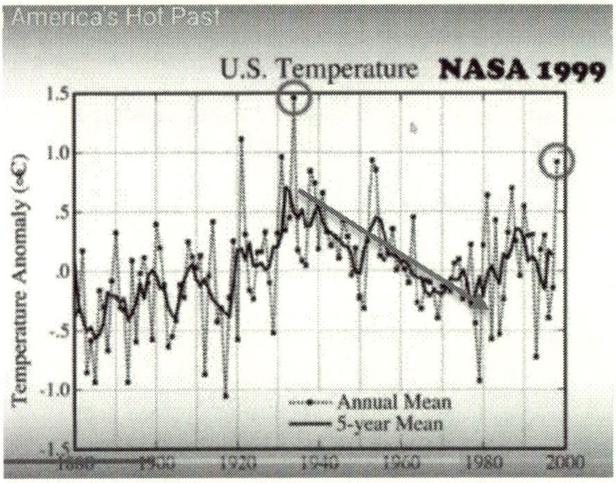

Let's start by looking at two comparable charts, where we see a side by side comparison of the official temperature records published by NASA and see what they tell us?

Fig-1-a [245] is the temperature record officially published by NASA in the year 1999. It clearly shows the max temperatures were recorded in the late 1930s, dust bowl years. Especially note that 1938-39 were more than 0.5 C higher than the max temperature for 1998. The second thing we notice is the declining temperatures from 1939 until the early 1980s when it quickly turned up, resulting from a significant El-Nino period. This data, was the source of frustration for J Hansen as it did not support his model that tied temp rise to CO2 increases[246]

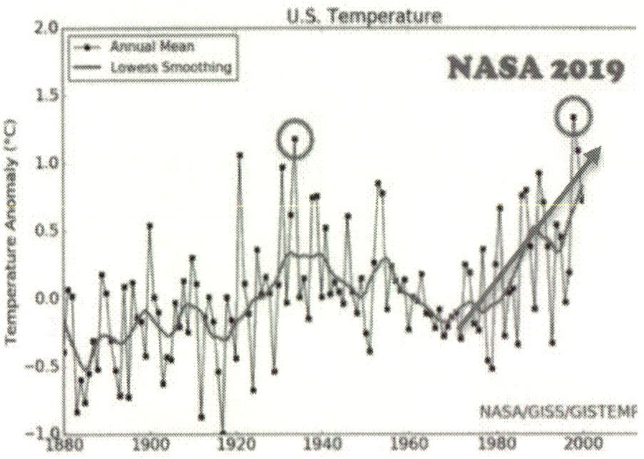

In **Fig 1-b,**[247] we see how NASA re-wrote history. Note that almost ½ C was shaved off the temperature of 1938-39 and increased the temperature of 1998 by about 0.5 C, creating a swing of more than 1.0 C and changing the slope of the curve to show an accelerating temperature trend compared to the prior downtrend.

In a dramatic paper 'SURFACE TEMPERATURE RECORDS: POLICY-DRIVEN DECEPTION?" by Joseph D'Aleo and Anthony Watts,[248] it goes into the detail of actions taken over the last decades that enabled NOAA/NASA to do this, which are fully described in the article. For example, the number of land-based reporting stations was dramatically reduced, and not only in the USA but worldwide. It allowed NASA to "guess" and fill in what the temperatures ***should have been*** at the closed stations. It also goes on to show which stations were closed, and why?

In **Fig 2,**[46] we especially note the dramatic temperature increase, coincidental with the station's closings by almost 1.5 C. The paper also discusses the relocations of many stations within the USA, with many being moved to hot spots, with numerous photographs of thermometers next to major heat sources, like paved roads and parking lots, near brick buildings, at airports near jet engine exhausts, and next to AC condensers, etc.

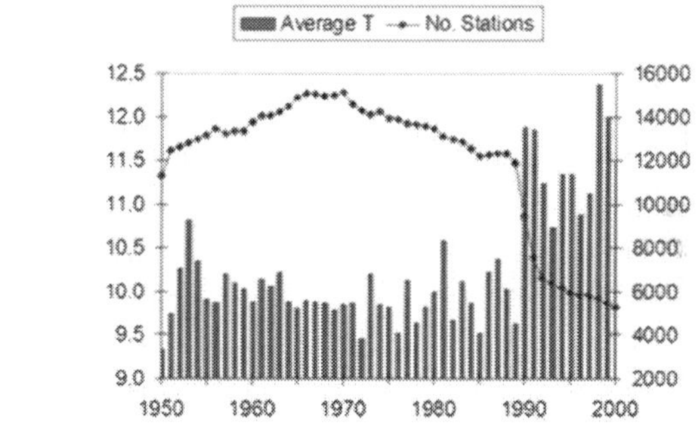

FIGURE 5 Plot of the number of total station ID's in each year since 1950 and the avera temperatures of the stations in the given year.

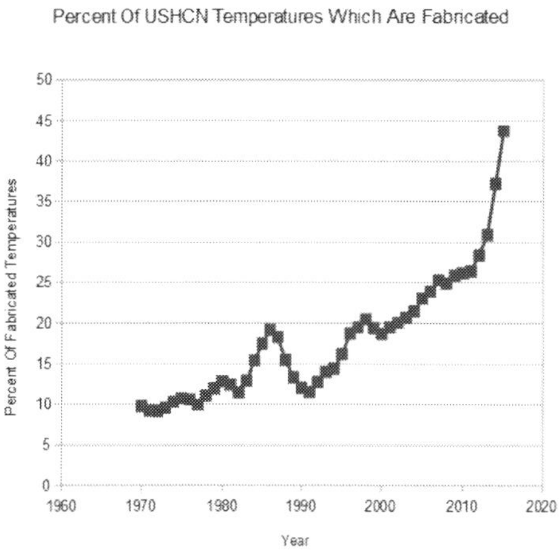

Let's look at a simple example in **Fig 3**. The stations that were closed since the 1990s, representing almost 45% of the surface temperatures, are fabricated. Meaning in their offices and labs, NOAA decided what the temperatures "should have been" in the deleted stations. Then to these fabricated readings, they make other "adjustments" discussed in detail above. Updated information, through 2019, tells us that the number of "fabricated" temperatures "readings" are now up to 61%. [249]

Let's ask the final question, are these adjustments to the surface temperatures made by accident, faulty instruments, or is there some plan or objective at work behind the scenes?

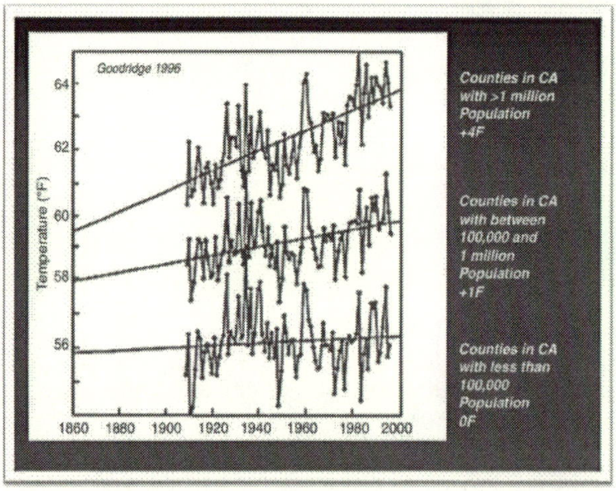

FIGURE 16 Jim Goodrich analysis of warming in California counties by population 1910–1995.

F[illegible] prior to 1980. Warming post 1980 was due to many issues unaccounted for. Compare to UAH value for 2009.

In **Fig 4,**[250] we see an interesting comparison of GISS in 1980 and 2010. In the blue line (ending in 1980), we again see the higher temperatures of 1938-39 along with the downslope to 1980. But by 2010, by the red line, we see the slope flipped and extended. But if you look hard, you will notice a most interesting dangling participle/note; the satellite says an overall temperature increase of + 0.26 C, which we must assume has to be from 1979 to 2009, 40 years, which are the satellite years.

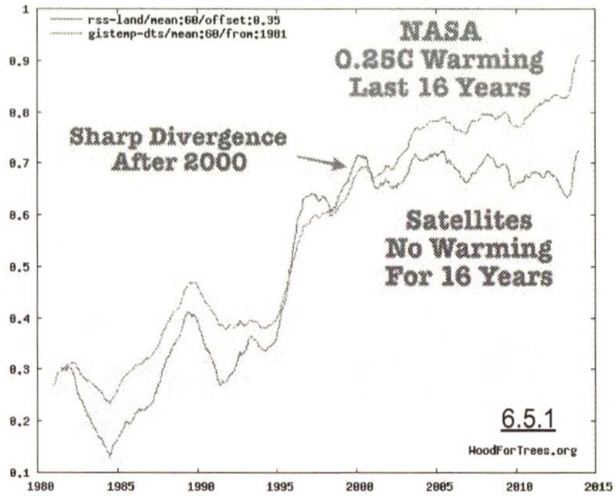

In **Fig 5,**[251] we note the urbanization effect. In large cities, we see an urbanization-effect growth of about 4.0 F since 1995. But in the rural areas, we see only about a 0.5 F increase. The article also goes on to show the reduction in the number of rural stations and an increase in urban stations.

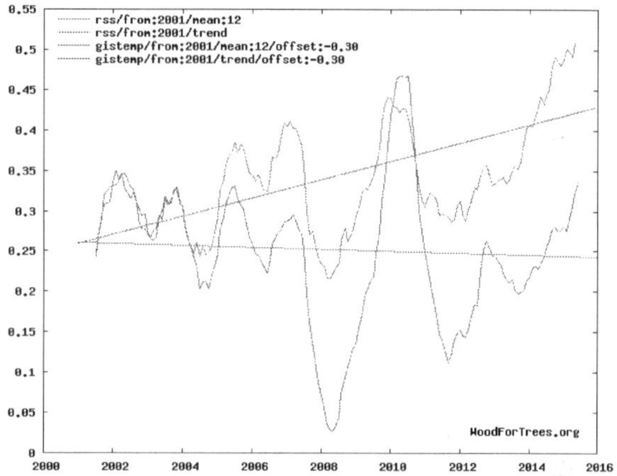

More evidence.

We present another piece of evidence in Figure 6.5.1.[252] In this example, we see the lack of reliability of the NOAA land and the sea-based data discussed above. The green line is the adjusted NOAA surface temperatures next to the satellite data shown in red. Here we see that "normalized" surface temperatures are routinely higher than the satellite data. Especially note the clear divergence after the year 2000 (the Climategate era that continues to this day). Satellite data is broadcasted directly by the satellites to the many countries that funded the satellites and continue to support them, year after year. Nobody, no organization or group, can screen, adjust, or manipulate satellite data.

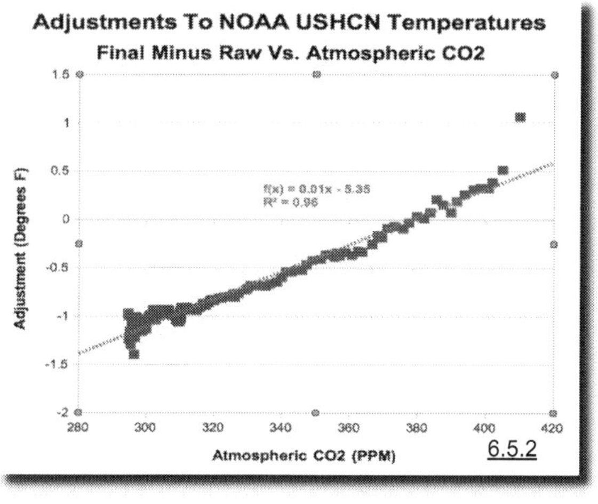

6.5.2

Also, satellite data is not just more reliable and accurate, but it is less susceptible to human error. Politicians and the media continue to beat the drums of human-caused global warming based on the land and sea temperatures, while NASA/NOAA remains silent on this divergence seen in **Fig 6.**[253] This appears to be clear evidence that since the years 2000, there's been no global warming. But the alarm bells and shrieks continue louder, and the consequences ever more threatening and immediate.

Now many will contend that satellites and surface instruments don't measure the same thing. However, the satellite adjustments are small and easy to make compared with the many "errors" of omission and commission of the sea and land surface temperatures.

In this last **Fig 6.5.2,**[254] we seem to have another hint. The blue dots show the values of the surface temperatures made by their computer models. And in the red line, we see the CO2 increase over the same period. Is this a sheer coincidence, or is it the target adjustment that needs to be made so they can continue their mantra that increasing CO2 is driving the temperature increase? And then, they turn the various adjustment knobs to described above to achieve the targeted temperatures they want?

You be the judge.

Besides the above discrepancy between the satellite temperature history and the "adjusted" NOAA temperature history, let's go back and revisit 6.4.4. Recall the discussion about this chart. The blue line was raw data, meaning the actual temperatures that were recorded on the exact days they were taken, and the orange line represents the adjusted or the manipulated NOAA temperatures. We now have three independent pieces of evidence of data fraud by NOAA.

6. THE DRAMA OF DR. WILLIE SOON

This is a sad commentary[255] on what happens to a scientist who dares to pursue a disciplined scientific approach to climate change when it goes against contemporary orthodoxy. But first, let's start with who is Robert Carter and Lord Monckton.

Who is Dr. Carter? [256] Joe Bast writes in part: *"It is with deep regret that I report the passing of a friend, colleague, and great scholar, Dr. Robert M. Carter. Bob died peacefully in a hospital surrounded by family and friends following a heart attack a few days ago. He was 74 years old. Bob was the very embodiment of the "happy warrior" in the global warming debate. He was a scholar's scholar with impeccable credentials (including a Ph.D. from Cambridge), careful attention to detail, and a deep understanding of and commitment to the scientific method. He endured the slings and arrows of the anti-science Left with seeming ease and good humor and often warned against resorting to similar tactics to answer them."*

Who is Lord Monckton? He is the third Viscount Monckton of Brenchley, a British public speaker, hereditary Lord, and a mathematical genius. But Lord Monckton is better known for his charismatic and satirical approach to the follies on the CO2 industry. He mocks their "science" and "mathematics," especially the sensational disaster speculations, then challenges their concept of reducing CO2. In recent years, his public speaking drew international attention, mainly because of his denial of climate change disasters. Maybe we should simply grant him a pass because he is so entertaining. Here are referenced some YouTube videos presented for your amusement and education.[257]

Dr. Carter and Lord Monckton have one thing in common; they, along with many notable climate experts, continue to be avid defenders of Dr. Willie Soon. Lord Monkton championed a petition letter to Harvard University titled "Petition to Harvard-Smithsonian in Defense of Willie Soon" May 5, 2015." In the introductory section, it states, "*Approximately 500 scientists and policy analysts signed this letter to members of the Harvard-Smithsonian Board of Regents defending Willie Soon, an astrophysicist falsely accused by Harvard-Smithsonian of having improperly not disclosed a source of his funding for his work at the Harvard-Smithsonian Center for Astrophysics. The signers ask for an investigation of misbehavior by senior managers of the Harvard-Smithsonian Center for Astrophysics.*"

Dr. Willie Soon was falsely attacked and prosecuted in the court of public opinion for years. His crime was to expose the false science of CO2 induced global warming. Using sound physics and data, he explains how the present warming trend is primarily caused by solar activity and other natural cycles. He does not support the popularly advanced dogma that we are at the edge of climate change destruction, and that the only culprit is human-made CO2. Willie attacks the consensus solution to radically transform and eliminate fossil fuels, even if trillions of dollars are needed. On November 5, 2013, The Boston Globe published an article[258] with the headline, *"Researcher helps sow climate-change doubt. Industry-funded Cambridge astrophysicist adds to partisan divide.*" Here, Dr. Soon was accused of not disclosing the source of the funding for his work against the fashionable notion that the rise in global temperatures is 100 percent driven by human-made CO2. In reality, he was being punished for not accepting the consensus CO2 dogma.

"Ad hominem" attacks [259] followed, as many presses, media, and bloggers quickly piled on to destroy not Dr. Soon's theories or data, but the man himself. Nobody bothered to review or test his data or his methods. They only sought to besmirch and discredit him as a scientist and a person. They aimed to cut off his future funding sources and employment opportunities. Meanwhile, he had complied with 100 percent of the disclosure requirements per his agreement with his employer, Harvard-Smithsonian Center for Astrophysics in Cambridge. The Human-made CO2 disaster lobbyists were helped by outlets like NPR, and the many newspapers that launched numerous attacks. As an example, The New York Times,[260] on Feb 21, 2015, went on a particularly vicious campaign to destroy Willie professionally. Why so much anger and venom against one person? Simple; to set an example for other scientists who might be thinking of pursuing an agenda that's not in line with the UN/IPCC consensus industry.

New York Times Repeats Scurrilous Greenpeace Attack[261] on Willie Soon Without Checking the Facts." Article *by* MYRON EBELL, *FEBRUARY 27, 2015 in* BLOG: *"New York's Times republished a Greenpeace press release on the front page of its Sunday, 22nd February edition that attacks Willie Soon of the Harvard-Smithsonian Center for Astrophysics for obtaining $1.2 million in funding for his research over the last decade from energy corporations, electric utilities, and charitable foundations related to those companies. The press release, cleverly disguised as an article supposedly written by Times reporters Justin Gillis and John Schwartz, also claims that Dr. Soon did not adequately disclose the sources of his funding in articles published in scientific journals."*

7. WHY NOT NUCLEAR?

Three fundamental questions need to be asked:

- What has been the real-world nuclear experience in the past half-century of operation, and how does it compare with other forms of electrical generation?
- Is nuclear power for everybody on this planet?
- Are we stuck with uranium-based nuclear technology, and do we have options?

The author's view is that nuclear power has demonstrated to be the safest,[262] cleanest,[263] and cheapest[264] method of generating electricity. It's unfathomable, then, why the Big E Environmentalists can be against nuclear power? It produces none of the CO_2 that they blame for the coming global warming disasters. Let's look at each of these three attributes in detail.

7.1 Safety. Let's start by challenging the premise of safety, which brought the industry to a near-complete end. Please follow this endnote to see an overview of a typical safety program at nuclear plants.[265] The safety of nuclear plants is backed by substantial evidence based on over 450 plants in thirty-three countries around the world with 20,000 years' operating time. We will look at the evidence and facts and try to put aside all the fearmongering foisted by the press, media, politicians, and the well-intentioned do-gooders.

Each plant requires a 4-point safety program:

- Operational Safety: Highly trained experts run nuclear plants. With the NRC's oversight and layers of safety precautions, a nuclear plant is one of the safest industries in the United States.
- Security: Several systems keep our plants secure, and top-notch security starts long before an armed guard stands to watch. Plant design, screening systems, behavioral observation, and highly trained forces protect our reactors from external threats.
- Cybersecurity: Our nuclear plants are well-hardened from cyber threats. They are designed as islands of operation disconnected from the internet. Technology moves fast, but our cybersecurity experts move faster.
- Emergency Preparedness: Each nuclear plant maintains a response plan for different emergencies. Pulling together federal, state, and local responders, these plans meet strict NRC and FEMA requirements.

There have been two primary and one nominal nuclear reactor accidents in about 50 years of operation, and here are the facts:

Fukushima:[266] What are the deaths and adverse health effects to date? Nobody died from the reactor damaged by the tsunami, and no one died from radiation exposure. The only adverse health effect has been psychologically induced by the media. Kazuo Sakai of Japan's National Institute of Radiological Sciences said, *"Since the disaster in Fukushima, we have observed no health effects from radiation, although we have heard reports some people fell ill because of stress from living as evacuees and because of worries and fears about radiation. We know from epidemiological surveys among atomic-bomb victims in Hiroshima and*

Nagasaki, if exposure to radiation is greater than 100 millisieverts, or 100 mSv, the risk of developing cancer will gradually rise. The risk of developing cancer will not increase if a person is exposed to less than 100 mSv. Most people measured were exposed to 20 mSv or less."

There was a total of 20,600 deaths, but that's not what was reported. Instead, the media reported false narratives to induce a nuclear hysteria. Worst of all was how particular objective truths were stacked and conflated. Moreover, choreographed word choices led casual citizens to believe their agenda-driven conclusions. Here are the epistemological numbers:

- The tsunami wave caused 20,000 deaths when it smashed through the impacted area, and later by the mass of water that followed the initial wave. To better understand the dynamics of a tsunami, please follow this endnote.[267]
- Another 600 deaths were caused due to a poorly planned and executed evacuation, and recovery plans.
- <u>Zero is the number of deaths</u> attributed to the nuclear plant accident (direct, indirect, and long-term radiation health effects).

Those are the facts, but the anti-nuclear lobby and media coverage hid the facts. This led the uninformed public to believe that thousands had died from the "Fukushima Nuclear Accident." The simple truth is that there was no Fukushima nuclear accident. But instead, there was a deplorable political decision in choosing the location for the nuclear plant. None-the-less, the induced psychological fearmongering and damage was unrelenting.

<u>Three Mile Island,</u> Pennsylvania, USA, 1979. Level of damage, nominal. It can only be described as a scene right out of an episode of *The Simpsons*. After the initial failure of a cooling pump, the backup pumps immediately went into operation, as designed. They quickly restored the core cooling and stabilized the plant. Had Homer Simpson just kept eating his doughnuts, drinking his Duff Beer, or kept sleeping, everything would have been fine. The plant was already automatically shutting down safely. But Homer got his switches mixed up. Instead of shutting off the broken pump, he shut off the backup pumps. And instead of learning from the experience and implementing active, viable training and safety programs, the ensuing hysteria took over. Unfortunately, it started the near-death spiral of the nuclear industry. Meaning endless demonstrations against any new constructions, countless lawsuits, boycotting anybody that showed any

support for the industry. But worst of all was the endless delays in development and licensing that threatened to ruin anyone investing in the nuclear industry.

Meanwhile, despite all this hype and tripe of the "Three Mile Island nuclear disaster," it had zero deaths and zero long term health consequences.[268]

Chernobyl,[269] Ukraine, was a significant event. This plant was doomed from the start, thanks to the sloppy design, lacking even any containment structure, and shabby construction. These shortcomings were made worse by flawed operation and maintenance, which resulted in the worst nuclear accident in the world. The massive demolition project that followed caused even more damage than the plant's operational failure. The result was two immediate deaths by the malfunction and twenty-nine by subsequent radiation-induced sickness of the clean-up crew. The worst nuclear accident in the world to date resulted in a total of thirty-one deaths.

Compare and contrast:

"Safety" is a relative term. When people say this activity is dangerous or might cause death or severe injury, it needs to be answered by the question, "Compared to what?" Safety and risks are factors, no matter what we are or are not doing. For example, there are safety concerns for commuting to work, climbing a ladder, shingling a roof, fixing a car, sleeping in your bed, etc. In June 2019, a family of three was killed in Tampa when a drunk driver crashed into their home as they slept. In figure 6.7.1,[270] we compare the number of nuclear deaths and radiation sicknesses to the various power generation technologies and is measured by the number of fatalities per Tera-Watt-year.

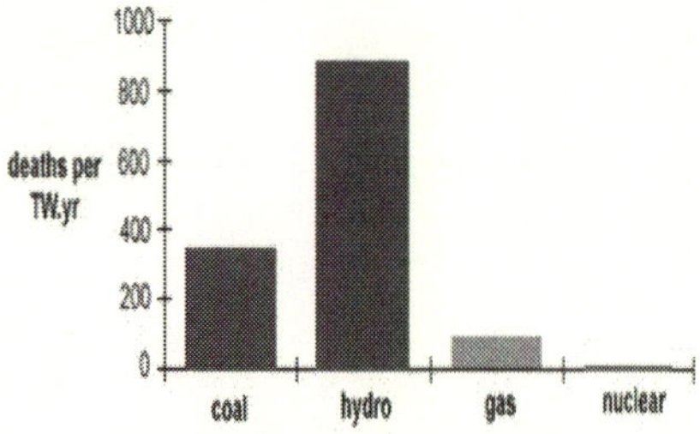

- Let's also compare to other industries:

Fishing, Alaska only	31 deaths/year

Law enforcement, USA only	128 deaths/year
Fire Rescue, the USA alone	10 deaths/year

- High Radiation Exposure Occupations:[271] Below is the industries with the highest radiation exposures. As a benchmark, airline crews are the most exposed population at 4.6 mSv/yr. Recall the reference, below 100 mSv/years is not a problem.
  –Airline pilots and crew
  –Industrial radiography
  –Medical radiology and nuclear medicine
  –Uranium mining
  –Nuclear power and fuel reprocessing plant, 3.6 mSv/yr.
  –Research laboratories (government, university, and private)

7.2 Challenge on emissions and pollution: Fossil fuel plants are notorious for pollution discharges and greenhouse gas emissions. These pollutants present a risk and a substantial cost to the environment. But let's take these apart and start with CO2, and restate that CO2 is not a pollutant. Many fossil fuel plants can install carbon capturing and sequestration equipment. But it's only an expensive, feel-good piece of equipment, and it's a waste of money. The good news is that we have the technology, industry, and will reduce the real pollutants to near zero. The real pollutants are soot, fly-ash, Nitrous-Oxides and sulfur, and various other particulate emissions. But it comes at a cost, including many acres of land for the settling ponds for coal-fired plants. Nuclear reactors have no pollution and no CO2 issues. However, there is a substantial cost associated with the treatment, handling, and storage of radioactive waste. But overall, it's much less costly and more manageable than all other competing technologies.

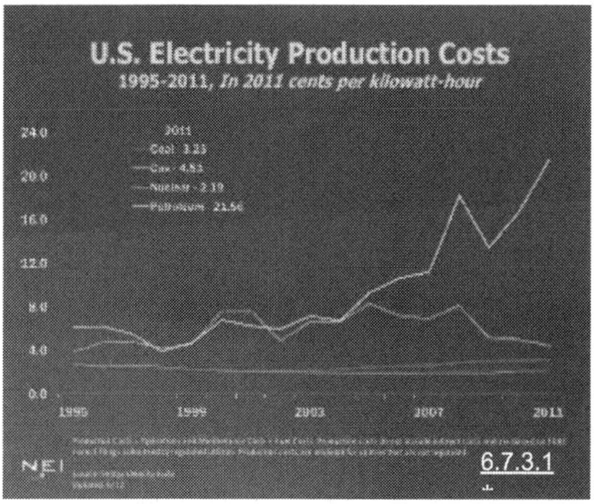

7.3 Challenge Costs, the premise that nuclear is the cheapest.[272] Please refer to 6.7.3.1,[273] where we see comprehensive data showing the total costs in the U.S. for the base-load electrical generating alternatives. Nuclear is beset by substantial costs and delays in the permitting process, public relations, and licensing. But once up and running, there is no cost competitor. Natural gas and coal are close, but we may want to reserve those fuels for export in the future. Especially natural gas, where we will likely have a better market in a few decades for automotive and transportation rather than wasting it in our electrical plants today. Second, we hope to reduce nuclear anxieties and the exhaustive nuclear licensing-clearing process. If we achieve that, we might reduce the nuclear generating cost even more. Nuclear is the ideal generating form, especially if we are to venture more and more into electric vehicles. In 6.7.3.2,[274] we see the leveled comparison of generation costs, including the renewables. However, what these charts don't show can be just as impactful. Here are a few examples:

- The graph does not show the subsidies paid by federal, state, and local entities for the renewables solar, wind, etc., which are paid for by consumers in some form of a "car
- bon tax."
- Land-based wind does not include the cost of the thousands of acres of land and countless miles of transmission lines. It also does not show the price and ecological damage for having all trees and hills erased so as not to affect their performance.
- Solar, wind, and other renewables do not include the cost of a backup fossil plant and the operational cost of running it in the spinning reserve mode. So, on top of the prices shown above, add the cost of a combined cycle plant of about $75 per Megawatt-hour, which nearly doubles the costs.
- There's the additional consideration that wind turbines take so much energy to manufacture and install, that they will probably never recover the amount of electricity that was used to construct them.

One final note on France:[275] At one point, France had a nuclear power goal of 100 percent and reached almost 80 percent. But later, France became the principal in spearheading the Paris Agreement[276] commitment. However, now it is planning to scale back its nuclear efforts gradually. See the article "Nuclear Power in France," updated June 2019. [277]

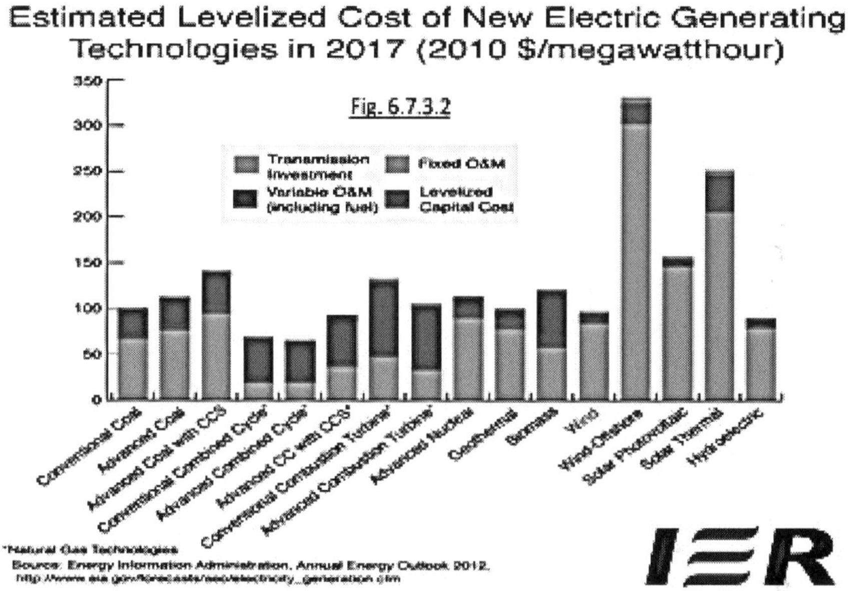

- Today, France derives about 75 percent of its electricity from nuclear energy because of a long-standing policy based on energy security. Government policy is to reduce this to 50 percent by 2035. But to date, nothing is done along this line.
- France is the world's largest net exporter of electricity for its meager cost of generation and gains over €3 billion per[278] year from this export.
- The country has been very active in developing nuclear technology and continues to receive significant export sales.

About 17 percent of France's electricity is from recycled nuclear fuel. France's energy mix in 2018 comprised 75 percent nuclear power and 8 percent from wind and solar. And because of its low nuclear generating cost, France today remains the world's biggest exporter of electric power.[279] Its biggest customer is Germany, which, more than a decade ago, made a political decision to go all out for wind and solar. But in recent years has scrambled to rebuild gas-fired combined cycle plants to make up for their electrical shortages. In fact, Germany contracted with Russia for a dedicated gas pipeline to fuel these new fossil plants. However, since the Paris Accord, France has been championing CO2 reduction by increasing its "carbon tax" on all fossil fuels. As a result, the average French consumer is paying almost $7 per gallon of gasoline, versus the USA at about $2.55 a gallon. These ever-increasing "carbon taxes" have sparked many protests and riots throughout France for nearly a year now and continue to this day.

7.4 Is nuclear for everybody? The answer is no!

- Nuclear is not an option for any underdeveloped or developing country. Significant hurdles include the high cost of upfront capital, years for permitting/licensing, and the complexities of technologies.
- Nuclear security is a significant barrier from an operational point, from acts of terrorism, and the dangers of recycling the spent fuels used to manufacture crude atomic weapons.
- Several countries are blessed with abundant, clean, reliable, renewable, hydroelectrical power. These include Russia, Norway, Iceland, Canada, Uruguay, Albania, Switzerland, and other countries where they have vast open areas, ample sunshine, and oil and gas reserves. Here they can have solar provide a substantial portion of their electrical supplemented by oil/gas combined cycle plants.
- There are a few relatively small countries with high population densities where the high cost of capital for a uranium double reactor plant might exceed their national requirements, such as Belgium, Luxembourg, Switzerland, and Norway.
- Stop forcing the underdeveloped countries to go all-in with wind and solar. The policies of the UN for the developed countries and the World Development Bank will not provide finance or grants for coal electrical plants. Please change these laws and practices immediately.
- In developed countries, hundreds of billions of dollars are wasted each year in an attempt to reduce CO2. But after decades of research and trillions of dollars, we have no data that CO2 is harming the environment or humanity. On the other hand, we have ample data that

lack of electricity is causing millions of deaths each year, especially in underdeveloped and developing countries.

7.5 Technology assessment, Question 3. What is the state of nuclear technology today, and is there an alternative to uranium reactors?
There were many good decisions made back in the 1950s-60s concerning nuclear reactors. Looking back and seeing where we are today, many of us would say yes. The commercial reactors followed the path forged by our military-led uranium technology. As an optimist, I believe it was the right decision then. We had no World War III, we had mutually assured destruction potential, but no buttons were ever pushed. There were several brush wars, a few of which lasted far too long. On top of that, it's getting better each year, especially for poor people around the world.
But that was the past, and the future starts today. Today, we have the capital and technology to reclaim our leadership in a thorium reactor technology, which we abandoned in the early 1970s. Another great decision by Richard Nixon! Unfortunately, today, we don't have the national will to even seriously debate on it. But China is now taking the lead in thorium reactor technology, followed closely by India. The Nordic countries are also looking at forming a thorium reactor consortium. What will we do? At the very least, we should start a national awareness program. The consequences of a no-decision will mean China wins, and we will lose out on the next energy industrial revolution and all the jobs, wages, and commerce it brings. Here in this footnote is a summary of the pros and cons of thorium versus uranium.[280] A recent Forbes article [281] is demonstrating the tactical advantages of portable thorium nuclear generators for the battlefields. It points out the possible savings of thousands of lives lost due to the dangers and vulnerabilities in transporting fuels for aircraft, tanks, trucks, et. Hopefully this military need may give us an additional incentive to develop and commercialize this promising new technology.

8. TRUTH, MARK TWAIN, AND TRUSTED SOURCES

8.1 Truth: Here, we are more than halfway on our journey. We have seen several instances where the public was misled or purposely deceived.

Example #1:[282] Above, we talked about how the "97 percent consensus" was calculated. Let's now take our own slightly different survey. Let's say we took a survey of 200 doctors and asked them all the same question: "Do vaccines have potentially harmful side effects?" Let's do a simple test: The survey population is 200.

- Some doctors had no time or interest to respond—let's say one hundred of them did not respond.
- Of the one hundred respondents, ninety-seven said, "Well, sure, they could pose a risk, but it's hard to know for certain." Some may say, "Taking vaccines is probably better than not taking them."
- So, here's a conclusion that might be drawn by someone with an agenda; 97 percent of doctors surveyed say taking vaccines could be dangerous to your health. A few even say in rare cases, it may cause death.
- Now, if our agenda is against the use of vaccines, and we have a big microphone like the United Nations, the press, TV, radio, the President of the USA, etc., we might get them to promote the message, saying, "Two hundred doctors surveyed, 97 percent say vaccines are risky, maybe even fatal."
- Would this be an accurate statement? Would it be ontologically correct? Is it a lie staged as a truth?
- What if 99.9 percent of the 200 doctors had their children vaccinated? Was this question asked in the survey? If not, why not?
- What if 98 percent said the benefits outweigh the risks? Was it asked? If not, why not?
- Was there a greater good at stake that outweighed the lack of a more transparent and data-driven message?
- Who benefitted from the lack of clarity? Who suffered because of it, and how?
- Could it be criminal?

Example #2: If I proposed to the EPA that we must remove the ban on DDT and restart its production and use, what would happen? If I did that, I assure you, within days, there would be a national furor. Big E-Environmentalists would be storming Capitol Hill. Capitol Hill would respond immediately and drag me in front of a hearing to be publicly reprimanded and humiliated. Teachers would be organizing their students to protest in front of my house. Somebody in the media would immediately start doxing me. Revealing all my personal information they could find, like where I live, where I work, where my children go to school. Essentially the purpose of this doxing is to invite some half-crazy people to do me and my family harm. My life would be ruined. You, dear reader, must be thinking that I am crazy!

EAH! Not-so-much. Here's why. The whiplash of unintended consequences.[283] Here is an example of the truth you are not told. Here is an excerpt from an article dated August 26, 2009, titled "Law of Unintended Consequences: Banning DDT": "Malaria remains the world's most devastating human parasitic infection. Malaria affects over 40 percent of the world's population.[284] The World Health Organization (WHO) estimates that there are 350 - 500 million cases of malaria worldwide, out of which 270 - 400 million are falciparum malaria, the most in years." Please read the entire articles referenced above. According to another example,[285] this one from PMC (the US National Library of Medicine National Institutes of Health) "Debating the Health Effects of DDT: Thomas Jukes, Charles Wurster, and the Fate of an Environmental Pollutant. By Elena Conis, MS, MJ.

It goes on to say, "*The controversy regarding DDT's continued use in the U.S. was one that pitted the chemical's risks against its benefits. On the surface, this was also the subject of the debate between Wurster and Jukes. To Jukes, few technologies had done as much as DDT to promote human health. To Wurster, few were as insidious and subtle in their effects on the ecosystem, of which both humans and wildlife were apart.*"

Example #3: In the above article on why all the fuss about CO2, why did the 97 percent IPCC consensuses remain silent on the many benefits of the increased CO2? Worst yet, why do they continue the hysteria against reinstating DDT because it "kills birds," but are deaf, dumb, and blind when their windmills kill hundreds, even thousands of them, every year? Even more egregious is their opposition to the lifesaving benefits of DDT to tens of millions of people infected every year by malaria. And their excuse is, no, we can't have DDT because it supposedly hurts the birds.

Example #4: We saw indications that the CO2 consensus group attacked the motives, funding sources, and the character of the "skeptics" and "deniers." However, the skeptics and deniers attacked only the consensus' data or lack of data. The skeptics made no ad hominem attacks against the consensus persons. What's the message here?

Example #5: We have hard data that shows that nuclear, especially thorium, is the safest, cheapest, most reliable, and most eco-friendly of any power generation method. So why does the media still portray the opposite? I am now convinced it's just a sample of their anti-humanism and their false god of the woodland, Gaia.

Sad to have this discussion. Above is a minuscule sample of how the media deceives us over and over. We note how one or two or three "truthful statements" are twisted, staged, ignored, or glossed over to fabricate a grand deception. An average person has no knowledge base from which to set their reference points nor the time to put together the many puzzle pieces. They should rely on the integrity of the scientists, press, and media. That was the purpose of "Freedom of the Press!" The purpose of the First Amendment of the Constitution was to allow the press to keep us informed. It was not a license to brainwash us with their agenda-driven propaganda, especially in the brainwashing of our elementary school children!

8.2 Mark Twain:[286] We still have so much to learn about the scientific process but fear not. As a dedicated student of the MTS (Mark Twain School) Scientific Method, help is on the way.

Many moons ago, I read the short stories by Mark Twain, and one of his tall tales taught me the importance of the scientific process. It was hilarious with Sam Clemens using his wit and irony to drive home a straightforward concept. With his unique gift, he wrapped it in his inimitable style and grandeur. At any rate, his message to me as a high school student was differential. The name of the story is, "Some Learned Fables, For Good Old Boys and Girls." Luckily you can find it on this website[287] without buying his complete short story book (although I highly recommend it). The story is divided into three parts, and this tale pushes the limits of how long a short story can be. It tells how the animals of the forest set out on a great scientific discovery journey.

It's about what the animals did to prepare for the trip and what happened during the journey. In the process, we find ourselves enormously amused while taught the simple truth of the need for a scientific method. In the story, we see the arrogance of the educated elites' tortoise and daddy-long spider, the deference paid to them by those who wanted to shine in their reflected glory. How they sought social standing by merely agreeing with the learned elders. And then there is the dung-beetle who upturns the entire social structure. Once you have read this story, you will find yourself reading the newspapers and listening to the TV news much more attentively and with added skepticism. No, I will not give any more spoilers. Read it and enjoy yourself and his newfound scientific and behavioral guiding principles. Most of all, see how many of your friends, portrayed in this tale, can you recognize.

8.3 Trusted sources:

As we have seen, the need for analytical reading is an absolute necessity in these polarized times. Left vs. right, liberal vs. conservative, moral vs. immoral. You don't have the time to sort them all out. So, let's identify some of my more trusted sources of information.

Newspapers and Other Media:

- On the center-left, we have *USA Today*. Since it does not have too many details, it's easy to read. Furthermore, it occasionally gives a general overview of the socio-scientific articles that are getting national attention. At times they will reasonably commit adequate journalism.

- On the center-center, we have *The Wall Street Journal* that seems to pay little attention to the reader's sociopolitical preferences. It doesn't overwhelm you with exact details. Instead, it zeros in on what's possible, what the consequential costs are, and what are the short-term and long-term social and economic implications of A vs. B.

- On the center-right is Fox News, and I have seen and read several climate discussions there, some with levity and some at a more profound level.

Websites:

- The Global Warming Policy Foundation, https://www.thegwpf.org/
- The Heartland Institute, https://www.heartland.org/topics/climate-change/index.html
- The University of Illinois Climate Science, https://experts.illinois.edu/en/publications/climate-science
- Yale University opinion survey, showing how politicized climate change has become, https://climatecommunication.yale.edu/visualizations-data/ycom-us-2018/?est=happening&type=value&geo=county
- Google / Yahoo climate charts https://images.search.yahoo.com/yhs/search;_ylt=AwrEeJ7CvxZdGTgAiA0PxQt.;ylu=X3oDMTByMjB0aG5zBGNvbG8DYmYxBHBvcwMxBHZ0aWQDBHNlYwNzYw--?p=google+climate+charts&fr=yhs-Lkry-newtab&hspart=Lkry&hsimp=yhs-newtab
- I continue to surf the NASA sites because they occasionally will provide reasonably factual data. But sharpen your skeptical reading skills. Ignore their sidebars and flashy headlines and look for the small printed notes on the peripherals. https://www.nasa.gov/subject/3127/climate/
- Alex Epstein and the Center for Industrial Progress. Alex has a unique way of looking at climate change and reflects his education in philosophy and the ethics of what is good and right for humanity https://industrialprogress.com/about/
- Don Easterbrook, a one-stop shopping center for climate data. http://myweb.wwu.edu/dbunny/
- Roy Spencer provides us with climate insight by presenting interesting articles, and you don't even know you are being taught. http://www.drroyspencer.com/
- https://wattsupwiththat.com It advertises itself as the most visited climate change website and is referenced in several places in this book.
- https://skepticalscience.com/global-cooling.htm Does a reasonably good job of explaining the scientific part of the CO2 alarmist mode. I like the way they provide explanations of critical scientific concepts at the beginner, intermediate, and advanced levels.

Climate change books. Please note that two of the books are geared primarily on the environment and humanity. I hope that these books and authors will help us reclaim the moral high ground from the CO2 consensus industry.

- Roy Spencer; *Global Warming Skepticism for Busy People*
- Alex Epstein; *The Moral Case for Fossil Fuels*
- Bjorn Lomborg; *The Skeptical Environmentalist*
- Don Easterbrook; *Evidence-Based Climate Science*
- Patrick Moore; *Confessions of a Greenpeace Drop Out*
- Rupert Darwall; *Green Tyranny: Exposing the Totalitarian Roots of the Climate Industrial Complex*
- Bruce Bunker, *The Mythology of Global Warming: Climate Change Fiction VS. Scientific Facts*
- Patrick Michaels: *Sound and Fury: The Science and Politics of Global Warming.*

Periodicals

- For decades, I subscribed to *National Geographic* and the *Scientific American* but wrote both of them off a few years ago for being too speculative and too sensationalizing.
- I continue to subscribe to journals of *Science* and *Nature* because occasionally, they present interesting papers with elements of real science. For example, *Nature* published the articles of Dr. Valentina Zharkova and Dr. Henrick Svensmark.

People I regularly follow on YouTube, their online lectures, and news articles:

Valentina Zharkova	Alex Epstein	Henrik Svensmark
Don Easterbrook	Willie Soon	Richard Lindzen
Roy Spencer	Christopher Monckton	Patrick Moore
Bjorn Lomborg	Jay Lehr	Mark Steyn

9. THE GREEN NEW DEAL

What is it? We must find out what's in this proposal, Green New Deal[288] pushed by the Democratic Party! What does it intend to accomplish, what's the likelihood of success, and at what price? Could it be another Trojan Horse deception? It's been put forward by vocal members of the Democratic Party and backed by 100 percent of their presidential candidates. It's presented to the public as "our last and only chance to save the planet and humanity." Is it even a serious proposal? Well, that all depends on where you go for your information and how informed you think you are. So, let's get a sample.

9.1 From USA Today,[289] "Green New Deal:[290] What is it, and what does it mean for climate change?" Reads the front-page headline from USA Today; So, here's a few opening paragraphs and questions and answers:

"The Earth is facing a climate change deadline, with a looming tipping point into a dramatically changed, less hospitable planet–and Democratic lawmakers are beginning what's likely to be a long discussion over how best to deal with it.

These first attempts have coalesced under the umbrella phrase a 'Green New Deal' championed by Rep. Alexandria Ocasio-Cortez, D-N.Y., and Sen. Edward Markey, D-Mass."

This group of Democrats introduced a resolution calling for a dramatic increase in the generation of electricity only with renewable fuels, such as wind, solar, and hydropower sources. That way, we can shift within ten years to energy systems that are "net-zero" CO2 when it comes to greenhouses gasses. They are dogmatic in their belief that human-made CO2 is the sole cause of climate change.

Now, what are we to think? We recall from the introduction of this book about the need for critical thinking and skeptical reading so we can understand what's said, what's not said, and what's nuanced so we can formulate the essence of the issue. In section 8 above, we read about the need to ask piercing questions that will help us unravel the truth behind what we are told and not told. Let's do our forensic analysis of the headline, the opening paragraph, and the first questions posed.

What does it mean for climate change?[291] Let's start its deconstruction since they present it as the essence of the issue. They are telling us that in the next decade, human-made CO2 will continue to induce global climate warming. It will threaten the very existence of not only our planet but all of its humanity and life. Here's the first thing it tells us: they are appealing to our emotions, our fears, to be exact. It's understandable; it's a newspaper—where the traditional standard has always been "if it bleeds, it leads." Now let's ask: what are the two most important drivers of our behavior? Many would argue that the first, the basest of our instincts, is self-preservation. Yes, it's fights or flight, and they hit this nail right on the head. What's our second most primitive drive? That would be to perpetuate the bloodline, the primordial drive for reproduction.

A perfect one-two punch, but they also feel the need to reinforce their approach, and they go to work on it. For example, USA Today saw the need to strengthen this second drive-by showing us a photo of our poor defenseless children that are doomed to extinction because of our callousness. Nice graphic touch, n'est-ce pas? Doubt me? Look at what salmon do to be the first to reach the best spawning zones. Or the beautiful and delicate monarch butterflies or the rugged Canada geese who travel thousands of miles to the instinctive but unknown nesting places. Or the elk, and bear, and lion, and fill in the rest who risk their lives and limbs for the privilege of mating and continuing their bloodline. Is USA Today appealing to our higher faculties of knowledge or reason? Hell no; they are appealing to our basest fears and needs. Does it appear that ethics, truth, or concern for the "doomed humanity" was ever considered as a factor in deciding what photo to insert here and for what purpose?

Deadline: "The Earth is facing a climate[292] change deadline," screams the opening sentence. To me, this shows the scorn the paper has toward its readers. Much like a snake-oil salesman telling the crowd that he only has five bottles left of his magical tonic. The subliminal message? Buy now, buy fast, no time to think! But our instinctive reaction today, based on what we have read so far, calls on the need for critical thinking and asking meaningful questions. Yes, we are prepared. So, in our mind, we say, "Really? Says who? What data do you have that I can trust?" We now know the background story. On one side are these consensus scientists, saying the world will end if we don't do what we are told. They bring us more hyperbolic disasters, and we don't have time to think about it. We need to fall in line quickly—no time to waste!

On rare occasions, we may read in the Wall Street Journal about experienced professors telling us that the CO2 threat is near zero. But who has time to read it? Who are we to believe? The consensus scientists are not stupid or ignorant. These consensus scientists, like newspaper writers and TV pundits, are responding to ensure their self-interests are served. There's no grand collusion, no vast climate conspiracies, nor purposeful deception orchestrated at any level. No, they are "good people" doing what's best for their families; to put food on their table, preserve their bloodlines, pay the bills, and gain social stature with minimum effort and costs.

Let's look at this phrase: "That's practically impossible, experts say, especially if nuclear power–which isn't mentioned in the plan and Green New Deal supporters oppose–isn't in the mix." Let's ask a two-part question. Why is it inserted here? At first, it looks like we are presented with a fair and balanced view. But it could also be a straw man. A straw man they will beat down later in the article or a follow-up article in tomorrow's edition. There, they will remind us about the Three Mile Island meltdown, the Chernobyl disaster, and foster another line of fear. But we also know that there are honest, financially independent, socially responsible, and emotionally secure scientists, humanists and naturalists out there. If we only take a little time and listen to what they are telling us, we'll come to know that no such disasters are coming.

Even if you want to believe that the CO2-driven disaster is right, there is not enough sunlight or wind power to keep seven billion people alive. So now they have put eugenics on the table! On a humanitarian scale, this is utterly alien. Who will decide which people will live or die? Will it be the capitalists, who are profiting from the CO2 story? Will it be MIT, Harvard, or Caltech professors? Will it be the politicians who tell us about the need to be socially responsible? How about the press that perpetuates the CO2 myth? The ugly truth is that the people who will be hit the hardest and first to die will be the poor in Africa and southern Asia, and some in South America. Next will be the poor in other second world countries. Next will be the poor in the developing countries; after that, the people of color in the developed countries.

U.S. Senator and presidential candidate Bernie Sanders saw the need, or should we say, the opportunity to weigh in on this scaring-eugenics theme. He declared that birth control and abortion in third world countries would be one of his top priorities if elected president. Doubt me? Check out what this first Google page reveals! Here are just a few sample headlines from this website, check out the many individual websites for yourself. [293]

– From Investment Watch; "Spreading the truth. Bernie Pushes Abortion, Etc. In 3rd World - Because..."Climate Change."

- From Newbuster.org, "Whoopi Defends Sanders, Population Control: 'Eugenics' Doesn't Have Anything to Do with Minorities!"

– From scoopraio.com; "Bernie Sanders announces support for global eugenics and depopulation, calls on accelerating abortions in countries populated by people of color."
– "Climate Crazies: CNN Pushes for Global Eugenics, Trillions in a bizarre. "

The article later reminds us about the looming danger to the planet by inserting a gratuitous photo of an open-pit coal mine.

9.2 The Wall Street Journal continues to be my go-to source for the economic implications of this science vs. that science. Their editorial columns are a great source of knowledge and insights. Here's an excerpt from one of the many reviews that commented on the article the Green New Deal in the WSJ by Kimberly Strassel. : "I Was Laughing So Hard I Nearly Cried:" WSJ'S KIMBERLEY[294] STRASSEL CAN'T GET OVER GREEN NEW DEAL" 02/07/2019 | ENERGY. The Wall Street Journal's Kimberley Strassel was not impressed by the rollout of the proposed Green New Deal." The Democrats rolled out the resolution, notably backed by freshman Democratic New York Rep. Alexandria Ocasio-Cortez. The commentary praises and criticisms rolled out. Strassel was firmly and decidedly in the latter's camp. In a tweet, she said:[295]

"By the end of the Green New Deal resolution (and accompanying fact sheet), I was laughing so hard I nearly cried. If a bunch of GOPers plotted to forge a fake Democratic bill showing how bonkers the party is, they could not have done a better job. It is beautiful."

9.3 Fox News:[296] *"Biden unveils climate change plan using Green New Deal as a framework after AOC criticism. Using the Green New Deal as a framework, the front-runner in the primary for the 2020 Democratic presidential nomination announced he's calling for a Clean Energy Revolution to confront this crisis and do what America does best–solve big problems with big ideas."*

9.4 The New York Times:[297] *"Major Climate Report Describes a Strong Risk of Crisis as Early as 2040"* by Coral Davenport; Oct. 7, 2018. The article opens with: *"INCHEON, South Korea — A landmark report from the United Nations' scientific panel on climate change paints a far more dire picture of the immediate consequences of climate change than previously thought."* The rest of the article is biased and delusional. For example, it confidently proclaims that global warming could increase by the end of this century by an additional 2.7 C! It goes on to say that we can prevent that if we spend 54-trillion dollars on reducing human-made CO2. This is utter nonsense to anyone who has taken the time and effort to understand the real climate change story we addressed in the first few chapters. The only part that made sense in this article was when it concluded by saying, "it would be politically difficult to achieve."

9.5 The New York Post:[298] Not to be outdone, here's the NYP headline, as reported by Whatsupwiththat, on June 4, 2019, in their hyperbolic disaster scenario: "*Climate change could end human civilization by 2050*," by moderator Charles. We'll just let this utter nonsense speak for itself.[299]

9.6 Summary: We now have three estimates of the costs to prevent this CO2 driven planetary disaster; $93 trillion, $6.7 trillion, and $54 trillion. The Wall Street Journal tells us it's technologically impossible to achieve the stated goals; The New York Times and Fox News report it as news, posing no direct questions or challenges to the statement. But the NYT highlights several pictures that show the damage they attribute to climate change. While USA Today states, it can't work because there's no nuclear power in the solution. But is this just a straw man? What seems clear is that this Green New Deal aligns with two major political and social forces:

- First, with the ecological extremists, who consider humankind as the number one enemy of the Earth. For them, the fewer people, the better! And, if deception and coercion are needed, they rationalize it by the sanctity of their cause and moral superiority.

- Second, these extreme environmentalists present nature as the idealistic state. They aim to defend it at all costs from the intrusion of men, their machinery, and greed. History is full of these dedicated zealots, reeking misery and death on the heretics who cross their noble causes. And, while

their cause is always presented on the superiority of their virtue, the implementing mechanism always ends up the same; loss of freedom, dungeons, deprivation, and death.
Plato needed slaves to make his idealist Republic work. St Augustine told us that the City of God is in perpetual earthy strife with The City of Men because of man's greed and sins.

Marx, Lenin, Mao, Castro, and even the Pilgrims of Plymouth spoke of the nobility of the working men and the holy cause of egalitarianism. But we know too well what followed. Perhaps we'll become more saintly in this 21st century, and by then, we'll be ready to achieve these utopian dreams. But one thing is sure; Environmental extremes will be the top issue in the 2020 national election.

10. REGAINING THE MORAL HIGH GROUND.

In this section, we bring together the thoughts and positions of two young, brilliant and sincere thinking individuals. These two are not climate scientists per se. But, like me, they have backed into the field of climate study because of their devotion to nature, humanity, and a sense of the economics of doing what's best for humanity at the least costs. I will try to consolidate their message as a foundation for recapturing the Moral High Ground that's been hijacked by the anti-humanists and anti-naturalists CO2 driven Consensus mob.

10.1 Alex Epstein[300] is an author, energy theorist, and industrial policy advocate. He is the founder and president of the Center for Industrial Progress, a for-profit think tank located in San Diego, California. Epstein is also the New York Times bestselling author of the book [301] "The Moral Case for Fossil Fuels" (2014). He advocates the use of fossil fuels like coal, oil, and natural gas for the benefit of humankind, especially those at the lower rungs of the economic ladder. For advocating this humanistic cause, he has been criticized and maligned. Alex Epstein was an adjunct scholar at the Cato Institute and a former fellow at the Ayn Rand Institute. Alex is unique in the field of climate science in that, after receiving his degree in Philosophy, he found himself gravitating toward a science-based climate of ethics. He argues for doing all that we can to improve the lives and conditions of humanity.

In his bestselling book, "The Moral Case for Fossil Fuels" (2014), there are many compelling statements, charts, and data. Yes, it's the message that puts him and his approach in a league of his own. Here are a few examples of a transparent thought process backed by science, economics, and a defined moral sense of values. We'll just let the charts and Alex speak directly to the reader.

"15 Chapter 3.1 Fossil Fuel Use and Human Progress – The Big Picture ALEX[302] EPSTEIN MARCH 28, 2016.

In 6.10.1, we see the relationship between the use of fossil fuels and life expectancy. This is astounding progress. Here we are using emissions CO2 as a proxy for the total consumption of fossil fuels. It clearly shows the dramatic increase in the factors that are the positive consequences of the increased use of fossil fuels.

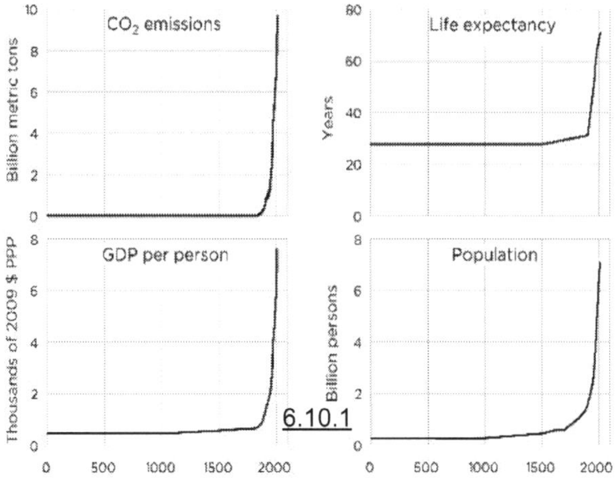

6.10.1

Alex always tries to look at the big picture with a sensible compass for reference, making sure that priorities and facts are right and aligned with what's best for humanity. He has no attachment to specific ideologies and looks at both the total benefits and detriments of any proposal. There he uses the benchmark, "Is it good for humanity or not?" These graphs clearly show that there's more than a causal relationship between the use of fossil fuels and life expectancy, GDP per person, and population growth. More fossil fuels consumed, especially in underdeveloped and developing countries, correlates heavily with improvements in life expectancy and quality of life. Lastly, he challenges us to examine all assertions and asks quantifying questions, like: is a 25 percent CO2 increase detrimental or good for humanity? How about if we double CO2 again, will that still be good? Yes? No? Show the details, the process, and data to answer these questions.

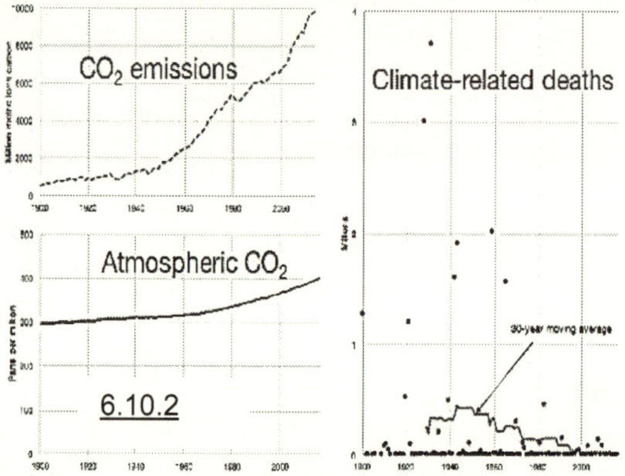

In 6.10.2, we see another astounding correlation between climate-related deaths and the use of fossil fuels. Here he shows us two proxies: CO2 emissions as a measure of the consumption level of fossil fuels and total atmospheric CO2. Here we see a steep decline in climate-related deaths. We recognize that with the increase in total CO2 and human-made CO2, we have reduced climate deaths by two to three million people per year.
How can anyone look at this chart and claim that fossil fuels are "bad" for humanity and bad for the planet? Well, that depends on your moral compass. If you see the population increasing to seven billion people, and if you believe that people are the enemies of your goddess Earth, then you need to reduce the number of people. But that's a whole new discussion for another day. But, all too often, Alex finds himself at odds with both the consensus industry, the IPCC climate change acolytes, and the pseudo-caring Environmentalists. But let's clarify the meaning of what a caring and humanistic "environmentalist" is.

Figure 1.6: U.S. Air Pollution Goes Down Despite Increasing Fossil Fuel Use / Figure 7.1: Decline in U.S. Air Pollution

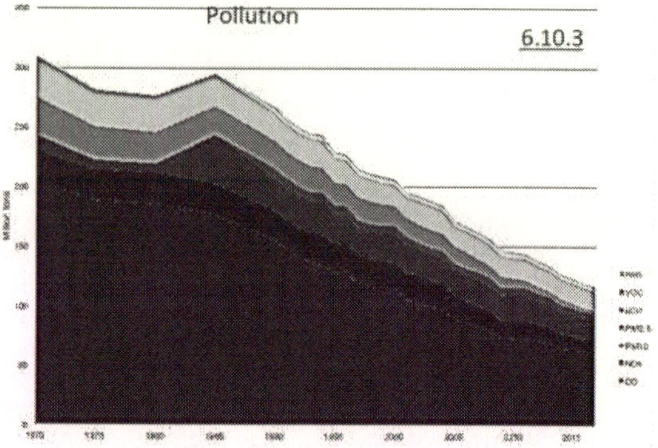

I care about a clean

environment. For years, I worked hard and considered myself a "small e" environmentalist. I want fresh air to breathe, clean water to drink, clean ponds to swim in, and forest trails that are free of waste, sludge, and garbage to walk along. I see myself as a part of nature and not an enemy of nature. I want to experience it and share it with my fellow-creatures. By contrast with the "big E" Environmentalists, who see nature as in "the perfect state" only if humankind is not part of it. By their definition, it's acceptable for a beaver to build a dam but not acceptable for humanity to do the same. It's acceptable for a beaver to cut down a tree, and, according to them, it's also fair to spike a tree. Why? So that if a person tries to cut it down, he is immediately screwed. He doesn't know the tree's been spiked and seriously injures himself in the process. Well, the prominent E Environmentalists shrug it off and say that's only part of the cost of saving the planet.

Another big lie: Fossil fuels destroy the environment. In 6.10.3,[303] we see a steady decline in all of the major pollutants since 1970. The chart is made even more dramatic considering the fact of the increasing use of fossil fuels over this same period.

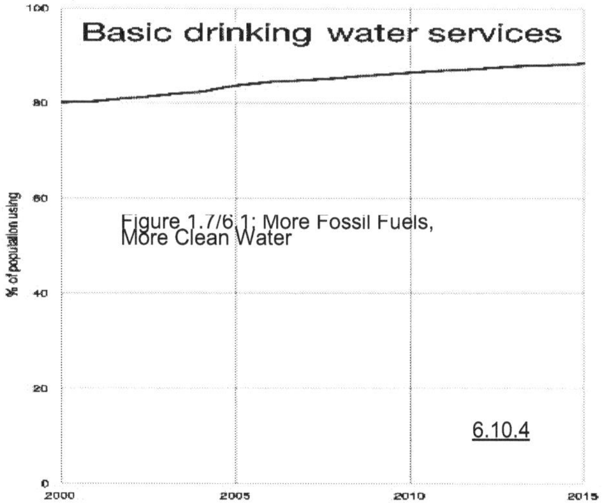

Figure 1.7/6.1: More Fossil Fuels, More Clean Water

In isolated cases in several municipalities, we heard terrible stories about polluted or contaminated water. In no way is that connected to fossil fuels. Instead, these localized incidents are caused by mismanagement of budgets and incompetent local administrators. In reality, as shown in 6.10.4.[304] The increase in the quality and quantity of drinking water also correlated with the same growth of CO2 emissions as the proxy for increased consumption of fossil fuels.

Environmental impact of windmills. There is one last and remarkable factor that goes against the widespread impression that fossil fuels are dirty and make the environment polluted. But again, data shows the exact opposite. Data shows that the more a nation uses fossil fuels, the cleaner their environment, drinking water, and the air they breathe. They also enjoy better hygiene and quality of life.

In 6.10.5, Alex shows us the amount of steel and iron required to build comparable electrical plants powered by wind, coal, and natural gas. It's astounding! A windmill needs about a hundred times more steel, iron, and other materials for the same amount of electrical generating capacity than a gas-fired fossil plant. Let's take a quick look at the comparable impact to the environment of a windmill plant. Compared to a gas-fired power plant, a windmill needs:

- One hundred times more mining of ores and coal, and the energy to extract and transport them.
- One hundred times more power for smelting, forging, and casting.
- One hundred times more cement and excavations and destruction of trees, and brush, and bulldozing of hills to clear wind obstructions.
- One hundred more transportation and installation labor and materials.

6.10.5

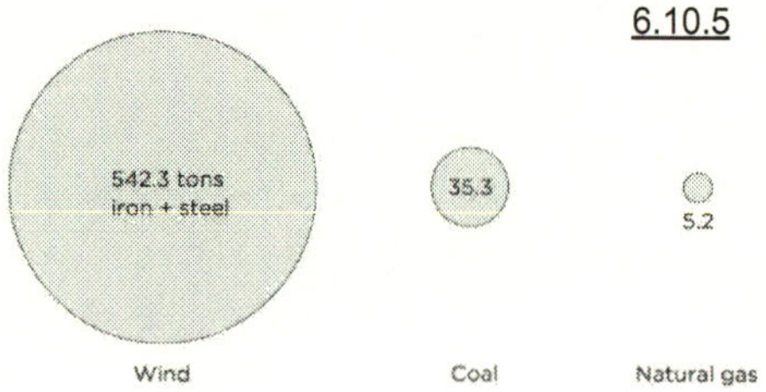

Figure 6.10.5[305] dramatically shows us of the impact on the environment and the expensive cost of electricity from building one of these windmills. And, after you have done all of this, you still need to buy, install and operate a back-up gas-fired plant and continue burning about 90% of the same fuel, generating nearly the same pollutants and CO2 as if the windmill was not even there and producing no electricity. Wind power will most likely never recover the energy it took to build it and with no measurable decrease in CO2 production.

Alex makes the economic, environmental, and humanitarian case that fossil-fueled electricity is the best option for humanity and can be done with little impact on the environment. The only viable alternatives are nuclear and hydro. But again, the big E Environmentalists are dead set against those too. But ask yourself, why would any environmentalist be against them? Because they don't want humankind to grow and prosper and further impinge on their Gaia Earth goddess. Not only does Alex see energy as the base of wealth and a good life in the industrialized and industrializing countries, but he also believes that it is our moral duty to make it available and affordable for the billions of people who today have none.

Today, coal is the fastest and cheapest way to get the most electricity to the billions of poor people around the world who have none. They desperately need it to improve their quality of life, extend it, and use it to kick-start their advancements in agriculture and industry. He says that we need to look at both sides of the equation. These are the tangible benefits to humanity, versus the costs, in money and lives, of doing nothing, other than preaching save the planet as people needlessly die. And why? Why must we have all this misery and death? If you listen to their words, these druids of nature give you a definite answer. They tell us straight forward there are too many people in the world.

A clean, healthy environment is one of the many benefits of modern fossil power plants because we have the technology, the capital, and the will to do it. This is in sharp contrast to the big E Environmentalists who say we must do nothing to unbalance nature's perfect state, which has become a new religion to these E-Environmentalists. So, to them, it's like the spiked tree; if poor people have to suffer and die, that's an acceptable price because their goals are noble and their cause righteous.

If you are interested in a clean environment, clean air, and clean water, you must have noticed that very few places have naturally occurring pure water and clean environments. Most of the "natural" water must be filtered, processed, and treated by electrically powered machinery to make it safe to drink. And then you need the pipelines and pumping stations to get it from where it is to where it's treated, and then to where it's needed. Then more pumps, pipes, and electricity to get the wastewater to the treatment plants before returning it into the natural cycle. Clean water doesn't usually come from nature; it comes with work, materials and energy. While the E Environmentalists make nature sounds like a 19th-century romantic and poetical phrase, it's devoid of any substance or thought. Instead, Alex sees it as an opportunity for humanity to improve the quality of life for the most people possible.

Imagine living a mere 150 years ago, when we were producing little to zero CO2, what was the day-to-day experience of humanity. The streets were full of smells and infections caused by human and animal waste. Plant and animal parts rotted in pits or were fed to pigs and poultry. People in their log cabins froze in the winter and sweltered in the summer heat. Drawing water from a well, by hand, sounds eco-friendly, but who knows what dead animals had fallen in there. How many people got sick and died from eating spoiled foods due to a lack of refrigeration and proper preservation? Life expectancy, one hundred years ago, was half of what it is today. If this is your picture of Gaia, I want no part of it. If I did, all I would need to do is move to any underdeveloped country.

Alex takes issue with the pessimistic minimalists who have been decrying that we will run out of fossil fuels. These are the same people, with the same mindset, who told us in the 1960 and 1970s that humankind had already exhausted the planet's resources. It didn't happen then, and it won't happen now! Especially when we have the energy, the will, and the technology to find and extract more fossil fuels, keeping us stocked for centuries, even millennia.

Put *The Moral Case for Fossil Fuels,* number one on your priority list.

10.2 Bjorn Lomborg:[306] Bjorn[307] was an undergraduate at the University of Georgia who earned an M.A. degree in political science at the University of Aarhus in 1991, and a Ph.D. degree in political science at the University of Copenhagen in 1994. Perhaps he is best known for his book *The Skeptical Environmentalist*" [308] and his many YouTube lectures. At times Bjorn earns the ire of skeptical scientists for being a firm believer that human-caused climate change is real and meaningful. But he keeps it within the bounds of rationality. More importantly, he has a keen method of putting it into a measured perspective. For example, how high will the ocean levels really rise? One foot—we can fix that problem at the country

level or the state level in a much cheaper and humane way than spending trillions on the elusive and debatable CO_2 alarm. His goals are simple and straight forward:
First of all, fix the immediate consequence of the problem instead of chasing after grandiose and impossible solutions. Secondly, look at both sides of the benefits/liability equation. For example, if 2,000 people are dying in Paris because of the heat increase, perhaps 20,000 fewer people will die in Normandy from the damaging cold. In this case, both have essentially the same and affordable solution: buy air conditioners for the poor in Paris and heaters for the people of Normandy at a lower cost and higher benefit for all. A straightforward fact has been hidden from the general public: cold climates kill ten times more people than hot climates, maybe even a hundred times.

Don't overdramatize danger in either the extent or the immediacy of time. Alarmists point to the risks of increasing hurricanes and use the damage cost to show it rising to the ceiling. That's a bogus comparison! A hundred years ago, a category five hurricane could have blown through Miami with minimal cost consequences. Why? Because back then, Miami was little more than a two-horse town, a few barns, and some shacks. But today there are millions of people, each trying to get the best locations and best buildings, near the beaches and spending millions on buying homes.

Bjorn demands that climate scientists get their facts and projections straight. For example, if the ocean levels rose seven inches in the last one hundred years, show me the data that in the next twenty, fifty, or a thousand years, it will be another foot or five feet higher. The Netherlands solved the problem of their rising sea level 200 years ago with their canals and levies. They were affordable and doable then and are a thing of beauty today. If a one-foot rise comes to New Orleans and Miami, they can solve the problem at the county, city, or state level the same way that the Netherlands did and let human ingenuity turn this problem into an

> **Author's note:**
> Here we see a totally different response than we saw in the Yale survey, 8.3 "trusted sources" where we saw a much higher ranking of climate change. The only conclusion that we can draw at this point seems to be that such surveys need an in-depth review and should not simply be taken on face value.

asset.

Bjorn also established the "Copenhagen Consensus," an organization that seeks to prioritize which of the world's problems impact the most people. Then prioritize them so they can be solved at the least possible costs and doing the most good for humanity. According to his studies, global warming is hardly the world's biggest problem. When people were asked to rank the top 20 priorities for the President, they focused on jobs, education, and health. Climate change came on the 19th.

Also, with their outreach program "The World We Want," the UN already has asked what the rest of the world thinks. More than 4-million people from every nation say the top priorities are better education and health care, less corruption, more jobs, and affordable food. At the very last place, as priority number 17 comes global warming. [3] Bjorn then makes the bold statement for us to soberly contemplate: "DO WE SAVE ONE PERSON FOR $10,000 OR 10 FOR $100? ECONOMISTS SHOULD NOT MAKE THIS DECISION, AND … SHOULD NOT RULE THE WORLD."[309]

If you genuinely care for humanity, please read his book,[310] *The Skeptical Environmentalist,* and take it from there.

3 https://nationalpost.com/opinion/bjorn-lomborg-global-warming-is-hardly-the-worlds-biggest-problem
https://www.ozy.com/provocateurs/bjorn-lomborg-and-the-list-that-could-save-the-world/60266/

~ 7 ~

ETHICS, SOCIAL, EDUCATION, AND POLITICS

Rated ESS: Over 21, Emotionally and Socially Secure

7.1 INTRODUCTION

Background: In Chapters 1-5, we examined the science of climate change. Basic questions were asked, and responses provided. We learned what causes weather and climate change and which factors are more consequential than others. We learned which factors can and can't be controlled by human activities. Just as importantly, we determined which events we can ignore because we can't control them, but we must prepare for their consequences. In Chapter 6, we delved into controversial subjects and exposed ourselves to the frailties and follies of humankind. But hopefully, we came away with a fair amount of self-deprecating humor and a lot of humility.

You may ask, why do we even talk about "humility" here and now? Because the societal pressures of our evolving "morality" are replacing grace and charity with hubris and anger. As a result, we see growing rifts, left vs. right, black vs. white, liberal vs. conservative, consensus vs. denier, etc. Team A tells us that we must take drastic actions on climate change to save the planet. Team A has a desperate need: "We must save humanity from human-caused climate change." But how was this "desperate need" created, especially in our wealthy industrialized and highly educated countries? Equally important, why is Team B refusing to comply? And why must we give the politicians the trillions of dollars they are demanding? These vast sums would destroy our economy and culture, and for what? To alleviate the fears and anxieties perpetuated by Team A and rammed upon the unsuspecting and the uninformed public by their press/media acolytes? They admonish those of us who refuse to comply. They tell us we must be greedy. They tell us we must be Republicans, and we must be slaves of the oil companies. Team B is accused of callousness, not caring about people, and not caring about the future of the planet. Team B is evil and needs to be destroyed!

Cross-generational values. Growing up in a small village, high in the Gran Sasso mountainside in post-World War II Italy, we faced many social and economic challenges. On several occasions, my family faced the unasked question, do we share two or three eggs with our neighbor who had none? One day, I asked my grandfather what we should do. "Silly boy," he remarked, "We give them a few eggs, and we do it with humility."

When I asked why again, he replied, "Silly boy, someday you will be in need. Then, on that day, you can accept your neighbor's gift with pride." We scrambled the remaining eggs, and our family shared the same frittata. I've been very fortunate in my life, never to have experienced the second part of that deal. But Hurricane Dorian reminded me how quickly fortunes could change. It showed me how fragile our businesses, homes, jobs, financial status, and our health and lives are. One thing I know for sure is that it's much harder to give with humility than accept with pride. I hope not to fall short on my grandfather's grace if I'm ever disadvantaged in such a situation.

Cultural values and structures. In this chapter, we take a deep dive into our societal values and structures and expose ourselves to the laws of the unintended consequences and outright deceptions. Our decisions and actions may well be a result of a well-thought-out plan. But all too often we are motivated by greed, personal aggrandizement, or just plain laziness and folly. Here we will discuss how climate change is being used and abused by politicians, virtue-signaled by social engineers, and monetized by opportunists. It's rated ESS for a reason, so be Emotionally and Socially

Secure and proceed with caution.

If in reading any one of these articles, you feel like you want to stop reading it because it upsets you or makes you feel guilty or just frustrated and sad, it doesn't! Instead, imagine how hard, how tiring it is for a little chick or duckling to break free from the eggshell. But how happy they then are to be free, alive, running around, and just being very cute. Here are the topics we will discuss in this Chapter.

~ The case for and against environmental activism
~ Social injustice, the environment, and socio-economic theft
~ The limits of sanity
~ Fraud and university research grants
~ Tyranny
~ The false promise of good intentions
~ The death of Socrates and education
~ Commentarii De Bello Civili.

The case for and against environmental activism

Part 1, A personal journey.[311]

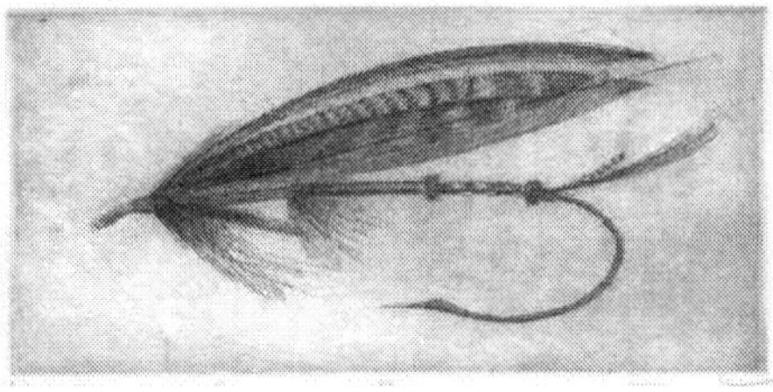

In 1976, after spending half a decade in the confined and polluted environments of France, England, and Italy, I looked forward to resettling my family near Schenectady, New York. There I planned to resume my weekend fishing trips to the pristine Adirondacks, a mere ninety-minute drive away. I had missed those days, and as soon as we settled in our new home, I jumped into my Pinto station wagon and headed north. Breathing in the cold, crisp autumn breeze was exhilarating. I headed to my favorite fishing spot, the confluence of the Indian River, and the Hudson River in the Wilderness section of the Adirondacks. As I walked through the underbrush and briers and fording little streams here and there, something changed, but I could not put my finger on it. I shook it off and forged ahead, knowing all the while that in late August, the waters would be low and warm. I was prepared for the lack of trout action but looking forward to the fast and furious smallmouth bass.

Just as I reached the two rivers, I heard the familiar alarm going off, signaling that the Indian River reservoir was going to release water into the Indian River. They did this regularly to replenish the Hudson River so that the downstream part would have enough water to keep it navigable. So, I just laid back on a mossy embankment and waited for the two to three hours it would take for the surge of water and the flood of kayakers to swoop down. I soon fell into a lazy nap but was suddenly awakened by the yelling and screeching of the kayakers as they rode the tidal storm. Then I quietly went back to sleep as they flashed out of my hearing range. As daylight was waning, I decided to pitch my tent, have a quick dinner, and get set for the night. After nearly seven years, I looked forward to glorious dawn with me and the majestic bald eagles fishing in the early morning light. I slept in peace to the tune of the chirping crickets, honking frogs, and dozens of other sounds from the ancient forest around me. I fell into a deep, relaxing, and undreaming slumber.

At first light,[312] I awoke to the sounds of fishermen already in the river. They were all joy, cackling about the eagles swooping through the mist into the river and catching fish. I could hear their cameras clicking furiously and wished that I had brought my camera too. After a quick breakfast of bread and cheese, I joined the three fishermen, having a great time catching largemouth bass. Upon speaking with them, I learned how the smallmouth bass had disappeared in the last few years and how the warmer water bigmouth bass had moved in along with pickerel and panfish. After a few hours of fishing, we all went back to my campsite, where we spit-roasted the fish we had caught, along with some wild mushrooms I had picked on the way back to camp.

What an excellent lunch when combined with the beer they brought, along with a few select cigars. Then they started talking about how things had changed in the preceding few years. They were especially worried about the acid rains, caused by the pollution coming in from Indiana and Ohio. One of them was a real naturalist who had joined the newly formed Mohawk Valley chapter of the Sierra Club to fight the pollution that's killing the Adirondacks. As the beer flowed freely and the cigars went up in smoke, I started talking about the work we were doing to solve this problem. Some of our active projects were how to reduce the pollutants from coal-fired plants. This included coal gasification, fluidized beds, scrubbers, electrostatic precipitators, etc. We were also redesigning the gas turbines to reduce the sulfur dioxides and nitric oxides that caused the "acid rains," at which point they encouraged me to join them and invited me to the next meeting of the Mohawk Valley Sierra Club.

The lions' den. Several weeks later, as I walked into the meeting hall, the signs and posters were intimidating. They all had an angry theme, some proclaiming a battle against the enemies of the environment, others "Death to the Earth killers;" "Shut down the polluters;" "Stop all coal and nuclear power plants," etc. Once the meeting started, several speakers described the demonstrations they had done, the events they had planned, and the companies targeted for protests and boycotts. Many members began shouting and howling to do whatever's necessary because their cause was just and righteous.

About an hour later, my Hudson River friend introduced me as an engineer working to address these ecological problems. I started to talk about the technology that was already available to reduce pollution in the air. I touched on the newer technologies to reduce the NO_X and SO_x. I spoke about improving plant efficiencies and saving the companies money so they could afford these pollution control devices. I told them about the substantial pollution reductions achieved in London in just a few years.

Soon a few started to shout me down, while a few others wanted to hear me out. I believed we would make faster progress if the Club pushed for pollution reduction instead of shutting the power plants down. There was some back and forth, and it looked like progress was made when one of the more radical members yelled out, "What about the nukes?" Keep in mind this was two years before Three Mile Island. At this time, there had been no significant nuclear accidents anywhere in the world. This was a time when nations were struggling to recover from the oil embargo, a time when the concern of the West was how Russia and Libya would soon control Western Europe, becoming dependent on their new gas pipelines. Many of us working in the field were of the mindset that only nuclear power could save us and get us off our limited supply of oil and gas.

I never saw it coming. I was immediately condemned as a spy, a plant for the coal and nuclear industry. They shouted me down. Several members of the executive board suggested that I leave immediately for my safety, at which point my Hudson River friend escorted me out of the building and suggested I forget the whole thing.

So here we are now, five decades later, and what have we learned?

- The protesters became more sophisticated, taking their fights off the street. Using highly paid lawyers and lobbyists, they moved their protests to the offices and backrooms of Capitol Hill.
- All too sadly, when it comes to the dogma of the environment or any other "holy cause," sanity, reason, facts, and logic do not amount to a hill of beans when pitted against the power of raw emotions.
- Scientific facts, technical data, and logical constructs are no defense against an angry, dogmatic movement.
- Dogmatic leaders have the mindset that, if you're not with us, then you're against us. Therefore, they have the "duty" to destroy opponents, professionally, financially, socially. Their accusation is, you have no right to exist and no reason to dispute our way of thinking.
- The more socially/politically skilled priests of the religion of their righteous causes may say that while our intentions are OK, we are misguided and need serious sociological and psychological reorientation.
- Cunning politicians have formed alliances with the press and cause advocates to harvest favorable coverage and votes.
- Shrewd businesspeople have capitalized on these causes, coming up with strategies and tactics to monetize the movement. They bask in their newfound wealth while John and Jane Doe will bear the burden of higher taxes and fees and reduced standards of living for the

general public.

Part 2, Patrick Moore and The Greenpeace Movement:

Patrick is an exciting and complex individual. In the early 1970s, he first gained world attention when Russian whalers fired harpoons over his head to kill a sperm whale he was defending. His swash-buckling actions later brought him into conflict with the U.S. military attempting to stop hydrogen bomb testing in the Pacific Ocean. A few years later, his rubber boat, named "Rainboat Warrior," was sunk by the French Navy when he interfered with their planned nuclear testing near New Zealand. There are claims and counterclaims whether he was one of the founding members of Greenpeace in the late 1970s or not. However, there's no argument that for years, he was involved in many internal policy decisions with Greenpeace. One fact remains indisputable; he was an integral insider in the organization and served as president of the Canadian chapter for nine years.

> Check out this excerpt from an article in Whatsupwiththat titled **"Greenpeace Claims Immunity from Lawsuits Because Its Claims Are 'Hyperbole'"**
>
> "A former member of Greenpeace's Board of Directors, Kenny Bruno, last year tweeted,
> ***'I don't want to abolish Exxon. I simply want to reduce it to the size where I can drag it into the bathroom and drown it in the bathtub.'***
>
> If it wasn't already abundantly obvious, these latest developments just go to show how much credulity Greenpeace has."

In 1986 he parted company with Greenpeace over issues of policy and tactics. He became involved in several enterprises and, to this day, remains a staunch and media-savvy public speaker against what he claims are the illegitimate policies of Greenpeace and a critic of their goals and tactics. He has written several books; *Confessions of a Greenpeace Dropout* and *The Sensible Environmentalist.* Patrick Moore calls global climate change the "*most difficult issue facing the scientific community today in terms of being able to predict with any accuracy what's going to happen.*" In 2006, he wrote to the Royal Society[313] arguing there was "no scientific proof" that humankind was causing global climate change and believed that it had "a much better correlation with changes in solar activity than CO2 levels."[314] He was also a staunch opponent of nuclear power, but for decades now, he has become an avid supporter. In the adjacent box, we see a recent summary of their initiatives and positions. Read the entire article by Katie Brown from March 3, 2017.[315]

In many ways, Patrick and I are cut from the same cloth—avid and dedicated to a healthy and vibrant environment. I also have to take my hat off to Patrick because he had the dedication and courage to do battle with the big-E Environmentalists, whereas I retreated from that battlefield long ago and am now trying to make up for the lost time.

7.2 ECO-MADNESS

The Boeing 737 max. Here we're going to discuss a startling example of the clinical link between environmental activism and the universal law of unintended consequence. Here we remind ourselves that just because our cause is just, our goals are noble and virtuous, our commitment is unbounded, and our efforts are unrelenting; it doesn't mean we are protected from unforced errors and tragic outcomes.

- We start with an article from the New York Post, By Miranda Devine, October 23, 2019[316], with the headline; *"Eco madness may be reason for disastrous Boeing 737 MAX safety issues."*

- It then follows up with: "*No one has said it explicitly yet, but this relentless pressure to reduce emissions appears to have been a significant factor in the disastrous safety failures of the Boeing 737 MAX aircraft, which resulted in two fatal crashes in the past year, claiming 346 lives.*"

It's a very comprehensive article, and I hope you read it. But let me give you the cliff notes version of this tragedy by traveling back in time to demonstrate the consequences of good intentions based on poor information.

- On 10 March 2019, Ethiopian Airline Boeing 737 max took off, but within a few minutes, the aircraft went out of control, nosediving to earth, killing 157 peoples.

- 5 Months earlier, in Indonesia, a Lion Air 737 max crashed into the sea during takeoff, killing all 187 persons on board. And like the first crash, a new flight computer program took control of the aircraft away from the pilots and drove them nose-first into the earth.
- This computer software was needed to prevent a "stall" during normal takeoffs. This unique software was required to correct for the aerodynamic problems of the plane that resulted from re-engining it with a bigger engine.
- Why did the plane need newer and more powerful engines? Because these more modern engines reduced fuel consumption, thereby increasing airline profits.
- But, just as importantly, as a consequence of the Paris Climate Change agreement, airlines were mandated to reduce the CO_2 emissions or pay a hefty "carbon tax," thereby wiping out those increased profit dollars.
- On top of that, airline passengers, Boeing stock owners, and the media/press were all demanding planes to become more eco-friendly.
- As clearly stated in the article, "*The eco-imperative for Boeing was more than woke posturing. Its customers, the airlines, were demanding better environmental performance because of regulations and mounting threats from climate-conscious institutional investors." Biofuels and electric planes aren't yet viable, so fuel efficiency was the only option."*
- *"The decarbonization imperative for Boeing was clear."* The new 737 max allowed Boeing, American, and other major airlines to market its 14 percent reductions in CO_2 emissions.
- The sales went through the roof. Boeing could not build and ship them fast enough. Moreover, it regained the market lead from Airbus, who had launched a similar eco-friendly aircraft a few years earlier, but not as impressive as Boeing's 14 percent CO_2 reduction.
- On March 13, 2019, the FAA grounded the aircraft. Boeing has been scrambling to minimize the damage ever since, but it remains grounded till today (February 25, 2020).

Let's play, "pin the tail on the donkey!"

Boeing: It's easy to note that Boeing made some unfortunate technical and programmatic and strategic mistakes that will cost them dearly, with even the potential for bankruptcy. Strategically, who would not agree that it was the right decision? After all, they were responding to their clients, the airlines demanding CO2 reductions. On this basis, we should clear them from any moral or criminal responsibilities, unless other information will be found during the ongoing investigation.

What about the airlines? They, too, will pay dearly for their actions and decisions, but like Boeing, we should also clear them of any moral or criminal guilt.

How about the UN's International Civil Aviation Organization, do they bear or share in the guilt? After all, they made it impossible for their aircraft to land on hundreds of airports around the world if the planes did not meet the new CO2 guidelines.

What share of our moral outrage do we heap on the IPCC/NASA/NOAA/climate activists and all the CO2 industrial climate change industry, for so purposely misleading the public of the evils of CO2 and the resultant fears and hysteria?

What about the media, the press, the Hollywood elites, the town/country/city school board committees, for indoctrinating our children about the false dangers of CO2?

What about our schoolteachers, who perpetuate and tolerate the false "science" of climate change and the uninformed or uninvolved parents who ignore or tolerate the false narrative?

But don't worry; there's enough blame to go around.

But wait, there's more. In chapters 1-6, we provided the scientific theory, the data, results from real-world measurements and experiences and experiments to prove that CO2 is no danger to any living thing. In fact, we went on to show that more and more CO2 will be beneficial for the entire Earth ecosystem. In Chapter 6 and the remaining of this Chapter 7, we will get into a few other economic, social, and societal factors and dangers presented to us by thy CO2 myth.

Above we saw an example of the law of unintended consequences on full display. And while there are many and less dramatic examples, there's one looming black storm on the horizon I want to give you a heads-up. I'm talking about the "The Green New Deal" we discussed in Chapter 6.9 above. If this "Deal" is adopted, the consequences will be so punishing on our country and our society that it will make the above Boeing example a mere whisper in the wind. In the "Deal," it won't be just a few major, faceless corporations that will suffer the consequences; it will be all of us in the US. It would also send it's punishing reverberations to every country and every person on this planet.

Read it a second time and turn your knowledge into an active verb.

7.3 SOCIAL INJUSTICE, THE ENVIRONMENT, AND SOCIO-ECONOMIC THEFT

Open your heart and your brain. Look at this photo, 7.3.1.[317] Look at it again, and again. Don't be lazy, don't be squeamish; look at each face; each has his or her unique gift from nature and God. I want you to view and think and reflect because this is my reference image as I'm writing this book. It's also the image I want you to think about after you read the next alarming headline about CO2. Or the next time your well-intentioned do-gooder friend,

7.3.1

politician, or overly educated moron pontificates about saving the planet with their green energy plan. Think of this and countless similar images the next time you're going to produce your climate change poster. Because they are already suffering and dying by the tens-of-thousands because of our collective hubris and misguided ignorance and "good intentions." In this short op-ed, I will draw your attention to the connection between this photo and why we need to rethink our views and actions regarding climate change.

Despite the many success we have made in the U.S. and other developed countries in reducing pollution, it will continue unabated for years worldwide. In many cases, it will get worse, maybe even for decades to come. That may be good for humanity in the long run. Was that heresy I just spoke? Am I now an enemy of the planet just as the Mohawk Valley Sierra Club accused me of being?

No way! First and foremost, I am a lover of humanity, and right alongside that, I'm a lover of nature. This is a false either-or decision, as many would have you believe. They are compatible and harmonious. But the manipulative press, politicians, and opportunists will continue to conflate and confuse pollution with CO_2. Why? Because **pollution IS always harmful** to the planet and for humanity. But as we demonstrated, the increased CO_2 in the past century has been a gift for the earth and humanity. We have documented scientific facts in this book, proving that CO_2 is not only useful but essential for life. We have presented data that confirms that more CO_2 is better for all life than too little CO_2!

Why have we been conditioned, like Pavlov's dogs, to confuse CO_2 with pollution? That's the question we will answer in this section. What follows may not all be scientifically proven facts backed by 100%-reliable data. They are my observations based on my general knowledge accumulated over the decades of my life. I now want to share them with those of you who have not yet completed your journey.

We demonstrated how, in the USA and other developed countries, we have the affluent class being subsidized for their good intentions by the working middle class. That is an immediate outrage, but it's far worse than that in third world countries. Let's look at the underdeveloped and developing countries and see how they, too, are exploiting the unfortunate and starving people around the world. "This is outrageous, preposterous, totally fake news," you might say. "Our wealthy, socially responsible people are generous with their money and their time. They are investing in climate change practices, policies, and products like recycling and banning plastic straws. They are good people!" But like an excellent surgeon or a forensic coroner, we are going to take out our sharp scalpel and see what's going on beneath the veneer presented to us by the self-promoting media, grant recipients, politicians, and activists.

The green delusion: To start with, let's draw a simple distinction between these two societies. For we, in the developed world, can afford to buy the backup power plants needed for our solar and wind electrical plants. Furthermore, we have the means to pay the continuing rising premium rates for this electrical generation. This allows us to enjoy these privileges for ourselves and our children and still have a cleaner environment at a price we can afford.

But let's look at the developing countries around the world and especially the weak ones. There the lives of hundreds of millions, maybe billions, of people are not so good. Each day they live on a knife's edge for their very subsistence. They have little food because they cannot afford the cost of tractors or fuel to power them, or fertilizers or the pumps for water and water treatment systems to supercharge their agriculture as we can. Adding to their plight is the lack of electricity needed for preservation, sterilization, refrigeration, transportation, and storage of the little food they have. Many get sick and die because of food spoilage.

To make matters worse, they don't have the electricity for clean water to drink, clean, or wash their clothes or dishes. They lack medicines and all the other blessings provided to us by affordable and reliable electrical power from fossil and nuclear plants. In the USA, life expectancy for women is nearly eighty-seven years old. In contrast, in many places such as Africa, South America, or Asia, women would be lucky to reach fifty-five.[318] They live in misery and die at a young age.

In underdeveloped countries, people do not have access to technologies to reduce pollution and alternatives to minimize CO2. Most likely, many do not even know what technologies are available or affordable and which to prioritize. When their country's UN representatives return from the UN conference, they repeat to their less educated people about the exotic beauty of green technology. They excitedly talk about how they don't need to spend their precious little money on expensive fuel costs and, on top of that, how the green electrical plants cost much less to install and operate and have zero pollution. So, when they get financial grants or near zero-interest loans from the World Development Bank, they will be told that they must use that money only for "green technologies."

But all too soon, they are faced with the fact that none of these "free green energies" can be used for more than a few hours a day. If they have already started the construction on their coal-fired plants, they are told to shut it down. Or even if they have not, the policymakers who were misled find themselves in a pickle. They had built up the expectations of their general population, and now they can deliver neither coal nor green energy. Maybe some commissions were already skimmed by their "upper/ruling class." What are these local rulers/decision-makers to do now? The sad answer is nothing good can come out of it. No matter what they do or not do, their poor people will continue to suffer the most because they won't get the electricity they need to climb out of their poverty and depressive existence. But rest assured, the manufacturers of these "green machines" in the developed countries, who built and sold the green generation equipment, got paid their full prices, and probably before it was even shipped.

<u>A sad and undeniable fact:</u> First and foremost, how dare we, in the lucky, affluent, and long-living comfortable world, be so quick to criticize the people of the underdeveloped world for trying to get some electric energy at a price *they* can afford? Or for criticizing them for polluting their environment with their cheaper and "dirtier" coal power sources. Contrast this hungry world with the world of the "caring savants" and "priests of climate change." Living in their lusty villas of Carmel, California, or the fashionable beaches of San Trope, France.[319] And all the while, sipping chilled chardonnay, jet-setting to Monaco, and yachting all over the world to preach to these unfortunates on why they need to reduce their "carbon footprint."

While on the sub-Saharan desert edge, the poorest of the poor are praying they can get some scraps to live another day. To "Les Misérables" all over the world, they extoll the virtue of reducing CO2 to save the planet when they are struggling to stay alive one more day. At the same time, these Hollywood whores continue to waste hundreds of billions of dollars each year trying to control the narrative that CO2 may someday cause some kind of harm to somebody. All the while, they guzzle fossil fuels in their hundred-foot yachts, 20,000 square-foot villas, and private planes.

A simple, humanitarian solution: Why don't we take some of that same CO2-reducing wasted money and grant it to the poor and starving people in these troubled countries? Let them use that money to install the cheapest energy sources, like coal-fired plants. Then they can reduce their misery, hunger, and live longer! Hell, here is a simple fact, and as John Adams told us, "Facts are a stubborn thing:"

- There is zero evidence that CO2 is harming us or will do so for centuries to come, if ever. Quite the contrary. The increased CO2 we experienced in the last several/warming decades are:
    - Greening the planet,
    - Increasing agricultural yields per acre,
    - Increasing the amount of arable land and food supply.
- There is increasing scientific evidence that in the next thirty to fifty years, the planet might experience a significant cooling period. As discussed in the publication *Investor Business Daily*,[320] we are told that we may already be at the doorstep of this global cooling.
- The cooling could last for decades, which would reduce the global food supply 20 percent or more.
- Consequently, who would be the first to suffer and die? Certainly not Mr. Country Club or Mr. Hollywood!
- Look at the wealth/income distribution by counties in 7.3.2.[321] Too many people are not aware of the many hundreds of millions of people

who are kept alive each day because of the overabundance of food production we have today in our developed countries.

Lastly, I find it astounding how naïve we are in our own pampered, advanced, industrial nations, especially the intelligent and well educated among us. Here we have many educated and moral people profiting from this global warming scare at the expense of the least fortunate among us.[322] I don't claim they do this out of hubris or arrogance. I dare say most of them are not remotely aware of the harm and exploitation they are perpetrating. Let's give them the full benefit of the doubt. Let's say they are doing it out of a well-intentioned effort to save the planet with factual, technical, and financial ignorance. No doubt, many of these people are championing this cause out of pure altruism. OK, that's good. And some are doing it out of a higher sense of moral principle to elevate their self-esteem and moral authority and raise their social status. And that's fine too if it causes no harm to humanity.

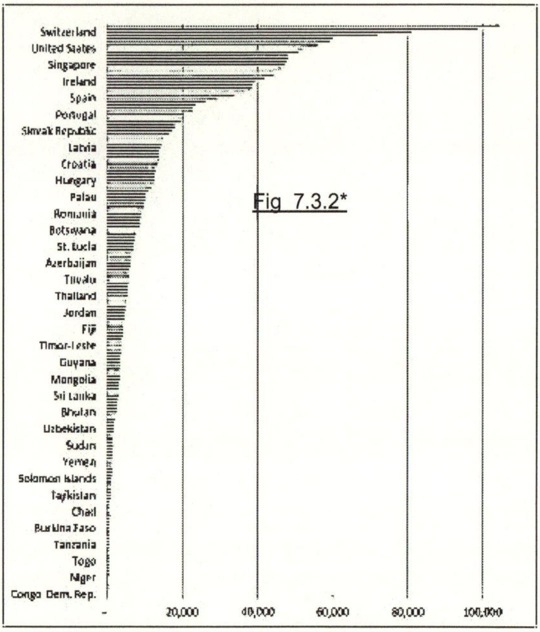

Fig 7.3.2*

A straightforward example of what we might do in the USA: first, the wealthy have the resources to install solar panels on their roof, thinking this will reduce their carbon footprint. It also allows them to display their moral superiority to their friends and neighbors. But then they are eager to get their money back by a tax rebate and a discount on their electrical consumption from their utilities. What they are probably not aware of is that these rebates and discounts are being paid by the people who can't afford to pay the costs of the solar panels and their installation. Then they have to fund the tax rebates to the wealthy who can afford them and pay the higher electric rates to subsidize the wealthy who can. I call this "social-economic theft."

Why am I writing this book? You now have a clear answer. It's a personal appeal to those of you who are intellectually curious, honest, and caring enough to challenge yourselves. I ask you to dig deeper into the real science of climate change. Understand more fully the economic, social, and moral consequences of what we have been doing, and make a rapid and decisive pivot. You can make a difference.

Thank you!

7. 4 THE LIMITS OF SANITY:

Preventive Environmental War: Below are a few select sections from the Abstract, Introduction, and Conclusion of a twenty-four-page "scholarly paper" provided by academia.edu, an online subscription service. The article is titled "Preventive Environmental War," by Adam Betz.[323] We'll take a few sentences so you can get the direction it's headed.

"Abstract:
This paper argues that there is a just cause for war to prevent the future hazards of anthropogenic climate change even if, because of the Non-Identity Problem, that cause is not grounded in the rights of future generations. The evidential demands for justifying preventive military action to forestall climate change have been met, as a majority of climate scientists affirm that climate change is underway and is likely to become seriously hazardous for future generations. Security forecasters also regard it as a likely threat to international stability."

Author's note: Reread it; does it say that?

"Introduction:

Preemptive war is commonly distinguished from preventive war in that the former aims to thwart a temporally imminent threat, but the latter aims to thwart a non-imminent, perceived future threat. When just war theorists discuss preventive war, they typically have in mind military action aimed at forestalling a perceived, non-imminent future threat of a kinetic or conventional armed attack. These perceived threats come paradigmatically from terrorist groups, whose unpredictability renders standard defensive responses less effective, as well as 'rogue states' whose governments demonstrate contempt for international law, or which would be especially dangerous if they acquired weapons of mass destruction. Among the Bush Administration's stated justifications for the Iraq War, for instance, was the claim that waging war now would spare the United States, and its allies, from facing a graver threat or waging a bloodier war in the future.[324] *Whatever the merits of this argument with respect to the Iraq war in particular, the general principle to which it appealed might, on rare occasions, be a sound one: it is better to prevent likely future threats before they materialize. For once they have materialized, it will be much more difficult, costlier, or even impossible to defeat them."*

"Conclusion:
The effects of climate change wrought by human emissions of GHG since the Industrial Revolution has already been felt around the world, especially in poorer regions: flooding in Bangladesh, Droughts in Sub-Saharan Africa and the Middle East, and 2017's succession of powerful hurricanes throughout the Caribbean and Gulf of Mexico may be only the tip of the (rapidly melting) iceberg. The IPCC and security futurologists are predicting more of the same and worse in the coming decades, with potential global catastrophes looming in the next few centuries."

Author's perspective: Please reread these few sentences and give them time to sink in. Better yet, get the full paper and draw your conclusions. Also, as I write this, it's Earth Day. In the Introduction of this book, "Overview," we read that many of us think that the Earth has never been in a better place. So, for Earth Day, why not celebrate and take some joy and pleasure for the achievements being made and prepare ourselves for the additional work that we have left? Instead, here we have a "scholarly paper" saying that we should start to discuss, maybe even start planning for a preemptive war against countries that throw too much human-made CO2 in the air. Really? Is there a boundary of sanity when it comes to climate change, or do we put on our white sneakers and just drink the cool-aid?

Mr. Betz is not alone. Moreover, who are the world's most severe polluters? Who's the poster child for the "enemy of the environment"? It's China, India, and Pakistan, and they are all nuclear powers. But perhaps most worrisome is that in addition to Mr. Betz, many intelligent and educated people support this line of thought. For them, I have a simple question; what the hell are you guys thinking? [325]

In pages 20-22 he lists numerous references with titles such as:

- Broome, J. (2012). *Climate Matters: Ethics in a Warming World* (New York: Norton).[326]
- Buchanan, A. (2007) "Justifying Preventive War." In H. Shue and D. Rodin (Eds.), *Preemption: Military Action and Moral Justification*, pp. 126-142 (Oxford: Oxford University Press).
- Coady, C.A.J. (2013) "Preventive Violence: War, Terrorism, and Humanitarian Intervention." In D. Chatterjee (Ed.), *The Ethics of Preventive War*, pp. 189-213 (Cambridge: Cambridge University Press).
- Kaempf, S. "The Ethics of Soft War on Today's Mediatized Battlespaces." In M. Gross and T. Meisels (Eds.) *Soft War: The Ethics of Unarmed Conflict*, pp. 104-118 (Cambridge: Cambridge University Press).
- Plus 52 more of the same.

Then on pages 23-24, there are several endnotes, such as:

- "For an interesting historical discussion which makes a compelling case that preventive war justifications and strategic thinking were common among U.S. leaders in World War II, the Cold War, and in the face of the North Korean threat during the Clinton Administration, see Trachtenberg (2007).
- In his presentation of the consequentialist argument for preventive war, (Walzer 2000: 77) offers a similar condition: "that to fight early, before the balance [of power] shifts in any decisive way,[327] greatly reduce the cost of the defense, while waiting doesn't mean avoiding war… but only fighting on a larger scale and at worse odds." Walzer presents the consequentialism argument without endorsement. His fundamental criticisms of it are taken up and fleshed out further in Rodin 2007.

- Arnold and Bustos (2013: 470) recommend 2001 as the date at which "business organizations that are responsible for substantial CO2 emissions have a moral obligation to be engaged in aggressive, proactive measures to abate their CO2 emissions." They regard this is a conservative timeline, as there was arguably decisive scientific evidence of anthropogenic climate change as early as 1988.
- And 20 more such notes.

Remember the TV show *Dallas* from back in the 1970s and the character J. R. Ewing in particular? His position was always crystal clear; "Once you get past that pesky ethics thing, life is so much easier." We'll end it here and pray for sanity.

7.5 FRAUD AND UNIVERSITY RESEARCH GRANTS

Duke University: Today, in the morning headlines, one item screamed out at me. "*Duke University, one of the most prestigious universities in the country, was fined $112 million for scientific research misconduct.*"[328] Of course, I immediately ran some checks to confirm the integrity of the article. But also, to see if this was a one-off or just one of many. Brief research showed that the problem has been pervasive for decades and on an increasing trend since the 1980s.[329] The misconduct can be as dramatic as the outright fraud of data or findings. They can also be as subtle as shading the conclusions to get a little more dramatic pop in the media.

In Chapter 5, we discussed just how big the climate change research industry is. We saw that it has been on an accelerating pace, reaching nearly $20 billion in 2019. But this is only a small portion of the total research grants allocated by the U.S. government to science. Unfortunately, human nature being what it is, large sums of money will often draw the seedy and greedy fringes with their elastic values. Other evidence of concern is that there has been an increasing number of peer-reviewed published papers that have been withdrawn. This trend is exposing a flaw in the peer-review process. Here are some additional sources where the reader may choose to see the full extent of this growing problem, both the legal and ethical implications.

- Christian Science Monitor.[330]
- "Why the epidemic of fraud exists in science today," by Jerry Bergman.[331]
- "False positives: fraud and misconduct are threatening scientific research," by Alok Jha, science correspondent, *The Guardian*, Thursday 13 September 2012 18.12 BS.[332]

Not all experiments work out the way you expect.

<u>The purpose</u> of this short article was simply to make the reader aware of the problem and that it's substantial and growing. We see the increasing concern in the research industry for the need for significant reform. Let's remember that this trend is unrelenting and disturbing.[333]

7.6 TYRANNY:

<u>Who controls the past</u> controls the future: who controls the present controls the past."[334] In the end, is it a warning about the mutability of information? In today's world, the quote reminds us that we need to question the authority of oligarchs continually, that we need to be able to recognize when we are being manipulated, and that the dangers of being manipulated, whether to act or not, can be devastating. Other significant points made: [335]

- *"1984 is a novel of a dark and threatening future, and Big Brother's slogans keep its masses of people under control by use of three-party slogans: "War is peace," "Freedom is slavery," and "Ignorance is strength." That reminds the reader, as Orwell certainly intended it to, of the Nazi party in World War II Germany. The Nazis had a number of party slogans with which it dulled the minds of the people: if someone gives you a slogan to chant, you don't have to think about the implications. You just chant."*

- *"Up until recently, only a few people were able to publish and be widely read. That was certainly true in the mid-20th century: only governments and government-supported businesses had the money to publish textbooks and determine what was in them. At the time, government-sponsored textbooks were just about the only way a high school student could learn anything about the past."*

Who controls information controls the present: Here in the next few pages, we'll briefly discuss the possibility of a third World War, the "war of information?" Our focus, however, will be limited to the "Civil War of information," the battle for the minds and actions and decisions on our own citizens. We'll open the discussion with this last-minute entry, published in the journal Nature, September 4, 2019, titled "Information Gerrymandering and Undemocratic Decisions." The citation is posted below in its entirety with no author's comments of any kind, leaving readers to draw their thoughts, questions, and values.

Key takeaways:[336] An insightful article by K. Kris Hirst, updated June 11, 2019. K. Kris Hirst is an archaeologist with thirty years of field experience. She is the author of The Archaeologist's Book of Quotations, and her work has appeared in Science and Archaeology.[337] Her core points are:

- The novel describes a dystopian future, where a single political party manipulates all citizens.
- Orwell was writing when a minority of people was controlling the information. Moreover, his novel contains references to Nazi Germany.
- The quote still reminds us that it is essential to identify or to know the sources of the information we receive.

Tyranny of information access: I want to emphasize the last bullet. If you're looking for information on climate change, or what's happening in the Middle East, where do you go? Easy question, right? So why are some notable people, including Senators and presidential candidates like Elizabeth Warren of Massachusetts, going after major tech behemoths like Google and Facebook? All the while, there's lots of talk of high-profile people wanting to break up these "information monopolies." While I don't generally subscribe to many of Senator Warren's views on government and the economy, she makes an excellent point here. As you read on, keep in mind that a wise man can learn from a fool; a fool can learn from nobody.[338]

Not a new issue. *US News & World Report* posted an extensive article on June 22, 2016, by Robert Epstein titled, "The new censorship: How did Google become the internet's censor and master manipulator, blocking access to millions of websites?" The article[339] maintains that Google has, at a minimum, nine different blacklists that restrict certain people from accessing some sites, that impact our lives. It does so without any input or oversight by any authority outside of Google itself. But let's give credit where credit is due; Amazon, Reddit, Twitter, Facebook, etc. have been accused of doing the very same thing by banning specific topics and outright blocking certain points of view. That helps shape the political discussions and affecting voting patterns for their desired outcomes. Many web search engines do the same thing; it's just that Google is the biggest bully in town.

https://jloog.com/explore/Reali

The reader is encouraged to seek out the entire *US News* article. Read it carefully and analytically and ponder on the many underlying implications. The article is found on the following link[340] but don't be surprised if it is taken down when you try to access it. So, here are the most likely "blacklists" maintained by Google at the time of publication of this book.

1. The autocomplete blacklist, keys-in on certain words or phrases that might be "offensive or vulgar." But during the 2018 election, it also froze up or shut down search words, like "Ted" was in the search bar as he was the Republican candidate for the U.S. Senate, Ted Cruz, and

thus attempting to influence elections.

2. Google map blacklist: This may be a good list to be on to prevent your property or house from being made visible to all so that you can request to opt-out of this feature.
3. YouTube blacklist: YouTube, owned by Google, allows users to flag "inappropriate words," and it seems most used on political subjects, without any high consistencies. For example, at times, pro-life clips are blocked now and then, but pro-choice never appears to be.
4. Google account blacklist: A few years ago, Google consolidated many of its products and services such as Gmail, Docs, and Wallet into one account, making it a great convenience to many users. But if you somehow violate your "terms of service agreement," which is so complicated, nobody has ever read and understood it, they can and will shut your account down. Then voila! You are locked out of all your documents, emails, and financials. WOW! Now, what are you going to do?
5. Google News blacklist: Suppose you are an avid supporter of a Democratic candidate for president. You go to the library to see what *The New York Times*, *The Washington Post*, and all the other liberal-leaning newspapers are reporting about them over the weekend while you were vacationing on Cape Cod. But the librarian sees you coming, knows what you are looking for, and with superhuman speed, sprints, grabs all the copies of the papers and throws them in the trash can. Well, if you're on this list, this is what Google can do to you, time and time again. Is this a First Amendment issue? You be the judge.
6. Adwords: Or, how to blacklist an entire industry. In May 2016, Google blacklisted an industry for anything to do with "payday" loans. Independent of how you feel about the industry, do they have the right to exercise their "moral authority" and suborn an entire industry to their whims?
7. Google AdSense blacklist: AdSense is a business arrangement that is highly marketed by Google. Once Google has approved your website, Google is allowed to place ads on your website and pay you for it. If you're good at it, you can make a lot of money. But numerous sites have filed lawsuits against Google contending that Google took down their websites to avoid paying their hit fees.
8. Search engine blacklist: Google has compiled an index of more than 45 billion webpages. That's three times their closest competitor, Bing.

The problem is Google makes "frequent adjustments" to their algorithms, without apparent notifications to companies. As a result of these changes, some companies suddenly find their revenues disappearing without any reason or forewarning. Our representatives and senators have asked EOs many times, but the answers tend to be, Oh! We made some coding errors, or we'll have to look into it and get back to you.

9. The quarantine list: On occasion, Google shuts down entire domains, claiming that said sites contain malware, are hacked, or are otherwise harmful to the user and blocks the user from accessing it. In researching for this book, I have received a few such lockouts, but only to sites that support the skeptical views on climate change.

In its summary: Mr. Robert Epstein[341] concludes with the statement: "No one company ... should have the power to put another company out of business or block access to any website in the world. Google's 37,000 employees with the right passwords or skills could laser a business or political candidate into oblivion or even freeze much of the world's economy." It goes on to say, "Some degree of censorship and blacklisting is probably necessary; I am not disturbed about that. But the suppression of information on the internet needs to be managed by, or at least subject to, the regulations of responsible public officials." The bottom line is, if you are relying only on Google or the public press and television networks for your information consumption, your perceived "facts" may not be as reliable as you would like to believe.

Political and social tyranny.[342] In a book sponsored by the Global Warming Policy Foundation and released in the UK in 2017, *Green Tyranny,*[343] the reader is given an insight into the abuse of power. Here we see the following flyer for the book launching. This should provide us with sufficient cause to ask, what are we doing?

Flyer: *Exposing the totalitarian roots of the Climate Industrial Complex. Book launch of Rupert Darwall's new book.*

Climate change was political long before Al Gore first started talking about it. In the 1970s, the Swedish Social Democrats used global warming to get political support for building a string of nuclear power stations. It was the second phase of their war on coal, which began with the acid rain scare and the first big UN environment conference in Stockholm in 1969. [344]

Where: House of Lords, Committee Room G, London SW1When: 1 November 2017–6:30-8:00 p.m.
Nuclear energy was to have been the solution to global warming. It didn't turn out that way, most of all thanks to Germany. Instead, America and the world are following Germany's lead in embracing wind and solar. German obsession with renewable energy originates deep within its culture. Few know today that the Nazis were the first political party to champion wind power, Hitler calling wind the energy of the future.

Post-1945 West Germany appeared normal, but anti-nuclear protests in the 1970s led to the fusion of extreme Left and Right and the birth of the Greens in 1980. Their rise changed Germany, then Europe and now the world is their goal. Radical environmentalism became mainstream. It demands more than the rejection of the abundant hydrocarbon energy that fuels American greatness. It requires the suppression of dissent.

Attendance by invitation only

7.7 THE FALSE PROMISE OF GOOD INTENTIONS

Clarity of thought: I always liked the way French writer, historian, and philosopher Voltaire had such a crisp form of cutting through the fog, especially the fog of self-deception and self-aggrandizement. He made a couple of interesting observations based on selected verses of the Bible. So, let's look at what the Bible has to say: [345]

Matthew 6.1;[346] *"Be careful not to practice your righteousness in front of others to be seen by them. If you do, you will have no reward from your Father in heaven."* Note that it did not say beware of bad men, or evil people, or wicked nations.

Matthew 7:15-20; *"Beware of false prophets, who come to you in sheep's clothing, but inwardly*[347] *are ravenous wolves. You will know them by their fruits.*" These verses speak clearly in their context, but let's see how the mind and wit of Voltaire would add to their clarity. He says, "I always make one prayer to God, a very short one, 'O Lord, make our enemies quite ridiculous!' God granted it." Later he follows that "Virtue is debased by self-justification."

Contemporary hypocrisy: We see each day how it has spread its leathery wings to all corners of the world. The reader is welcome to read the entire article, titled "Collateral Damage: Poor Biggest Victims of Britain's Insane Climate & Energy Policies."[348] but be warned, it only gets worse.

The poor get screwed. "The climate change act at ten: History's most expensive virtue signal," is an excellent article By Rupert Darwall.[349]

Darwall has written to assess the benefits and consequences to the UK ten years after passing the UK's 'Climate Change Act.' He has written extensively [350]for publications on both sides of the Atlantic, including *The Wall Street Journal*, *The National Review*, *The Daily Telegraph,* and *The Spectator* and is the author of the widely praised *The Age of Global Warming: A History* (2013)[351] and *Green Tyranny: Exposing the Totalitarian Roots of the Climate Industrial* [352] *Complex* (2017). Here is the executive summary of the climate change act at ten, and the reader is encouraged to read the entire thing."

"The Climate Change Act (CCA) is ten years old. Parliament passed it overwhelmingly, only five MPs voting against it in the House of Commons (see Appendix I).
If truth is the first casualty of war, the poor are the biggest casualties of the CCA. By now, fuel poverty was to have been a thing of the past. Both the

Labor and Coalition governments had a target to abolish it. Thanks to the CCA and other anti-fossil-fuel policies, it lives on and is worsening.
Fuel poverty is strongly influenced by energy prices, but decarbonization policies drive up energy costs. Rather than be honest, in 2013, the Coalition government dropped the standard measure of fuel poverty for a new one less sensitive to energy costs, instantly halving the number of people officially defined as experiencing fuel poverty.
The government and official bodies have consistently understated the cost of forcibly phasing out hydrocarbons from Britain's energy mix. In advising the government on the draconian 80% emissions reduction target by 2050, the Committee on Climate Change (CCC) reckoned that it would only cost 1–2% of GDP – assuming rational policies. But, as last year's Helm review on energy costs shows, 'rational' is not a word that remotely describes the mélange of current policies, which, Helm says, perpetuates 'the unnecessarily high costs of the British energy system.'
Both the CCA and the CCC reinforce the disastrous tendency of politicians to pick winners, something the EU also does with its 2009 renewable energy targets. These were foisted on the EU by Germany, which was concerned that its renewable energy policies were disadvantaging Germany business.
Wind and solar create hidden costs within the system – and we still don't know how much they are. When the German Energiewende was launched, the Green energy minister said it would put the equivalent of a scoop of ice cream on monthly energy bills. Nine years later, his CDU successor was saying the Energiewende could cost up to one trillion euros.
After Tony Blair signed Britain up to a 15% renewable target, Department of Trade and Industry officials reckoned it would triple the cost of meeting the UK's emissions target and argued that the renewables commitment risked making the EU's Emissions Trading System (ETS) redundant. Similarly, with the CCA, unless the quantity of ETS Emissions Allowances (EAs – essentially permits to emit carbon dioxide) is reduced, for every tonne of carbon dioxide not emitted in Britain, an extra ton can be emitted elsewhere in the EU. In terms of cutting global emissions, the CCA doesn't do anything. Yet the economic case for the CCA rests on the fiction that it does.
The official impact assessment puts a price tag of £324–404bn on the CCA, which the government concedes is a lower bound estimate; it also excludes transition costs. But the claimed climate benefits are pure fiction. The upper bound of the £404–964bn range of climate benefits assumes effective global

action. Even so, the UK will apparently contribute 42% of the total global benefits. This makes the CCA a bargain for other countries and a lousy one for the UK, but also assumes away the existence of the ETS and the likelihood of 100% carbon leakage to the rest of the EU.
The impact assessment is correct in pointing out that any benefits from the CCA are global, not national. As yet, there has not been any credible official study on the overall costs and benefits of global warming to Britain, which, it is plausible to believe, could derive many advantages from some modest warming. This did not prevent Ed Miliband, the Energy and Climate Change Secretary, from untruthfully claiming that the CCA's benefits to British society would outweigh its costs. "

"The impact assessment also makes the obvious point that absent effective global action, any economic case for the CCA collapses. Short of repeal, the CCA locks the UK into unilateral decarbonization irrespective of what other countries do – embedding blind unilateralism into the law of the land ...
That blindness also affected the promoters of the CCA, who, almost to a man, were and remained fervent supporters of Britain's EU membership. Eight years before the Brexit referendum, they were afflicted by 'fog-in-the-Channel' syndrome: the CCA was conceived as if Britain wasn't in the EU and fully participating in the ETS. Thus, the principal beneficiaries of the CCA are other EU countries who are getting a free ride courtesy of British business and households.
Indeed, the CCA's real purpose is not to cut global greenhouse gas emissions. Rather it is to demonstrate British climate leadership. While politicians flatter themselves as climate saviours, the costs are borne in worsened business competitiveness and squeezed household budgets that weigh most heavily on the poorest in society. In one regard though, the CCA has succeeded in its aim as a demonstration project. No other serious country will do anything quite so foolish in the name of saving the climate."

<u>Hollow aggrandizement</u>: Below is an interview by Professor Medani P.[353] Bhandar to show that self-asserting nobility has no borders and no cultural or national boundaries. I'll spare you the time by first giving my observations based solely on the headline and the abstract.

<u>Author's Comments:</u>

Note 1: "*The entire world is our home.*" That may be what you want it to be, what you aspire. OK. But as you write this nonsense, people in your country and countries all over the world are fighting their neighbors for reasons they have long forgotten, or goals based solely on hatred and malice. This is "virtue signaling" at the basest level, or in Voltaire terms, "Virtue based on self-deception."

Note 2: "*All living beings are our relatives.*" A beautiful, humanistic desire rooted again in idealism and self-deception and virtue signaling. That's never been the case, historically anyplace on earth, and at any point in time! Just look at the evidence by what's going on in your country day after day, year after year, century after century? What philosophy, policies, practices are you advocating that gets us there? Be specific, be practical, be clear, and have a plan!

Note 3: "*Worry about climate change.*" When has worrying ever accomplished anything? What are you doing to solve the problem? Have you defined the problem? Are your solutions based on facts and science or, again, more ego-puffing?

Note 4: "*Pollution problems in the major cities in India, Nepal, Bangladesh, and Pakistan.*" Pollution has absolutely nothing to do with the advocacy of CO2 reductions and nothing to do with climate change except at the slimmest margins. If you have a pollution problem, many affordable solutions are available that have nothing to do with CO2 and are practical and affordable.

Note 5: "*Abstract.*" A nonsensical combination of words that, in sum, means nothing other than the words "environment" and "climate change" that are inserted here and there for some reason. And this is what they are teaching to our sons and daughters around the world. Sad!

My request to the dear professor: Have you studied science? If yes, have the courage and be true to your studies. If you have not, get a solid education in the hard sciences and then come back with a fruitful teaching approach. What I see here and thousands, perhaps millions of people around the earth with good intentions, that can only lead us to ever more magnificent follies.

"Bashudaiva Kutumbakkam" The entire world is our home, [note 1] *and all living beings are our relatives.* [Note 2] *Why we need to worry about climate change,* [note 3] *with reference to pollution problems* [354] *in the major cities of India, Nepal, Bangladesh, and Pakistan* [Note 4]

Medani P. Bhandari
Akamai University, Hilo, Hawaii, USA, and Sumy State University, Ukraine.
Email medani.bhandari@gmail.com [355]

"Abstract [Note 5]
In this interview format opinion paper, Professor Medani P. Bhandari, directly or indirectly reveals the interconnected impact of the geographical, and socio-cultural environment on personal motivation building. As such Prof. Bhandari tells the story of why and how he became interested in the conservation of nature and natural resources, what was the problems and how he overcome and continuously working on the same track with same focus in his entire life; however, it might be the story of each environmentalist who has tried to continue environment conservation action and activism and academic scholarships together. Prof. Bhandari is a lifelong conservationist, expert of climate change impact, social empowerment, and educationalist, who has devoted his entire life for the conservation of nature and social services. This true story tells how personal background makes people's perceptions of nature and society and what role a spiritual / tradition, Indigenous knowledge can motivate.[356] *Prof. Bhandari has published about 50 papers in international journals, published four books and poems volumes. A brief biography and contact details of Prof. Bhandari is included at the end of this interview. Prof. Bhandari states, "My intention, of life, is to pay back; give or contribute to the society in fullest whatever I have, earned, or experienced." Hopefully, readers will enjoy reading and will be benefited from this true an intrinsic motivational story with the evidence of scientifically grounded facts. A brief bio of Prof. Bhandari is available at the end of this interview."*

8. THE DEATH OF SOCRATES AND EDUCATION

<u>8.1 Why Socrates had to die:</u> It's been a perplexing and hotly debated question for the last 2,400 years. Argued and discussed by some of the most intelligent and reasoned thinkers: Plato and Aristotle, then onto the Romans, and the scholastics, and the age of enlightenment. Later by the modern and post-modern philosophers. So here we are today in the post-post-modern era, and some might add, in our most-reasoned period of western civilization. And we still ask why.

<u>And why, of all things,</u> would we ask this question here in a book dealing with climate change? I'm glad you asked because it's as relevant today as it was over 2,400 years ago. In 399 B.C., Athens was in turmoil and confusion. This first experiment in democracy had just suffered a crushing military defeat at the hands of the totalitarian, anti-humanistic Spartans. The Athenian citizens were struggling with the core concept of freedom. Had they chosen the best path? Are the weaknesses of democracy so profound that it's unsustainable for little more than a century or two at best?

Socrates spent his life studying, contemplating, and teaching the essence and nature of ethics but never wrote anything down. Fortunately, some of his brilliant students did, especially Plato. In this book, *The Last Days of Socrates*, Plato walks us through the civil process of Socrates charged on two counts. The first charge was that he had corrupted the youth of Athens[357] and the second with impiety against the State's gods. In Athens, these two elements were nearly inseparable. The book is comprised of four dialogs named: the Euthyphro, the Apology, Crito, and lastly, the Phaedo. Together they take us through the trial. The Euthyphro explores the definition of justice versus the nature of his offense. In the Apology, Plato then puts words in the mouth of Socrates to find a reconciliation of his and his societal values, and the person versus the soul. In the Crito, we see a personal discussion between Socrates and his friend

Crito as they explore the very definitions of justice, injustice, and just penalties. It ends with the "Phaedo," where he argues the case of the immortality of the soul before he rejects the opportunity given to him to escape. Instead, he commits his final act of scorn as he drinks the hemlock.

We're not relitigating the Socratic conundrum. Instead, we discuss it briefly to draw the concerning parallel with the present-day assaults on our rapidly changing societal values. And with particular concern with the erosion of confidence in our public education system. Just as relevant today is a question like the Athenians were asking, when are responsible citizens allowed to challenge the unjust governing laws imposed by the power of money or corruption. And while I may not be a great philosopher or a mediocre one at that, I see how Socrates exposed the failure of the Athenian leadership and their representative embodiments to the human frailties.

These shortcomings beleaguered the Athenians then and are now challenging us today. Here we face many of the same questions, including the role of our education. How can it be improved? Who would benefit, and who would suffer from any changes? Just as importantly, we are told that climate change is an existential threat like they saw the Spartans. But for us, it's not just for our country, but the entire planet, and we are told it's our fault. Worse yet, we are threatened that anyone who challenges the claim of CO2 impending disaster is an evil opportunist, denier, racist, or psychopath who, like Socrates, must be destroyed. And like Socrates's "Apology," we are told that our hemlock consists of giving up our electricity, cars, jets, cows, our civilization, our values, and social structures.

Behind the headlines: So, let's look beyond today's blaring headlines, anti-social riots, op-eds on a polarized government and polarized people, and re-ask the questions the Athenians could not answer: Is democracy too taxing for the average citizen? For democracy to work, it requires study, though, a solid fact-based education with a precise, logical construct. In other words, it needs a lot of work on the part of the citizens. Perhaps it requires more effort than the average citizens were willing to invest in, with their minds, their bodies, and their money. In Athens, they just wanted everybody else to come up with the fix that would put the burden on somebody else and make the challenges go away.

Our Founding Fathers struggled with the same challenges and limitations of democracy. In handing off the new nation, they said, "We gave you the best system we could come up with, and it will last only as long as you have the desire and fortitude to make it last." The Athenians did not; neither did the senate and tribunes of Rome nor the Carthaginian senate. And so, they paved the way for the Pericles and the Caesars, Cromwell, Hitler, and Stalin. Please take special note of the below Breitbart article to see what's on the horizon for us if left unchecked.

8.2 Why are we even talking about public education in the USA, and what does that have to do with climate change? My go-to answer is, "Education is the foundation upon which we build our lives, our families, our future and our environment." For forty years, I work in a company that required me to travel to more than forty different countries, and some of these countries many times over. On these travels, I would always arrange my schedule to stay at least one weekend on each trip so that I could see their people, civilizations, and cultures. I find it as no surprise to see South Korea at the number one position in education and industry and Japan just right behind. My Korean and Japanese counterparts went to extraordinary measures to make sure their children went to the best schools. There they had to take the most demanding courses, no silly subjects with little prospect of a career position, and once there, it was their job to get the highest grades. The parents would accept nothing less.[358]

I recall reading English versions of the local newspapers in South Korea, in which there were numerous examples of prominent people arrested for bribing the best schools to accept their children. In Japan, many young professionals are sent abroad when they are quite young, so they could return to Japan before their children reach the third grade. They didn't want to expose their children to their perceived failures of our soft-Western educational system.

In China, it was the usual practice (and still might be) for teachers to "blackmail" the parents of very bright children. If they didn't pay up, they didn't get the excellent grades the students had earned, thereby hamstringing them for life. In Italy and France, where I lived for several years, I got to see their school systems in operation. In France, for example, each child was tested in the seventh grade, and their life and future would be shaped by how they scored on this two-day series of tests. Those at the bottom were sectioned off to the trade schools where they would become electricians, plumbers, mechanics, carpenters, etc. Those who achieved high grades in math and sciences were prepared and later sent to the technical colleges. Those who excelled in arts and literature went to the classical colleges, and the lucky few who excelled in both could go wherever they wanted.

Is the USA getting worse? NO! I'm not advocating that we adopt anything like these drastic measures, but the standing practice of our schools in the U.S. has degraded year after year. It has severely been impacted, especially in the past two generations. As seen through the eyes of the previous article, "The false promise of good intentions," our vacuous approach is also spreading around the world, leaving countless uneducated and unemployable students burdened with massive school debts. Unfortunately, I don't see an easy way out because of the structural and societal problems we have built and continue to reinforce around them. See a recent study [359] comparison of the top-ranking countries in the world in the field of public elementary education. As we see there, the U.S. is ranked fourteenth. Many similar studies show that if we looked at science and math only, we would be listed on the thirtieth level, or even worse.

8.3 Our political pawns: If you are reading this book, the chances are pretty good that you have or expect to have children or grandchildren. With this assumption, I ask you to get involved with your local schools and see not just what is taught, but also how the children are taught. But today, perhaps just as importantly, be suspicious of the media/press. Mehmet Murat Ildan,[360] author and social commentator, warns us, "Beware of pro-government media in your country because it does not open your eyes, it just makes you blind."

- Are your children being taught, or are they being indoctrinated? Are they being taught the skills needed to develop critical, analytical, and independent thinking? Or are they led on a group-think path? Are they being taught logical constructs and how to differentiate between what we want to believe from the ontological truth that exists around us, whether we like it or not?

- Do politicians use public school children as pawns for their political agenda? I'm especially concerned with grades K-5, where the mind is most susceptible to imprints of ideologies.
- Our future is in the hands of your children who, today, are spending too much time being indoctrinated on social issues and not educated sufficiently in the hard sciences, math, and other skills needed to build a successful career, family, and enriching your society.
- Are they taught to use the scientific approach, do their research, gather and analyze the data, come up with their theory, and test it against their test data? And at all costs, avoid the pea-shell game of the "education" charlatans?
- Are "socially conscious" parents and teachers aware of the education crisis, or are they contributing to the problem?

Greta Thunberg at the United Nations: "*You Are Stealing Our Future:" Greta Thunberg, 15, Condemns the World's Inaction on Climate Change.*" Please watch this four-minute video[361] as a fifteen-year-old girl lambasts the world leaders for inaction on climate injustice. As you watch it, please note a few unexpected things.

- Her sincerity, clarity of thought and expression, and her dedication and the eloquence in delivering her plea.
- As she progresses, we see her passion building up in her facial and bodily expressions.
- Looking closely, you start to see what the driving force for her passion is; it's fear.
- This child is terrified by the dogma impregnated in her mind and spirit.
- One last thought; are we to believe that this near-perfect presentation was the product of a child's

spontaneity? Or are we free to ask: how many hours of speechwriting and coaching was she subjected to by the many invisible adults who prepared her so well to be the perfect pawn for this incredible performance?

- By the end, I was greatly saddened for her and the torturing fears and scars she will carry for the rest of her life.

Social and Emotional Learning (SEL),[362] or as I like to call it, "a competition for the participation trophy." Below, we see a partial reprint of an article published by Breitbart,[363] and I'll just let a few sentences speak for themselves about the damage that has been done in the last few decades. The scary part is that we have educated, intelligent, licensed adults seriously discussing the need for implementing Social and Emotional Learning (SEL) now even in math and science.

"Panelists at the South by Southwest (SXSW) EDU 2019[364] *conference this week urged educators to make Social and Emotional Learning (SEL) part of every core subject in K–12 classrooms."*

"SEL 'has no academic components and is clearly facing a tough sell by companies trying to drink from the public trough,' Dr. Sandra Stotsky, professor of education emerita at the University of Arkansas, told Breitbart News."

Author's commentary.
"Why are you doing this to your children?"

"Increasingly, more schools are adopting an aggressively progressive curriculum. In Minnesota, School leaders adopted

the 'All for All' strategic plan—a sweeping [365] *initiative that reordered the district's mission from academic excellence for all students to 'racial equity.'" The Weekly Standard reported in February [2018].* [366] *Children in kindergarten are expected to become "racially conscious" and examine their "white privilege." And leftists' radical agenda is taking hold in a less blatant but not less toxic way in the rise of social and emotional learning (SEL), which presents just as much danger to parents, kids, and the education system as Common Core".*

"SEL teaches kids to feel and not to think," Mull wrote. [367] *"Traditional public schools, apparently determined not to teach kids history, how to read, spell, add, subtract, multiply, or anything useful, instead take on the role of the psychotherapist (and not a good one)."* Drawing courtesy. [368]

<u>The Wall Street Journal,</u>[369] "An Education Horror Show: A case study in public school failure and lack of accountability," by The Editorial Board, July 7, 2019.

In this piece, *The Wall Street Journal* takes a particularly scathing look at one example of our failed education system. Below are a few paragraphs from this extensive article.

- *"The National Education Association held its annual convention this past weekend, and the Democratic presidential candidates made their pilgrimage to promise the teachers union more money—and even more money. One word we didn't hear on stage was 'Providence,' as in the Rhode Island capital city whose public schools were recently exposed as a horror show of government and union neglect."*
- *"Peeling lead paint, brown water, leaking sewage pipes, broken asbestos tiles, rodents, frigid and chaotic classrooms, and student failure were all documented in a 93-page review by the Johns Hopkins Institute for Education Policy. The review was conducted in May at the request of the Rhode Island education commissioner, and it deserves attention nationwide as an example of government failure."*
- *"No surprise, then, that only 5% of Providence eighth-graders on average scored proficient in math in the 2015 through 2017 school years."*
- *"One culprit is policies that discourage student discipline. Rhode*

Island Democrats in 2016 passed legislation backed by the American Civil Liberties Union that limits school suspensions, which progressives claim discriminate against minorities. Teachers are reluctant to punish students, and violence and misconduct make it harder to retain good teachers.[370]"

"The Biggest Problems Facing the Public-School System? [371] Screams the headline in this report. Below are selected paragraphs giving substance on the need for parents to fight back against the private interests of the "education lobby." In the U.S., 181 is the baseline number of required school days.

- *"The American public-school system is far from perfect, but the list of top issues is constantly changing. Some say that the emphasis on standardized testing is destroying the quality of public education while others believe that schools are too crowded, and parents are too uninvolved."*
- *"Many countries outside the United States have much higher requirements for school days. Canadian requirements are usually around 188 days and students in England have 190 scheduled school days. But if you travel a little further from the U.S. you'll come to China where there are 221 school days and Japan where there are 223. Korea has the highest number of scheduled school days at 225".*
- *"Research conducted by the Pew Research Center revealed a declining interest in education among Americans. In regard to which topics had the most interest, the top three were the U.S. economy, terrorism, and job creation."*
- *"The sad truth is that there are many problems in the American education system. Some of these problems are overwhelmingly large and often interlinked with other issues. Unfortunately, there may not even be much that you can do personally to improve these problems. What you can do is educate yourself and become an advocate for the American public education system."*

The bottom line; get involved. You, Mr. and Mrs. Parent, need to take responsibility for the education of your children. The good news is that you are not alone. Many organizations share their values, concerns, and goals. Your children are not just your most prized possessions. They are your future. Your happiness is no greater than the joy of your least happy child.

9. DE BELLO CIVILI

9.1 History repeated, again?[372]

Commentarii de Bello Civili, which translates to "Commentaries on the Civil War," is the title of the second and lesser-known book written by Julius Caesar dealing with their civil war and ranking far behind his first book on the Gallic Wars. So, what? Why bring this up at this time, you might ask? Excellent, thought-provoking, critical-thinking question. There are many uncomfortable parallels today between the state of the U.S. Republic and that of the Roman Republic of 2,000 years ago. Today we have a split Congress, more concerned with political infighting, personal enrichment, and self-promoting than the welfare of the republic and the people it's supposed to represent. The Roman senate was obsessed with arresting and trying to impeach Caesar for his "illegal wars" in Gaul. Sounds familiar with what's going on in Washington and around the country for the past several years.

The book describes in detail, at least from Caesar's point of view, the great undertakings that he was planning for the ordinary citizens. It included freeing up more land for them that had been hoarded by the wealthy nobility and Senators, the need to rebuilding crumbling infrastructure, and resettling veterans to Poland, where they could start up their farms. And most in parallel with today, drain the swamp—literally, draining the Pontine Swamp, rebuilding the Roman sewage system, and release of all private debts, which today we call free housing, free schools, guaranteed bread, and circus. After several years of fighting the political battles, it finally led to an all-out bloody civil war that lasted six years and killed more Romans than many of their wars of conquest.

9.2 Failure to learn from history is not to learn from history. Today I see many uncomfortable parallels between the USA and the Romans at the turn of the B.C./A.D. period. They faced the same social issues, the same civil matters, the battle for the votes of the plebs, and the lust for power and glory by the rich and powerful, and the price they paid for their ignorance and arrogance in treasure and lives. Read Caesar's book, as it demonstrates the value of history, and how to learn from the mistakes of others from the past instead of our lurching forward to our follies. As has been said too often, "The failure to learn from history is the failure to learn from history." We need to keep this in mind as we are embarking on our new social wars led by the many banners like, "Save the planet," "Drain the swamp," "Free tuition/healthcare/debt forgiveness, the Green New Deal," and dozens of similar deceptions.

~ 8 ~

HISTORY: CLIMATE CHANGE AND UN/ IPCC

Rated DR — Dramamine Required

~ INTRODUCTION ~

We're now going to look into the past, the gossip, the backstabbing, and the fun part of the UN/IPCC. Sit back, put your feet up, have a pickle, and enjoy the rollercoaster ride.

1. THE FOUNDING OF THE U.N.'S - IPCC.

The UN/IPCC has three, Key Advisory Committees, to ensure that the Secretary-General's Climate Actions deliver major outcomes on enhanced climate ambition.

- Steering Committee, "is the political arm" chaired by the Special Envoy to the Secretary General.
- Climate Science Advisory Group provides science expertise in areas of climate science, mitigation and adaptation.
- Ambition Advisory Group, "political activists" deliver transformational, impactful, and actionable outcomes.

In the article "Manufacturing consensus: the early history of the IPCC," January 3, 2018, by Judith Curry,[373] we are going to draw back the curtain and expose the goings-on in the smoky backrooms and the dungeons of the IPCC. I hope you read the entire article. It's easy reading, no math, no serious science, and no graphs to interpret. Instead, it reads like a murder-mystery novel, with just a splash of palace intrigue. But we'll summarize its key points, which we attack with the clinical skills, hyperbole, and farcical humor worthy of Mark Twain.

Before we dig in, I want to tell you why we are delving into this quagmire. First, because Dr. Curry was a member of the UN/IPCC Climate Science Advisory Group. The article implies that not only did she ignore all the politics and infighting, but she wasn't even aware of how extensive and consequential it was. In late 2009, after seeing how the IPCC Steering and Ambition Committees were routinely compromising and corrupting the climate change science to advance political and financial agendas, she quit. Soon after, she became an outspoken and vocal critic of the IPCC, their hysteria, and the false human-made CO2 disaster agenda.

Secondly, it appears that Dr. Curry may have learned a lot more about the depth and extent of the IPCC corruption while reading the book, *Searching for The Catastrophe Signal: The Origins of The Intergovernmental Panel on Climate Change.* Or, as Dr. Curry would graphically describe it as a "*Summary: scientists sought political relevance and allowed policymakers to put a big thumb on the scale of the scientific assessment of the attribution of climate change.*"

<u>Author's Notes:</u> The IPCC painted itself into a corner when it proclaimed that it needed to find temperature data before it could attribute CO2 as the cause of climate change. IPCC scientists worked for decades trying to find this "attribution" without success until Dr. Hansen manufactured the distracting solution, called "the hockey stick." The graph created the illusion that CO2 was driving the temperature change and, in effect, putting the CO2 cart ahead of the climate change horse.[374]

<u>Judith Curry</u> got her Ph.D. in Geophysical Sciences from the University of Chicago and was the former chair of Atmospheric Sciences Department at The Georgia Institute of Technology. For years now, she has been a frequent critic of the IPCC, especially for its sole reliance on the anthropogenic CO2-driven global warming scare. Dr. Curry considers the

effect of human-made CO2 as minimal at best, while the consensus industry ignores the many natural cycles known to affect climate change.

Dr. Curry participated in the US Senate Hearing "Data or Dogma," on December 8, 2015, and in the past ten years has been a frequent target of the consensus group. In her opening remarks to the US Senate, she had the following discussion outline in her prepared remarks:

"*My testimony focuses on the following issues of central relevance to the state of climate science:* [375]
- *Consensus, uncertainty, and disagreement*
- *Unsettled climate science: the importance of natural climate variability*
- *Scenarios for the twenty-first-century climate*
- *The broken contract between climate science and society."*

Following a 2017 interview on NPR,[376] Richard Harris writes: *"Curry certainly has the credentials. She is a professor and chairwoman of the School of Earth and Atmospheric Sciences at the Georgia Institute of Technology. She also runs a side business as a private weather forecaster but doesn't deny the basic principles of climate change. 'If all other things remain equal, it's clear that adding more carbon dioxide to the atmosphere will warm the planet,' she told the committee. But she went on, not all things are equal. She says there's so much uncertainty about the role of natural variation in the climate that she doesn't know what's going to happen. She says a catastrophe is possible, but warming could also turn out to be not such a big deal. And she focuses on uncertainties and unknowns far more than on the consensus of climate scientists, who say 'we know enough to be deeply worried."*

Article by Dr. Curry: Let's start by going through a few items, to which we'll add our perspective.

"The 1970's energy crisis. In a connection that I hadn't previously made, Lewin provides historical context for the focus on CO2 research in the 1970s, motivated by the 'oil crisis' and concerns about energy security. There was an important debate surrounding whether coal or nuclear power should be the replacement for oil."

Author's perspective: In late 1973, shortly after the oil embargo hit the U.S., my wife and I drove from Schenectady, New York, to Port Elizabeth, New Jersey, to load our car on a ship. We were moving to Belfort, France, where I was going to work on building the prototype of the world's first 100-megawatt (137,000 horsepower) gas turbine for electrical generation. The big challenge we faced that day was, would we be able to buy enough gas to make it to the port on time? Luckily, we had been advised to bring some extra fuel in the trunk of the car, and we barely made it. However, two weeks later, we were not as lucky. As we drove from Belfort to the port of Le Havre, France, to pick up our car, we ran out of gas. What was to be a fun four-hour drive took two days and two unexpected hotel bills because we could not get the fuel we needed.

Two years later, we did it. We fired up the world's most powerful gas turbine engine on schedule and on budget. That handsome young man with the black hair and tie is yours truly at the assembly of a sixty metric ton rotor with its stator counterpart. As we lowered it about one centimeter per minute, we had to maintain axial and diametrical accuracies of about the width of a human hair.

Shortly after we completed the initial testing, I was asked to move to Florence, Italy. There, for the next three years, my focus was on two natural gas pipelines (one from Siberia to

Austria and the other from Algeria to Italy). Another essential item on my plate was to work with the oil companies and their engineering consultants on enhanced oil extraction techniques. This involved high-pressure reinjections of natural gas into the oil wells to push more oil out of the sand and rocks and store the gas in the oil wells to be retrieved years later. Remember, this was almost fifty years ago, and we had no concept of fracking technologies at that time.

"But in the struggle between nuclear and coal, the proponents of the nuclear alternative had one significant advantage, which emerged because of the repositioning of the vast network of government-funded R&D laboratories within the bureaucratic machine. It would be in these 'National Laboratories' at this time that the Carbon Dioxide Program was born. This surge of new funding meant that research into one specific human influence on climate would become a significant branch of climatic research generally. Today we might pass this over for the simple reason that the 'carbon dioxide question' has long since come to dominate the entire field of climatic research—with the very meaning of the term 'climate change' contracted accordingly."

Author's perspective: In the late seventies, I was back in the USA and deeply involved in the many facets of "how do we replace oil?" One part of my job was exploring coal gasification concepts and fluidized bed combustion. At the same time, I was also negotiating a nuclear licensing agreement with a European company. All went very well, and a few years later, I found myself house-hunting near Palo Alto, California, where I was to head up international licensing of our nuclear technologies. Fortunately, even with the raise that came with the promotion, it came nowhere near the additional costs of moving to and living in California. So back to Schenectady for a few more years of coal and oil stuff. I say "fortunately" because, several months after my house-hunting trip, the Three Mile Island incident occurred, and about nine months later, 3,000 employees in our nuclear division were laid off and I would have been one of the casualties.

"<u>This focus was NOT driven by atmospheric scientists:</u> The peak of interest in climate among atmospheric scientists was an international climate conference held in Stockholm in 1974 and a publication by the 'US Committee for GARP' [GARP is Global Atmospheric Research Programme] the following year. The US GARP report was called 'Understanding climate change: a program for action,' where the 'climate change' refers to natural climatic change, and the 'action' is an ambitious program of research."

"<u>The emergence of 'global warming</u>.' In February 1979, at the first ever World Climate Conference, meteorologists would, for the first time, raise a chorus of warming concern. The World Climate Conference may have drowned out the cooling alarm, but it did not precisely set the warming scare on fire."

<u>Author's perspective:</u> Sweden and, in particular, Olof Palme, had a driving desire to replace Sweden's oil and coal-fired plants with nuclear power. As a consequence, Sweden took the lead in organizing the world's first climate change conference in Switzerland in 1979. For years Palme beat the CO2 global warming drum on the international stage, all the while building support for his nuclear plan. A few years later, Palme was murdered in the streets of Stockholm, and the whodunit continues to this day.

"<u>Origins of the IPCC</u>; With regards to the origins of the IPCC: Jill Janager gave her view that one reason the USA came out in active support for an intergovernmental panel on climate change was that the US Department of State thought the situation was 'getting out of hand,' with 'loose cannons' out 'potentially setting the agenda,' when governments should be doing so."

"While the politics were already making the science increasingly irrelevant, Bert Bolin and John Houghton brought a focus back to the science."

<u>Author's perspective:</u> The political arm of the IPCC took full control over the scientist about a year before the first assessment report was due in 1990. When the initial report was finally published, a year late, it was not the simple scientific pamphlet the scientists had in mind. Instead, the "politicians" had turned it into a large piece of bureaucratic art. The sheer volume of hundreds of thousands of unnecessary wordiness, however conveniently provided cover for them to insert their messages and nuances. This process often contradicted or eliminated outright the message that the real scientists had written. But, by having its bogus messages spread over thousands of pages and different volumes and chapters, it was too taxing for most people to follow. As a result, the IPCC provided the media/press with simple, clever, and convenient sound bites.

Key take-aways from the article include:

http://www.clker.com/clipart-

- Yes, some of the scientists complained about how their data was "managed" by the political and advocacy working groups. But the scientists also loved the attention, notoriety, and the tons of funding the IPCC was providing.
- The UN/IPCC decoupled the AGW/CO2 climate debate from the real science that had first started the concern.
- Dr. Hansen had become a rock star, and many of his fellow scientists wanted to share in the spotlight, even though they were dissatisfied with Hansen's lack of scientific verification.
- The manipulation of the historical temperature data used by Hansen to generate the hockey stick was so blatant that major past climate events like the Roman and Medieval Warming and the devastating Little Ice age of the 1620s - 1740s were made to disappear.
- Especially peculiar is how the infamous hockey stick chart skirted the fundamental problem of detecting the "catastrophe signal" that the IPCC scientists could not find.
- I hope I gave you sufficient enticement to read the entire article of the shady history of the U.N. and the IPCC in particular.
- Especially noteworthy are two books by A. W. Montford; "The Hockey Stick Illusion," and especially its sequel, "Hiding the Decline."

2. Q & A: DEBATE OVER CLIMATE PANEL BIAS

Following is an excerpt from an article by Jessica P. Johnson et al., titled "Q&A: Debate Over Climate Panel." July 18, 2011.[377]

Author's Notes: The article sheds light on what appears to be a hubris bias against the real climate scientists versus the political hacks who dominate the policymaking interpretations. In this report, the IPPC confidently proclaims that by 2050, solar and wind power could replace 77 percent of the total world energy requirements. I invite you to read the complete article because it shows the utter contempt that these IPCC "scientists" have for all of us. They have convinced themselves that we, the average intelligent persons, are so gullible that we will believe anything they tell us. For my part, I will point out a sample of the absurdities they are selling us masquerading as science. As an example, let's set the stage for estimating what the growth of the USA's electrical generating capacity from 2018 to 2050 will be. Then, as a second step, we'll try to forecast how much could be supplied by sun and wind power.

- In 2018, the actual entire USA generation of electricity from solar was 1.6 percent, and from wind was 6.6 percent for total renewable electricity of 8.6 percent of the nation's needs. The fact remains that this 8.6 percent, while it's the world's highest, has not significantly increased its percentage share in the last decade. Despite substantial federal and state incentives, premiums, and mandates, this needle has not moved up.[378]
- The USA electrical demand is expected to grow at 2 percent per year for the next thirty years, reaching a total growth of 82 percent by 2050. That means solar and wind would have to nearly double their existing installations to maintain their present 8.6 percent share.

- In the USA, all fossil fuels today account for 66 percent of our electrical power generation needs, and these fossil fuels account for about 80 percent of the human-made CO2.

Maybe they were anticipating that our transportation needs would have us at about 100 percent electric autos by 2050.

- The shocking reality is that this UN/PCC position paper relied on an article written in secret by the delusional Greenpeace movement without any reviews whatsoever, not even by the IPCC's scientists. Secondly, they also went out of their way to hide the fact that the source material for this UN/IPCC position paper was 100 percent authored by Greenpeace.[379]

3. FINAL EXAM TIME

If you have made it this far in the book, then you should be prepared to take this final exam to qualify for our prestigious award of Ph.D. CEW, "Climate Expert Wannabee."

In the below Figure, we have our standard thermometer. Choose your position on this scale from the following three options:

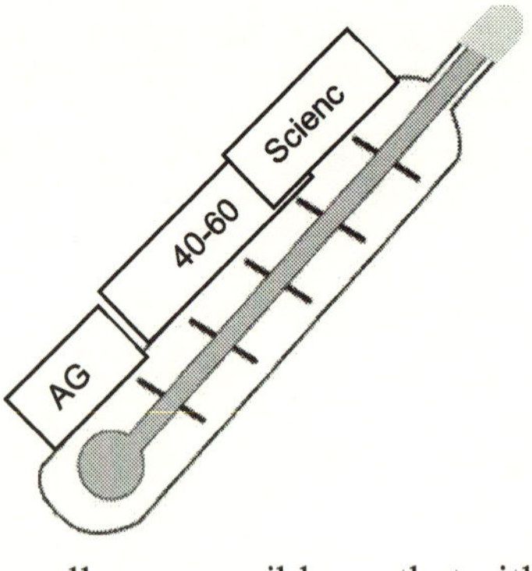

a) Science: This choice says that you generally believe that CO2 is a minor contributor to climate change and the increase in CO2 and global warming has been favorable to life on Earth. Skip the rest of this chapter, go straight to Chapter 9, and collect $200.

b) 40-60: Choose this if you believe that both human-made CO2 global warming and the natural cycles are about equally responsible or that either is solely responsible for climate change. You need more information to make a decision. My advice decide the source of your doubt. If it's the science, go back to the first few chapters and then come back and retake the test. But if you're concerned more about a possible change to your social status, then please see if any of these statements apply to you: a) You need more tattoos, b) Do you have any big girl/boy pants yet, or c) How's life in your parents' basement?

c) **AG:** You believe that human-made CO_2 is responsible for the inevitable global disaster that you will face in twelve years. At the end of the book is a short pledge sheet for you to fill out and sign. It states that you are ready to give up all your money, cars, trips, burgers, house, A/C in the summer, heating in the winter, etc. And secondly that you understand that having given away all your STUFF, the climate will still keep doing what it's been doing for millions of years, no matter what you do or don't do.

4. THE IPCC SHOULD LEAVE SCIENCE TO SCIENTISTS

Read the article "*The IPCC Should Leave Science to Scientists*," from the publication *American Thinker*.[380]

Author's comments: This is an astonishing indictment of the IPCC process and is reminiscent of the court of the Queen of Hearts in *Alice in Wonderland.* You may recall in the book the Queen of Hearts saying, "Off with her head," and then goes on to say, we can have the investigation and trial at a more convenient time. The article goes on to say:

"In an article last summer, which focused largely on the tactics of eco-maniac Al Gore, I explored the depths to which the GW [Global Warming] attack machine will delve to silence its detractors. Gore target and former IPCC member, Dr. Richard Lindzen said that alarmism dissenters have, "seen grant funds disappear, their work derided, and themselves libeled as industry stooges, scientific hacks or worse."

https://i.pinimg.com/736x/00/0c/8e/000c8e5ce63f75b4e12f82248676b433--

Author's comments: This is even worse than the Queen of Hearts' "Off with her head." It's like the Queen of Hearts ordering her soldiers to burn down the man's house and farm before the rebel is executed so his family would also starve.

"Lindzen has been quite vocal about 'global-warming alarmists intimidating dissenting scientists into silence' and, unlike many of his brethren, has steadfastly refused to succumb. Not surprisingly, the Alfred P. Sloan Professor of Meteorology in the Department of Earth, Atmospheric, and Planetary Sciences at MIT is now an outspoken critic of the IPCC."

Author's comments: Lindzen is retired; he and his family are financially secure and are not dependent on the CO2 climate research grants the way the younger scientists are.

"It was Lindzen who blew the whistle on irregularities in both the 2001 summary and report when he testified before the Senate Environment and Public Works Committee in May of that year. After stating that the IPCC was created to support negotiations concerning CO2 emission reductions, he gave an astonishing account of the pressure placed upon the scientists who drafted the report."

Author's comments: In my research for this book, when I saw Dr. Lindzen's home address on his Petition to President Trump, I realized he was my neighbor in Newton, Massachusetts, living just a few houses down on the shore of Crystal Lake. Just a simple reminder of how small our planet has become, and how interconnected we all are and how fragile/dangerous the world can be if you stray from the "consensus."

5. RAISING THE ALARM:
Sample articles and headlines from around the world

a. "U.N. Predicts Disaster if Global Warming Not Checked."[381] By Peter James Spielmann, United Nations (AP) *June* 29, 1989, AP:

UNITED NATIONS (AP). "A senior U.N. environmental official says entire nations could be wiped off the face of the Earth by rising sea levels if the global warming trend is not reversed by the year 2000."

Author's Notes: I guess what we did leading up to 2000 must have worked since satellite data shows global warming stopped in 2000. What was it that we did in 2000? Nothing! So, let's keep doing more of the same.

"Coastal flooding and crop failures would create an exodus of 'eco-refugees,' threatening political chaos, said Noel Brown, director of the New York office of the U.N. Environment Program, or UNEP."

Author's Notes: I guess what we did must have worked, since not only did we see zero climate refugees, but we also saw a vast greening and leafing of the Earth and reduced desertification. How did we achieve this great climate outcome? We did nothing; let's do more of the same. This recommended inaction is for climate change only and not to be confused with repairing the many damages done to the environments around the world. For example intensive overgrazing especially by sheep and goats.

"He said governments have a 10-year window of opportunity to solve the greenhouse effect before it goes beyond human control."

Author's Notes: In 1989, we were told we only had twenty years to stop CO2 and avert climate disasters.[382] So here we are twenty years after the deadline, and we have been in a slight cooling period for the past twenty years.

"As the warming melts polar icecaps, ocean levels will rise by up to three feet, enough to cover the Maldives and other flat island nations, Brown told The Associated Press in an interview on Wednesday."[383]

Author's Notes: NASA satellite confirms that since 2000, temperature readings indicate a significant cooling of the Earth's upper atmosphere. And here we now have, "NASA confirms – Sea levels FALLING across the planet." October 12, 2017.[384] It appears that lately, climate alarmists can't catch a break.

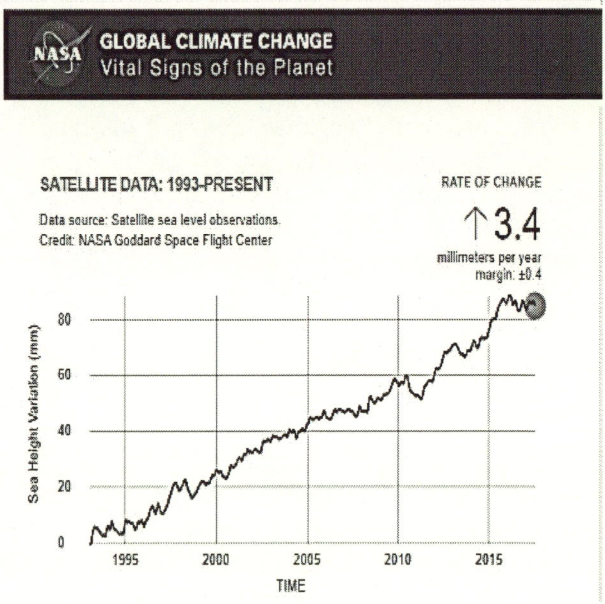

b. "The IPCC's latest climate hysteria." By Paul Driessen.[385] Oct 14, 2018; Townhall:

"Intergovernmental Panel on Climate Change Special Report 15 claims the latest disaster "tipping point" is just 12 years away. If governments around the world fail to make "rapid, far-reaching and unprecedented changes in all aspects of society," human civilization and our planet face cataclysm, the IPCC asserts."

Author's Notes: Perhaps this is a good time for the reader to pause and reflect on some of the poor decisions we might have made in our past. What was our mindset when we made those poor decisions; were we calm, clear thinking, and reflective, or emotionally charged up with anger or fear?

A turning point in my life was when I read the book "*Dune*" by Frank Herbert. That was the first time I came across the word "ecologist," as the author described his plan to restore water on this desert planet. I checked my Webster's New World Dictionary, and no form of that word was to be found. But after reading several more pages, I figured it out and thought it was cool. It later became a seminal moment in my life as my love for nature and involvement in our environment grew profoundly. A few years later, I read a sequel titled "*Dune Messiah,*" where Frank Herbert again caught my attention. This time it was a short phrase murmured in a corner by a secondary character whispering to himself while observing influential people arguing over something important, "Reason is the first victim of strong emotions." So I want to extend my thanks to Mr. Herbert for introducing me to these two concepts, which have been foundational in my personal life, my professional development, and family relationships.

c. "NYT reporter demands we become 'hysterical' over 'climate change.'"
By Thomas Lifson. Nov 26, 2018; American Thinker:[386]

"Stop thinking! Act out of fear" and "become hysterical" is never good advice! If a salesperson uses these sorts of arguments, it's time to walk away from the deal. But that's what one advocate of global warming hysteria – literally hysteria – was publicly urging yesterday. And not just in print, but on Meet the Press, the oldest continuously broadcast program in the history of television yesterday. The implicit rejection of rational discourse on an issue of public policy by a writer for what used to be the nation's premier newspaper is another historic first for the broadcast."

Author's Notes:[387] In November 2018, the journal *Nature* published a paper by Dr. Zharkova that predicted global cooling starting in the early 2020s, which could last twenty-five to fifty years. Do news outlets inform their audience on climate change? Do teachers educate our children to seek truth and make the right decisions? You, dear reader, answer these questions to yourself, not in silence or a whisper in a corner, but loudly and clearly!

d. "U.N. chief predicts 'total disaster' if warming not stopped."
By Seth Borenstein and Edith M. Lederer, Associated Press, Updated: May 8, 2019, Philadelphia Inquirer:[388]

"U.N. chief predicts 'total disaster' if warming not stopped. United Nations Secretary-General Antonio Guterres speaks during an interview at United Nations headquarters on Tues, May 7, 2019."

Author's Notes: Only a year ago did NASA start to hedge their position on global warming, in essence, saying that global cooling may soon come as a result of a lazy Sun.[389] This is precisely the same forecast and rationale used by Dr. Zharkova in a paper first published a few months earlier in the journal "*Nature.*"

f. The IPCC's latest climate hysteria.[390] By Robert Richard Lindzen: Oct 14, 2018; Ice Age Now:

"Implausible conjecture backed by false evidence and repeated incessantly … to promote the overturn of industrial civilization."

Author's Notes: No comment required.

~ 9 ~

CLIMATE FORECAST AND DISCUSSIONS

Rated TTGR: Time to Get Real

1. INTRODUCTION

Walk in the sunshine of science and truth

I'm going to really need some Zumba after this!

Forecasting is a dangerous business! All the more reason to approach this question as Mark Twain would; attack it with hyperboles and good humor.

Now, forecasting is like trying to decide what number will come up on the next throw of the dice, or the next card you draw, or the next ball you roll. So, let's put ourselves in the proper setting. Yup, here we are in the Climate Change Saloon in downtown Las Vegas. In case you didn't know, "Las Vegas" means "the green and fertile valley" in Spanish. See, the Spaniards also had a great sense of humor and irony. But not the CO2-consensus industry. These people are humorless and self-referential, much like the Puritans of old. With a stern look and judging eyes, they tell us that it was climate change that turned the lush valley into a desert after we invented automobiles.

Here is another little secret: American taxpayers have been losing money in the CC Saloon for over thirty years, and the vast majority don't even know it. Every year they pony up their ante with their climate change research-industrial-political dollars and comply with silly laws and regulations in the name of "save the planet." But other than that, nothing tangible comes from these climate change tax-dollars. That is nothing except more climate change urgency and hysteria. The ordinary folks just kept losing their ante, which was quickly gobbled up by the CO2 consensus industry. For the first many years, it didn't hurt much, and most weren't even aware of it.

But all of a sudden, some fool got jacks or better and is now raising the bet by $10 trillion. Then some bigger fool raises to $56 trillion; then the Green New Ordeal comes along with a 93 trillion dollar bill—what are we to do? We're now being asked to bankroll these climate change mobsters with more money than we have, to solve a problem that doesn't exist!

Further, anyone who raises any questions is condemned, put in the public stocks for humiliation, and personal and family destruction. Why? Because they threaten us, if we don't precisely do what we are told, we're all going to die! In schools, on TV, on social media, they indoctrinate our children that we're destroying their planet and their lives. Remember, this is serious money, so we, citizens of the earth, need to do some serious reckoning here.[391]

What are we to do? Remember, Greta Thurnburg's persuasive speech at the U.N.? **"You have stolen my dreams!"**[392] And, even if you don't remember many of her words, I trust you will remember the fear and outrage on her face. When these Gen-Z youths come home from school, scared for their future, and angered with us for destroying their lives, what do we tell them? What father wants to confront his daughter's rage and fears? And that's why you need to read and re-read this book because with the knowledge you will gain, you can take away her fears and resentments.

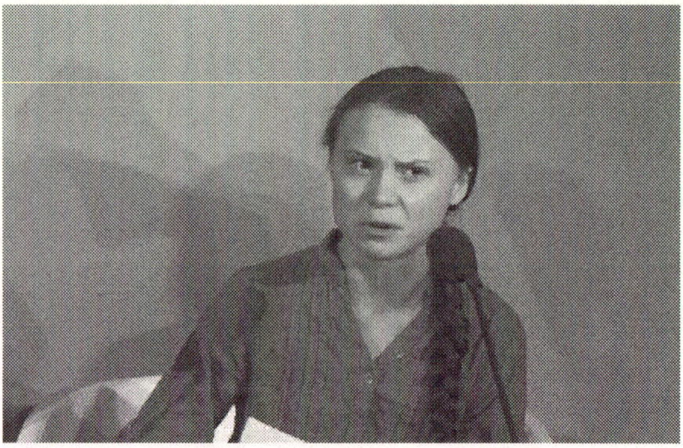

2. THREE KEY QUESTIONS

But where to start? Before we can decide where we're going to be in the next twenty, forty, or a hundred years, we need a perfect understanding of three simple things:

1. Where are we today?
2. How did we get here?
3. Where are we going?

Let's start with Question 1: As stated many times throughout this book, for the last hundred years or so, the Earth has been in a near-perfect place. Humanity, the biosystem, and every creature is thriving, and the extra CO2 of the last several decades has helped green the planet. But then we are shown the intimidating Michael Mann "hockey stick," see 9.1.1[393], and we are told we're on the precipice of runaway global warming.[4] The graph shows this relatively flat temperature curve over the last 1,000 years. But then, in the previous fifty-seventy years, we see the scary temperature jump, and we're told the planet will soon be scorching.

But let's give credit where credit is due. This hokey stick chart is a masterpiece of deceptive propaganda and beautifully staged as "science." Compare this hockey stick 9.1.1 with 9.1.2[394]. The first thing to notice is that, except for some fudging of the surface temperature records by NOAA, the two charts show almost the same data. Both graphs demonstrate a temperature increase of about 0.8° C in about the last 150 years. But there are some very noticeable differences both in facts and fabrications, let's dig for clarity. First, the hockey stick chart is presented on a minute laboratory scale, where the average person has no context. Then it's given an even more threatening appearance by the use of the flame-red color at the end.

---

[4] Recall in Chap 3.15 we discussed the scientific principle of a runaway global warming. But then in Chap 6.2 we explained that its consequences were trivial because 1) there's very little man-made CO2 and 2) there's only a small amount of a special infrared light that warms up CO2, and 3) that infrared light is already nearly saturated.

Now the second chart shows almost the same data, except it's displayed on a temperature scale where we live, where we work, play golf, go to the beach, etc. It's on a level that is easily understood and contextualized by the average person. Suddenly the "hockey stick" is not so intimidating after all. In fact, over the past eighteen years, the blade part of the hockey stick has been whittled down from a maximum temperature increase of 0.8 C in 1998-1999.

In 9.1.1, we readily note that something's not quite right?

- First, the graph conveniently cuts off in the year 2,000 right at its peak and does not show the temperature decline from 2000-2019. In the Climategate scandal emails, the term that NOAA used was "hide the decline."

- We then notice that something resembling the Mauder Minimum but is shown about 200 years later than it was, and not as cold as it was. What happened? To approximately 0.6° C (Jan-2020).

- Second, on this graph, we can't seem to find the Medieval Warm Period. It should be located at the extreme left about 900 years ago. Where did it go?

- Let's repeat this statement in sharpened context: all of the global warming hysteria is based on a temperature increase of about one-half a degree centigrade in the past 150 years. To the average American, this may have meant an extra fifty dollars per year for air conditioning in the summer and maybe saving thirty dollars in winter heating. Overall, the

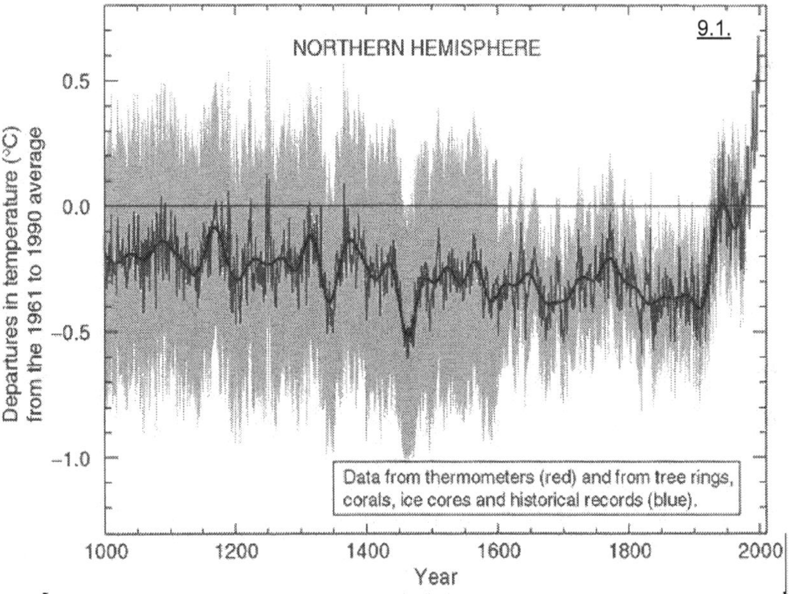

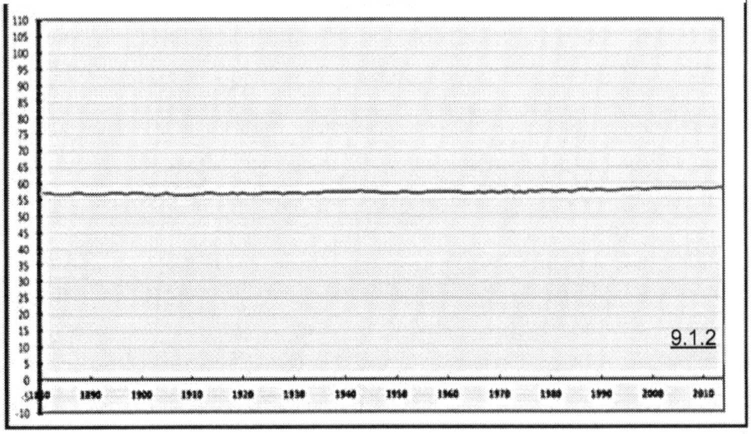

change is minimal, and the consequences are trivial.

3. HISTORICAL EVIDENCE

Question 2. How did we get here? We are told we live in a period of "unprecedented" hot climate—the warmest in history. The human-made CO2 will produce ever more scorching temperatures and catastrophic sea-levels on us. But is that true? Let's check out what the temperatures were in the more recent past—say, the last 10,000 years after we came off the last ice age. Let us take a close-analytical look at the now-familiar figure 9.2.1[395]

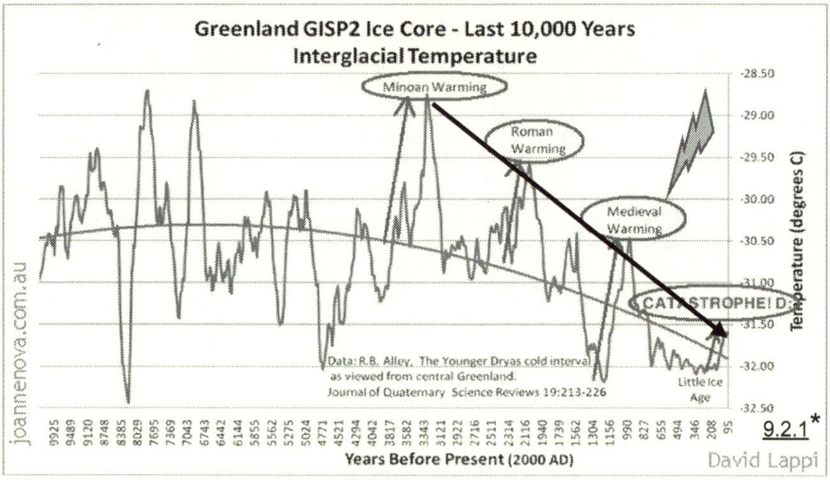

9.2.1*

Woah! Now, this looks amazing. Here we see ourselves in the lower right corner. There we see a tiny temperature uptick of about half a degree Celsius, labeled "CATASTROPHE! D." But as we look back, we see that the Earth had been in many periods that were much warmer than today! Note especially that each of the previous four warming periods has been on a declining scale (black arrow). It looks like the Earth has been in a long-term cooling trend for the last 4,000 years. And more astounding, we see that this latest global warming period (1978 to 1998) has been the weakest recovery in the series.

Let's take a very close second look at the warming period labeled "Medieval Warming," highlighted by the yellow lightning bolt at about 900 years ago. We now expose a contradiction with the hockey stick chart. Figure 9.2.1 shows the Medieval Warm Period was about one degree Celsius warmer than the "CATASTROPHE! D" temperatures. But the consensus has been telling us that the present, human-made CO_2 driven temperatures have been "unprecedented," "record-breaking," "historical."

Let's now go back to the hockey stick chart and try to find where this "Medieval Warm Period" is. But where is it? It should be on the far-left side, about 1,000 years ago. It should be very noticeable since it's about one degree Celsius higher than the present temperatures. At this point, I still see no reason for me to bet $100 trillion; do you? But let's dig into the details some more. Let's look back a little further.

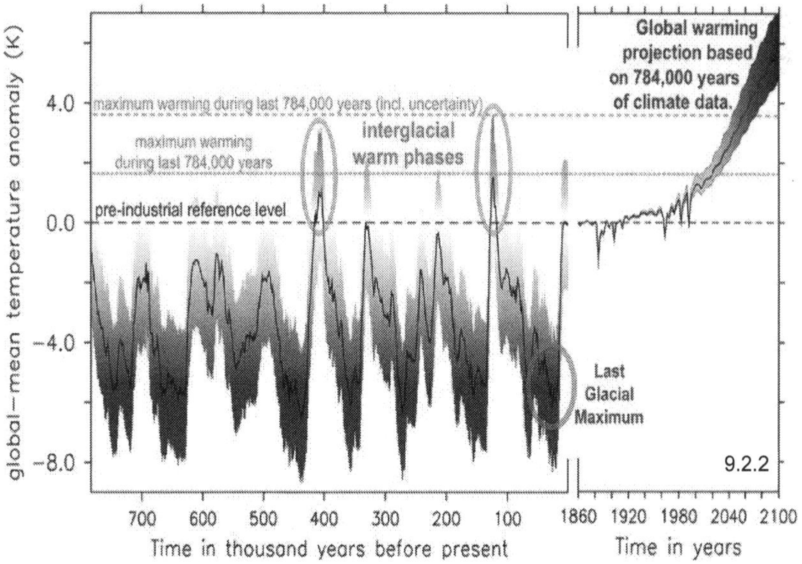

Let's now go back to the hockey stick chart and try to find where this "Medieval Warm Period" is. But where is it? It should be on the far-left side, about 1,000 years ago. It should be very noticeable since it's about one degree Celsius higher than the present temperatures. At this point, I still see no reason for me to bet $100 trillion; do you? But let's dig into the details some more. Let's look back a little further.

Take a long look at the last eight hundred thousand years. Ladies and gentlemen, boys and girls, mesdames et messieurs: Houston, We Have A Problem! Looking at 9.2.2,[396] it certainly seems like we have a problem. It looks like we might be on the edge of another cyclic ice age, which seems to come about every 100,000 years. Just as importantly, look at how short the "warm" periods are compared to the prolonged cold periods.

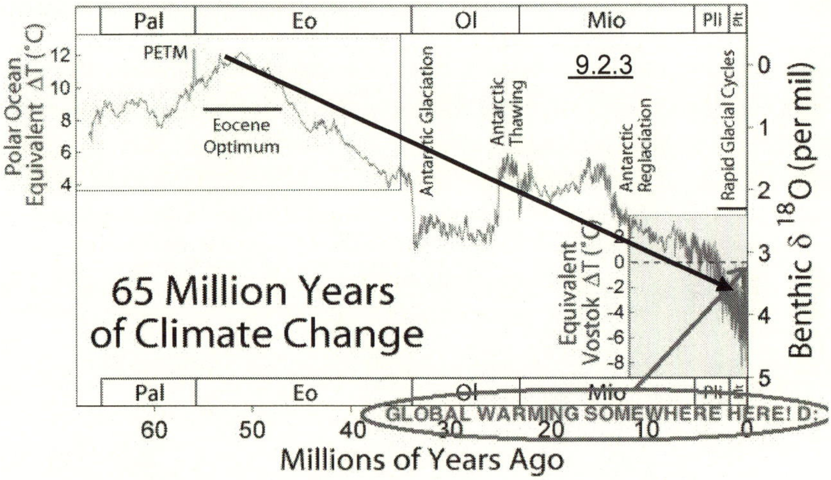

Now check out Fig. 9.2.3,[397] where we see that the Earth has been on a cooling trend of about ten to twelve degrees for the previous fifty million years (black arrow)! Then compare that with a small temperature increase of the 20th century.

Historical records confirm that the claim of an "unprecedented" global warming disaster is a bust.

4. SCIENTIFIC EVIDENCE

But wait! Based on the above historical data, it's now clear that the present warming threat is not threatening at all. But, before going back to Las Vegas and the CC Saloon, let us make one last check on the science.

A. The skeptic scientists tell us: [398]

- Water vapor accounts for 90-95 percent of all the greenhouse warming effect.
- Total CO2 accounts for about 3.5 percent of the world's greenhouse effect.
- Human-made CO2 accounts for about 0.06 percent of the total CO2 greenhouse imbalance (Table 4.16.1).
- CO2 is only heated by a limited supply of short-band infrared radiation reflected from the Earth, and that about 90 percent is already saturated. This means even if we double or quadruple the human-made CO2, the incremental greenhouse heating will still be trivial.

- Nearly 95 percent of the heat arriving at the planet is from the sun. For the last several decades, the sun was at high solar activity. As a result, it produced more TSI and generating powerful solar flares, solar winds, coronal mass ejections, and magnetic fields.

These effects and forces resulted in a warmer planet Earth and its sister planets in the solar system.

- We are now in a period of low solar activity, and we are told it may even be a grand solar minimum, which seems to occur about every 400 years. This will mean:
    - Reduced TSI energy arriving from the sun to the Earth.
    - More galactic cosmic rays will penetrate the Earth's system, causing increased cloud formations. Consequently, more rain and more clouds and more TSI will be reflected into space, creating some incremental global cooling.
    - The increase of the Earth's snows and glacial fields will also increase the TSI reflected outer space.
- Meanwhile, the increased CO2 will continue to help the agricultural production and somewhat mitigate the effects of a slight temperature decline.
- Lastly, the increased heat of the last 100 years has been absorbed and is stored in our warming oceans. So, if and when there is a noticeable global temperature decline, the oceans will slowly release this heat over many decades and mitigate any adverse effects of this cooling.

<u>The skeptic's perspective, the only questions left to answer are:</u>

- How cold will it get?
- How long will it last?
- How do we prepare and protect seven billion people and the planet's animals from the coming cold?

B. <u>The CO2-consensus scientists</u> give a fuzzy and fudged historical temperature record with a staged hockey stick graph to traumatize us into submitting to their outlandish demands. Further, they do not provide us with any data about:

- The natural cycles of the Earth, the energy storage capacities of the oceans.
- They tell us nothing about the many benefits of increased CO2, or how the oceans modulate the amount of atmospheric CO2.
- They never talk about the sun, its dramatic magnetic cycles, the changes in TSI; how the sun protects us from galactic cosmic rays at high activity levels; or how it exposes us to more of them during low activity periods.

- Nothing is ever mentioned about any of the astronomical cycles and how those affect weather and climate.
- They pretend the Earth is the only thing in the universe, or somehow the Earth is contained and protected within a Ptolemaic celestial bubble. The only thing we need to fear is CO_2 and other human activities.

The only thing they tell us is:

- Man-made-CO_2 – bad, nature – good. Must protect Mater Gaia (Mother Earth goddess) from the bad people.
- How horrible humanity has been to the Earth with all of that dirty coal, and oil and gas, and farting cows and cars and flying machines.
- How fast the Earth is cooking in human-made heat, shut up and do what we're told, and we need to be carbon-free in the next ten or twelve years, or it's the end of everything.

So here are their predictions as best as I can understand them:

They forecast a temperature increase of about three to seven degrees by 2100. But it's hard to pick a number since they use over a hundred different computer models, none of them work, and then they take the average of these models. Pick your number.

- They tell us the sea levels will rise, coastal cities will inundate and be destroyed, and millions of people will need to relocate to the Blue Ridge Mountains in Tennessee and learn to play the banjo.
- They give us no scientific data about the sun, the astronomical cycles, never a word about galactic cosmic rays or reduced TSI, or which wavelengths are more impactful than others.

- They never told us about how the historical CO2 levels went from 280 ppm to 380 ppm right after NOAA changed the way they measured CO2 levels in 1958. More NOAA fudging?
- We must reduce human-made CO2 in twelve years, or we all die, this is a straight-up lie.
- Lies, fears, and threats are the tools and instruments of their science.

5. ***Scientifically speaking, the claim of an "unprecedented" global warming disaster is a bust.***

K TO VEGAS AND THE CC SALOON.

Ladies and gentlemen, and everyone in the middle, it's time to place your bets. Here's how I will wager the one hundred dollars in my pocket:

IPCC forecast:

See figure 9.5.1,[399] the red line is the IPCC-Consensus forecast and shows an increase of one degree through 2025, projecting a growth someplace above three to seven degrees by 2100.[400]

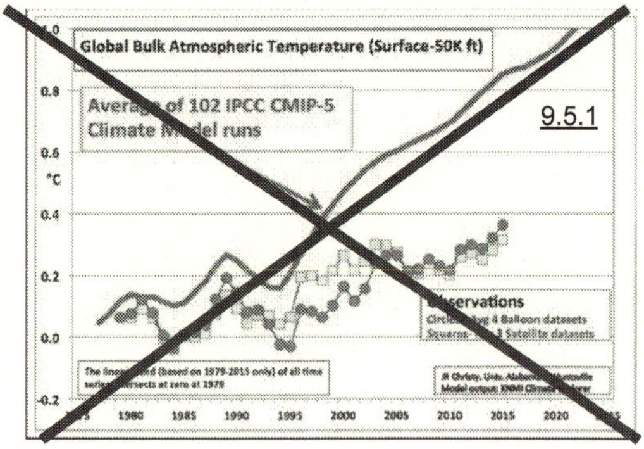

I bet zero dollars on this foolish concept and urge all of you to reject the madness, no matter who presents it and how well it's packaged.

Dr. Easterbrook's forecast

First, I'm placing *a twenty-five-dollar bet* on the forecast by Dr. Easterbrook, the revised blue line in 9.5.2.[401]

This forecast also tends to be generally in line with the estimates by Dr. Valentina Zharkova, but with a temperature reduction of about half of what she predicted in 2018.

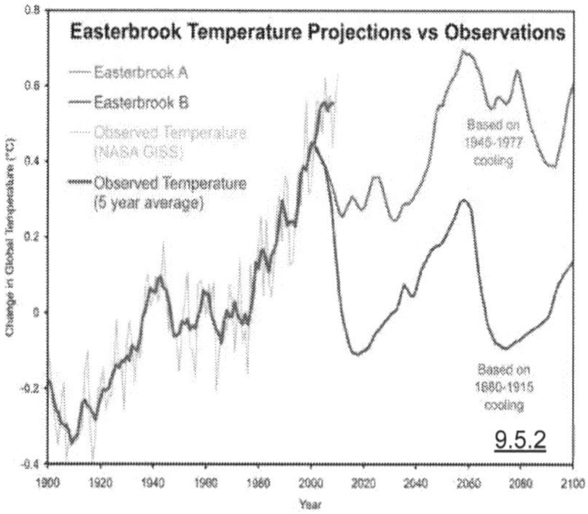

9.5.2

Dr. Zharkova's forecast.

Upcoming modern Grand Minimum
To occur in 2020 – 2055
This is a unique event in solar-terrestrial connection → reveal the pros and cons of solar dynamo models
Big impact on the terrestrial temperature via SI and reduction of magnetic field
Shortage of vegetation periods can lead to possible food shortage in 2028-2032
Need inter-government efforts to avoid disasters

9.5.3

Second, I am placing ***a twenty-five-dollar bet*** on the forecast presented in Fig. 9.5.3.[402] This is the original forecast Dr. V. Zharkova gave at the Global Warming Policy Foundation and published in the journal *Nature* in 2018 at about a -1.0 to 1.5 C drop.

Third I'm placing **my last fifty-dollar bet** on the expected revised forecast by Dr. Zharkova, which is anticipated to show mostly the same estimates as above (–0.5 to –1° C). Still, the temperature drop will not be as cold as her original 2018 forecast.

Let's wrap it up.

1. We were in a sustained period of global warming, driven primarily by high solar activities from 1978 to 1998.
2. We have been in a slight cooling period since about 2000.[403]
3. The only question is how cold it will get, what will be the rate of annual declines, and how long will it last until the next warm recovery cycle.
4. I'm estimating a decline of about the same general shape as the Dr. Easterbrook forecast (blue), but bottoming out at about the same temperature levels seen in the 1900-1920 period as shown if 9.5.3.

5. CONCLUSION:

This is the easy part, so we'll get right into the fun and facts and consequences of global warming ignorance.

There is no danger of impending CO2 global warming for centuries to come, if ever. The CO2 disaster-driven threats are hyperbole and disguised motives. Enjoy your life, your-day-to-day experiences, and be vigilant for the climate change charlatans and opportunists. They want to take your money and your freedom as payment for the made-up threats that exist only in their lies.

This Photo by Unknown Author is licensed under CC BY-SA-NC

Yes, the ancient Trojans naively brought the Greek horse into their citadel, but at least it was free.

We have already replaced the ancient Trojans as history's biggest fools, having already paid hundreds of billions to the charlatans to build their CO2 horse.

Do you now really want to pay additional trillions of dollars to tear down and demolish our lives, our liberties, our economy, and our civilizations in the chase of this CO2 Kool-Aid?

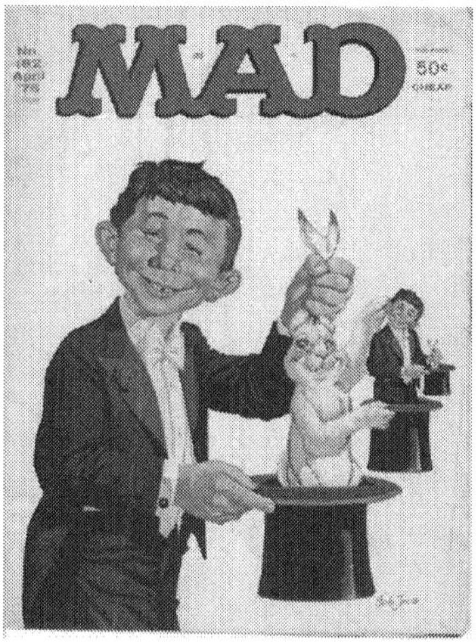

Don't be this guy.[404]

~ 10 ~

FIELD GUIDE

Rated GTFS – Get the Facts Straight

1. INTRODUCTION

THE VOYAGE OF THE BEAGLE by Charles Darwin documents his scientific findings and journal report based on his five-year journey. It provided Darwin with the textual reference and fundamental data that he later used to formulate his famous book and theory, *The Origins of the Species.*

Fig FG.1

The Beagle[405] sailed from Plymouth, England, on December 27, 1831, under the command of Captain Robert FitzRoy. While the expedition was initially planned to last two years, it lasted almost five—the *Beagle* did not return until October 2, 1836. Darwin spent most of this time exploring on land (three years and three months) and eighteen months at sea. The book is a vivid travel memoir as well as a detailed scientific field journal covering biology, geology, and anthropology. Written at a time when Western Europeans were exploring and charting the whole world, this book demonstrates Darwin's keen powers of observation. Although Darwin revisited some areas during the expedition for clarity, the chapters of the book are ordered by reference to places and locations rather than by date.[406]
Our purpose here is to document our detailed notes and keen observations of our journey through the discovery of climate change. Because, like Darwin, learning takes its deepest roots when we write things down in two steps. The first step, like any good scientist (and Darwin certainly was) is to document what one observes when one observes it. The second and perhaps more important step is to organize the notes in some logical way. This allows the traveler-scientist to reflect on his documented observations and try to make some sense of it, both in individual parts and in its totality.
We will not come anywhere near the scope or the brilliance of Darwin's masterpiece. Nonetheless, we will document our journey and contextualize the meaning of what we observed and learned. These notes can later be reviewed and referenced in any discussion we will have in the future, especially in teaching and educating our children and grandchildren.

2. THE VIEW FROM 30,000 FEET[407]

1. The bottom line. Climate-wise, it's all good! No global warming to worry about. Yes, we've been in a modest warming period for the past 150 years, and it reached a maximum increase of 0.8° C in 1998 and has since come back down a net gain of about 0.5°C by mid-2019.
For the next thirty to fifty years, we are forecasting a slight temperature decrease, going back to the levels of the early 1900s. Unfortunately, each day, we are pummeled by

prophets of doom and fearmongering "environmentalists" with the proactive participation by a deceptive media, self-serving politicians, and the greedy CO2 industrial complex.

But, now that we have a well-grounded understanding of the science of climate change, we can casually dismiss all the fearmongering by the climate change industry, dishonest press, and self-serving politicians with facts and good humor.

2. Summary of findings. Humanity has never had it so good, thanks to the advancements of real science. Humanity is prospering like never before, and the biggest winners in the fossil-fueled industrial evolution have been the middle class and the poor.

The idea that "scientists" identified human-made CO2 as the singular cause of global warming as causing a planet-destroying force is absurd. The entire concept that humankind can control weather or climate is the height of arrogance and hubris.

3. The real causes of climate change.[408] It's got little to do with either naturally occurring CO2 or human-made CO2. It's the sun, baby! That big yellow ball in the sky has been and continues to be the single most significant determinant of climate change. As the sun goes, so do we. The diatribe that human-made CO2 is destroying the planet is a myth at best. The greenhouse effect is real, and without it, the Earth would be in a perpetual ice age, with no life on Earth of any kind. But the greenhouse effect is 99.99 percent controlled by the many astronomical, solar, and the Earth's natural cycles. Yes, human-made CO2 does have some effect, but it's too small even to measure, making it inconsequential.

4. More science stuff. In the past few decades, tremendous progress was made in advancing the real science of climate change. We have learned a great deal about the solar cycles from Dr. Zharkova, and the vital role that cosmic rays play in climate change from Dr. Svensmark. We also learned about other effects of galactic cosmic rays, like stimulating nucleations,

volcanic, and tectonic activities. Over and over, we find strong correlations between the sun's magnetic events and major volcanic and tectonic movements. We are also learning that the whole of the sun's magnetic cycle may be how the sun reacts to the gravitational tugs from specific planet groupings. Similar to how we see the moon's gravity causing the Earth's ocean tides.

5. Just the facts, ma'am. Polar bears were doing just fine and benefitted from the global warming of 1978-1998. We discussed the minuscule role that total CO2 plays in climate change, and the unmeasurably small contribution made by human-made CO2.

We put CO2 to the test, and there is zero evidence that the increased CO2 has caused any problems for humankind or the Earth's bio-system.

We also explained the many blessings brought by the increase in global CO2 with higher agricultural yields, reductions in world famine, and an overall greening of the planet. It would be great if the atmospheric CO2 amount would double, but that is beyond the control of humankind.

6. CO2 has run out of gas.[409] We summarized the origins of the CO2 hysteria and explained why, even if we double or quadruple the amount of CO2 presently on Earth, it would still be beneficial.

7. The origin of the "CO2 impending disasters." We found out that, in the 1970s, it was the nuclear industry that started the whole CO2 global warming scare. They did this to gain a competitive advantage over coal-fired electrical power plants.

We also summarized how the entire CO2 hysteria is based only on the UN/IPCC flawed computer models. There's not a scintilla of scientific data to back up any of their alleged "science."

We also discussed the Climategate scandal, where NOAA manipulated the historical temperature records to deceptively show CO2 as the only cause of climate change.

8. Misleads and head-fakes. Here we discussed how the average taxpayer had been purposely misled and taken advantage of by this spurious CO2 climate change industry for personal gain and wealth. We also talked at length about how the climate change industry deceived even the brilliant and well-educated people. The climate charlatans took advantage of the fact that their targeted audience was too busy with their daily activities to check out their deceptions and lies.

We also talked about how the CO2 industry takes advantage of the political processes of the U.S. Government to manipulate billions of research dollars, and where about 90 percent of the funds are channeled to chase the CO2 rabbit.

9. The need for an insurance policy. Here we debunked the concept that we need to have an "insurance policy" on the remote chance that human-caused CO2-driven climate change will destroy our planet.

As intelligent, educated, and rational people, why would we spend trillions of dollars on an insurance policy just in case 2 + 2 equals 5? The entire premise is absurd and delusional.

10. Socioeconomic theft. This book is a how-to manual to enrich and aggrandize yourself if you have neither ethical limits nor any moral compass.

11. The World Development Bank. Here we saw a startling example of how the poor people in underdeveloped countries are deceived and exploited by selfish persons. I recall a saying I read somewhere in my remote past, but don't remember the source. In substance, it said, "Let evil people go about their evil in the name of evil but beware of what they do in the name of good."

But as a substitute, I offer this fascinating article titled "10+ Warning Signs You Are Dealing With An Evil Person," written in Higher Perspective,

October 4, 2017.[410] Please read this article; it's an eye-opener, and yes, evil people continue masquerading in sheep's clothing.

12. Back to science. Facts, data, and evidence are indisputable; nuclear power is the safest, cheapest, and most reliable source of electrical power. So why is it not an integral part of the Green New Deal? Find out why.

13. Political arrogance and infectious stupidity. Here we asked five simple questions that terrify the CO2 industry. Take the test.

14. Environmental preemptive war. Can you believe this? We discussed about "scholarly papers" advocating preemptive wars against nations who continue to pollute the planet.

Never mind that the three biggest polluters that account for most of the pollution on Earth are nuclear powers.

15. What did we learn from the "Climategate" scandal? Specific tasks by NASA and NOAA that fabricated the illusion that the increased CO2 is responsible for global warming.

They then devised and executed an elaborate strategy to seek out the climate change "denier" scientists, and then attempted to destroy them personally, professionally, and financially.

16. The myth of "clean, renewable energy." Here we explored the real-world experience of countries, like Germany, who launched nationwide programs to "go all-in for green," and the sad realities of unintended consequences.

Be forewarned!

The charlatans of the CO2 -global warming hysteria are ready to pivot on a dime, manufacture new fears and look for ways to exploit this newly-found global cooling opportunity.

17. Human frailties and follies were put on full display, including how even excellent education and intelligence are of no protection against willful ignorance. We discussed the power of fear and how expert charlatans create it, manage it, and milk it.

But, once we understand the tools and tactics of the CO2 industry mob, we will be better prepared and can defend ourselves from their deceptions.

18. The self-righteous ego ride.[411] Another to-do manual on how to gain moral superiority and social status at minimal costs. A short play in three acts.

"Which of tonight's specials is the most sanctimonious?"

19. Time to take out the crayons. The economy, demographics, and tax consequences of the winners and losers of the CO2 climate scam.

20. WTF. WWYT? [5]

[5] WWYT – What Were You Thinking.

A reprimand to my baby-boom generation, a plea to our Gen X generation, and a prayer for our Millennial and Gen-Z generation.

21. The growing consensus for global cooling. Eleven short, thought-provoking articles from highly respected sources showing the increasing trend that more and more people are turning skeptical on the CO2 global warming threat.

NASA, along with many respected publications, is finally admitting that "global warming" ended in 1999.[412] They state "because our sun became lazy" in the past twenty years. Many accredited scientists are predicting this cooling trend to continue for some time, and a healthy scientific debate is developing around why it's getting cold, how long will it last, and how cold will it get.

3. THE BOTTOM LINE

Here's the good news, the not-so-bad news, and the bad news. The bad news for humanity, your family, and the children around the world is this: when it comes to climate change, you can't run, and you can't hide from it. Not physically, not emotionally, and not metaphorically.

The good news[413] is shown on the pictured cover of the book by Dr. Spencer[414] with the understated message: Go live your life, have fun with your friends and family, and don't sweat the global warming climate drama. Physically, in the past century or two, we had our share of weather and climate ups, like the warm periods of the 1930s and the happy 1980s and 90s, continuing to this day. We've also had a few downs like the cooler 1960s-1970s. This was when we first heard predictions of a coming new ice age. And we now have a climate change "pause" of the past twenty years. But overall, it's been near-perfect for humanity and the entire planet.

Sociologically and psychologically speaking; however, it's a very different story. In the 1960s and 70s, doomsday prophets first broke into the scene. They warned and threatened us that humankind was to end because we had already polluted our planet beyond repair. We were told that the earth had too many people, and we had already overreached the limits of our food production capabilities. We were excoriated for having exhausted all of our natural resources, especially oil, clean water, clean air, and fertile farmlands.

In the mid-1970s, the weather-climate change terrorists-scientists first came on the scene, telling us that we were on the verge of the next Ice Age. But then, in only a few years, we were bombarded by how global warming will destroy humankind, the environment, and all life on earth. And, if that was not alarming enough, the stakes were raised again. The revised headlines of 1989 read, "Humanity only has twelve years left to fix the problem, or all life on earth will perish." And the only way to fix the challenge was to immediately and entirely commit trillions of dollars and transform our lives, our industries, and our culture into a zero-carbon ecosystem!

Each new day for the past thirty years, we are pummeled with new hyperboles by television talking heads, newspaper reporters, demonstrators, politicians, and Hollywood celebrities. All with their hair on fire, screeching the climate change alarms, bombarding us with the singular message that human-made CO_2 will end the world. Each new day the impending disasters get more colossal, more imminent, and the voices ever more loud and shrill. This induced CO_2 hysteria has gone past many limits of sanity. Governors, U.S. Senators, Congressmen, former Presidents, and would-be Presidents are constantly teeing up multi-trillion-dollar and cultural-shattering legislation proposals. The headlines scream, "Last chance to save the planet" or "We only have twelve years left to eliminate CO_2 before it eliminates us." Metaphorically, the planet is so much bigger than Moby Dick, and their cause to save us from ourselves is presented as ever more noble, and ever more righteous.

Let's take a quick inventory. We'll do it by the numbers and see where we are. Here we need the active participation of our readers. First, if you got this far in the book, put up one finger, or put up two fingers if your hair is not on fire. Now, if you are listening to the news and reading the papers and listening to the politicians a little more skeptically, put up one more finger. Or put up two if you are doing it very suspiciously and give yourself a hug. If the Green New Deal sounds reasonable, subtract one finger. If it looks and sounds good, subtract two fingers. And if the Green New Deal sounds really-really great—put down this book and seek immediate psychiatric attention.

But, if you read as a minimum the Introduction and Chapters 1 - 5, have all your fingers and enjoy your sense of humor with family and friends, then this book served you well. Now that you understand the basic science of climate change, this knowledge lets you see through their many, and outrageous, lies and nonsense spread each day from the scientific truths you have learned, your mind is at peace. You are now confidently capable of dismissing or explaining the climate change myths casually and with good humor. You'll be in a place where all the planetary disasters and socioeconomic mumbo-jumbo heaped on you each day is only the wind in the willows. You will have achieved nirvana.

4. SUMMARY OF FINDINGS

We'll now make a listing of all that we learned in the preceding chapters, and we'll categorize each point as a Data or Data plus my Opinion. There's no need to repeat the farcical half-truths, fake headlines, and fearmongering that continues to be heaped on us. Items with no indicator are Facts or Data as validated in the preceding chapters. To get started, let's recall these definitions from the Introduction:

Data: Are facts, figures, relationships, etc. that are obtained by measurements, mathematics, and experiments used to support or to challenge a theory or a scientific law or a consensus. ***Take special note; output from climate models are not data.*** When computers first started to emerge in the 1960s, a particular phrase was immediately coined: GI-GO, Garbage In - Garbage Out. It was an entertaining way to remind us to code our programs carefully and accurately.

But today, as Dr. Willie Soon likes to say, the IPCC climate models have a new coin; GI-DO, or Garbage In - Dogma Out. Heck, we can equally quote Simon and Garfunkel: "*Then the people bowed and prayed to the neon god they made.*"

Opinions: These are the choices we make, where the preponderance of available evidence appears to favor position A over B. But in all cases, it's a preference, and it's not Data!

I am scoring the findings. So, with this in mind, let's boldly explore the universe and ourselves. Note that a hashtag (#) will mark the areas where I'm expressing my opinions or (Data + my Opinions).

Climate change is real and is here, and so is climate warming and climate cooling and climate annoying. They can all be okay or terrifying, and everything in between. But let's put it into perspective.

We're good. The people and the Earth today have never been in a better place. Populations are growing and living longer. They lead happier, healthier, and safer lives. They are doing so because of the advancements made by humankind in the hard sciences like physics, chemistry, metallurgy, biology, agriculture, etc. This scientific base has allowed us to design and build incredible instruments, machinery, materials, and processes, powered primarily by readily available, reliable, and affordable fossil fuels and nuclear power. These fuels have given humankind a force multiplier. Today one person does what would have required a hundred or a thousand workers in the past. Besides, we can now do tasks that were impossible or unimaginable a century ago.

Force multipliers. Fossil fuels have provided humanity with the ability to extend our physical capabilities by a hundred-X and our intellectual capacity by a million-X. In some applications, it may be a billion-X, and in other instances, by an infinite-X, because we can now do things, we could not do without fossil fuels, even with a million people. We can fly from New York to Rome in six hours; we can land on the moon; we can mine in the Arctic regions, or reach the edge of "quantum supremacy."[415]

These force multipliers have provided us with more and better foods, improved hygiene, cleaner air, cleaner water, better medical care, longer lives, and a higher quality of life by improved shelters and all the many comforts. All of these "wonders" are made possible by our fossil-fueled and nuclear-powered industries and an abundance of affordable and reliable electricity. Hopefully, going forward, as we strive for an even cleaner environment, we will return to more nuclear electrical power. This cheaper and cleaner electricity will be especially beneficial for electric cars and other electrical transportation industries.

Good for everybody. In the past, the rich and powerful lords and ladies always had force multipliers; they were called slaves. The wealthy and the powerful always had it good, and the wealthy of today have it even better. With our affordable and reliable energy, they now have air conditioning, central heating, excellent hospital care, dental care, etc. What about the middle class? Well, only a few of them even existed in the pre-industrialized world. But today, with our force multipliers, these are the people who design, build and operate the industrial-entrepreneurial-commercial industries that continue to provide excellent life and livelihood to all of us.

But today it's the "poor people" whose lives have most improved. Think about the irony that one of the biggest health challenges of the poor has been turned on its head. Historically their most significant threat was starvation and deprivation. Yet today, we have the Mayo Clinic[416] advising us that being overweight is a significant health issue and reminds us of the importance of portion control. In the U.S. and many industrialized countries, individuals on some form of public assistance generally have all the necessities of life and many of the comforts as well. Notice the word "industrialized" in the previous sentence; you can only have an industrialized country if you have plentiful, reliable, and cheap energy.

Developing and underdeveloped countries have also made tremendous progress. This, too, happened because of "fueled industrialization." And how can we have continued and accelerated industrialization without fossil and nuclear energy? A few countries, like India, China, and Pakistan, have about half of the world's seven billion people! Until a few decades ago, starvation for millions was always their biggest threat. But look at this excerpt from a report by the World Development Bank: "*India is a global agricultural powerhouse. It is the world's largest producer of milk, pulses, and spices, and has the world's largest cattle herd (buffaloes), as well as the largest area under wheat, rice, and cotton. It is the second-largest producer of rice, wheat, cotton, sugarcane, farmed fish, sheep & goat meat, fruit, vegetables and tea.*" [417]

- *"Africa Needs Fossil Fuels to End Energy Apartheid"* headlines an article in the Scientific American by Lisa Friedman, ClimateWire, August 5, 2014.[418]
- McKinsey & Company, in their 2015 assessment report states in part: *"This means that almost 600 million people in sub-Saharan Africa lack access to electricity."*[419]

What do these reports tell us? Without electricity, they have no hospitals, no food preservation or refrigeration, no clean water for sanitation. Even today, much of their cooking is done by burning dried animal dung. It means their life expectancies are marginal, and their quality of life is not so good.

But what do our anti-power environmentalist fanatics want to do? They want the world to return to some idyllic, pre-industrialized state, even if it means that millions of these poor people continue to live in misery and die at a young age. We must not let these anti-humanists succeed. I also want to rein in the explosive population growth, but how did we do it in the industrialized countries? We did it by creating wealth through an industry that allows advancements in education, especially education for the women of the world.

First, do no harm! We in the industrialized countries can help accelerate development in these developing countries at no extra cost. All we need to do is stop wasting valuable time and money on the silliness of chasing the CO2 rabbit. We should gift a portion of the billions of dollars now squandered on the CO2 wild-goose pursuit. That would enable these nations to get cheap electricity, clean water, and fertilizers that will save their lives and improve their quality of life.

So, you want to control the climate, do you? After all, what is climate, other than weather patterns and cycles over a long period? We can all talk about the weather and talk about the climate, but one thing we can't talk about is Anthropogenic Weather and Climate Control. Somebody has already filled that job. But, even if we can't control climate change, we can surely prepare for it and adapt to it. More importantly, if we do it well, Darwin will give us his prestigious "survival award."

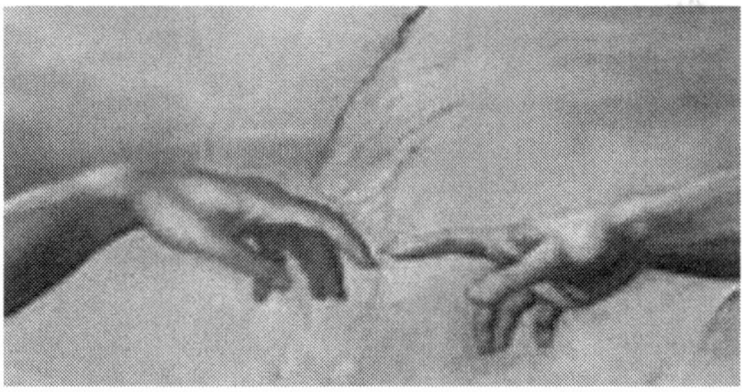

5. MORE SCIENCE STUFF

In the past few decades, significant advancements have been made in the science of climate change. No doubt, a significant driver of these advancements has been in response to the CO2 myth. This myth is primarily marketed by the UN's IPCC, the 97 percent consensus team, academia, and the climate change industry. Whatever their motivations, we have learned that new and real scientific advancements were and continue to be made in the actual science of climate change. For brevity, we'll mention some of the more important ones and the key scientists.

At the top of the list, we have Dr. Valentina Zharkova and her assistant Dr. Helen Popova. They developed a calculative formula for predicting the timing and strengths of the solar magnetic cycles. Let me repeat that. Dr. Zharkova did not come up with a computer model, or a statistical curve fit on historical data. Instead, she derived a calculative function based on solar physics and dynamics, much like the formula *Area = Length X Width,* or $A = \pi r^2$. With this formula, they accurately reconstructed the recorded climate history of the past thousands of years with a 97 percent accuracy then went on to forecast the next hundreds of years with the same expected accuracy. But I fear at some point; it may need to be adjusted for the future onset of the Milankovitch Cycles.

Next on the honor roll, we have Dr. Henrick Svensmark, who first pioneered the link between galactic cosmic rays (GCR) and climate change. After twenty years, his theory seems confirmed by his experiments and by the tests at CERN. These experiments confirmed that when cosmic rays enter the Earth's atmosphere, they collide with the atmospheric gasses, creating tiny aerosols. These aerosols act as “seeds” around which water vapors start to condense. The process continues and keeps clustering together to build bigger and denser clouds.

More clouds = more problems. More cloud cover means more reflecting of the sun’s rays back into outer space. As a result, less solar energy reaches the Earth, and the Earth’s system (air, lands, and oceans) gets colder. But this does not mean that the clouds would be uniformly distributed around the world. The cloud disparity would result in colder temperatures and more rain in one area, but warmer and drier climates at other locations. Both of which will reduce agricultural yields and may cause widespread hunger. This interaction between lower solar activity and galactic cosmic rays dovetails with Dr. Zharkova’s formula, which is predicting low solar activity for cycles 25, 26, and most likely 27. She tells us that we will know for sure in a few years if we will have a Dalton or a Maunder type of cooling, and whether it could last twenty-five to fifty years or more.

Next, let’s put P. D. Jose, Milutin Marjanov, and Dr. Stefani on the same pedestal. They have advanced the theory tying the solar magnetic cycles to the celestial planetary cycles. It appears that Drs. Zharkova and Tallbloke undertook a joint effort to validate this concept. But Dr. Stefani and his team may have beat them to the punch.

Alongside them, we also want to mention some of the “martyrs” of the climate change social wars. They include Drs. Soon, Curry, Lindzen, Tallblocke, Easterbrook, and many others who were the targets for professional and personal destruction by the CO2 consensus industry for defying and exposing their deceptions.

<u>Finally,</u> let's give a special shout-out to Drs. Lindzen, Easterbrook, Spencer, Lehr, and many other dedicated climate scientists. In addition to their many contributions to climate science, these gentlemen need to be recognized for their bravery under fire and their communication skills. They have represented the real climate science well in Washington and the political policy establishments. They bore the brunt of the media, the press, and the 97 percent mob in bringing the climate change truth to the general public, Congress, and the U.S. President.

6. JUST THE FACTS MA'AM

Here we will now document some simple truths that we discovered in our climate change journey, in no particular order:

<u>Polar bears</u>[420] are not and were never endangered by global warming; over the past thirty years of warming, the population has grown from 5,000-10,000 to 20,000-40,000.[421] Global warming has generally benefitted polar bears and other marine mammals.

<u>The greenhouse effect</u> is authentic and consequential. Without it, the planet would have an average temperature of about -15°C instead of the healthy and comfy 15°C we enjoy today, and without it, we'd all be dead.

<u>There's just too little CO2.</u> We learned that total CO2 (human-made plus nature-made) is only a minor contributor to the greenhouse effect. Total CO2 is responsible for about 3.5 percent, and human-made CO2 is responsible for about 0.02 percent of the greenhouse effect. The planet Earth has been and still is in a CO2 starvation mode.

We answered the big question: Has the CO2 increase of the last hundred years been harmful to humankind and the Earth's bio-system or beneficial? The answer is clear; more CO2 is better for the planet and all of its life forms. Less CO2 is harmful to all kinds of life.

We put it to the test:422 We stated that all four of the below conditions must be met to consider CO2, and especially human-made, as a significant problem that we must address. We now have a definitive answer.

Condition-1: An increase in temperature *must follow* an increase in CO2. Conversely, a decrease in temperature *must follow* a reduction in CO2.

Response: Scientific data confirms that temperature always leads, and the quantity of CO2 follows. When the oceans get warmer, they release more CO2, and when they get colder, the oceans reabsorb it.[423]

Result: CONDITION NOT MET

Condition-2: The ice core record of the measured CO2 must accurately reflect what the atmospheric CO2 was at the concurrent time.

Response: Ice core measurements of CO2 are used exclusively by NOAA, NASA, the IPCC, and the media. It does not accurately represent the actual atmospheric CO2 levels of the past ages. Alternative proxies, such as stomatal morphology or similar, should be used to counter-check the polar ice records. Secondly, there is considerable debate on how these two hugely different measuring systems (ice core until 1958 and actual readings post 1958) were "stitched" together.

Result: CONDITION NOT MET

Condition-3: The CO2 increase must have been caused by humankind.

Response: We have demonstrated that total CO2 (natural + human-made) at best only accounts for 3.5 percent of the overall greenhouse effect. The human-made CO2 equals about 0.02 percent of the full greenhouse effect.

Result: CONDITION NOT MET

Condition-4: The increase in atmospheric CO2 (human-made, or total) must be harmful to humans and other living things on Earth.

Response: It's been confirmed that the increased CO2 of the last century has been beneficial for all life on Earth. The elevated CO2 has contributed to improved agricultural yields and a sizable increase of the greening of the planet and cooling of the Earth.

Result: CONDITION NOT MET.

Conclusion: Not one of the four conditions has been met! The human-made CO2 threat is nonexistent.

Notwithstanding the many short-term ups and downs, the overall temperature trends of the past 100 to 150 years have been steadily upward until 1999. By short-term, we mean solar cycles lasting from eleven years to about every 400 years and a few more in between. I don't mean to trivialize these short-term swings, because they can be damaging and deadly, like the Little Ice Age (1650-1720) was. It may also be benign or as beneficial as the global warming seen in the 1978-1998 period. But as we read in Chapter 9, the global temperature over the past 4,000 years has been on a downward trend, dropping by about 3°C from the Holocene high. The twentieth-century warming is an insignificant up-blip on this downward trend.

The Milankovitch cycles, which act on about 20,000 to 100,000-year periods, may be responsible for the devastating 100,000-year and 50,000-year ice age cycles. For these cycles, there is nothing that humanity can do to prevent them or even mitigate their destructive cold cycles. Let me say that another way, over the past 10,000 years, each warming cycle has been a benefit for humankind and the planet. Conversely, each cooling period brought famine, wars, and misery. In the case of the Milankovitch cycles or the shorter term colder solar cycles, we will need to either prepare and adapt or perish by the millions in the best cases, or possibly billions in the worst case. The good news is that we don't need to worry about the Milankovitch cycles for many thousands of years.

With regards to the CO2-AGW (Anthropogenic Global Warming), On the positive side, we can all agree that it has a dominant marketing theme, is well-organized, has world-class spokesmen like Obama, Gore, and Hollywood celebrities. We say impressive because, like all great Hollywood scripts, it identifies one straightforward villain and one "human empowered solution." But the real news is that human-made CO2 has no measurable cause-effect relationship with global climate change.

Human-made CO2 is negligible, meaning humankind does not have the technologies or the energies or resources to produce enough of it to make any measurable difference, even if we wanted to. Yes, the greenhouse effect is real, and it's consequential, and without it, the Earth would likely be in a perpetual ice age. But having said that, here's the reality that adults and children alike need to realize. Whether we fire up the nukes or the fossils fuel plants and cars or build 100,000 windmills per year in the grand scheme of things, human-made CO2 means nothing tangible.

7. CO2 HAS RUN OUT OF GAS[424]

Above we stated that there is not enough CO2 to make a noticeable difference. But you may ask, what happens if humanity keeps producing more and more CO2; could that topple the apple cart? And isn't that why we need to implement an "insurance policy and do it quickly"?

No! That's the simple answer. CO2 is only heated by a limited supply of narrow bandwidth IR light waves. There simply is not enough of this IR to saturate all the CO2 molecules we already have today. What if we double it? NO, it will still make no measurable difference. What if we double that again? NO! Here's what saturation means, it's like once you have painted your house with three coats of red paint, adding yet another layer or ten more will not make it redder. Or, if once you have filled up a glass with water, or soaked a sponge, pouring more water on them will not make them any wetter.

Based on Data, experiments, and analysis and not the hype or pathology, has the increased CO2 of the last fifty years done any damage? After 30 years and hundreds of billions of research dollars spent, there's not one scintilla of data-evidence that it has caused anybody or anything any harm. Has the increased CO2 bestowed any benefits to our planets? The answer is an overwhelming NO and YES. But if the answer is no, it has done no harm, and yes, it has had substantial benefits, why would the press/media not tell us that? Great question-answer? Crickets! [425]

Moreover, why do the IPCC and their allied "97 percent consensus Scientists" continue to tell and threaten us with the impending disasters caused by increased levels of CO2? The answer is straightforward because it does not support the narrative that serves their vital interests. In this book, we examined the history and origins of the IPCC. We saw how the political factions came to dominate the IPCC philosophy, policies, and reporting over the objections of the real climate scientists, even those still affiliated with the IPCC.

The origin of the CO2 hysteria dates back to the 1970s, following the devastating oil embargo, when the International Oil Cartel stopped shipping nearly one hundred percent of their crude oil to the industrialized countries. In the wake of that embargo, industrialized countries believed there was not much oil or gas supply left. It was necessary to find an alternative energy source. At that time, the main competitors were coal and nuclear to unseat king oil.

To gain a competitive advantage, the nuclear industry invented the CO2 global warming scare. This CO2 theme was immediately picked up by environmental lobbyists, who pressured the governments to fund studies with hundreds of millions of dollars and later with tens of billions of dollars. Academia jumped on the CO2 dollar gravy train, as did lobbyists, politicians, and industry, and they all found their home in the IPCC. The rest is history, and the U.S. government will likely award about $20 billion in climate research in 2020, with about 90 percent still going to the CO2 crowd.

No harmful effects have been documented or even theoretically attributed to increased CO2. On the benefits side, NASA satellite data confirms the elevated CO2 has "greened" the planet's forests, fields, farms, and pasture lands by the equivalent to half the size of Australia. NASA data also reveals that deserts have receded because of the increased CO2. More CO2 allows plants to grow in drier areas because at higher CO2 levels, plants need less water. This is especially important to increase farms and pastures for hunger relief for the poorest people. They don't have the means for pumps to access well-water. Think about what sub-Saharan poverty, hunger, and misery look like.

The increased CO2 has also increased the growth of worldwide ocean planktons and aquatic plants. In turn, the plants and planktons increased the oxygen and food supplies in the oceans resulting in increased populations of fish, ocean mammals, and polar bears.

Cause of global warming. What about the continuing claim by the CO2 alarmists that it is the single cause of "global warming"? Dr. J. Lehr used a famous quote by Richard Feynman in his presentation to the U.S. President Trump on climate change in 2017: *"It doesn't matter how elegant your theory is. It doesn't matter how smart you are. If it doesn't agree with experiments, it's wrong."*

8. THE ORIGIN OF THE CO2 IMPENDING "DISASTERS"[426]

How did it start, and why? And how, under all the scrutiny of real science and the exposures of outright fraud, does it persist?

It all started by the nuclear industry. As stated above, it first started with the CO2 fearmongering by the nuclear industry, which opened the floodgates for research and production funding.

Enters the IPCC. Then we learned how the IPCC began as a valid international-cooperative scientific project. But within a few years, it was turned into a political machine controlling tens of billions of dollars each year in the direction of CO2 global warming. Only later was global warming renamed to CO2 climate change when it was seen that global warming had become global cooling or global pause. But what if there was no understandable, no singular, no human controllable climate villain? What would happen to the billions of dollars entrusted to the IPCC or the politicians or the "consensus scientists"? Again, good question – more cricket answers!

We then learned about the plot within the IPCC, NASA, NOAA, and East Anglia University in the "Climategate" scandal. This hacker, who remains anonymous, published one thousand scathing emails and eighty internal documents. These emails revealed a clear pattern of deception showing manipulated historical climate records and created whole new sets of "historical temperature records." Why? For the sole purpose of matching them to the CO2 increase and of matching their narrative. Sad, but no one has gone to jail!

The CO2 alarm is based only on human-made computer models. They were designed to forecast the ever-increasing global warming and endless increases in ocean levels. To date, not one bit of scientific observation, no experiments, not even statistical curve fittings of historical data, has been used to generate their models. Imagine this: more than one hundred different versions of these computer models were designed for billions of dollars to fabricate their climate change projections. But each model was known to be flawed and inaccurate. So, the IPCC took the average of these erroneous models to make their "forecast."

[#] WTF? That's like using a hundred blindfolded people to decide which path to take in a forest at night! When these IPCC models were put to the test to re-predict the historical temperature records, they failed miserably. If they can't even replicate the known historical record, why should we trust them to forecast the unknown future with trillion-dollar policy consequences?

We then learned how a coordinated campaign was launched to libel and smear the real climate scientists; the ones who had the integrity and independence to disagree with the CO2 impending disasters. These brave people were labeled "skeptics" and "deniers." Campaigns were launched in the media/press/internet to discredit their careers and reputations. It was a coordinated attack attempting to destroy them personally, professionally, and financially.

Human-made CO2 theory has lost all scientific legitimacy. Today the human-made CO2 approach is like a chicken with its head cut off. It's still running around in circles, refusing to believe that it's dead. But in their wake, the CO2 villain has become a mighty political, sociological, economic, and pathological hot potato. So, let's go into some of these CO2 science details:
CO2 has increased by more than 40 percent since the industrial revolution. That's what NASA, NOAA, and the IPCC keep blasting. They blame it all on the human-made industries, cars, airplanes, and cows. But we have demonstrated that all greenhouse gasses have increased by similar amounts, thus proving that global warming is not caused by human-made CO2. The simple fact is that the vast majority of these increases came from the sun-warmed oceans in the last fifty to a hundred years. One example is dramatically seen as Pacific Oscillator and the vast El Niño of the 1990s. The other source of error and confusion is how the CO2, from the historical polar ice data, was calculated and stitched together with the latest data in the late 1950s.

CO2 is not a pollutant. Soot, fly-ash, and smoke are pollutants, but CO2 is not a pollutant.

- Today we have the technology to reduce the real pollutants to almost zero. We can do it more cheaply than building redundant solar farms or windmills, plus fossil plants to back them up.
- CO2 is purposely and deceptively conflated with pollution. When they do this, they are deliberately deceiving us.
- The "97 percent scientific consensus" that global warming is caused by human-made CO2 is bogus. Recall the survey of 31,000 scientists and 9,000 Ph.D.'s and the Lindzen petition to the U.S. President signed by hundreds of real climate scientists.

9. MISLEADS AND HEAD-FAKES

The average person who supports the CO2 theory is purposely misled and misinformed by dishonest media, greedy industry leaders, scheming politicians, and self-aggrandizing do-gooders. They see it as a way to make more money and have more power and gain a higher social status.

As an example, I recently spoke to a friend with a Ph.D. and who works in the medical industry. He's a capable and ambitious, busy young man with a family to raise and a career to build. I asked him about the CO2 hysteria and what he thought about it. He replied that the increased CO2 cause sounded reasonable to him but never paid much attention to it. He said we need to do more to protect our fragile environment. After a five-minute discussion, his view was quickly turned because he has the scientific foundation to appreciate what I was telling him. When I asked him to review my book draft, he said, "Sorry, I just got a new project, and I'm swamped but will buy the book when it comes out. "

How is it possible for this brilliant, highly educated young man to be so wrong on such an important issue? The answer is simple but unsettling. It's what he was taught in grade school and high school. In his chosen science field, he was not exposed to any of the "climate science." Today as he's working in his medical specialty, he is repeatedly told about the evil CO2 by the media and politicians, friends, and neighbors who are similarly educated. He's like I was two years ago.

But why does Industry support the CO2 scenario? Because they make more money selling both a solar (or a wind) plant plus the mandatory backup fossil. And if they want to add more bells and whistles, like carbon-capturing and sequestration, then more sales for them. And if they also want battery storage, they add it to the bill. In this manner, they can turn a potential $150 million sale for a combined cycle gas plant into a sale of $300 or $400 million. The more, the merrier.
Politicians support the CO2 myth to get more government funding to buy more votes, and of course, they will get more campaign contributions from the emerged CO2 industry.
Career-minded young scientists (like my neighbor) support the CO2 myth to get easy access to the ever-increasing research grants to fund their studies.

This helps them advance their careers and pay their mortgages, country club fees, house bills, and free social kudos to boot.

By contrast, the vast majority of the "skeptical" scientific studies are done by retired professors or financially secure scientists, who can afford to be honest.

The simple fact is that 90 percent of all U.S. government-funded climate change grants still go to projects that support the CO2 myth. This is an outrage, and we must get this to at least fifty-fifty.

10. # THE NEED FOR AN INSURANCE POLICY

Most people who support the CO2 theory are misled, and misinformed and cunning politicians have solidly jumped on board. Every Democratic politician has fully embraced and, all presidential candidates have launched several versions of the "Green New Deal."

- The argument is made that we should take preemptive measures just in case the CO2 threat is the real driver of the coming run-away global warming. They tell us the world needs an insurance policy. This usually is a good thought process only if the insurance premium costs outweigh the expected costs of the risks.
- But spending 20-50-90 trillion dollars on the "Green New Deal," insurance premium will bankrupt the country and maybe cover one or two percentage, or none of the so-called CO2 risk. This is just silly.

But I have a perfectly valid alternative insurance policy that has all of the following advantages:

- It's totally carbon-free, absolutely zero CO2 output without the need for complicated, expensive and challenging measures to maintain carbon capturing and sequestration equipment,
- It requires a tiny fraction of the land compared to wind or solar. Besides, it requires no fossil-fueled backup plant because it's the singularly most reliable means of generating electricity,
- It is the safest and least expensive electrical generation mode,
- It is ecofriendly, zero emissions of any kind,
- Kills no birds, kills no bats, kills no fish, kills no bald eagles,

- The generating costs are likely to decrease in the future as we make technological upgrades,
- It will not bankrupt us, it will not endanger our economic or industrial infrastructures, but will give it a boost benefitting everyone.

It's called nuclear power! And hopefully, in 15-20 years, we will start thorium reactors, which are even less expensive to build, operate, and maintain than the present uranium reactors. Also, it will allow us to recycle the spent uranium fuel. So, while thorium generates electricity, it will also solve the uranium spent fuel problem. Spent uranium fuel has enormous costs and risks because it has a dangerous half-life of thousands of decades. But, we can recycle this uranium spent fuel by using it as fuel in a thorium reactor. So while it's generating electricity, it will simultaneously reduce the uranium half-life to a manageable 300-400 years.
Now, this is an insurance policy we cannot afford to pass up.

11. # SOCIOECONOMIC THEFT

Sadly, we also learned about the use of "human-made CO2 climate change" as a tool for socioeconomic theft.

- In the U.S., the middle class and the poor are subsidizing the rich to be richer, the politicians to be more powerful, the elites to be seen ever more virtuous, and socially responsible.
- The rich get tax rebates when they buy a Tesla and a lower electrical utility rate on their monthly electrical bills. But the poor bloke that can only afford to buy a 1968 Datsun gets screwed. No tax rebate. He also has to pay higher taxes and higher utility rates to offset the credits to the Tesla buyer. Then he must bear the scorn of being a climate denier or an enemy of the environment.
- Same issues with subsidized solar panels. The rich get savings and kudos; the poor get screwed!
- California recently passed requirements for constructing new homes. No solar panels on the roof mean no permit. Again, no problem for the rich. They get their tax rebate, their lower electrical rates, and lots of social kudos. But Joe lunch-bucket now can't afford the new house. He must buy an old fixer-upper and subsidize the rich and bear the social scorn.

- We are also profiting by ripping-off the people of the developing and underdeveloped countries as detailed in item 12, below.

12. [#] THE WORLD DEVELOPMENT BANK (WDB)

The WDB was set up to help less developed and underdeveloped countries to fund projects to help improve their lives. One of the most essential and immediate ways to do this is to provide them with cheap and reliable electricity. Now look at this map and tell me you don't just want to cry. At night there are practically zero lights in Africa. Almost none in most of South America. These people are living in the dark ages. They have no electricity to keep food and medicines from spoiling and no power for the pumps for water for drinking, hygiene, or irrigation. No electricity means no hospitals, no x-rays, no CAT scans of any kind, no emergency delivery capability means higher infant and mother mortality rates. It also means no way to escape from subsistence-level farming. They will continue to live in misery and die at a young age.

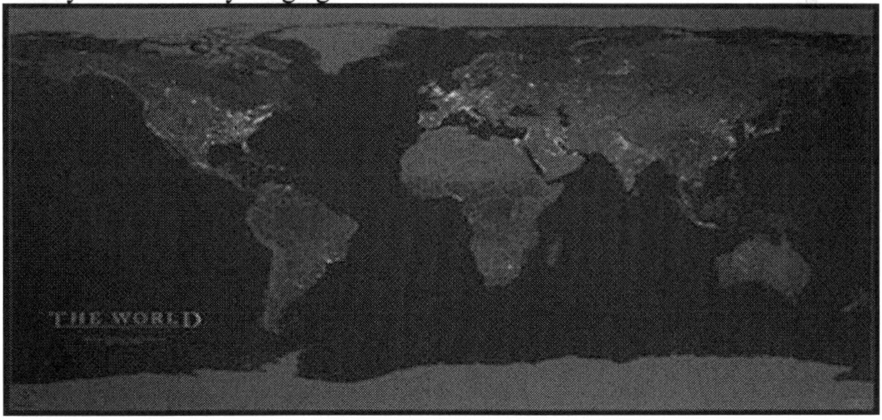

The WDB was set up to fix these critical humanitarian issues. Before the IPCC/CO2 scam, they were making slow but decent progress. Affordable coal, oil, or gas-powered plants were launched, providing them with affordable, reliable electricity.

Wasted money, wasted time, lost lives. Many of these coal plants used to take three to four years to build in the USA. But because of the third world inefficiencies, it might take them maybe double the time. But with the ever-tightening EPA regulations and litigations of the last few decades, it's now taking five years or longer years in the U.S. But, the WDB was forced to implement similar environmental requirements in countries with near dysfunctional governments. The U.S. benchmark of five to ten years jumped to fifteen to twenty years and resulted in many of these WDB projects to be abandoned. Why?

During this period of EPA induced delays, the entire regulatory scope was changed. It now requires that the WDB grants and loans can only be used for solar or wind plants. To their credit, the WDB sought relief, saying they should at least be able to complete the coal plants that were already being constructed. Unfortunately, the IPCC is not relenting and forcing governments to stop those constructions. So, these poor people not only never got the electric plants they were promised fifteen to twenty-five years ago but are now forced to change to unreliable and intermittent solar or wind power.

So, billions of dollars' worth of incomplete structures are seen on their countryside as a sad reminder to these people, of how many lives were lost because of the whimsical regulations and outright silly rules of the rich-industrialized countries. So how did these silly-CO2-chasing rules benefit these wretched people that the WDB was to have helped? It didn't! It resulted in a kick them while there're down with their cynicism that prioritized silly ideals over saving human lives.

[#] <u>Let's discuss the root problem</u> of the big "E" Environmental activists and explore the how's and whys of migrating to these extreme positions. The simple answer is they don't care about people, humanity, or starving children. Why? Because in their twisted value system, humans are the enemy of the planet. The fewer humans, the better it is for "the planet." If millions of humans must die, well, so be it! I know I'm at risk for a five-yard delay of game penalty. But please indulge me one more minute, because this is what puts fire in my belly and tears in my eyes. Look at this absurdity! The WDB wanted to keep forging ahead and completing those fossil power plants that were already started and delayed. But no! These Environmentalists are now crucifying the WDB because the WDB wants to continue building these cheap fossil fuel power plants to help these poor starving people.

These poor people can't afford the luxury of the "green power" plus their backup fossil fuel plants. Nor can they afford expensive scrubbers and precipitators and filtering and carbon-capturing gadgets as we can in the overdeveloped and self-indulgent countries. They need affordable, cheap, and reliable electricity and they need it ASAP!

13. BACK TO SCIENCE.

Nuclear is the cheapest, cleanest, and safest source of electrical power. But it is plagued by bad press that's driven by the same wrong-minded environmental extremists plus the same media and the uninformed public, just like we saw in the above CO2-driven scam.

- Nonetheless, uranium reactors are proven to be safer than all other electrical generating plants, including solar. Have you any idea how many solar panels and windmill installers die each year from slipping and falling from solar roofs or towering windmills? [427]
- But in truth, nuclear plants do have one major problem, and that's the spent fuels that remain dangerously radioactive for thousands of years.
- Uranium-fueled reactors were selected sixty years ago for electrical power generation because of the technology similarity with the U.S. military uranium requirements. But today China and some European countries are now seriously studying the thorium-based liquid-salt reactors for electrical power generation.
- But now, here's another magnificent piece of irony, that we discovered on this journey! Based on actual tests conducted in the Oak Ridge National Laboratories in Tennessee in the 1960s, the science of the thorium reactors was validated, and it offered many advantages over uranium reactors.
  - It was demonstrated to be much cheaper to build and operate than a conventional uranium reactor. And, unlike uranium, thorium has an

unlimited supply of fuel, it's very affordable, and is readily available.

- More importantly, it is safer, and the nuclear wastes of the uranium reactors can be recycled in a thorium reactor to generate more power. In the process, it will reduce their dangerous radioactive life from thousands of years to a much more manageable 200-300 years, making it much more eco-friendly.
- Yes, we can excuse and find solace in the fact that thorium was abandoned at a time of the U.S.-Soviet Cold War-dominated mindsets. When assured, mutual self-destruction was the order of the day, and perhaps it was the right decision. But that's not the world or the reality of today, and let's ask the fundamental question now! Why not invest in thorium reactors instead of the pipe dreams of "going green"?
- Let's step up and ask the old question, "Why not thorium?" Why not divert some of the billions of dollars wasted on the CO2 shell game and use a part of that money to fund thorium reactor research on a priority basis?
- Otherwise, we may soon be locked out by the Chinese and Europeans from this vast new industry. Ironically, its technical base was developed here in the USA.

14. POLITICAL ARROGANCE AND INFECTIOUS STUPIDITY[428]

Here in the U.S., we have a major political party saying CO2, and all fossil fuels are the villain. They must destroy the CO2-based industries no matter how many billions or trillions it will cost. No matter if the foundational economic structures of our society are irreparably harmed. We can't read the minds or intentions of these doomsday prophets, but we can certainly ask some good questions. There are many excellent and reputable scientists who, at first, signed on to the anthropogenic CO2-fueled global warming. But over the years, many left the "consensus Kool-Aid" movement and became vocal and proud "Skeptics" and "Deniers." So here are some basic questions:

Question 1: Why did many scientists, like Dr. Curry and Dr. Lindzen, leave the CO2 bandwagon gravy train, but other equally accredited scientists like Dr. Mann or Dr. Hansen, chose to stay the course? Was it the easy funding research dollars that increasingly flowed from the U.S. government to the "consensus scientists"? Did it assure them a stable and rewarding career and salary? Was it the fame and notoriety that followed the highly visible President Obama and the Hollywood elites? Was it some higher-more noble calling? How will we ever know?

Question 2: The IPCC started to find the root causes and the extent of global warming led by a team of able world-class scientists. So, why within only a few years did it become the fiefdom for bureaucrats from more than 180 countries. Capable scientists write the IPCC reports, which are then edited and polished by career politicians, often ignoring or overriding the reports that were drafted by able and fair-minded scientists. Equally important, why was the charter of the IPCC explicitly written to address only: Anthropogenic Global Warming (AGW)? Why was it specifically chartered not to investigate any of the other and real causes of climate change?

Question 3: Even with my limited knowledge of climate science, I can see the many holes in the CO2 AGW story. Surely the many scientists who stayed the IPCC course know it much better than I. So, what gives?

Question 4: Why did some of these very learned scientists, (Dr. M. Mann of Penn State, Prof P. Jones CRU/East Angle University, Dr. U. Wall NOAA/NCDC, and many others) participate in rewriting historical climate data records? Did they want to show a direct connection of CO2 increasing with global warming? More importantly, why are they still doing it today with the surface-based instruments? And why are they still getting away with it?

Question 5: Why are worldwide politicians, especially in the U.S., becoming ever bolder and shriller with their fearmongering? Daily we are reminded that the world will end in ten years unless we dump all cars, all planes, and all cows, as outlined in the "Green New Deal." Why such a call to battle for the elusive CO2 dread with a cost approaching fifty to a hundred trillion dollars?

15. ENVIRONMENTAL PREEMPTIVE WAR[429]

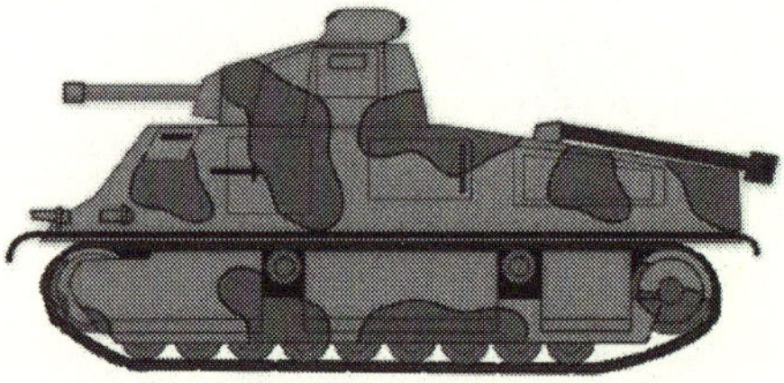

Now to follow up on the above silliness with insanity. We have today *"serious and scholarly papers"* and *"scholarly books,"* talking about possible needs and justifications for a "Preventative Environmental War."[430]

Worsening the concern is that these are written by university and college professors and political historians. Here is the overview of one such article published in the *Journal of Military Ethics*, 2019, by Adam Betz.[431] *"This paper argues that there is a just cause for war to prevent the future hazards of anthropogenic climate change even if, because of the Non-Identity Problem, that cause is not grounded in the rights of future generations. The evidential demands for justifying preventive military action to forestall climate change have been met, as a majority of climate scientists affirm that climate change is underway and is likely to become seriously hazardous for future generations."*

These guys are not talking about a verbal war or metaphorical war, but blockades, and shooting things! Really? What will you do against big time-nuclear armed polluters like China, India, and Pakistan?

- Are you serious? Are you sane? (See Chapter 7.4, "The limits of sanity.")

16. WHAT DID WE LEARN FROM THE "CLIMATEGATE" SCANDAL?

The scandal revealed, in over five-thousand emails and countless documents, that data was purposely manipulated by individuals and organizations, as detailed in Chapter 8.I. NASA and NOAA undertook a task to "normalize" historical temperature records and fabricate new historical temperature records. They did this to dramatize the temperature increase in the last decades of the twentieth century. As revealed in the leaked emails, they had specific tasks to achieve their goals, and here they are:

Data Tampering:

- Delete the Daulton Minimum
- Erase the Maunder Minimum
- Obscure the historic high temperatures of the dust bowl 1930s
- Accelerate the warming of the 1978 and ongoing
- "Hide the decline." Were specific words used to hide the fact that global warming stopped in 1999, and were actions taken to conceal the declining temperatures after 2000?

Identify and dox specific individuals, labeled "Climate Deniers" or "Skeptics" who would later be targeted:

- For professional, career, personal, and financial destruction.
- By fabricating rumors, lies, and false narratives against them.
- By calling into question their credibility by raising doubts about funding sources and affiliations.
- For starting coordinated press/media/internet attacks to spread accusations, rumors, and narratives against them.
- Primary targets included Judith Curry, Willi Soon, Richard Lindzen, Valentina Zharkova, Rog Tallbloke, and others.

Concocted a four-point strategy to support the human-made CO2 narrative:

1) Makeup and magnify tear-jerking stories and outrages like human-caused polar bear extinction, especially heart-wrenching stories about cute cubs eaten by their starving daddy bears. Stoke fears by predicting the loss of millions of lives because of starvation and loss of farmlands.

2) Use talented photoshopping to get the images out. For example, New York City under twenty feet of water, or half of Florida disappearing beneath an angry ocean.
3) Paint vivid images of hundreds of millions of "climate refugees" tracking along in deserts that were once fertile farmland and pastures before human-made CO2.
4) Then, as a bonus, they throw virtue and nobility signaling to aggrandize their holy cause to save the planet.

17. THE MYTH OF "CLEAN, RENEWABLE ENERGY"[432]

For reference, the reader is invited to review Chapter 3, Question 13, where we see the heavy price paid by Germany, Sweden, and other countries for pursuing their "green energy" decisions and related issues with wind and solar power. Wind farms are a waste of money, a waste of land, and a waste of fossil-fueled energy. Let's do an energy balance for a typical wind turbine of about 1.5 megawatts. The structure is 400-450 feet tall and weighs somewhere around 250-300 tons of steel, concrete, and especially aluminum. Consider the millions of megawatt-hours (MWh) of electrical energy, fossil fuels, and nuclear energy used to get the materials to the site.

- Each turbine will need about fifty to sixty acres of land, and it must be clear of all trees and obstructions. So, out come the chain saws and bulldozers and dynamite to clear the surrounding environment. Also, the adjacent lands cannot be used for anything else because of the dangers associated with the breakage of a wind turbine blade.
- Let's now assume we have thirty of these turbines constituting about a 50 MW plant on a 2,500- to the 3,000-acre field, and, based on available data, we can expect this plant to run on average three to five hours a day. But what happens when the wind is not blowing? No problem. We build a standby fossil fuel-powered 50 MW combined cycle plant.
- So, we need two 50 MW plants (one solar and one fossil) to produce 50 MW of power. We more than doubled the cost of the equipment and one hundred-fold increase of arable farmlands.

- But then the fun starts. To assure that our entire electrical power grid does not blackout if the wind stops blowing, we need to have the fossil fuel plant ready to go online in seconds. A typical startup of such a fossil plant could take an hour or more. So, to make it available immediately, we need to have the fuel plant in partial operation, i.e., running at about 90-95 percent power while the windmill is chugging.
- Now the backup fossil plant is running off-design point. This results in inefficient burning, thereby generating more emissions than it would if running at full power.
- At this point, we are burning almost as much fossil fuel in this backup reserve mode as we would if there was no wind turbine there. So, after making this double investment in capital and the land, maybe we have a few megawatt-hours per day of net output from the wind turbine.
- The question now dominates: will it ever generate enough net output electricity over a twenty-five to thirty-year life cycle to recover the original energy that it took to build the windmill? Probably not, and then you have all the expenses and power required of tearing it down. You also have to figure out how you are going to dispose of all those tens of tons of steel-reinforced concrete foundation.
- No problem—we fire up the fossil powered jackhammers!
- We note the silliness for "free, renewable, clean, green solar power." But unlike the wind turbines, at least the solar farms don't kill the thousands of birds and bats as the wind turbines do.

And the final blow to common sense, an article published on October 29, 2019, titled; *"CA Solar Panel Push Still Leaves Residents In The Dark As Grid Shuts Down For Fires."*[433] It opens up with the following two sentences, and yes, it says that. State laws mandate all new housing must have solar panels that can supply 50% of your electrical requirements by 2020. But, here's the irony, if PG&E has to shut off your electricity for any reason, like wildfire danger reduction, you can't get any useful electricity from your roof panels; you are electrically dead like everybody else!

As I reported in March of 2018, the light-on-wisdom, heavy-on-compulsion, government of California recently mandated that all new homes must be at least 50 percent solar-powered by 2020, which not only is an immoral command on peaceful homebuilders and buyers, it is an imposition of higher expenses and energy inefficiency.

And, now, it turns out that solar-paneled California residents were sadly mistaken in anticipating that their "solar homes" would have electricity when the power corporation PG&E shuts down supply "to lower fire risk."

18. # HUMAN FRAILTIES AND FOLLIES[434]

In our journey, we witnessed the full breadth and depth of the many and varied human frailties. Some made us laugh out loud, and some just brought a small smirk on our faces. Others made us upset, angry, or outraged, and some brought sadness in our hearts and tears in our eyes. Overall I would venture to say that perhaps the one surprise that stood out on this journey of discovery is how little progress humanity has made in the past several thousand years in terms of intellectual development and spiritual growth. And while that may take a whole new book to do it justice, let's enumerate the top few surprises.

Education and intelligence are no defense against ignorance or stupidity. We are perhaps the most educated people to ever inhabit the planet! But willful ignorance is rampant. Too many people are too confident in what they think they know that they refuse to hear what does not conveniently fit in their box. Worse, they will hate the person who challenges their comfort blanket and tries to take them out of their safe spaces, or even intrude into their safe zones. Too often, we find brilliant minds, and well-educated persons fall victim to the outright silliness of fearmongering, self-deception, and self-aggrandizement.

- Fear is the strongest human emotion because if properly used and manipulated, fear can turn intellect and all the other emotions on their heads. Congruent with this is that there seem to be a few synapses in the brain that have super sensitive receptors to the fear virus.
- We need to tell children scary bedtime stories. We need a high priest to tell us which virgin we need to throw into the volcano to satisfy the gods. We need to have politicians tell us who the bad guys are who will come, rape, kill, and steal so that we build an army and destroy them before they destroy us.

- <u>Good charlatans understand and appreciate the power of fear</u> and rely on our individual and collective intellectual laziness to:
  - Create the fear
  - Reinforce the fear
  - Make it ever more imminent and scarier
  - And if the charlatans do this well, they'll get us to do whatever they want because they promise if we do what we are told, they will take away our fears.

19. # THE SELF-RIGHTEOUS EGO RIDE

Now let's wrap this up with a personal story I experienced with my dear friends at the country club. This deals with one of my favorite subjects: socioeconomic theft, better known as "how to kick the poor and steal their pennies when they're not looking." So here we go with some comic relief with a morality play in three spontaneous acts:

<u>Act I:</u>[435] We have Mr. Country Club, and he's feeling good because he just bought a Tesla. In case you didn't know, Teslas are so totally eco-friendly, so cool. They have zero emissions, zero pollutants, and produce zero CO2, and they cost a ton. Just call my friend, Mr. Environment Sensitive Guy. So, he's feeling pretty good about himself and tells his buddy at the club how he also saved mucho bucks by buying the Tesla and got a ten percent energy rebate. Plus, on top of protecting the environment, he'll be saving money on his monthly electric bill with the eco-rate discount. His buddy, Mr. Me-too, says, Nice!, I just got a research grant from State University for $500-K to do a study on the global warming/CO2 effect on the pink and yellow salamander in my backyard. I think I can now also afford to buy a Tesla.

<u>Act II:</u> Mr. Country Club goes home and sees a flyer saying that he qualifies for a tax credit and a utility discount if he puts solar panels on his roof. He

does some simple math and shows he recovers his investment in –four or five years, and after that, he benefits from the discounted utility rates. Nice!

Act III: Meanwhile, Mr. Joe Lunch-bucket is driving to the club to cut the grass in his 1968 Datsun. He's paying income taxes to subsidize the Tesla rebate, paying the premium electrical rate and the U.S. government grant to fund Mr. Me-too for the research on the pink and yellow salamander. So, what can we do to remedy this injustice?

20. TIME TO TAKE OUT THE CRAYONS

And have some real fun! We'll call it ~~Alice in Wonderland:~~ Alice in the Anthropogenic CO2 Food Chain. As you read their profiles, see which characters you can identify among your friends and relatives and yourself. Heck, we could turn it into a friendly little board game.

The top 2 percenters:[436] These are the barons of the industry—Al Gore, Warren Buffet, Jeff Immelt, the carbon exchange traders, top Hollywood celebs, kings and sheiks of the oil cartels, sports superstars, trust fund kids, etc. The ones who expect to make even more money from the CO2-hoax game.

The top 5 percenters:[437]
These are the knights of the industry; CEO wannabes, celebs wannabes, Hollywood producers, U.S. Senators, tenured professors, late-night "comedians," etc.

The top 10 percenters; [438]Congress reps, cable news talking heads, NYT-WaPo columnists, radio-TV talking mouths, untenured professors, redemption-seeking bureaucrats, city mayors, state reps/senators, etc.

The top middle-ish percenters: [439] Factory-union members, Congress/Senate aides, city hall workers, teachers retired too young, social assistance beneficiaries, college graduates with degrees in sexology and gender studies but who can't tell the difference between a fig newton and Newton's physics.

Bottom whatever left percents:
You're living in your parent's basement, can't get a job or a date, can't pay back the college loans on a McMac salary. You vote for the Green New Deal and wait for the Living Minimum Wage, want free college tuition, and demonstrate to legalize pot.

21. WTF-WWYT?[6]

---

[6] WWYT = What Were You Thinking?

In this concluding segment, I want to give some particular parting messages to my baby-boomer generation and comrades.

- You freaking SOBs. You really screwed things up (visualize here Charleston Heston in front of the toppled Statue of Liberty in the movie *Planet of the Apes*, all broken up) by the destructive power of ignorance, arrogance, and dismissiveness.
- You squandered your inheritance from the "greatest generation" parents and wasted it in self-indulgent silliness and laziness! And when that money ran out, you committed generational theft by stealing money from your children and grandchildren. Nice!
- You screwed up our educational system and our value system to satisfy your intellectual laziness and heaped the following generations with debts they can never repay, wrecking their educational opportunities.
- Instead of now charging at the CO2 windmills in search of redemption, why not read this book? Read also a few books on education and communication and invest some time with your children and grandchildren and repair some of these mistakes?
- I am placing my hopes and bets and my prayers, not so much on you, not even on Gen X, but the Millennials and Gen Z.
- You screwed them and their value system beyond repair. I now pray to God that the Millennials and Gen Z will see the collective folly of this failed and failing generation.
- I hope they can restore our educational, value systems, and our humanity.
- God bless you, Millennials, and Gen Z, and forgive us for our trespasses.

22. GROWING CONSENSUS FOR GLOBAL COOLING

1. NASA Sees Climate Cooling Trend Due to Low Sun Activity.[440]

Written by James Murphy on October 2, 2018,[441] in Latest News. Below are the opening sections of the article. We knew that it was only a matter of time before we would see this news coming. NASA has been running interference for the IPCC and the 97 percent consensus team for more than twenty-five years. But now, even NASA has started to acknowledge the reality that global cooling is here finally.

However, NASA is not quite ready to fully embrace the future temperature decline. Instead, it is choosing its words carefully to depict this cooling period of the last twenty years as a mere "pause" or a short-term "setback on the CO2 global warming march." If you're a tech nerd, this article is a must-read.[442]

"The climate alarmists just can't catch a break. NASA is reporting that the sun is entering one of the deepest Solar Minima of the Space Age, and Earth's atmosphere is responding in kind.

"We see a cooling trend," said Martin Mlynczak of NASA's Langley Research Center. "High above Earth's surface, near the edge of space, our atmosphere is losing heat energy. If current trends continue, it could soon set a Space Age record for cold."

"The thermosphere always cools off during Solar Minimum. It's one of the most important ways the solar cycle affects our planet," said Mlynczak, who is the associate principal investigator for SABER.
Who knew that that big yellow ball of light in the sky had such a big influence on our climate?"

<u>2. Did global warming stop in 1998?</u>[443]

Author: Rebecca Lindsey, *Economist -September 4,* 2018. "No, but thanks to *natural variability* (note 1) *volcanic eruptions,* (note 3), *relatively low*

> <u>Author's Observations:</u>
> Note 1: "Natural variability generally refer to the Milankovitch sun-earth cycles and includes solar orbit, precession, obliqueness, solar Barycenter wobble, etc. which are major determinants of climate change and totally outside of man's control.
> Note 2: This is the sun's internal dynamo which we discussed in detail. Presently it's greater in the scope of climate change than the Milankovitch cycles. On a longer term time scale, we are not so certain.
> Note 3: Volcanic eruptions are short period events so they would affect weather temperatures, but not climate change.
> Note 4: NOAA generally uses land-based temperature records which they have been manipulating for years. Had they used the satellite data, it would have shown a decline in thermosphere temperature starting in 2000.

solar activity (note 2), the rate of average global surface warming from 1998-2012 was slower than it had been for two to three decades leading up to it …"

"How much slower depends on the fine print: which global temperature dataset you look at, whether it includes the Arctic and the specific periods you compare. Regardless, the big picture of long-term global warming remained unchanged."

3. <u>Who pressed the pause button?</u>[444] Mar 6, 2014. In this extract from an article in the *Economist*, we see clear evidence of a temperature pause or decrease, thus questioning the entire premise of anthropogenic CO2-driven global warming.

"BETWEEN 1998 and 2013, the Earth's surface temperature rose at a rate of 0.04°C a decade, far slower than the 0.18°C increase in the 1990s. Meanwhile, emissions of carbon dioxide (which would be expected to push temperatures up) rose uninterruptedly. This pause in warming has raised doubts in the public mind about climate change. A few skeptics say flatly that global warming has stopped. "

"This is the opposite of what happened at first. As evidence piled up that temperatures were not rising much, some scientists dismissed it as a blip. The temperature, they pointed out, had fallen for much longer periods twice in the past century or so, in 1880-1910 and again in 1945-75 (see chart), even though the general trend was up. Variability is part of the climate system, and a 15-year hiatus, they suggested, was not worth getting excited about….."

4. <u>*Discover* Magazine, is it time to rethink CO2-driven global warming?</u>[445] This extract from a 2018 article, by Tom Yulsman, March 12, 2018, is yet another article in the developing trend that questions what's all the fuss

about CO2. Essentially it asks the question, is it time for us to rethink that CO2 drives global warming and primarily by human-made CO2?
"This is not to say that I and the other writers and editors here at Discover view science as being infallible. Far from it. We recognize that as a human endeavor, science is prone to error born of vanity, preconceived notions, confirmation bias, a herd mentality, etc. Scientists know this better than anyone, so skepticism is one of their cardinal values. So is the recognition that even today's most widely accepted theories may have to be modified or even replaced tomorrow if new evidence requires it.
Journalists are also supposed to be skeptical and self-critical. We should frequently ask ourselves things like, "How do I know this? Am I sure? Maybe I should check because I could be deceived by my preconceived notions."
"And so, in this case, I thought it would be useful to delve deeper into what scientists know of the link between carbon dioxide and climate over the geologic timescale, and CO2's overall role as a kind of..."

5. The Next Grand Solar Minimum, Cosmic Rays, and Earth Changes [446] (an introduction).[447] By: *Sacha Dobler on 14, January 2018:*

"What to expect in a Grand Solar Minimum? How does an increase in galactic cosmic rays affect the Earth's climate and also tectonic activity/thermostat for the planet?"

Author observation: This article provides a simplified explanation of the highly technical paper presented by Dr. Zharkova. It essentially says that about every 400 years, a grand solar minimum likely occurs. It's centered on the sun's low magnetic field activity, which reduces the sun's magnetic field and solar winds over the Earth.[448] This allows more cosmic rays to reach the Earth, causing an increase in cloud formation, thus cooling the planet. From the article:
"Here is a simplified description of the basic mechanism:"

"A solar maximum is a period within the 11-year solar cycle of high solar magnetic field and high sunspot count. Sunspots are highly magnetic and visually dark spots or 'holes' in the photosphere of the sun, where solar flares can erupt.

A solar minimum is the low activity trough of the 11-year solar cycle (Schwabe Cycle). A Grand Solar Minimum is a period of several successive very low Schwabe Cycles, usually coinciding with phases of climate disruption and – in the long run -cooling. An example is the Maunder Minimum (c. 1645 and 1715) that coincided with the coldest phase of the Little Ice Age. The Little Ice Age, from which we have been emerging since c. 1850, was the coldest period of at least the last 8,000 years, possibly the entire Holocene. Grand Solar Minima recur in clusters roughly every 200-400 years. 27 Grand Minima have been identified during the Holocene (Usoskin et al. *2007). Thus, we were in Grand Solar Minimum about 1/6 of the total time."*

6. Cosmic Rays and Earth Changes449 (an introduction) In the following technical paper, the authors make a case for the relationship between volcanic/earthquake activities and cosmic rays.450 By Kovalyov, M. (corresponding author). In previous writing, we have explained in detail how, during periods of low solar magnetic activities, there is an increase in GCR that reaches the Earth's system. The authors here make a connection between cosmic rays and volcanic/seismic activities on Earth.

"This article describes the authors' observation that the seismic activity seems to show better correlation with cosmic rays, as measured by cosmic rays' intensity and abbreviated by CRI rather than with solar activity as measured by sunspot numbers and abbreviated by SSN. The two are correlated as shown in 1; high SSN correlates with low CRI, Cosmic rays are comprised of the extra-solar cosmic rays originating outside of the Solar System and the solar cosmic rays produced by the Sun. Near Earth CRI is known to be modulated by cyclical solar activity with the average cycle of about 10.85 -10.975 years long.[1] *We shall refer to such cycles as primary solar cycles. The physical mechanism of the solar activity is unknown but is currently believed to be solely of purely solar origin, with several theories attempting to explain it. Cosmic rays actually are not rays at all but particles, 90% of which are protons, 9% are alpha particles. A bit more careful analysis of Figure 1 shows that the maxima/minima of CRI lag the minima/maxima of SSN by a few months. The time lag, explained in Figure 2, further confirms the current paradigm that the solar activity modulates CRI. Recent work [6], however, suggests that not only SSN modulates CRI but also CRI affect.*

7. Astrophysicists link volcanic eruptions and Grand Solar Minimum [451]
By David Hilton, *Originally published May 23, 2018*
"The eruption of Mt Kilauea in Hawaii has provided some stunning imagery for news reports. What is left out, however, is that the Kilauea eruption is part of a global trend of increased volcanic eruptions and a harbinger of more to come.
Also omitted from news reports on the eruption is an explanation of the cause. According to a team of Japanese astrophysicists, though, the cause is not a mystery. They demonstrated conclusively in 2011 that explosive volcanic eruptions are triggered by cosmic rays.
Cosmic rays are high-energy radiation that originates from outside our galaxy. They travel in streams from intergalactic sources, like rivers through the cosmos fueled by supernovae. The uptick in volcanic activity we are witnessing globally is being driven by higher rates of these cosmic rays hitting the planet. The increase in cosmic rays that the Earth is experiencing right now, moreover, is being caused by a period of diminished solar output our solar system entered in 2017. This decline in solar output can be measured by counting sunspots and is known as a Grand Solar Minimum (GSM) That we have entered a GSM as of last year is not controversial. It's mainstream news ..."

8. Sunspots, planetary alignments, and solar magnetism: A progress review,[452] Vistas in Astronomy, Volume 35, Part 1, 1992, Pages 39-7, by P.A.H.Seymour* M.Willmott † A.Turner* Another must-read.
Abstract[453] *"This paper discusses a new theory of the solar cycle which is based on the concept of resonant coupling between the tidal forces due to the planets and the evolving magnetic field of the Sun. The theory combines the advantages of two earlier classes of theories and also overcomes the disadvantages of these classes. In order to set the new proposals in context we describe briefly the salient features of sunspots, the solar cycle and some of the theories relevant to the presentation of the new theory. We also introduce aspects of canal tidal theory since these form the basis of our proposal."*

Author's comments: The previous four papers appear to make a vital link between the solar magnetic activity as being related or caused by the gravitational forces induced by key planets, including Earth, Venus, Mars, and Jupiter. More must-reads for nerds. Please follow; the pieces are coming together.

9. And then there's physics.[454] Posted on June 6, 2019, by Willard. An abstract stakeholder's dialog. Vladimir, or V, is the expert.

Author's comments: A thought-provoking article on the scope, duties, and ethics of science and the consequences of letting the "experts" define the solution boundaries. Instead, the policies should be set by independent policymakers. I do not generally agree with this approach used by the IPCC as an example of what happens to science when corrupted by politics, money, and bureaucrats. Fig .26. [455]

"My point can be reduced to the following Moorean sentence, the paradigmatic example being "it is raining but I don't believe it is raining":

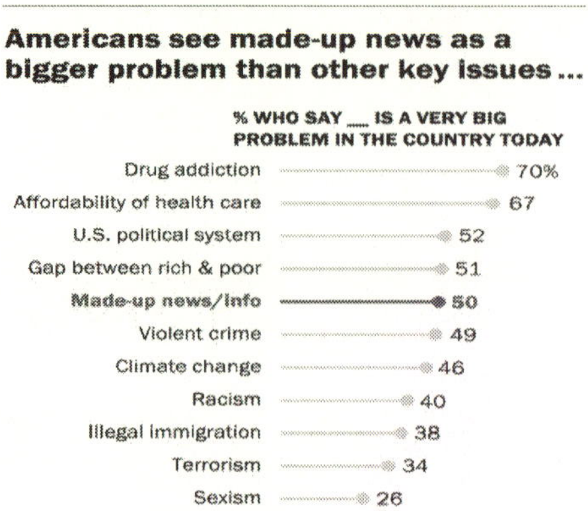

10. Trust in the press/media, Pew Research456, June 5, 2019: *Many Americans Say Made-Up News Is a Critical Problem That Needs To Be Fixed.*
Politicians viewed as major creators of it, but journalists

are seen as the ones who should fix it.
Article By Amy Mitchell, *Jeffrey Gottfried, Sophia Fedeli, Galen Stocking And Mason Walker.*

"Many Americans say the creation and spread of made-up news and information is causing significant harm to the nation and needs to be stopped, according to a new Pew Research Center survey of 6,127 U.S. adults conducted between Feb. 19 and March 4, 2019, on the Center's American Trends Panel.
Indeed, more Americans view made-up news as a very big problem for the country than identify terrorism, illegal immigration, racism and sexism that way. Additionally, nearly seven-in-ten U.S. adults (68%) say made-up news and information greatly impacts Americans' confidence in government institutions, and roughly half (54%) say it is having a major impact on our confidence in each other."

11. Google Trends: Below is a chart showing the level of interest developing over the last eight years, indicating a definite spike in searches related to the entire field of climate change. This chart is prepared by Google and is called "Climate Hoax, search term." I would consider this chart a simple indicator of a growing population of climate skeptics, especially when taken in context with the above Pew research, and that's an excellent thing.

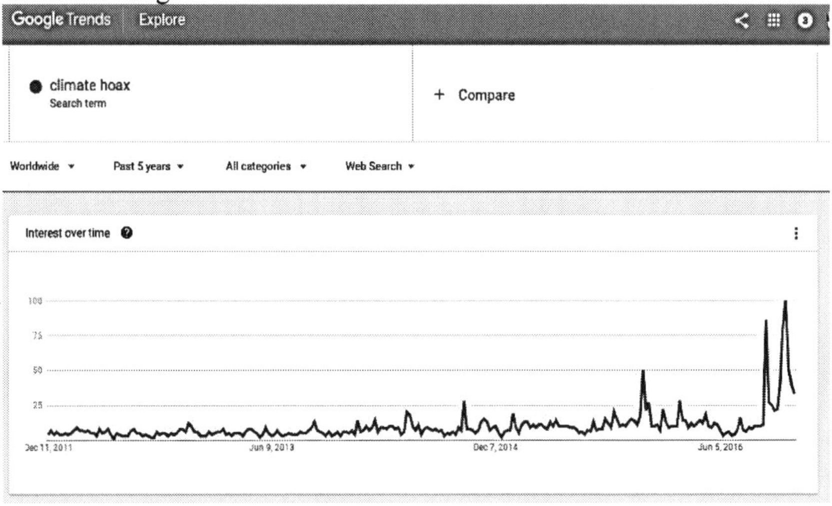

12. Increasing doubt of global warming and concern for climate cooling. Below is a search engine sample of results from Googling "new ice age coming."

a) Are we Heading into a New Ice Age? — Steemit. https://steemit.com/informationwar/@oyddodat/are-we-heading-into-a-new-ice-age
b) https://skepticalscience.com/heading-into-new-little-ice-age-intermediate.htm Part of the Little Ice Age coincided with a period of low solar activity termed the .... growing, then yes, the 10,000-year process of glaciation may have begun.
c) Astrophysicist – Mini Ice Age is now accelerating - Important video ...
d) https://www.iceagenow.info/astrophysicist-mini-ice-age-is-now-accelerating-important-video/Dec 2, 2018 ... Contrary to what the politicians are trying to foist on you, a new mini ice age – a new Maunder Minimum – has already started. Astrophysicist ...
e) Astrophysicist - Mini Ice Age accelerating - New Maunder Minimum ...
f) https://www.iceagenow.info/astrophysicist-mini-ice-age-accelerating-new-maunder-minimum-has-started/May 3, 2018 ... "What we have happened – NOW! – is the start of the mini ice age…it began around 2013. It's a slow start, and now the rate of moving into the ...
g) Little Ice Age? No. Big Warming Age? Yes. - Bulletin of the Atomic...
h) https://thebulletin.org/2018/12/little-ice-age-no-big-warming-age-yes/Dec 17, 2018 ... Image from "History and Antiquities of New England," published 1856. ... surface) could reach its coldest temperatures since records began in the 1940s. ... But the term Little Ice Age is a misnomer, and some climate scientists ...
i) The New Little Ice Age Has Started - ScienceDirect
j) https://www.sciencedirect.com/science/article/pii/B9780128045886000173The quasi-centennial epoch of the new Little Ice Age has started at the end 2015 after the maximum phase of solar cycle 24. The start of a solar grand minimum ...
k) https://www.theguardian.com/environment/climate-consensus-97-per-cent/2018/jan/09/the-imminent-mini-ice-age-myth-is-back-and-its-still-wrong
l) https://www.theguardian.com/environment/climate-consensus-97-per-cent/2018/jan/09/the-imminent-mini-ice-age-myth-is-back-and-its-still-wrongJan 9, 2018 ... Zharkova was also behind the 'mini ice age' stories

in 2015, based on her ... worth of human-caused global warming, and once its quiet phase ended, ... for a new U.S. environmental series that will explore the worrying health ...

m) Little Ice Age - Wikipedia
n) https://en.wikipedia.org/wiki/Little_Ice_AgeThe Little Ice Age (LIA) was a period of cooling that occurred after the Medieval Warm Period. Although it was not a true ice age, the term was introduced into scientific literature by François E. Matthes in 1939. It has been conventionally defined as a period extending from the 16th to the ...... "The 'Little Ice Age' maximum in the Southern Alps, New Zealand: ...
o) Every time we have a little heatwave, the media act as if .... https://www.americanthinker.com/blog/2019/07/every_time_we_have_a_little_heat_wave_the_media_acts_like_this_is_the_worst_one_ever.html
p) Every time we have a little heat wave, the media act as if https://www.climatedepot.com/2019/07/22/every-time-we-have-a-little-heat-wave-the-media-act-as-if-this-is-the-worst-one-ever/
q) Forget Warming, Here Comes Cooling: Scientists Announce Little Ice ... https://cornwallalliance.org/2019/03/forget-warming-here-comes-cooling-scientists-announce-little-ice-age-in-coming-decades/
r) https://cornwallalliance.org/2019/03/forget-warming-here-comes-cooling-scientists-announce-little-ice-age-in-coming-decades/Mar 27, 2019 ... The current warming trend began in the 19th century when the Little Ice Age— which had prevailed for at least two centuries— came to an end.
s) Are We on the Brink of a 'New Little Ice Age?' - Woods Hole ...
t) https://www.whoi.edu/know-your-ocean/ocean-topics/climate-ocean/abrupt-climate-change/are-we-on-the-brink-of-a-new-little-ice-age/When most of us think about Ice Ages, we imagine a slow transition into a colder ... Evidence has mounted that global warming began in the last century and that ...
u) A new little ice age has started: How to survive and prosper during the ...
v) https://www.amazon.com/new-little-ice-age-started/dp/1515158519The debate is over. Science has been proven right by the events of the last eighteen years. Climate is changing global warming does not exist, but a New Little ...

w) A New Little Ice Age Has Started: Lawrence Pierce - The ....
https://www.youtube.com/watch?v=lR3Z0zHkKZ0

13. Forecasted solar activity by Dr. Zharkova, showing the recorded solar activity for cycles 22, 23, and 24. Her formula then goes on to predict cycles 25 and 26 showing a continuation of the declining solar activity. As she stated, this chart would forecast a Dalton type of minimum with five consecutive down cycles. Not shown on this chart, however, is her forecast for cycle 27, where she also predicts to in line with period 26, which is the basis for the Maunder minimum forecast.

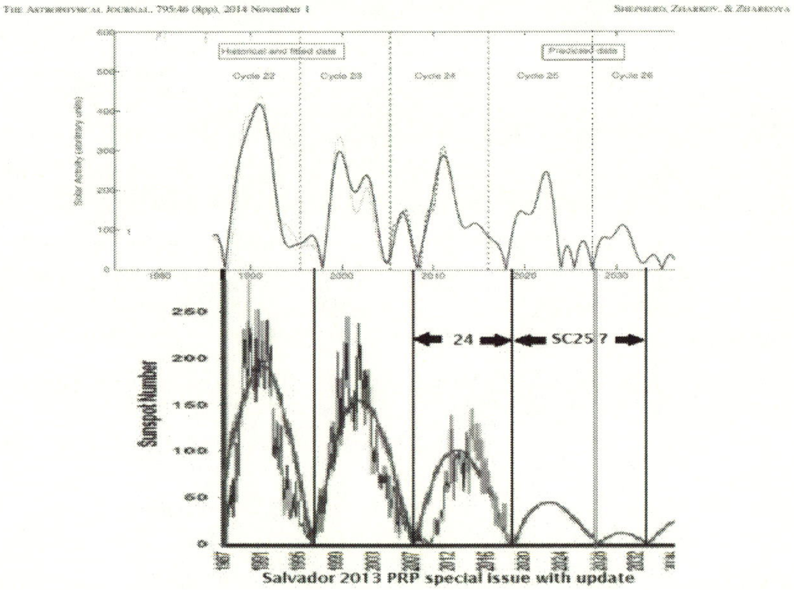

14. Trends in GCR entering the Earth system: Cosmic Rays "Off the Chart." [457] From the Oulu, Finland, Neutron Monitoring Station, cosmic ray counts are "off the chart" at the highest levels measured since the data was first recorded in 1964. Cosmic ray counts are inversely related to solar activity, as the solar wind and magnetic field deflect GCR. Cosmic rays have been related to cloud formation, which reflects rays from the sun and therefore leads to a cooling of the Earth. Note the high counts present during the 1970s' cooling period. Do the "record" recent high counts of cosmic rays presage global cooling?

years

23. A PLEA FOR GLOBAL REASON AND SANITY

1. World-wide health crisis. On 5 December 2019, Mail Online carried an article by Connor Boyd, reporting the worldwide and growing epidemic of measles. They report that in 2018, more than 140,000 were killed by measles. They say that a significant cause of this deadly and very infectious disease is "dangerous anti-vax propaganda." The World Health Organization (WHO) and the US Centers for Disease Control and Prevention (CDC) reports, "unprecedented crisis is set to enter its third year." The article went on to say:

- World-wide cases reached were 9,769,400 in 2018.
- Cases have risen by 2 million (29%) since 2017.
- A major cause of the increase is the "Anti-vaxxers spreading entirely unproven claims that vaccines are dangerous."
- Many organizations are advocating the unsubstantiated claim that vaccines are dangerous, and dosages are declining at an accelerating rate over the past several years.

In 2018, Travelvax issued an alarm, "Mosquito-borne virus alert, measles in south. The main point is to warn travelers in many parts of the world are at risk for contract measles, and many other deadly diseases are caused by mosquitos."

2. Who's the culprit? What we see is another example of the unintended consequences of deceptive, dangerous, and fearmongering lies perpetrated by the press/media/elites and the consequences suffered by the uninformed public.

The first is that vaccines are dangerous, thus scaring uninformed parents into not vaccinating their defenseless children and the resulting tragedies.

Second is that DDT is terrible for the environment and, as an example, says how it's "been proven" to kills birds. We discussed at length the consequences of this lie in Chapter 6.8.1, example, #2.

Third – this entire book. We examined the history of the Earth's climate change. Then we studied the real underlying science of climate change —

thus allowing us to confidently state that the premise of CO_2 induced climate disaster is a total falsehood.

Then, we made it crystal clear that any solution to reduce CO_2 levels, like the "Green New Deal," is not only unbearably expensive, but it wants to use a non-solution to solve a problem that does not exist.

In summary, if you have read this book this far, give yourself a hug, but don't leave it there. We ask you to use the information from this book to spread the truth, educate your children and grandchildren, and become an advocate to expose and stop the lies and spread the truth.

Thank You!

Annex A. Climate change fun facts!

Predictions from climate change alarmists go awry so often that at this rate, the only way they'll be able to save themselves from ridicule and embarrassment is if they make their doomsday predictions so far out in the future that they'll be dead before we can check them.

This Photo by Unknown

http://blog.electricitybid.com/index.php/2013/08/23/electricity-co2-tax/

1. Top 10 biggest climate alarmist predictions gone spectacularly wrong:[458]

This Photo by Unknown Author is licensed under

By Frits Ahlefeldt

Biologist Paul Ehrlich predicted in the 1970s that: "Population will inevitably and completely outstrip whatever small increases in food supplies we make," and that "The death rate will increase until at least 100-200 million people per year will be starving to death during the next ten years." *Not do much!*[459]

In January 1970, Life reported, "Scientists have solid experimental and theoretical evidence to support…the following predictions: In a decade, urban dwellers will have to wear gas masks to survive air pollution…by 1985 air pollution will have reduced the amount of sunlight reaching Earth by one half…."

NASA says, the atmosphere is getting cleaner.[460]

Source:

http://www.oxfamblogs.org/fp2p/?tag=climate-

In January 2006 Al Gore predicted that we had ten years left before the planet turned into a "total frying pan." Somehow we survived it.

NASA says the climate is cooling.[461]

This Photo by Unknown Author is licensed under

In 2008, a segment aired on ABC News predicted that NYC would be underwater by June 2015.

Author's note, seas up by 7 inches in the last 150 years.

This Photo by

In 1970, ecologist Kenneth E.F. Watt predicted that "If present trends continue, the world will be about four degrees colder for the global mean temperature in 1990, but 11 degrees colder by the year 2000, This is about twice what it would take to put us in an ice age."

Author's note "Baloney!"

In 2008, Al Gore predicted that there is a 75% chance that the entire north polar ice cap would be completely melted within 5-7 years. He at least hedged that prediction by giving himself "75%" certainty.

Source:

NASA says polar ice is growing[462]

On May 13′ 2014 [463] *France's foreign minister said that we only have 500 days to stop "climate chaos." The recent Paris climate summit met 565 days after his remark.*

Authors remark, Horsefeathers!

In 2009, National Aeronautics and Space Administration Goddard Space Flight Center head James Wassen warned that Obama only had four years left to save the Earth.

Author's note: God bless our scientist in chief!

Source:

On the first Earth Day its sponsor warned that "in 25 years, somewhere between 75 and 80 percent of all the species of living animals will be extinct."

Author's note, indeed, a proven concept.

This Photo by Unknown Author is licensed under CC BY NC ND

<u>Another Earth Day prediction from Kenneth Watt:</u> "At the present rate of nitrogen buildup, it's only a matter of time before light will be filtered out of the atmosphere and none of our land will be usable."

USA/Europe, Japan was never cleaner. China, India – yuk.

And no, we're not just nitpicking absurd predictions made by cranks. <u>A study in the journal Nature Climate Change reviewed 117 climate predictions and found that 97.4% never materialized.</u>

Source:

http://www.seppo.net/e/un-

Is it even fair to call it climate "science" at this point?

2. Famous Predictions on Climate Change:[464465]

a. *The 1975 Newsweek article entitled "The Cooling World," which claimed Earth's temperature had been plunging for decades due to humanity's activities..."*

"Experts suggested grandiose schemes to alleviate the problems, including "melting the arctic ice cap by covering it with black soot or diverting arctic rivers," Newsweek reported. It added, "The longer the planners delay, the more difficult will they find it to cope with climatic change once the results become grim reality."

Author's note, sounds familiar? — except that the "climate change" alarmists were warning against global cooling?"

http://www.clipartpanda.com/clipart_images/caveman-53486505

b. *New ice age and worldwide starvation:*[466] *In the 1960s and '70s, top mainstream media outlets, such as Newsweek, hyped the imminent global-cooling apocalypse. "Even as late as the early 1980s, prominent voices still warned of potential doomsday scenarios owing to man-made cooling, ranging from mass starvation caused by cooling-induced crop failures to another "Ice Age" that would kill most of humanity."*

c. *Holdren predicted that a billion people would die in "carbon-dioxide induced famines" as part of a new "Ice Age" by the year 2020. Among the top, global-cooling theorists were Obama's current "science czar" John Holdren and Paul Ehrlich, the author of Population Bomb, which predicted mass starvation worldwide. In the 1971 textbook Global Ecology, the duo warned that overpopulation and pollution would produce a new ice age, claiming that human activities are "said to be responsible for the present world cooling trend."*

The pair fingered "jet exhausts" and "man-made changes in the reflectivity of the Earth's surface through urbanization, deforestation, and the enlargement of deserts as potential triggers for his new ice age.

d. *Global warming — temperature predictions: Perhaps nowhere has the stunning failure of climate predictions been better illustrated than in the "climate models" used by the UN. ...All of them "predicted" varying degrees of increased warming as atmospheric concentrations of carbon dioxide (CO2) increased.*

Author's note, the problem is that every single model was wrong — by a lot.

e. *Almost laughably, in its latest report, the UN IPCC increased its alleged "confidence" in its theory, action experts such as Christy could not rationalize. "I am baffled that the confidence increases when the performance of your models is conclusively failing," he said.*

"I cannot understand that methodology.... It's a very embarrassing result for the climate models used in the IPCC report." "When 73 out of 73 [climate models] miss the point and predict temperatures that are significantly above the real world, they cannot be used as scientific tools, and not for public policy decision-making," he added .."

f. *The end of snow: The IPCC has also hyped snowless winters. In its 2001 report, it claimed: "milder winter temperatures will decrease heavy snowstorms."*

Again, though, the climate refused to cooperate. The latest data from Rutgers' Global Snow Lab showed an all-time new record high in autumn snow cover across the northern hemisphere in 2014, when more than 22 million square kilometers were covered. Worldwide, similar trends have been observed. Global Snow Lab data also shows Eurasian autumn snow cover has grown by 50 percent since records began in 1979.

g. *The melting ice caps: Another area where the warmists' predictions have proven incorrect concerns the amount of ice at the Earth's poles. They predicted a complete melting of the Arctic ice cap in summers that should have already happened, and even claimed that Antarctic ice was melting rapidly.....As far as the Antarctic is concerned, in 2007, the UN IPCC claimed the ice sheets of Antarctica "are very likely shrinking," with Antarctica "contributing 0.2 ± 0.35 mm yr. - 1 to sea level rise over the period 1993 to 2003.*

The reality was exactly the opposite. In a statement released in October, NASA dropped the equivalent of a nuclear bomb on the UN's climate-alarmism machine, noting that ice across Antarctica has been increasing for decades. In 2014, the Arctic ice cap, apparently oblivious to Gore's hot air, continued its phenomenal rebound, leaving alarmists struggling for explanations.

h. *Increased storms, drought, and sea-level rise: The ice sheets have not cooperated with warmists, and neither have other weather-related phenomena, such as mass migrations owing to sea-level increase. On June 30, 1989, the Associated Press ran an article headlined:*

"UN Official Predicts Disaster, Says Greenhouse Effect Could Wipe Some Nations Off Map."

But: "Consider a paper published in March of 2015 in the journal Geology. According to the study, the Funafuti Atoll has experienced "the highest rates of sea-level rise" in the world over the past six decades. Rather than sinking under the waves, the islands are growing. "No islands have been lost, the majority have enlarged, and there has been a 7.3% increase in net island area over the past century," the paper says."

i. *Prominent Princeton professor and lead UN IPCC author Michael Oppenheimer, for instance, made some dramatic predictions in 1990. By 1995, he said, the "greenhouse effect" would be "desolating the heartlands of North America and Eurasia with horrific drought, causing crop failures and food riots." By 1996, he added, the Platte River of Nebraska "would be dry, while a continent-wide black blizzard of prairie topsoil will stop traffic on interstates, strip paint from houses and shut down computers." The situation would get so bad that "Mexican police will round up illegal American migrants surging into Mexico seeking work as field hands."*

Eh, not so much: "When confronted on his predictions, Oppenheimer, who also served as Gore's advisor, refused to apologize….."

j. *Countless other claims of AGW doom affecting humans have also been debunked. Wildfires produced by AGW, for instance, we're supposed to be raging around the world.*

As Forbes magazine pointed out recently, the number of wildfires has plummeted 15 percent since 1950, and according to the National Academy of Sciences, that trend is likely to continue for decades. [467]

k. *On hurricanes and tornadoes, which alarmists assured were going to get more extreme and more frequent, it probably would have been hard for "experts" to be more wrong.* But "On January 8, 2015, meanwhile, the Weather Channel reported: "In the last three years, there have never been fewer tornadoes in the United States since record-keeping began in 1950."

l. *Maybe just one more prediction.*
"There is not the slightest indication that nuclear energy will ever be obtainable. It would mean that the atom would have to be shattered at will." - Albert Einstein, 1932.

Yes, Albert, we know you are really - brilliant. But you, too, need to remember Richard Feynman when he said, "no matter how elegant your theory is, no matter how smart you are, if it's not supported by data, it's worthless" or something like that.

Get your head out of the tabloids and cartoonish press/media

Annex B- Detailed reference materials

Chapter 1

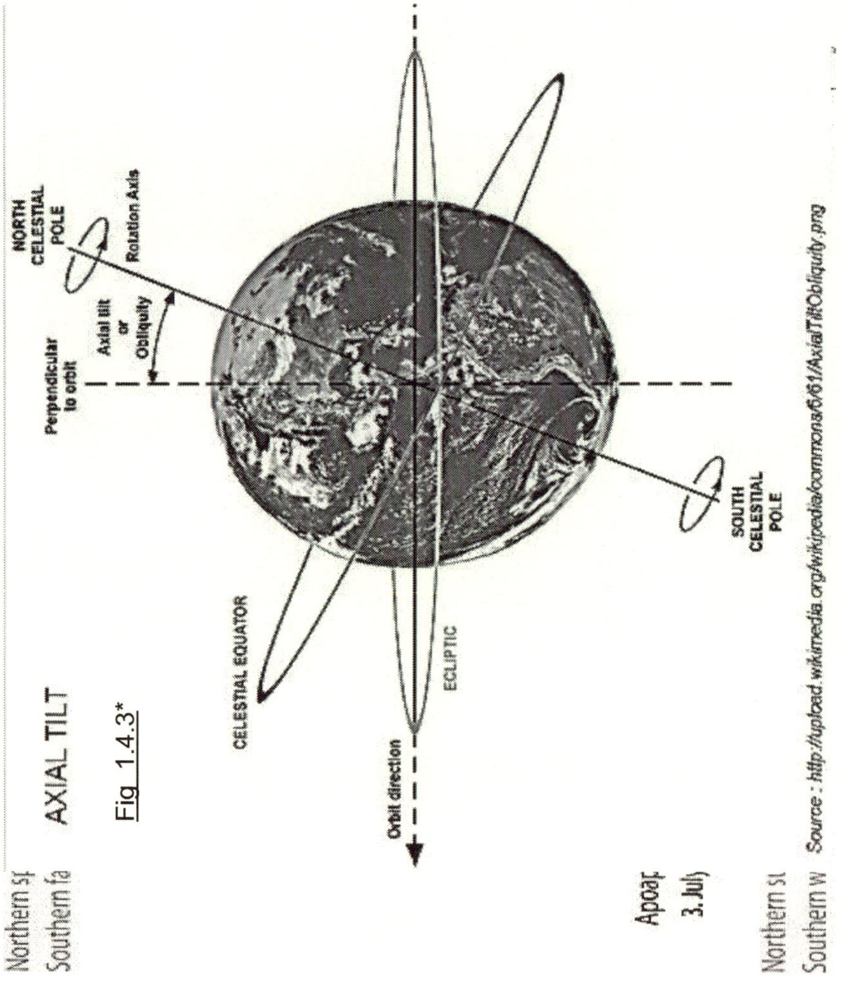

Chapter 2

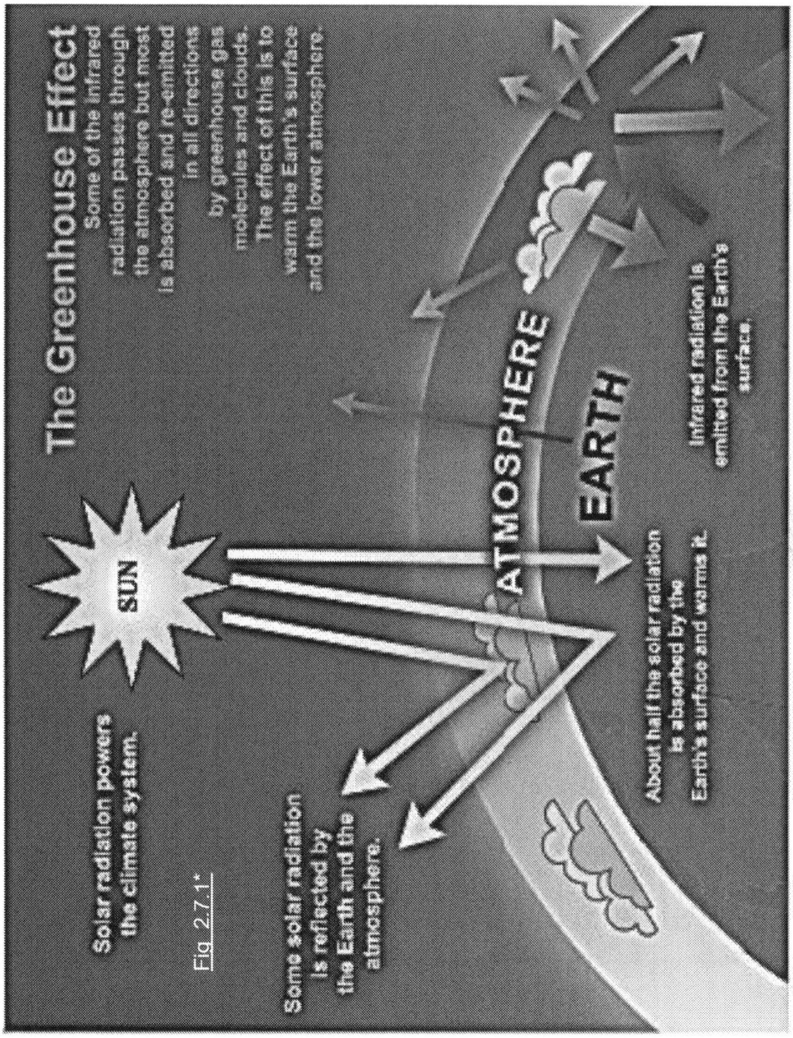
The Greenhouse Effect
Some of the infrared radiation passes through the atmosphere but most is absorbed and re-emitted in all directions by greenhouse gas molecules and clouds. The effect of this is to warm the Earth's surface and the lower atmosphere.
Solar radiation powers the climate system.
SUN
Some solar radiation is reflected by the Earth and the atmosphere.
ATMOSPHERE
EARTH
About half the solar radiation is absorbed by the Earth's surface and warms it.
Infrared radiation is emitted from the Earth's surface.

Fig 2.7.1*

Photo credit: http://www.ipcc-wg1.unibe.ch/publications/wg1-ar4/faq/wg1_faq-1.3.html

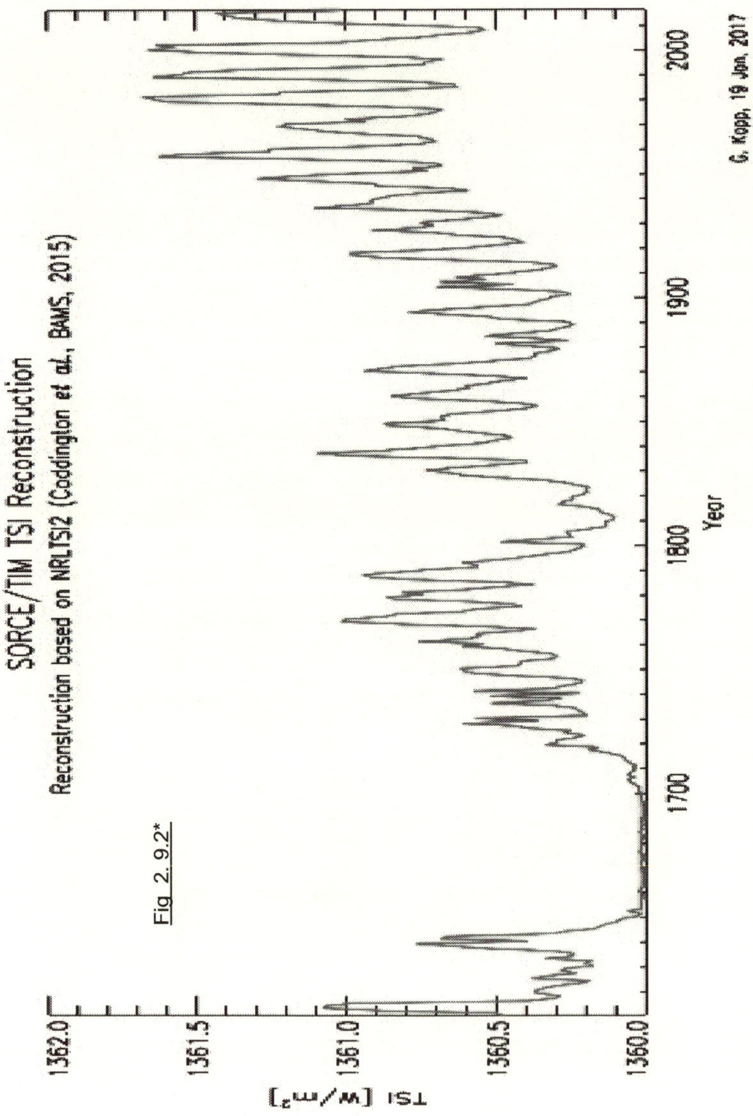
SORCE/TIM TSI Reconstruction
Reconstruction based on NRLTSI2 (Coddington et al., BAMS, 2015)
TSI [W/m²]
1362.0
1361.5
1361.0
1360.5
1360.0
1700
1800
1900
2000
Year
G. Kopp, 19 Jan, 2017

Fig 2. 9.2*

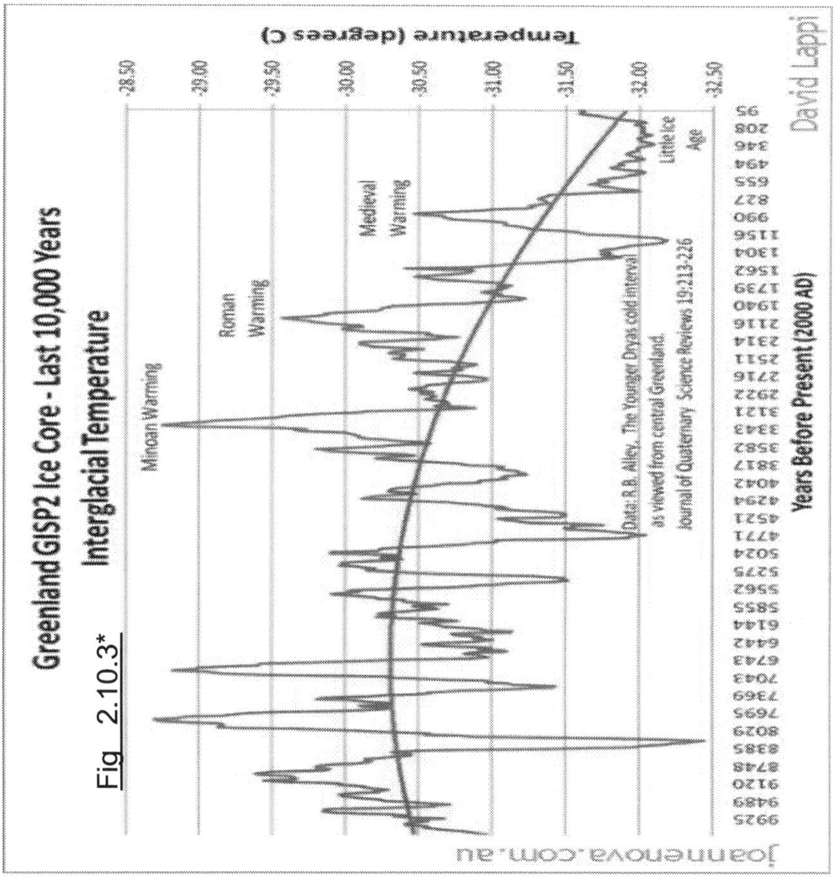
Greenland GISP2 Ice Core - Last 10,000 Years
Interglacial Temperature
Minoan Warming
Roman Warming
Medieval Warming
Little Ice Age
Data: R.B. Alley, The Younger Dryas cold interval as viewed from central Greenland, Journal of Quaternary Science Reviews 19:213-226
Temperature (degrees C)
Years Before Present (2000 AD)
David Lappi
joannenova.com.au

Fig 2.10.3*

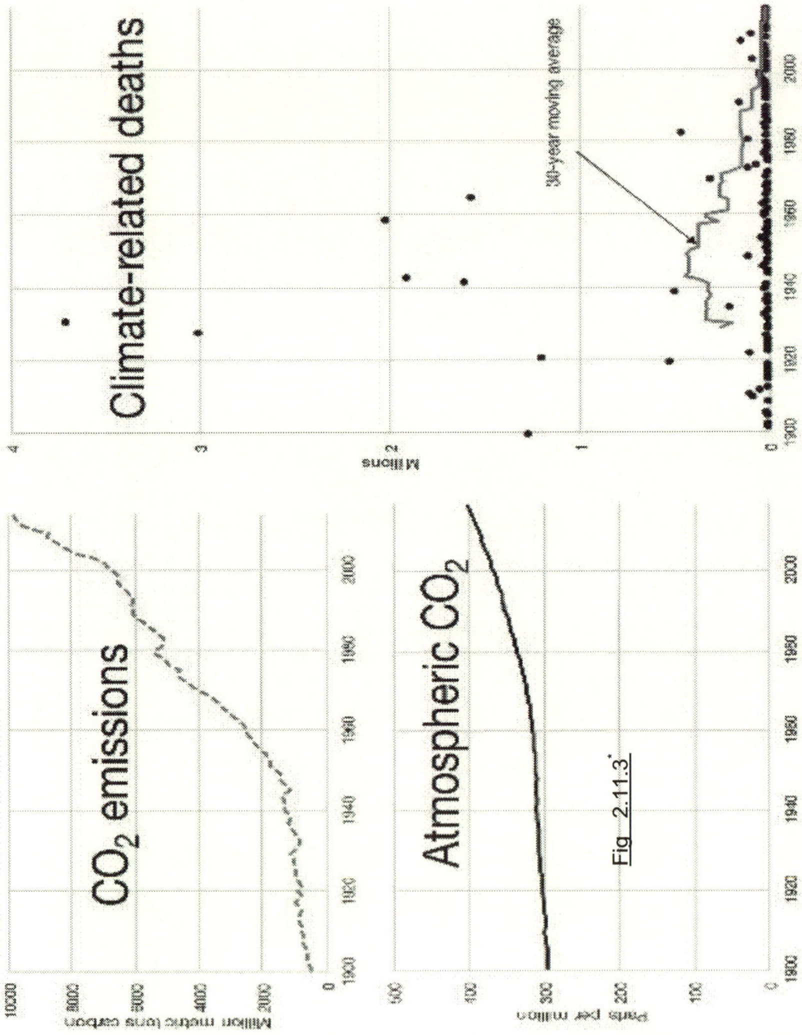
CO2 emissions
Million metric tons carbon
Atmospheric CO2
Parts per million
Climate-related deaths
Millions
30-year moving average

Fig 2.11.3*

Chapter 3

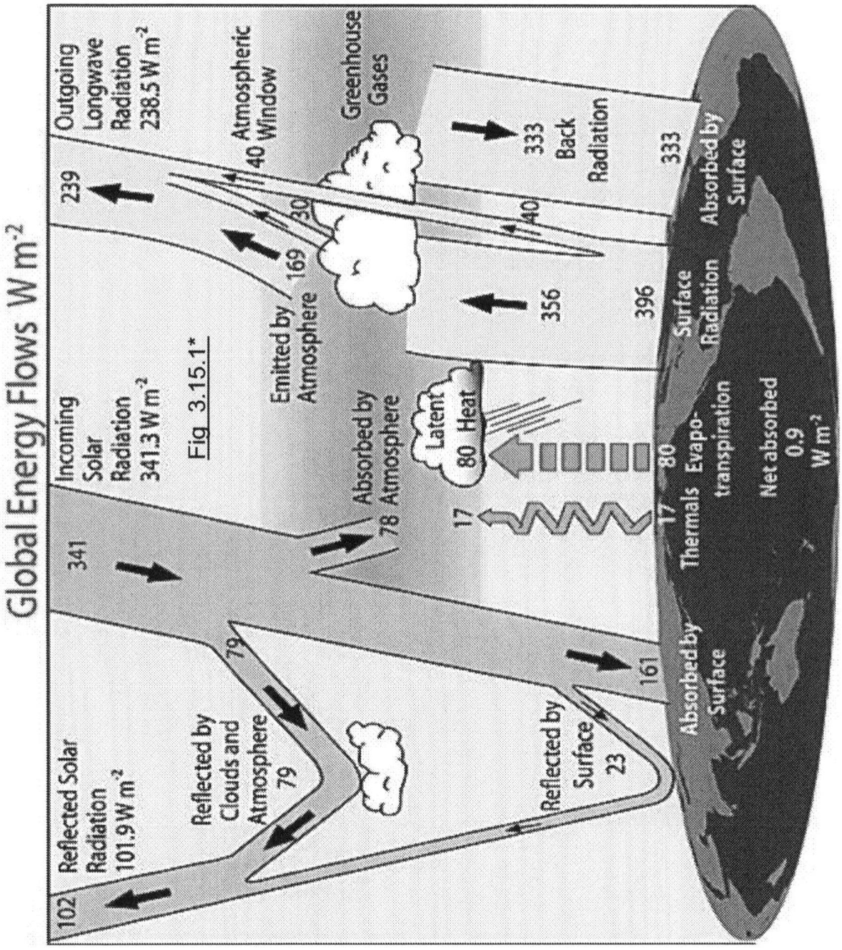
Global Energy Flows W m-2
Reflected Solar Radiation 101.9 W m-2
102
Reflected by Clouds and Atmosphere 79
79
Incoming Solar Radiation 341.3 W m-2
341
Outgoing Longwave Radiation 238.5 W m-2
239
Reflected by Surface 23
161
Absorbed by Surface
Absorbed by Atmosphere 78
17
80
Latent 80 Heat
Emitted by Atmosphere 169
30
40 Atmospheric Window
Greenhouse Gases
356
396
Surface Radiation
40
333 Back Radiation
333
Absorbed by Surface
Thermals
Evapo-transpiration
Net absorbed 0.9 W m-2
Fig. 3.15.1*

Chapter 4

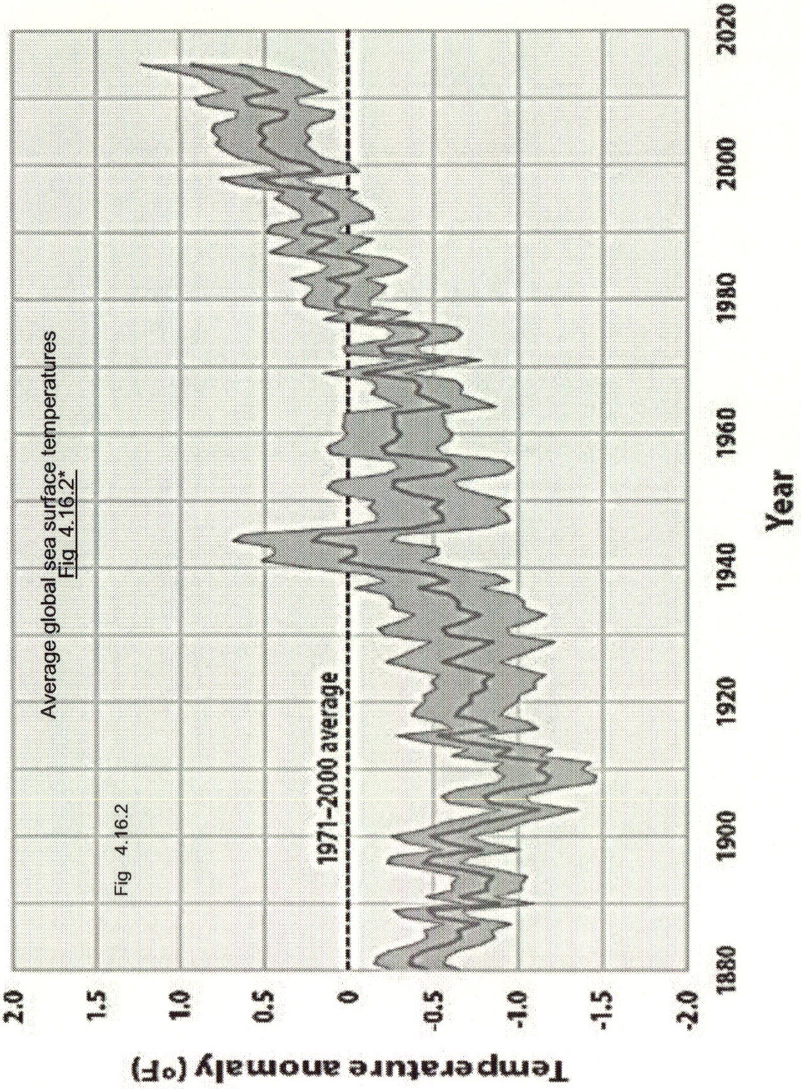
Average global sea surface temperatures
Fig 4.16.2*
Fig 4.16.2
1971–2000 average
Temperature anomaly (°F)
2.0
1.5
1.0
0.5
0
-0.5
-1.0
-1.5
-2.0
Year
1880
1900
1920
1940
1960
1980
2000
2020

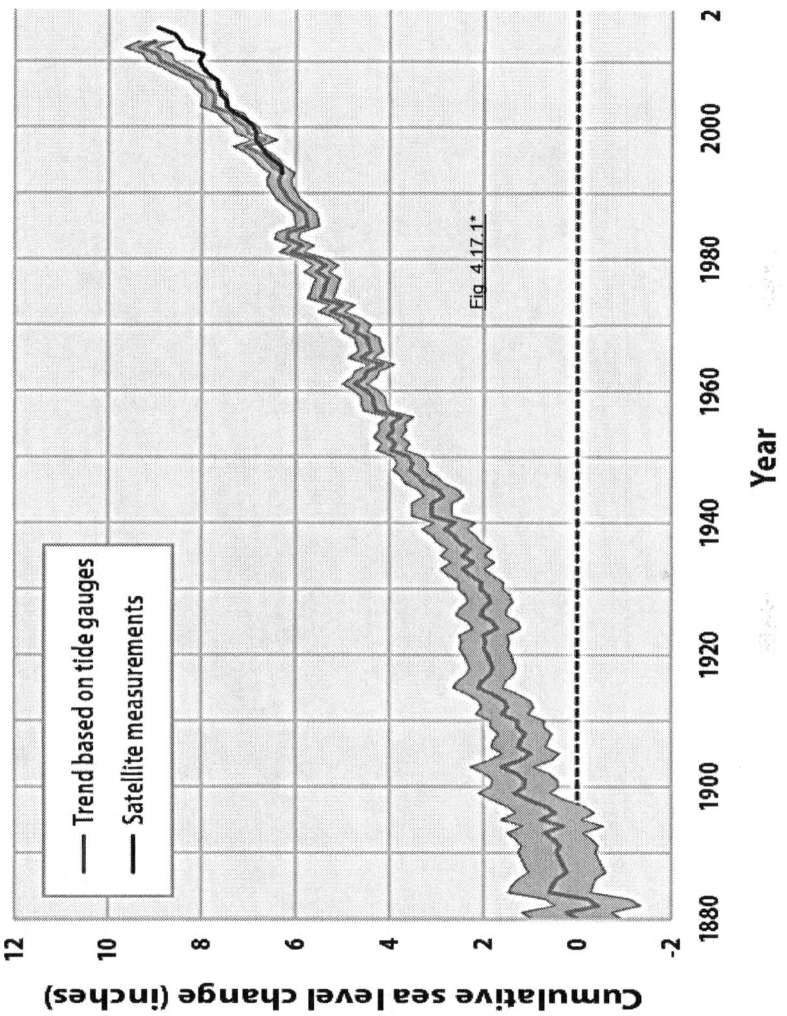
Trend based on tide gauges
Satellite measurements
Fig. 4.17.1*
Cumulative sea level change (inches)
12
10
8
6
4
2
0
-2
1880
1900
1920
1940
1960
1980
2000
2
Year

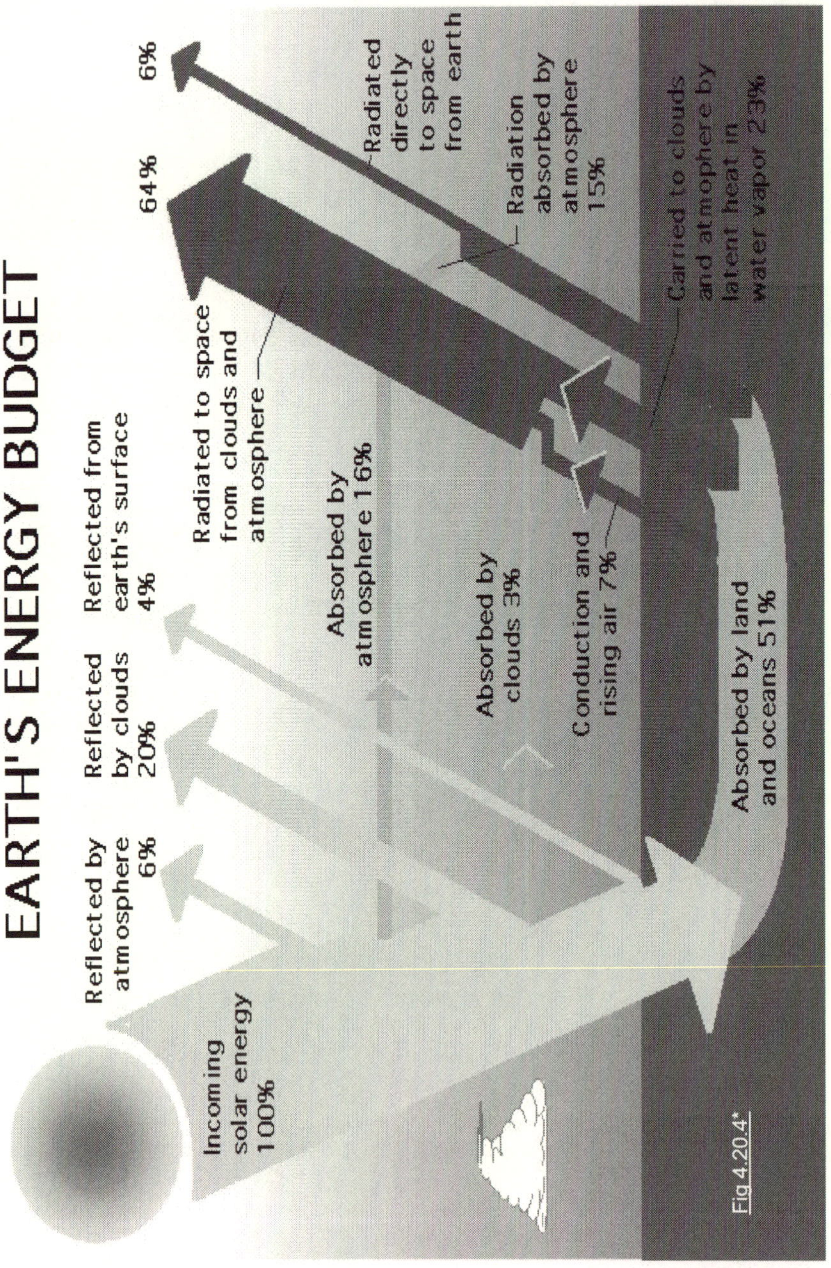

EARTH'S ENERGY BUDGET
Incoming solar energy 100%
Reflected by atmosphere 6%
Reflected by clouds 20%
Reflected from earth's surface 4%
Radiated to space from clouds and atmosphere
64%
6%
Radiated directly to space from earth
Radiation absorbed by atmosphere 15%
Absorbed by atmosphere 16%
Absorbed by clouds 3%
Conduction and rising air 7%
Carried to clouds and atmophere by latent heat in water vapor 23%
Absorbed by land and oceans 51%

Fig 4.20.4*

Chapter 6

Courtesy, WWW.johnenglander.net

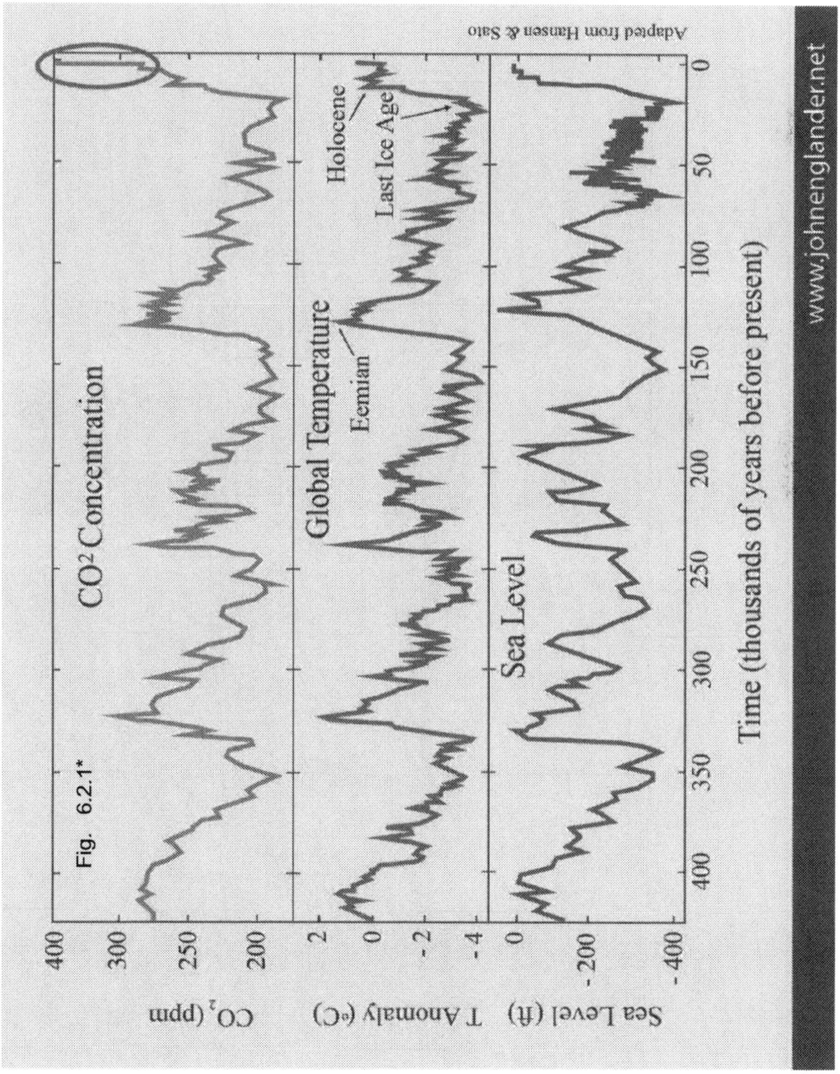

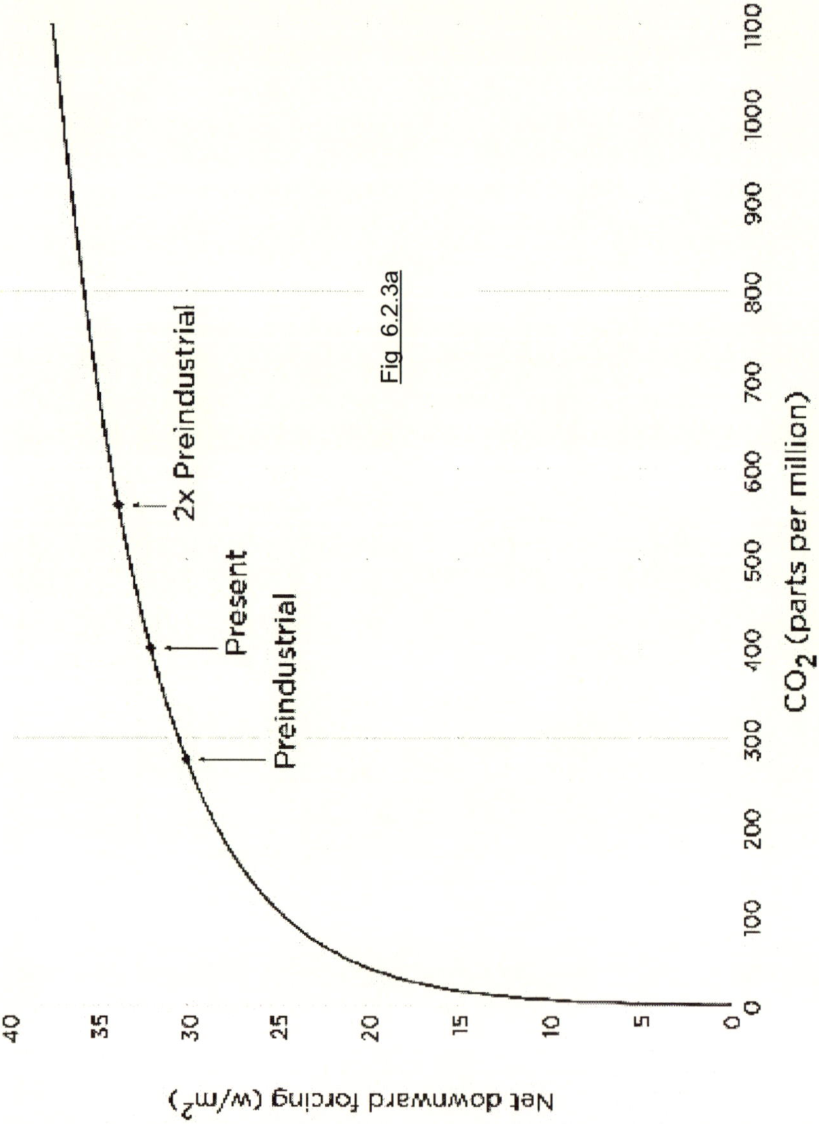
Net downward forcing (w/m²)
40
35
30
25
20
15
10
5
0
0
100
200
300
400
500
600
700
800
900
1000
1100
CO2 (parts per million)
Preindustrial
Present
2x Preindustrial

Fig. 6.2.3a

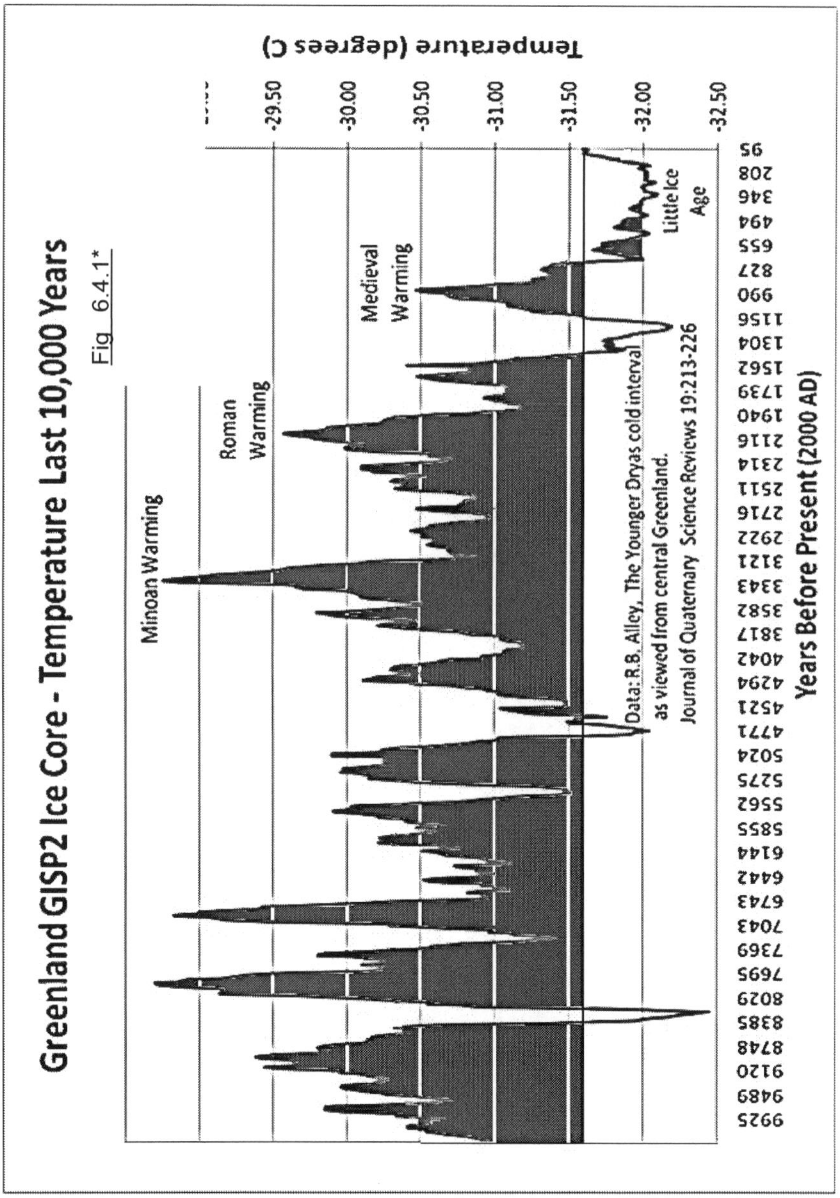
Greenland GISP2 Ice Core - Temperature Last 10,000 Years
Fig 6.4.1*
Minoan Warming
Roman Warming
Medieval Warming
Little Ice Age
Data: R.B. Alley, The Younger Dryas cold interval as viewed from central Greenland.
Journal of Quaternary Science Reviews 19:213-226
Temperature (degrees C)
-29.50
-30.00
-30.50
-31.00
-31.50
-32.00
-32.50
Years Before Present (2000 AD)
9925
9649
9120
8748
8385
8029
7695
7369
7043
6743
6442
6144
5855
5562
5275
5024
4771
4521
4294
4042
3817
3582
3343
3121
2922
2716
2511
2314
2116
1940
1739
1562
1304
1156
990
827
655
494
346
208
95

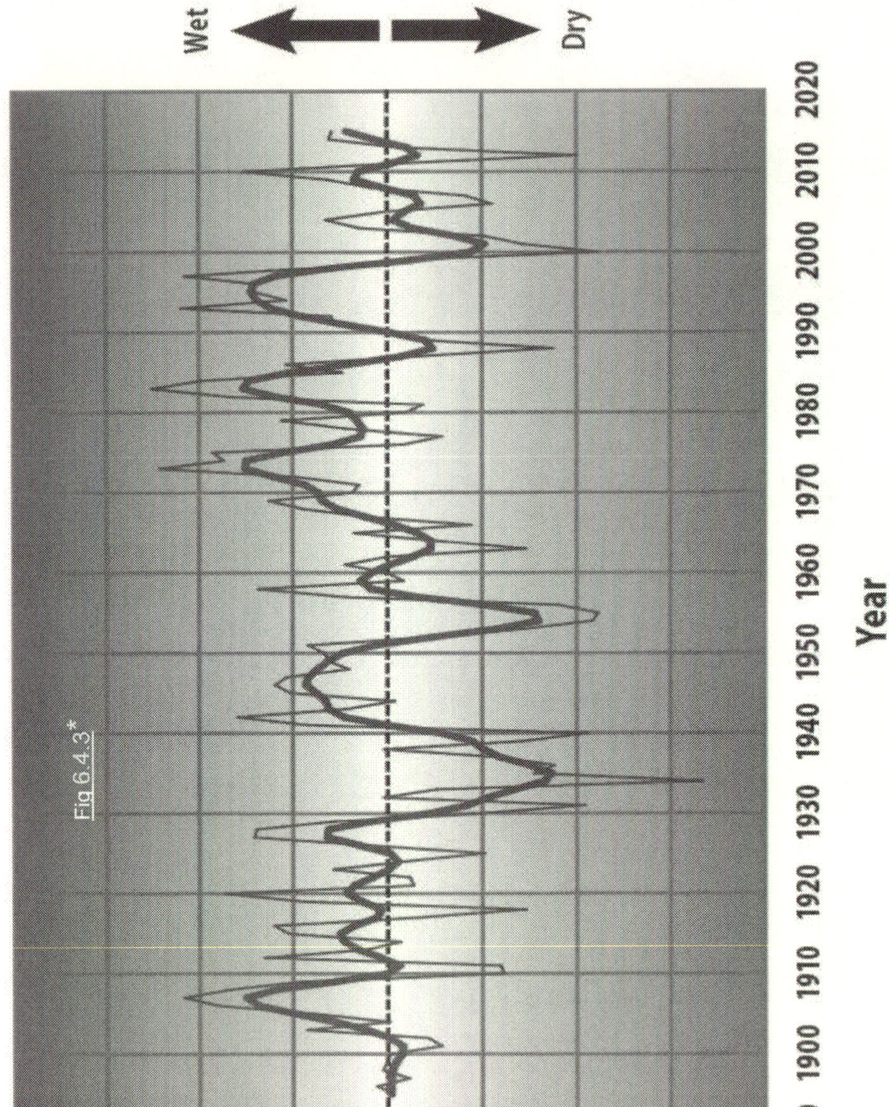
Fig 6.4.3*
Wet
Dry
Palmer Drought Severity Index
Year

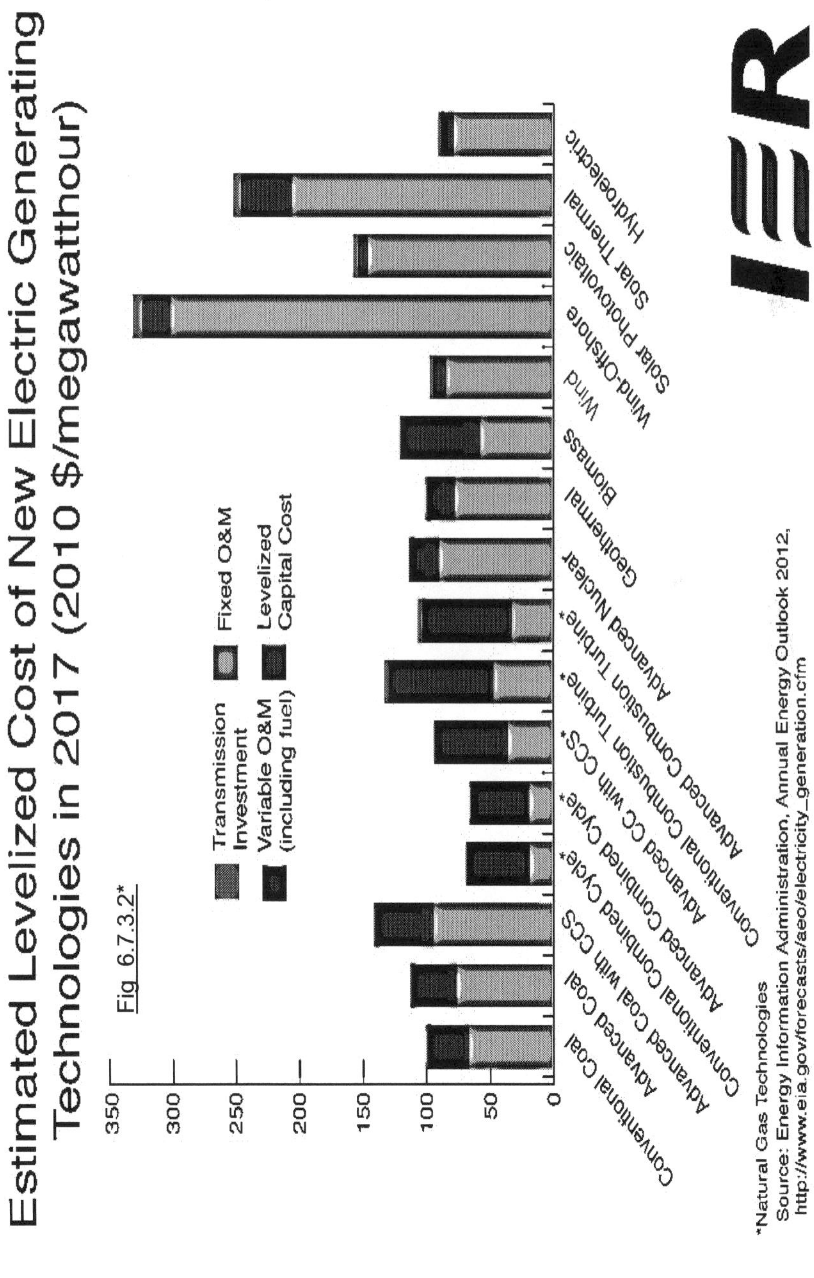

Estimated Levelized Cost of New Electric Generating Technologies in 2017 (2010 $/megawatthour)
Fig 6.7.3.2*
Transmission Investment
Fixed O&M
Variable O&M (including fuel)
Levelized Capital Cost
350
300
250
200
150
100
50
0
Conventional Coal
Advanced Coal
Advanced Coal with CCS
Conventional Combined Cycle*
Advanced Combined Cycle*
Advanced CC with CCS*
Conventional Combustion Turbine*
Advanced Combustion Turbine*
Advanced Nuclear
Geothermal
Biomass
Wind
Wind-Offshore
Solar Photovoltaic
Solar Thermal
Hydroelectric
*Natural Gas Technologies
Source: Energy Information Administration, Annual Energy Outlook 2012,
http://www.eia.gov/forecasts/aeo/electricity_generation.cfm

Banish all of your worries about global warming, rising sea levels, climate change, and the end of life on Earth by the year 2030 (See details below)

(100 dots vertical and 100 dots horizontal = 10,000 dots)

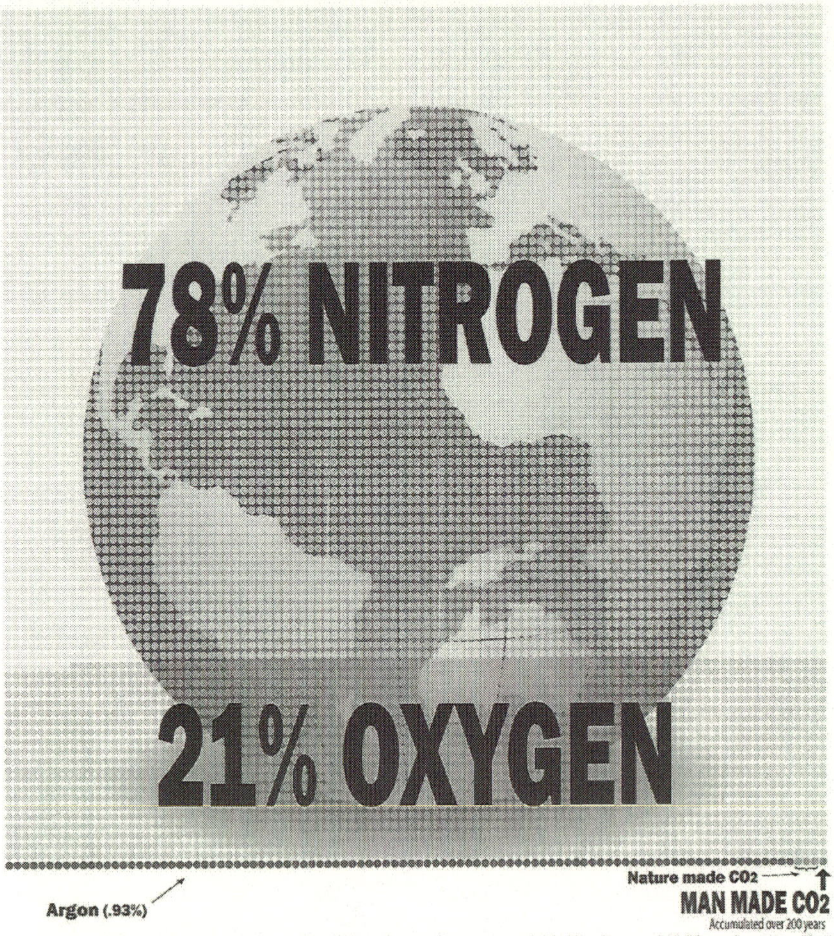

The above graphic representation of Earth's atmosphere reveals in the lower right hand corner that the accumulated carbon dioxide from man's activities, i.e. the burning of fossil fuels over the last 200 years, amounts to only 1.25 parts per 10,000. This 1 dot out of 10,000 illustrates that the amount of man made CO2 in our atmosphere is much too small to cause the imagined catastrophes attributed to it.

Created for the public's education by Jay Lehr, Ph.D., Senior Policy Analyst for the International Climate Science Coalition

Fig 6.10.1, The Moral Case for Fossil Fuels, Curtsey Alex Epstein

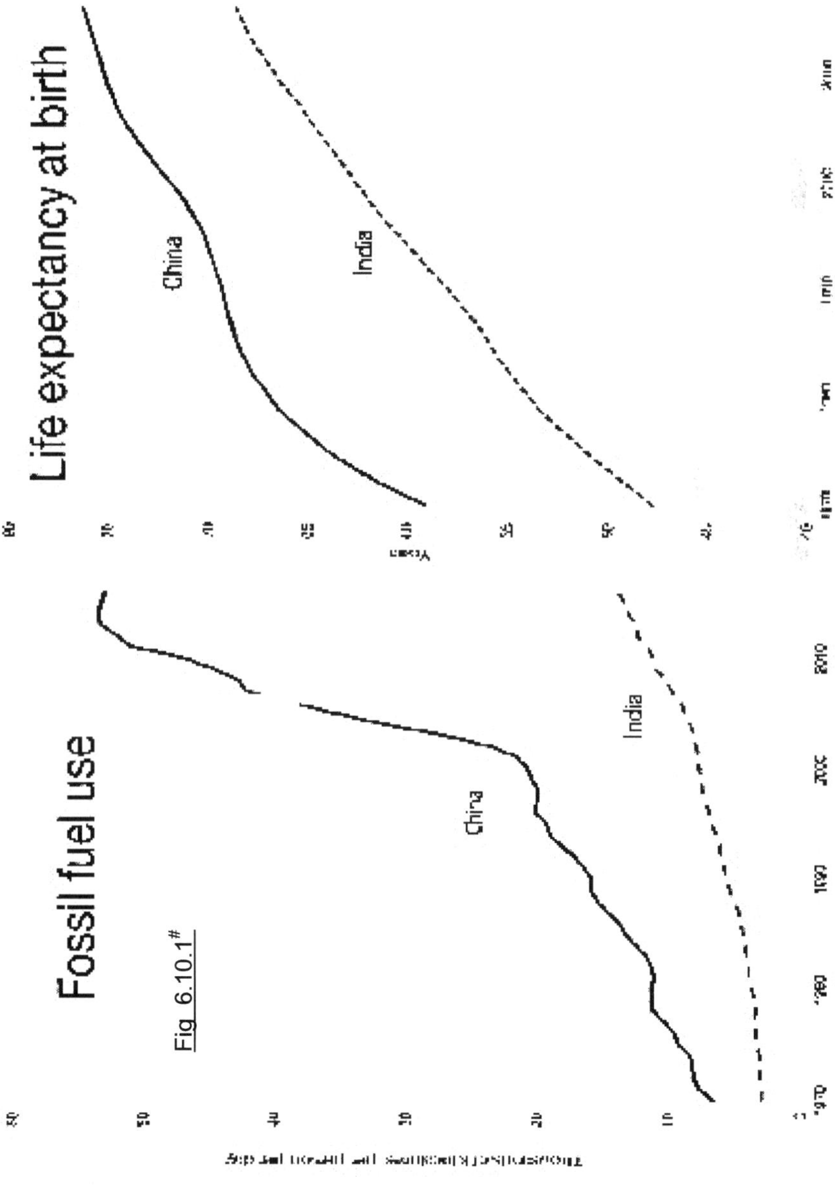

Chapter 7

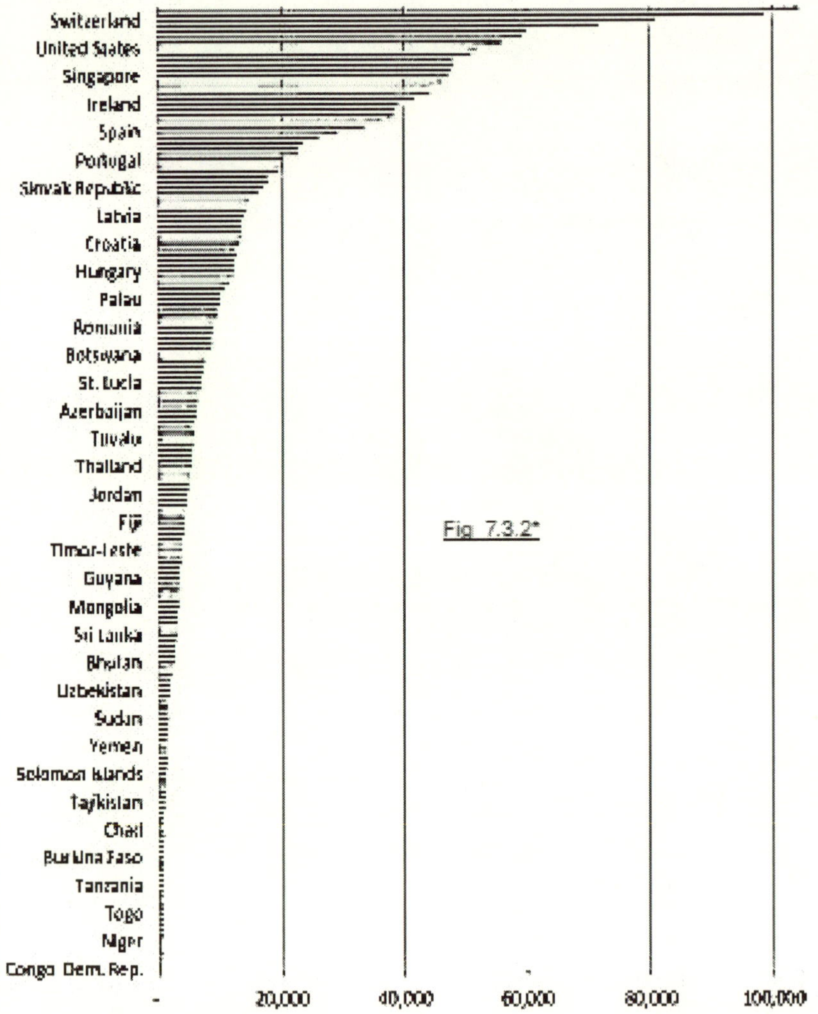
Switzerland
United States
Singapore
Ireland
Spain
Portugal
Slovak Republic
Latvia
Croatia
Hungary
Palau
Romania
Botswana
St. Lucia
Azerbaijan
Tuvalu
Thailand
Jordan
Fiji
Timor-Leste
Guyana
Mongolia
Sri Lanka
Bhutan
Uzbekistan
Sudan
Yemen
Solomon Islands
Tajikistan
Chad
Burkina Faso
Tanzania
Togo
Niger
Congo Dem. Rep.
-
20,000
40,000
60,000
80,000
100,000

Fig. 7.3.2*

Chapter 8

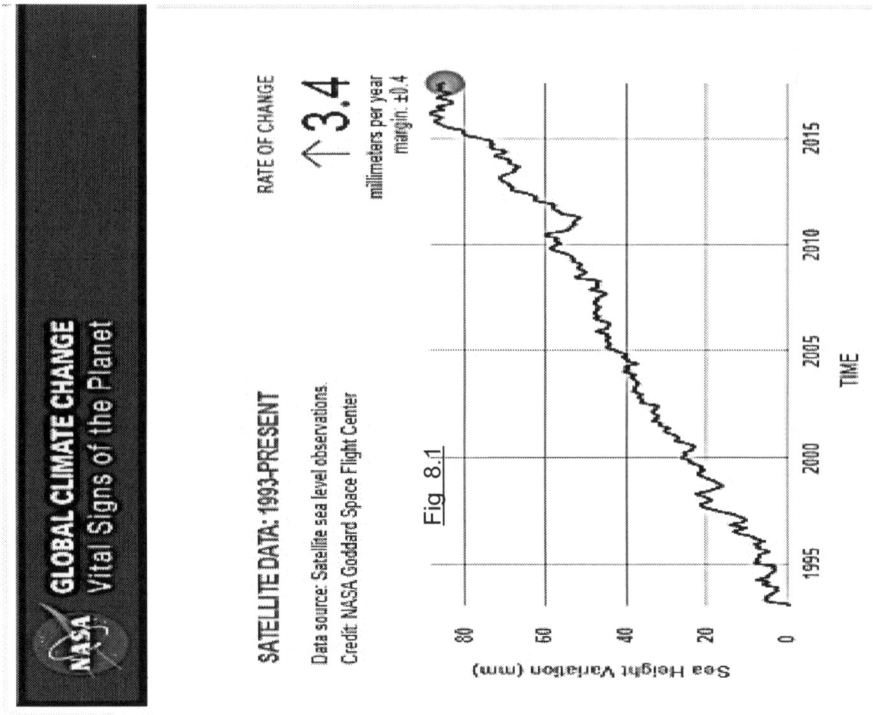
NASA
GLOBAL CLIMATE CHANGE
Vital Signs of the Planet
SATELLITE DATA: 1993-PRESENT
Data source: Satellite sea level observations.
Credit: NASA Goddard Space Flight Center
RATE OF CHANGE
↑3.4
millimeters per year
margin: ±0.4
Sea Height Variation (mm)
0
20
40
60
80
1995
2000
2005
2010
2015
TIME

Fig 8.1

Chapter 9

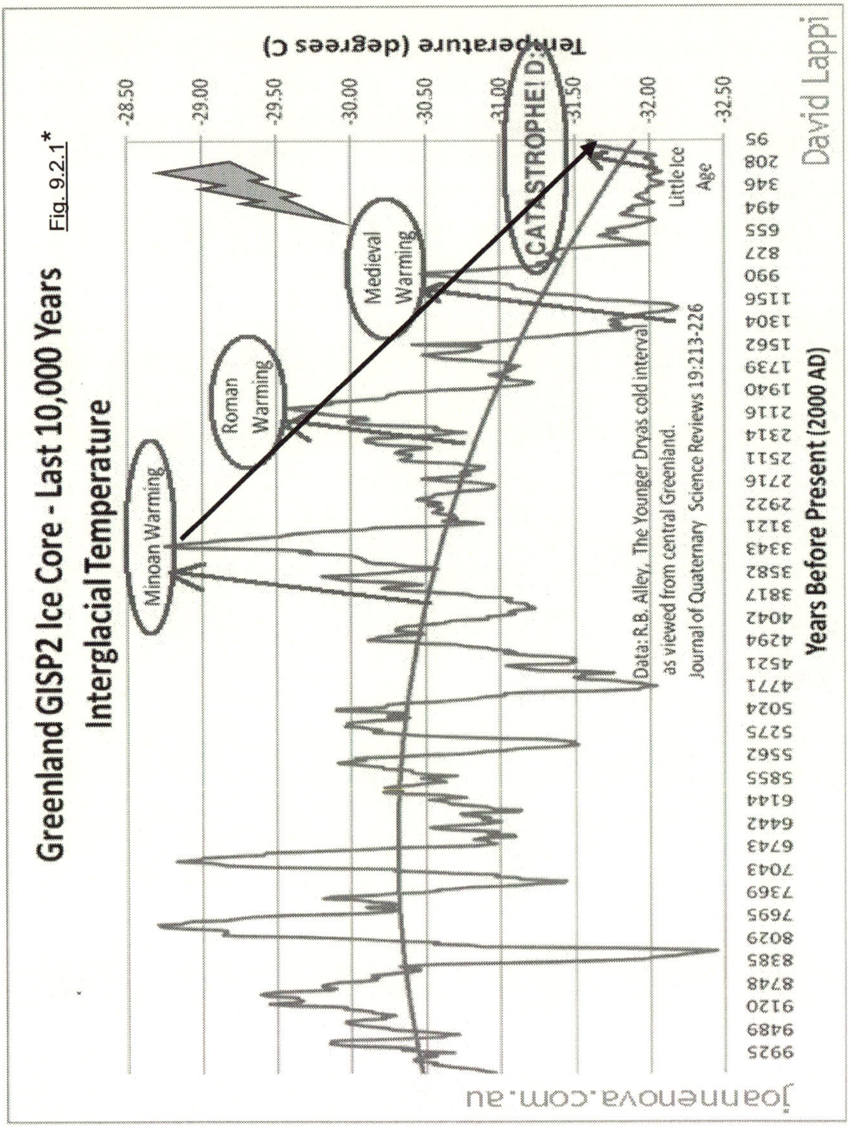
Greenland GISP2 Ice Core - Last 10,000 Years
Interglacial Temperature
Fig. 9.2.1*
Minoan Warming
Roman Warming
Medieval Warming
Little Ice Age
Data: R.B. Alley, The Younger Dryas cold interval as viewed from central Greenland.
Journal of Quaternary Science Reviews 19:213-226
Temperature (degrees C)
-28.50
-29.00
-29.50
-30.00
-30.50
-31.00
-31.50
-32.00
-32.50
Years Before Present (2000 AD)
David Lappi
joannenova.com.au

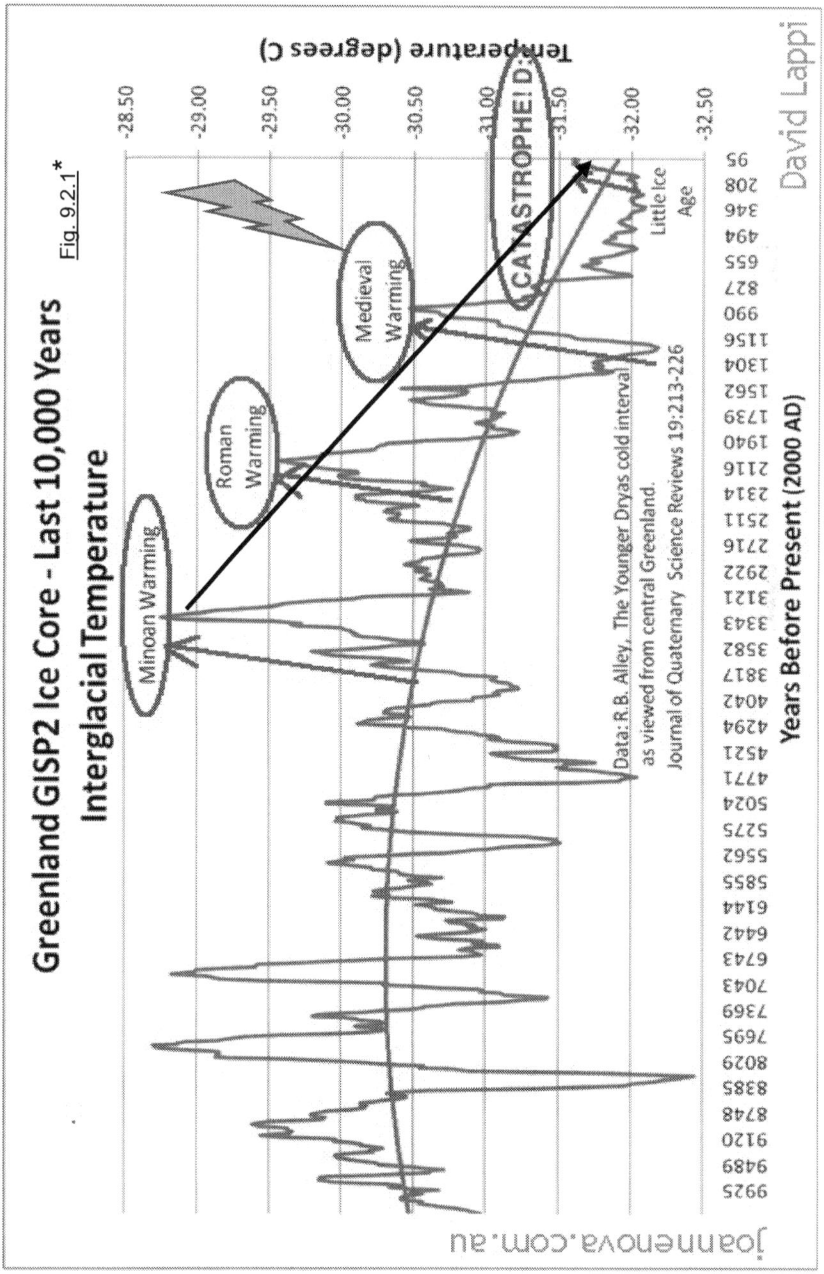
Greenland GISP2 Ice Core - Last 10,000 Years
Interglacial Temperature
Fig. 9.2.1*
Minoan Warming
Roman Warming
Medieval Warming
CATASTROPHE! D:
Little Ice Age
Data: R.B. Alley, The Younger Dryas cold interval as viewed from central Greenland.
Journal of Quaternary Science Reviews 19:213-226
Temperature (degrees C)
-28.50
-29.00
-29.50
-30.00
-30.50
-31.00
-31.50
-32.00
-32.50
9925
9489
9120
8748
8385
8029
7695
7369
7043
6743
6442
6144
5855
5562
5275
5024
4771
4521
4294
4042
3817
3582
3343
3121
2922
2716
2511
2314
2116
1940
1739
1562
1304
1156
990
827
655
494
346
208
95
Years Before Present (2000 AD)
joannenova.com.au
David Lappi

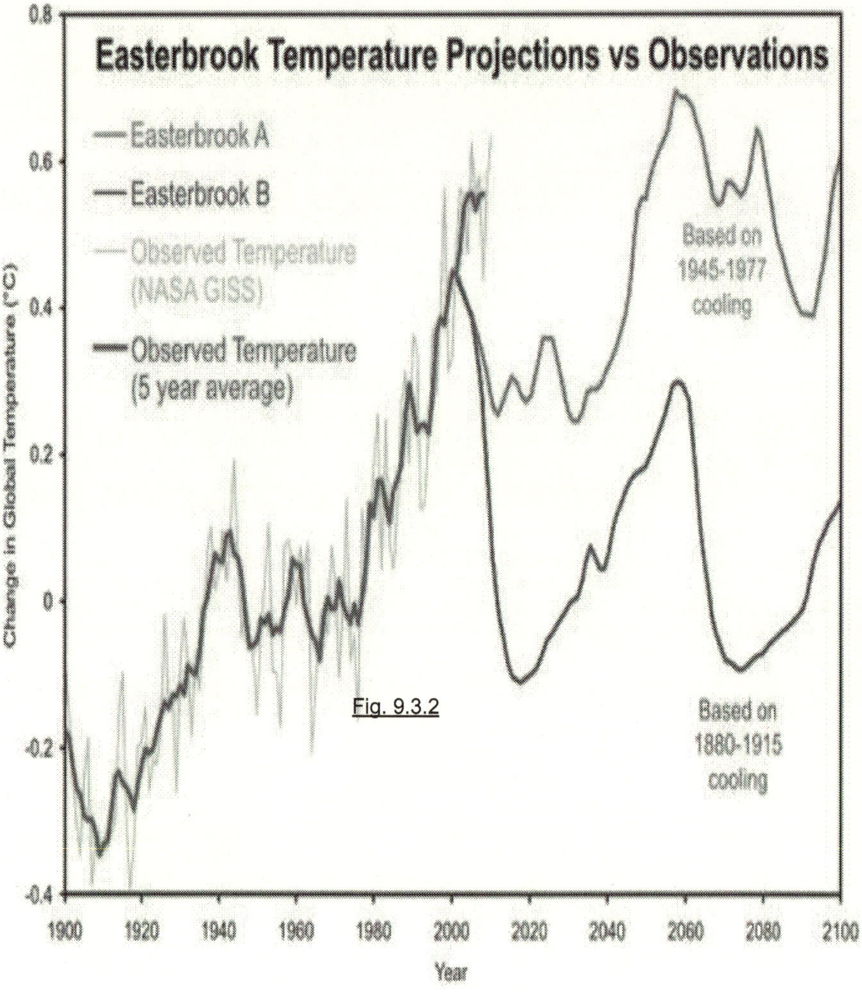

Easterbrook Temperature Projections vs Observations
Easterbrook A
Easterbrook B
Observed Temperature (NASA GISS)
Observed Temperature (5 year average)
Based on 1945-1977 cooling
Based on 1880-1915 cooling
Change in Global Temperature (°C)
0.8
0.6
0.4
0.2
0
-0.2
-0.4
1900
1920
1940
1960
1980
2000
2020
2040
2060
2080
2100
Year

Fig. 9.3.2

NOTES

1 Fig I-1 The effects of time pressure on reading comprehension and saccadic eye movement. Source: Physiology Lessons for use with the Biopac Student Lab PC under Windows® 98SE, Me, 2000 Pro or Macintosh® 8.6 – 9.1 ELECTROOCULOGRAM (EOG) The Influence of Auditory Rhythm on Visual Attention Revised 3/11/2013 D. W. Pittman Ph.D. Wofford College. Source https://webs.wofford.edu/pittmandw/psy330/exps/2011/HRexp2.htm
2 Author, Nov 3, 2019
3 Author, Oct 30, 2019
4 Fig I-2 This is the letter that was sent to every Bishop in the U.S. in May/June-2012. "More signs of the times and Climate Change covers whatever happens." http://timbernard.org/ltr-Bishops-2012.htm https: Original source: //pin.it/f2uyc2pwdhizw7
5 https://publicdomainvectors.org/de/tag/Schule
6 Fig I-4 http://images.clipartpanda.com/happy-earth-cartoon-cutcaster-vector-800923134-Earth-Jumping.jpg
7 Published 25 April 2016- Greening of the Earth and its drivers. By Zaichun Zhu, Shilong Piao [...] Ning Zeng. Nature Climate Change volume6, pages791–795 (2016) Source https://www.nature.com/articles/nclimate3004
8 When crocodiles roamed the Arctic, Published in Newscientist ,18 June 2008 https://www.newscientist.com/article/mg19826611-200-when-crocodiles-roamed-the-arctic/
9 When was the Ice Age according to the Bible? | Yahoo Answers. https://answers.yahoo.com/question/index?qid=20190624180020AAiAQz7
10 https://www.dailysignal.com/2019/04/22/on-earth-day-gloomy-predictions-havent-come-to-pass/ On Earth Day, Gloomy Predictions Haven't Come to Pass Nicolas Loris / @NiconomistLoris / April 22, 2019 / 26 Comments
11 Fig I-5 https://www.publicdomainpictures.net/en/view-image.php?image=139333&picture=stick-family
12 Fig I-5 https://www.publicdomainpictures.net/en/view-image.php?image=139333&picture=stick-family
13 Fig I-8 Source; http://www.clker.com/clipart-543540.html#7s8d6f87 ball-outline.html
14 Fig I-9, Are You Scaring Your Customer's Inner Caveman? By Liraz Margalit Credit;ttps://www.neurosciencemarketing.com/blog/articles/inner-caveman.htm
15 Original quote by W. Edwards Deming. Later adopted as a poster theme by NASA. https://quotes.deming.org/authors/W._Edwards_Deming/quote/3734
16 https://clipartion.com/free-clipart-13971/
17 "Democracy's plight" by Rush Holt, SCIENCE 363:433 (2019). Source: https://science.sciencemag.org/content/sci/363/6426/433.full.pdf
18 Fig I-11 Why is America a Republic and Not a Democracy? September 30, 2014. http://niagarafallsreporter.com/Stories/2014/SEP30/whyIsUSA.html
19 The Road to Bad Science Is Paved with Obedience and https://thenextregeneration.wordpress.com/2014/07/08/the-road-to-bad-science-is-paved-with-obedience-and-secrecy/
20 https://tallbloke.wordpress.com/2013/07/
21 https://publicdomainvectors.org/en/free-clipart/Yelling-kid/65808.html

---

22 http://wethepublic33.blogspot.com/2015/04/the-two-candidates-that-are-not_16.html
23 Author, Oct 28, 2019
24 https://publicdomainvectors.org/en/public-domain/
25
https://images.search.yahoo.com/yhs/search;_ylt=AwrJ4NYkDsNdCEwA4zA2nIlQ?p=greenwash+cartoon&fr=yhs-Lkry-newtab&hsimp=yhs-newtab&hspart=Lkry&imgl=pd&fr2=p%3As%2Cv%3Ai
26 Climate Change: How Do We Know? https://climate.nasa.gov/evidence/

27 https://www.newscientist.com/article/dn20413-warmer-oceans-release-co2-faster-than-thought/
http://www.drroyspencer.com/2009/05/global-warming-causing-carbon-dioxide-increases-a-simple-model/
28 Texas A&M Expert: Rainfall from Harvey Shattered Every ....
https://wattsupwiththat.com/2017/09/07/texas-am-expert-rainfall-from-harvey-shattered-every-record/
29 https://work.chron.com/climatologist-vs-meteorologist-16462.html
30 Author, Nov 5, 2019.
31 Author Oct 10, 2019
32 Author, Nov 3, 2019
33 https://www.publicdomainpictures.net/en/view-image.php?image=87854&picture=&jazyk=NL
34 Author, Oct 29, 2019
35 https://skepticalscience.com/print.php?r=58
36 https://publicdomainvectors.org/en/free-clipart/Hand-holding-tape-meter-vector-clip-art/5462.html
37 http://www.clker.com/clipart-thermometer-in-beaker.html
38 Real Climate science, article "The problem with the NOAA graph is that it is fake data. NOAA creates the warming trend by altering the data. The NOAA raw data shows no warming over the past century." Web site: https://realclimatescience.com/2016/12/100-of-us-warming-is-due-to-noaa-data-tampering/
39 Chart of 420,000 year history: temperature, CO2, sea level, John Englander, Site https://www.johnenglander.net/chart-of-420000-year-history-temperature-co2-sea-level/
40 Source "The Sun Today, Solar facts and space weather, by C. Alex Young, PhD. credit chart: http://bit.ly/1pQn7wy
41 The Earth's tilt with respect to its orbit. Image credit: Dennis Nilsson
Source: https://slate.com/technology/2012/12/winter-solstice-2012-the-axial-tilt-of-the-earth-is-the-real-reason-for-the-seasons.html
42 http://pubsapp.acs.org/subscribe/archive/ci/31/i09/html/09cartoons.html?
43
https://images.search.yahoo.com/yhs/search;_ylt=AwrEeBwlG8NduEUAdAQPxQt.;_ylu=X3oDMTByMjB0aG5zBGNvbG8DYmYxBHBvcwMxBHZ0aWQDBHNlYwNzYw--?p=drawing+thermometer+pot+public+domain+cartoon&fr=yhs-Lkry-newtab&hspart=Lkry&hsimp=yhs-newtab#id=90&iurl=https%3A%2F%2Fclipart-library.com%2Fimg%2F1547819.png&action=close
44 https://publicdomainvectors.org/en/free-clipart/Blacksmith-silhouette/56216.html

45 Physics world, EARTH SCIENCES, RESEARCH UPDATE- Article "Radioactive decay accounts for half of Earth's heat". 19 Jul 2011, by Hamish Johnston. Site - https://physicsworld.com/a/radioactive-decay-accounts-for-half-of-earths-heat/

47 https://publicdomainpictures.net/en/view-image.php?image=56296&picture=witch-stirring-brew
48 https://aggie- horticulture.tamu.edu/earthkind/landscape/dont-bag-it/chaptr-1-the-decomposition-process
49 https://sciencing.com/earth-receive-heat-sun-4566644.html, David Sarokin; Updated April 24, 2017
50 https://sciencing.com/protects-earth-harmful-solar-flares-2515.html, Tammie Painter; Updated March 10, 2018
51 https://earthobservatory.nasa.gov/features/Clouds by Steve Graham March 1, 1999
52 Do You Know What Is Greenhouse Effect ? April 1, 2016 http://factsnme.com/know-greenhouse-effect/
53 Water-cloud cycle https://the-importance-of-water.weebly.com/the-water-cycle.html
54 https://science.howstuffworks.com/nature/climate-weather/meteorologists/cloud-seeding1.htm BY JACOB SILVERMAN & ROBERT LAMB
55 https://www.space.com/31369-why-the-earth-has-a-force-field.html,Paul Sutter, Astrophysicist | December 14, 2015

56 Photo of aurora borealis. https://www.quora.com/Planetary-Science-How-does-earths-magnetic-field-protect-us-against-solar-wind
57 https://phys.org/news/2016-08-solar-impact-earth-cloud.html August 25, 2016 by Morten Garly Andersen, Technical University of Denmark

58 Cautions: Nerds only zone- https://en.wikipedia.org/wiki/Earth%27s_energy_budget#7s8d6f87
59 http://environ.andrew.cmu.edu/m3/s2/02sun.shtml
60 Earth's Upper Atmosphere Cooling Dramatically By Andrea Thompson December 17, 2009 Science & Astronomy https://www.space.com/7685-earth-upper-atmosphere-cooling-dramatically.html
61 https://www.nasa.gov/mission_pages/Glory/solar_irradiance/total_solar_irradiance.html
62 Nasa The Sunspot Cycle (Updated 2017/03/15) https://solarscience.msfc.nasa.gov/SunspotCycle.shtml
63 https://www.nationalvanguard.org/wp-content/uploads/2015/02/solar_cycle_24.gif
64 http://lasp.colorado.edu/home/sorce/files/2011/09/TIM_TSI_Reconstruction-1.png
65 NASA - Total Solar Irradiance: The Sun Also Changes. https://www.nasa.gov/mission_pages/Glory/solar_irradiance/total_solar_irradiance.html
66 NASA - Total Solar Irradiance: The Sun Also Changes. https://www.nasa.gov/mission_pages/Glory/solar_irradiance/total_solar_irradiance.html
6767 https://images.search.yahoo.com/search/images?p=don+easterbrook+climate+chnge+charts&fr=mcafee&imgurl=http%3A%2F%2F1.bp.blogspot.com%2F_XU9x8G7khv0%2FSc1LULr15HI%2FAAAAAAAABs4%2F7LwRIO6GsDk%2Fs400%2FDon_Easterbrook2_033.jpg#id=218&iurl

=https%3A%2F%2Fc3headlines.typepad.com%2F.a%2F6a010536b58035970c01310f4ff7a6970c-400wi&action=click
68
https://images.search.yahoo.com/search/images?p=Greenland+GISP+last+10+years+chart&fr=mcafee&imgurl=https%3A%2F%2Fi0.wp.com%2Fwww.whaleoil.co.nz%2Fwp-content%2Fuploads%2F2013%2F08%2Fgisp-last-10000-new.png#id=0&iurl=http%3A%2F%2Fjonova.s3.amazonaws.com%2Fgraphs%2Flappi%2FGisp-ice-10000-r..png&action=click#7s8d6f87
69 Cuyahoga River Fire. By Michael Rotman https://clevelandhistorical.org/items/show/63
70 https://www.epa.gov/transportation-air-pollution-and-climate-change/accomplishments-and-success-air-pollution-transportation
71 More fossil fuels; fewer climate related deaths. https://i2.wp.com/industrialprogress.com/wp-content/uploads/2018/07/figure-1.9-color.jpg
72 Alex Epstein: "The Moral Case for Fossil Fuels" | Talks at .... https://www.youtube.com/watch?v=s6b7K1hjZk4
73 https://electroviees.wordpress.com/2013/05/16/generating-electricity-from-a-bicycle-dynamo/
74 NASA - Total Solar Irradiance: The Sun Also Changes. https://www.nasa.gov/mission_pages/Glory/solar_irradiance/total_solar_irradiance.html
75 https://www.quora.com/What-is-the-contribution-of-wind-energy-in-combatting-climate-change
76 https://notrickszone.com/2011/04/05/merci-france-germany-now-dependent-on-foreign-nuclear-power/
77 https://www.npr.org/sections/money/2011/10/27/141766341/the-price-of-electricity-in-your-state#7s8d6f87
78 C https://www.dissentmagazine.org/article/green-energy-bust-in-germany#7s8d6f87#7s8d6f87
79 https://www.npr.org/sections/money/2011/10/27/141766341/the-price-of-electricity-in-your-state
80 https://www.dissentmagazine.org/article/green-energy-bust-in-germany#7s8d6f87#7s8d6f87
81 https://www.cleanenergywire.org/news/renewables-briefly-cover-100-germanys-power-demand-2nd-time/french-export-cheap-nuclear-power-germany-could-surge

82 https://tradingeconomics.com/germany/gdp-growth
83 High Renewable Energy Costs Damage the German Economy, https://www.energycentral.com/c/ec/high-renewable-energy-costs-damage-german-economy
84 https://wattsupwiththat.com/2019/05/04/swedish-power-shortages-looming-because-of-their-renewable-energy-push/
85 https://en.wikipedia.org/wiki/Topaz_Solar_Farm
86 https://www.iflscience.com/technology/worlds-largest-solar-farm-goes-online-california/
87 https://en.wikipedia.org/wiki/Cost_of_electricity_by_source#7s8d6f87 Table 59.
88
https://search.yahoo.com/search;_ylt=A0geK.CM_yRegsgAdTJXNyoA;_ylc=X1MDMjc2NjY3OQRfcgMyBGZyA21jYWZlZQRmcjIDc2ltdG9wBGdwcmlkA2lIWXZvdUdFUnBtZV9mYkgwMHNicEEEbl9yc2x0AzAEbl9zdWdnAzQEb3JpZ2luA3NlYXJjaC55YWhvby5jb20EcG9zAzAEcHFzdHI

DBHBxc3RybAMwBHFzdHJsAzUxBHF1ZXJ5A2dpYW50JTIweWVsbG93c3RvbmUlMjB2dWxj
YW5lJTIwdG8lMjByeHBsb2RlJTIwY2xpbWF0ZSUyMGNoYW5nZQR0X3N0bXADMTU3OTUz
Njg4Mw--?p=giant+yellowstone+vulcane+to+rxplode+climate+change&fr2=sb-top&fr=mcafee&type=E211US105G0
89
https://images.search.yahoo.com/search/images;_ylt=AwrE1xtmD2RdWhkATcFXNyoA;_ylu=X3oDMTEyajBycjRtBGNvbG8DYmYxBHBvcwMxBHZ0aWQDQTA2MDdfMQRzZWMDc2M-?p=climate+change+chart+for+the+past+1000+years&fr=mcafee#id=1&iurl=https%3A%2F%2Fcolemanscornerdotcomdotbr.files.wordpress.com%2F2014%2F12%2Fchart-last-1000-years.jpg&action=click
90 https://www.washingtontimes.com/news/2016/may/31/mars-also-undergoing-climate-change-ice-age-retrea/
91 Author, Oct 27, 2019
92 Convection Facts for Kids. https://kids.kiddle.co/Convection
93
http://www.lordgrey.org.uk/~f014/usefulresources/aric/Resources/Teaching_Packs/Key_Stage_4/Weather_Climate/03.html
94 http://i.imgur.com/MT5qfo4.png
95
https://images.search.yahoo.com/yhs/search?p=public+domain+cartoons+climate+drawings+climate+control+knobs&fr=yhs-itm-001&hspart=itm&hsimp=yhs-001&imgurl=http%3A%2F%2Fcurryja.files.wordpress.com%2F2014%2F09%2Fsensitivity-cartoon.jpg#id=-1&iurl=http%3A%2F%2Fcurryja.files.wordpress.com%2F2014%2F09%2Fsensitivity-cartoon.jpg&action=click
96
https://www.marefa.org/%D8%B8%D9%84_%D8%A7%D9%84%D9%85%D8%B7%D8%B1
97
https://www.cpc.ncep.noaa.gov/products/analysis_monitoring/ensocycle/nawinter.shtml
98 https://water.usgs.gov/edu/watercycleoceans.htm
99 Posted by Derrek Barry, label global warming, Gulf Stream, https://nebuchadnezzarwoollyd.blogspot.com/2007/05/gulf-stream-out-of-circulation.html
100 https://www.nasa.gov/mission_pages/sunearth/science/atmosphere-layers2.html
101 https://www.natickma.gov/346/Stormwater-Management-for-Kids
102 https://www.natickma.gov/346/Stormwater-Management-for-Kids
103 http://www.clker.com/clipart-629211.html
104 https://commons.wikimedia.org/wiki/File:Latitude_and_Longitude_of_the_Earth.svg
105 http://www.clker.com/clipart-670306.html
106 https://scied.ucar.edu/longcontent/energy-budget
107 https://www.nrdc.org/stories/greenhouse-effect-101#whatis
108 https://www.quora.com/What-role-does-human-activity-play-in-the-current-global-warming-trend
109 https://www.scientificamerican.com/article/how-bad-of-a-greenhouse-gas-is-methane/
110 https://www.epa.gov/ghgemissions/overview-greenhouse-gases
111 Table by the Author, data Source: Figure 7.3 , IPCC AR4; downloaded from-https://skepticalscience.com/human-co2-smaller-than-natural-emissions-intermediate.htm

112 NASA confirms that the increase in CO_2 is increasing plant life on earth, decreasing deserts. https://www.nasa.gov/feature/goddard/2016/carbon-dioxide-fertilization-greening-earth

113 Swedan, Nabil H. (2019), On the carbon cycle and its interactions with the biosphere, download: https://www.academia.edu/39398051/On_the_carbon_cycle_and_its_interactions_with_the_biosphere

114 https://www.engineeringtoolbox.com/gases-solubility-water-d_1148.html

115 Data source: NOAA, 20166 Web update: August 2016 https://www.epa.gov/climate-indicators/climate-change-indicators-sea-surface-temperature

116 https://www.globalchange.gov/browse/indicators/indicator-global-surface-temperatures

117 USGCRP Indicator Details | GlobalChange.gov. https://www.globalchange.gov/browse/indicators/indicator-global-surface-temperatures

118 Data source: Blane Perun's TheSea March 7, 2016; https://www.thesea.org/90-volcanic-activity-occurs-oceans/

119 Source: Figure 1, FAQ 2.1, IPCC Fourth Assessment Report (2007), Chapter 2 https://www.acs.org/content/acs/en/climatescience/greenhousegases/industrialrevolution.html

120 https://skepticalscience.com/search.php?t=c&Search=ice+core

121 https://www.newsweek.com/climategate-revisited-new-theory-explains-tree-ring-controversy-250208

122 Neutron star cosmic rays penetrate the earth and come out in china, Carl Sage, video from you tube video at https://video.search.yahoo.com/search/video;_ylt=AwrJ61jHJWhdX24AiBZXNyoA;_ylu=X3oDMTEyajBycjRtBGNvbG8DYmYxBHBvcwMxBHZ0aWQDQTA2MDdfMQRzZWMDc2M-?p=do+cosmic+rays+travel+deep+into+oceans&fr=mcafee&guccounter=1&guce_referrer=aHR0cHM6Ly9zZWFyY2gueWFob28uY29tL3NlYXJjaDtfeWx0PUEwZ2VLLmVNSldoZGE1c0FYUmhYTnlvQTtfeWx1PVgzb0RNVEUzT1Rsc05tWnFCR052Ykc4RFltWXhCSEJ2Y3dNMEJIWjBhV1FEUVRBMk1EZGZNUVJ6WldNRGNtVnNMV0p2ZEEtLT9wPWRvK2Nvc21pYytyYXlzK3RyYXZlbCtkZWVwK2ludG8rb2NlYW5zK3ZpZGVvJnR5cGU9RTIxMVVTMTA1RzEwJmVpPVVURi04JmZyMj1ycy1ib3R0b20lMkNwJTNBcyUyQ3YlM0F3JTJDbSUzQWF0LXMmZnI9bWNhZmVl&guce_referrer_sig=AQAAAKAcCt32SrHObcqqvUUUgWG8usB8rZvCztRpwmGKy4CWtDiB3QB1rJGIjG7jKsWcvJrj2LOB3QrV6McvarbpeQhU5QDZlzMhwxYJxpO9H6JnjJaYxlWnxrUoixtQMBRWZonbCYuBFxGPUsb1CbLp8wyfpVCmPg4BTbkxTHRYY4l6#id=38&vid=dc88c9fffcfbc7bc106d1bd19d594372&action=view

123 'Fire Under Arctic Ice: Volcanoes Have Been Blowing Their Tops In The Deep Ocean." June 26, 2008. Source: Woods Hole Oceanographic Institution https://www.sciencedaily.com/releases/2008/06/080625140649.htm

124 https://www.nasa.gov/topics/earth/features/vapor_warming.html

125 https://sealevel.nasa.gov/understanding-sea-level/global-sea-level/thermal-expansion
Thermal Expansion | Global Sea Level – NASA Sea Level .... https://sealevel.nasa.gov/understanding-sea-level/global-sea-level/thermal-expansion

126 https://www.engineeringtoolbox.com/water-specific-volume-weight-d_661.html

127 NASA Sea Level Change Portal: Thermal Expansion. https://sealevel.nasa.gov/understanding-sea-level/global-sea-level/thermal-expansion
128 http://www.clker.com/clipart-746850.html#7s8d6f87
129
https://www.answers.com/Q/How_many_days_a_year_is_Antarctica_above_freezing
130 2.2: The States of Matter - Chemistry LibreTexts.
https://chem.libretexts.org/Bookshelves/Introductory_Chemistry/Book
percent3A_Introductory_Chemistry_Online!_(Young)/02
percent3A_The_Physical_and_Chemical_Properties_of_Matter/2.2
percent3A_The_States_of_Matter
131 https://climate.nasa.gov/news/2361/study-mass-gains-of-antarctic-ice-sheet-greater-than-losses/
132 Study: Mass gains of Antarctic ice sheet greater than ....
https://climate.nasa.gov/news/2361/study-mass-gains-of-antarctic-ice-sheet-greater-than-losses/
133 https://www.usatoday.com/story/tech/news/2019/03/26/climate-change-greenland-glacier-growing-but-its-only-temporary-jakobshavn/3275098002/
134 https://www.usatoday.com/story/tech/news/2019/03/26/climate-change-greenland-glacier-growing-but-its-only-temporary-jakobshavn/3275098002/
135 USA Today on March 26, 2019, "....Natural cyclical cooling..."
136 https://historyofmassachusetts.org/how-boston-lost-its-hills/
137 Quantifying uncertainties of sandy shoreline change projections as sea level rises, 10 Jan, 019
https://www.nature.com/articles/s41598-018-37017-4
138 https://www.earthmagazine.org/article/mississippi-delta-drowning
139 Morrison's Island Public Realm and Flood Defence Project. https://s3-eu-west-1.amazonaws.com/arup-s3-lower-lee-frs-ie-wp-static/wp-content/uploads/lee_valley/Morrisons-Island-Appendix-C-Transport-Assessment-Report.pdf
140 https://www.nature.com/articles/s41598-018-37017-4
141 https://www.sciencedirect.com/science/article/pii/S1342937X10001966
142 Question; Is this your religion? Take the test. - Page 13.
https://www.debatepolitics.com/environment-and-climate-issues/191192-question-your-religion-take-test-13.html
143 Albrecht Kossel - Wikipedia. https://en.wikipedia.org/wiki/Albrecht_Kossel
144 CERN is "Conseil Européen pour la Recherche Nucléaire (French: European Laboratory for Particle Physics; Geneva, Switzerland) CERN"
145 https://principia-scientific.org/do-cosmic-rays-trigger-earthquakes-volcanic-eruptions/#7s8d6f87

147 A n artist's concept of the shower of particles produced when Earth's atmosphere is struck by ultra-high-energy cosmic rays. Credit: Simon Swordy/University of Chicago, NASA Source: SciTecDaily https://scitechdaily.com/solar-particles-infiltrate-earths-atmosphere-causing-a-gle/
148 Do volcanic eruptions coincide with low sunspot activity?
https://www.iceagenow.info/volcanic-eruptions-coincide-sunspot-activity/
149 Can Astronomical Tidal Forces Trigger Earthquakes ....
https://www.scientificamerican.com/article/can-astronomical-tidal-forces-trigger-earthquakes/

150 Can Astronomical Tidal Forces Trigger Earthquakes ....
https://www.scientificamerican.com/article/can-astronomical-tidal-forces-trigger-earthquakes/
151 https://en.es-static.us/upl/2012/10/two_tidal_bulges_earth.jpeg
152 Predicting Cyclone Induced Flood: A Comprehensive Case ....
https://link.springer.com/chapter/10.1007 percent2F978-981-10-1113-9_3
153 Credits: David B. Whyte, PhD, Science Buddies, download from:
https://www.sciencebuddies.org/science-fair-projects/project-ideas/EnvSci_p051/environmental-science/how-does-the-tilt-of-earth-axis-affect-the-seasons#7s8d6f87/
154 The total daily amount of extraterrestrial irradiation on a plane horizontal to the Earth's surface(H0h) for different latitudes. https://www.itacanet.org/the-sun-as-a-source-of-energy/part-2-solar-energy-reaching-the-earths-surface/
155 Solar Power. Date : 2014-08-04
https://www.steam-generator.com/solar-power/
156 Total Solar Irradiance Data
http://lasp.colorado.edu/home/sorce/files/2011/09/TIM_TSI_Reconstruction-1.png
157 Principal Uncertainties in Climate Models
http://homework.uoregon.edu/pub/class/es202/forcings.html

159 What causes Teslas to explode? https://www.sun-sentinel.com/business/fl-bz-tesla-crash-battery-explosions-20180509-story.html
49 How Lithium-Ion Batteries Turn Into Skin-Searing Firebombs
https://www.wired.com/2017/03/lithium-ion-batteries-turn-skin-searing-firebombs/160
https://electrek.co/2018/06/16/tesla-model-s-battery-fire-investigating/
161 https://www.wired.com/2017/03/lithium-ion-batteries-turn-skin-searing-firebombs/#7s8d6f87
162 http://cliparts.co/clipart/2331318

163 Will Weinstein Finally Kill the Old Boys' Network? - The ....
https://www.theatlantic.com/entertainment/archive/2017/10/will-harvey-weinstein-finally-kill-the-old-boys-network/542805/
164 https://www.ceotodaymagazine.com/2019/05/the-ultimate-guide-to-public-speaking/
165 https://convergentdivergent.wordpress.com/2014/02/27/public-satire-examples/
166 Author, oct 17, 2019
167 http://www.clker.com/clipart-woman-baking.html
168 http://www.clker.com/clipart-575666.html
169 900 Tons of material to build just 1 windmill | Peak ....
http://energyskeptic.com/2015/900-tons-of-material-to-build-just-1-windmill/
170 U.S. Government Funding of Climate Change - Climate Dollars.
https://www.climatedollars.org/full-study/us-govt-funding-of-climate-change/
171 U.S. Government Funding of Climate Change - Climate Dollars.
https://www.climatedollars.org/full-study/us-govt-funding-of-climate-change/
172 Erasing The Medieval Warm Period | Real Climate Science.
https://realclimatescience.com/2018/12/erasing-the-medieval-warm-period/
173 https://www.thegwpf.org/content/uploads/2018/03/HelmReviewS.pdf
174 https://www.publicdomainpictures.net/en/view-image.php?image=177414&picture=brexit-2

176 " Climate-Industrial Complex" Wasting £100 Billion And ....
https://notalotofpeopleknowthat.wordpress.com/2018/03/05/climate-industrial-complex-wasting-100-billion-and-shutting-down-debate-warns-lilley/
177 Lessons From The U.K Cost Of Energy Review | Friends of ....
https://blog.friendsofscience.org/2018/03/08/lessons-from-the-u-k-cost-of-energy-review/
178 Homepage - Wigan St Patricks ARLFC. http://www.wiganstpats.org/ "Climate-Industrial Complex" Wasting £100 Billion And ....
https://notalotofpeopleknowthat.wordpress.com/2018/03/05/climate-industrial-complex-wasting-100-billion-and-shutting-down-debate-warns-lilley/
179 Homepage - Wigan St Patricks ARLFC. http://www.wiganstpats.org/
180 https://clipartion.com/free-clipart-28758/
181 The Top 15 Climate-Change Scientists: Consensus &amp ....
https://thebestschools.org/features/top-climate-change-scientists/
182 Before the Flood - Top 10 Climate Deniers. Article by BRENDAN DEMELLE Executive Director, DeSmog
https://www.beforetheflood.com/explore/the-deniers/top-10-climate-deniers/
183 Michael Mann: The Top 15 Climate-Change Scientists: Consensus &amp ....
https://thebestschools.org/features/top-climate-change-scientists/
184 Before the Flood - Top 10 Climate Deniers.
https://www.beforetheflood.com/explore/the-deniers/top-10-climate-deniers/
185 Roy Spencer; Before the Flood - Top 10 Climate Deniers.
https://www.beforetheflood.com/explore/the-deniers/top-10-climate-deniers/
186 https://thebestschools.org/features/top-climate-change-scientists/#7s8d6f87 Source article: The Top 15 Climate-Change Scientists: Consensus & Skeptics, by James A. Barham.
187 Jay H. Lehr: Before the Flood - Top 10 Climate Deniers.
https://www.beforetheflood.com/explore/the-deniers/top-10-climate-deniers/
188 Jay H. Lehr: Biography - Jay H. Lehr, Ph.D. - prfamerica.org.
https://prfamerica.org/biography/Biography-Lehr-Jay.html
189 Biography - Jay H. Lehr, Ph.D. - prfamerica.org.
https://prfamerica.org/biography/Biography-Lehr-Jay.html
190 Syukuro Manabe: The Top 15 Climate-Change Scientists: Consensus &amp ....
https://thebestschools.org/features/top-climate-change-scientists/
191 Syukuro Manabe: People – Sensorweb Research Laboratory.
http://sensorweb.engr.uga.edu/index.php/people/
192 Don Easterbrook: Home | Don J. Easterbrook, Emeritus Professor of Geology| WWU. http://myweb.wwu.edu/dbunny/

193 Michael Mann; The Top 15 Climate-Change Scientists: Consensus &amp ....
https://thebestschools.org/features/top-climate-change-scientists/
194 Richard Lindzen - Wikipedia. https://en.wikipedia.org/wiki/Richard_Lindzen
195 John Francis: The Top 15 Climate-Change Scientists: Consensus &amp ....
https://thebestschools.org/features/top-climate-change-scientists/
196 Judith Curry - Wikipedia. https://en.wikipedia.org/wiki/Judith_Curry
197 The Top 15 Climate-Change Scientists: Consensus &amp ....
https://thebestschools.org/features/top-climate-change-scientists/
198 Carbon Dioxide is a Cooling Gas According to NASA : Cold ....
https://coldclimatechange.com/carbon-dioxide-is-a-cooling-gas-according-to-nasa/

199 Summary of the natural cycles from Youtube video, at minute markers 42.57 as presented by frollyphd climate science 5 https://www.youtube.com/watch?v=wbQ-KviHT5I
200 https://www.youtube.com/watch?v=s6b7K1hjZk4
201 Mob Power,
https://publicdomainvectors.org/ko/%EB%AC%B4%E%A3%8C%20%ED%81%B4%EB%A6%BD%EC%95%84%ED%8A%B8/%EC%A3%BC%EB%A8%B9-%EB%A7%88%EC%9D%B4%ED%81%AC/50580.html
202 Rebuttal to the attack on Dr. Don Easterbrook, by Anthony Watts / April 8, 2013
https://wattsupwiththat.com/2013/04/08/rebuttal-to-the-attack-on-dr-don-easterbrook/
203 WSJ: Climate Science In Denial. Global warming alarmists have been discredited, but you wouldn't know it from the rhetoric this Earth Day. By Richard S. Lindzen, Updated April 22, 2010.
https://www.wsj.com/articles/SB10001424052748704448304575196802317362416
204 WSJ: The Political Assault on Climate Skeptics; Members of Congress send inquisitorial letters to universities, energy companies, even think tanks.
https://www.wsj.com/articles/richard-s-lindzen-the-political-assault-on-climate-skeptics-1425513033
205 Dr. Richard Lindzen, Newton, MA 02461 Washington, DC Dear ....
https://www.eenews.net/assets/2017/02/23/document_gw_06.pdf
206 When climate change becomes personal. Attacks on skeptics do a disservice to scientists and their profession https://www.washingtontimes.com/news/2015/jun/10/anthony-sadar-attacks-on-climate-change-skeptics-a/
207 Climate Change-Denying MIT Prof. Richard Lindzen Is Suddenly Popular, Still Wrong. Fact-checking the claims of a well-credentialed skeptic.
https://www.inverse.com/article/11643-climate-change-denying-mit-prof-richard-lindzen-is-suddenly-popular-still-wrong
208 Dr. Richard Lindzen responds to the MIT letter objecting to his petition to Trump to withdraw from the UNFCC.
https://www.climatedepot.com/2017/03/09/dr-richard-lindzen-responds-to-the-mit-letter-objecting-to-his-petition-to-trump-to-withdraw-from-the-unfcc/
209 http://www.clker.com/clipart-203983.html
210 Chart by John Englander, temperature, CO2 and sea levels for past 420,000 years.
http://www.johnenglander.net/chart-of-420000-year-history-temperature-co2-sea-level/
211 How do we know that recent CO2 increases are due to human activities?
Filed under: Climate Science 22 December 2004 -
http://www.realclimate.org/index.php/archives/2004/12/how-do-we-know-that-recent-cosub2sub-increases-are-due-to-human-activities-updated/
212 John Englander chart
https://images.search.yahoo.com/search/images?p=chart+CO2%2C+temoerature+and+sea+level&fr=mcafee&imgurl=http%3A%2F%2Fwww.johnenglander.net%2Fwp%2Fwp-content%2Fuploads%2F2017%2F04%2F420-kyr-Englander-Triple-Chart-rev2017-US-Units-1024x774.png#id=0&iurl=http%3A%2F%2Fwww.johnenglander.net%2Fwp%2Fwp-content%2Fuploads%2F2017%2F04%2F420-kyr-Englander-Triple-Chart-rev2017-US-Units-1024x774.png&action=click
213 CO2 lags temperature - what does it mean? What the science says...
https://skepticalscience.com/co2-lags-temperature.htm
214 Life on Earth was nearly doomed by too little CO2. Guest Blogger / June 30, 2017, Guest Essay by Dennis T. Avery. During the last ice age, too little atmospheric carbon dioxide

almost eradicated mankind. https://wattsupwiththat.com/2017/06/30/life-on-earth-was-nearly-doomed-by-too-little-co2

215 Anthropogenic CO2 warming challenged by 60-year cycle; Earth-Science Reviews Volume 155, April 2016, Pages 129-135 https://www.sciencedirect.com/science/article/pii/S0012825216300277

216 Carbon Dioxide in the Ocean and Atmosphere. http://www.waterencyclopedia.com/Bi-Ca/Carbon-Dioxide-in-the-Ocean-and-Atmosphere.html

217 https://www.epa.gov/ghgemissions/overview-greenhouse-gases

218 https://video.search.yahoo.com/search/video;_ylt=A2KIbZw.DIVdpLEAd2lXNyoA;_ylu=X3oDMTEyZTRrYWpsBGNvbG8DYmYxBHBvcwMyBHZ0aWQDQTA2MDdfMQRzZWMDc2M-?p=Epstein+and+the+moral+case&fr=mcafee&guccounter=1&guce_referrer=aHR0cHM6Ly9zZWFyY2gueWFob28uY29tL3NlYXJjaD9mcj1tY2FmZWUmdHlwZT1FMjExVVMxMDVHMTAmcD1FcHN0ZWluK2FuZCt0aGUrbW9yYWwrY2FzZQ&guce_referrer_sig=AQAAAIAynDUVmOv07gHWXyXX3uSaE7oRxNxCEoFYVqJtrnOVTqqwFIHIqx4mxURud94S3eTOc2t-htGkS0By9dGLDj0iNa9m_ijQp6DDr0kIuoxatWBWL6VkaBM3UCSqme1LiTOYMBAAbF6YsOLpEtUuEZdszncRSqdDetDi2fsldta-

219 Paris Climate Pact Must Be Stopped – American Free Press. http://americanfreepress.net/paris-climate-pact-must-be-stopped/

220 http://www.saburchill.com/chapters/chap0025.html

221 Alex Epstein, home page; https://www.facebook.com/thepursuitofenergy

222 Patrick Moore, we need more CO2 https://www.academia.edu/11915593/DR._PATRICK_MOORE_-_THE_POSITIVE_IMPACT_OF_HUMAN_C02_ON_THE_SURVIVAL_OF_LIFE_ON_EARTH._We_need_more_not_less_as_photosynthesis_is_essential_to_all_life

223 https://www.academia.edu/40377384/THE_GLOBAL_WARMING_SCAM_by_Vincent_Gray_pdf._My_annotations_added.The_global_warming_scam_is_the_result_of_the_widespread_belief_in_a_new_religion_based_on_the_deification_of_a_nebulous_entity_The_Environment_#7s8d6f87

224 THE GLOBAL WARMING SCAM by Vincent Gray Climate Consultant 75 Silverstream Road, Crofton Downs, Wellington 6035, New Zealand Email vinmary.gray@paradise.net.nz (Revised October 2008). Source: https://friendsofscience.org/assets/documents/GlobalWarmingScam_Gray.pdf

225 LEADING SCIENTISTS, including 60 Nobel winners, doubt trace amounts of CO2 emissions cause over heated climate. New Research shows "extreme value of CO2 to all life forms, but no role in any change of the Earth's climate." Alarmism "statistically questionable." https://www.academia.edu/30183146/LEADING_SCIENTISTS_including_60_Nobel_winners_doubt_trace_amounts_of_CO2_emissions_cause_over_heated_climate._New_Research_shows_extreme_value_of_CO2_to_all_life_forms_but_no_role_in_any_change_of_the_Earth_s_climate._Alarmism_statistically_questionable.

226 Where Did '97 Percent' Global Warming Consensus Figure Come From? "Cook's 97 percent consensus claim was rebutted in subsequent analyses of his study. A paper by five leading climatologists published in the journal Science and Education last year found that Cook's study misrepresented the views of most consensus scientists. The definition Cook used to get his consensus was weak, the climatologists said." https://dailycaller.com/2014/05/16/where-did-97-percent-global-warming-consensus-figure-come-from/

227 When A Third Becomes 97 Percent: A Con That Changed the ....
https://www.breitbart.com/politics/2016/05/21/third-becomes-97-percent-bald-faced-lie-changed-western-world/
228 According to figures from the US Department of Education Digest of Education Statistics: 2008, 10.6 million science graduates have gained qualifications consistent with the OISM polling criteria since the 1970-71 school year. 32,000 out of 10 million is not a very compelling figure, but a tiny minority - approximately 0.3 per cent.
http://www.usmessageboard.com/threads/looks-like-the-cats-out-of-the-bag.698172/page-33
229 https://medium.com/real-in-other-words/sailing-on-the-river-denial-with-clinton-foundation-friends-d9cdfca4b247

230 3/26/2013 Dr Easterbrook testimony on climate science to U.S. Senate
231 Don Easterbrook | DeSmog. https://www.desmogblog.com/don-easterbrook
232 Three Facts Prove Climate Alarm Is a Scam | Newsmax.com.
https://www.newsmax.com/LarryBell/climate-global-warming-ipcc/2016/05/31/id/731497/
233 July 16, 2011 The Global Warming Hoax: How Soon We Forget
By F. Swemson
https://www.americanthinker.com/articles/2011/07/the_global_warming_hoax_how_soon_we_forget.html#ixzz612fpmvnE
Follow us: @AmericanThinker on Twitter | AmericanThinker on Facebook
https://www.americanthinker.com/articles/2011/07/the_global_warming_hoax_how_soon_we_forget.html
234 Global Warming Natural Cycle — OSS Foundation.
http://ossfoundation.us/projects/environment/global-warming/natural-cycle
235 Climate myths: It was warmer during the Medieval period, with vineyards in England
EARTH 16 May 2007. Read more: https://www.newscientist.com/article/dn11644-climate-myths-it-was-warmer-during-the-medieval-period-with-vineyards-in-england/#ixzz612ix5FPP.
https://images.search.yahoo.com/search/images?p=don+easterbrook+climate+chnge+charts&fr=mcafee&imgurl=http%3A%2F%2F1.bp.blogspot.com%2F_XU9x8G7khv0%2FSc1LULr15HI%2FAAAAAAAABs4%2F7LwRIO6GsDk%2Fs400%2FDon_Easterbrook2_033.jpg#id=0&iurl=http%3A%2F%2F1.bp.blogspot.com%2F_XU9x8G7khv0%2FSc1LULr15HI%2FAAAAAAAABs4%2F7LwRIO6GsDk%2Fs400%2FDon_Easterbrook2_033.jpg&action=click
236 Climate Change Indicators: Drought. This indicator measures drought conditions of U.S. lands.
https://19january2017snapshot.epa.gov/climate-indicators/climate-change-indicators-drought_.html
237 Delingpole: NOAA 2.5 Degrees F Data Tampering – 'Science Doesn't Get Any Worse Than This'
https://www.breitbart.com/politics/2018/03/21/delingpole-noaa-2-5-degrees-f-data-tampering-science-doesnt-get-any-worse-than-this/
238 https://realclimatescience.com/wp-content/uploads/2017/01/Screen-Shot-2017-01-03-at-3.31.51-AM.gif
239 Easterbrook crashes the U.S. Senate global warming party.
www.youtube.com/watch?v=dSVkSCN_hLQ&ab_channel=1000
240 https://www.theguardian.com/commentisfree/cif-green/2010/jul/07/climategate-review-expert-verdict

241 https://www.newsmax.com/larrybell/cato-dqa-mit-noaa/2016/02/01/id/712153/#7s8d6f87
242 Stats Tampering Puts NOAA in Hot Water | Newsmax.com. https://www.newsmax.com/LarryBell/CATO-DQA-MIT-NOAA/2016/02/01/id/712153/
243 This is the detailed 209-page paper By JS D'Alio And A. Watts. http://scienceandpublicpolicy.org/images/stories/papers/originals/surface_temp.pdf
244 https://thsresearch.files.wordpress.com/2017/05/chap3-published-in-elsevier.pdf
245 https://thsresearch.files.wordpress.com/2017/05/chap3-published-in-elsevier.pdf Page 112
246 https://stevengoddard.wordpress.com/2012/06/11/why-hansen-had-to-corrupt-the-temperature-record/
247 https://thsresearch.files.wordpress.com/2017/05/chap3-published-in-elsevier.pdf Page 115
248 http://scienceandpublicpolicy.org/images/stories/papers/originals/surface_temp.pdf
249 https://realclimatescience.com/2019/02/61-of-noaa-ushcn-adjusted-temperature-data-is-now-fake/
250 https://thsresearch.files.wordpress.com/2017/05/chap3-published-in-elsevier.pdf A Critical Look at Surface Temperature Records Joseph D'Aleo CCM, AMS Fellow, 18 Glen Drive, Hudson, NH 03051, USA. page 134
251 https://thsresearch.files.wordpress.com/2017/05/chap3-published-in-elsevier.pdf Page 111
252 https://www.breitbart.com/politics/2018/03/21/delingpole-noaa-2-5-degrees-f-data-tampering-science-doesnt-get-any-worse-than-this/
253 https://stevengoddard.wordpress.com/2016/01/08/satellites-versus-surface-temperatures/
254 https://www.breitbart.com/politics/2018/03/21/delingpole-noaa-2-5-degrees-f-data-tampering-science-doesnt-get-any-worse-than-this/

255 https://clipart-library.com/pictures-of-scared-people.html
256 Dr. Robert Carter. Source; https://wattsupwiththat.com/2016/01/19/dr-robert-carter-scientist-climate-skeptic-pioneer-friend-r-i-p/
257 https://video.search.yahoo.com/yhs/search?fr=yhs-itm-001&hsimp=yhs-001&hspart=itm&p=youtube+who+is+lord+monkton#id=2&vid=8d31be825fed8c975f97d6e529d1882d&action=click
258 https://www.bostonglobe.com/news/nation/2013/11/05/harvard-smithsonian-global-warming-skeptic-helps-feed-strategy-doubt-gridlock-congress/uHssYO1anoWSiLw0v1YcUJ/story.html
259 http://advanceindiana.blogspot.com/2012/03/not-one-of-gary-varvels-finest-hours_17.html#7s8d6f87
260 "NYT Smears Scientist Willie Soon for Telling the Truth About 'Global Warming'" https://www.breitbart.com/politics/2015/02/21/nyt-smears-scientist-willie-soon-for-telling-the-truth-about-global-warming/
261 http://www.globalwarming.org/2015/02/27/new-york-times-repeats-scurrilous-greenpeace-attack-on-willie-soon-without-checking-the-facts/
262 Safety of Nuclear Power Reactors (Updated June 2019) http://www.world-nuclear.org/information-library/safety-and-security/safety-of-plants/safety-of-nuclear-power-reactors.aspx
263 Is nuclear power zero-emission? No, but it isn't high-emission either.

May 20, 2015 4.05pm EDT https://theconversation.com/is-nuclear-power-zero-emission-no-but-it-isnt-high-emission-either-41615
264 Table 1. Updated estimates of power plant capital and operating costs, page 6. https://www.eia.gov/outlooks/capitalcost/pdf/updated_capcost.pdf
265 Is nuclear energy safe? The answer is unequivocally yes. https://www.nei.org/fundamentals/safety
266 https://www.energycentral.com/c/ec/deaths-nuclear-energy-compared-other-causes#7s8d6f87
267 https://www.sms-tsunami-warning.com/pages/tsunami-effects#.XGq_1uhKiM8
268 https://www.newsweek.com/three-mile-island-accident-deaths-location-facts-nuclear-meltdown-anniversary-864161
56 https://ourworldindata.org/what-was-the-death-toll-from-chernobyl-and-fukushima

270 http://www.world-nuclear.org/information-library/safety-and-security/safety-of-plants/safety-of-nuclear-power-reactors.aspx
271 https://www.energycentral.com/c/ec/deaths-nuclear-energy-compared-other-causes#7s8d6f87
272 https://www.eia.gov/outlooks/capitalcost/pdf/updated_capcost.pdf#7s8d6f87
273 https://www.instituteforenergyresearch.org/wp-content/uploads/2012/08/elec-prod-graph.png

274 https://www.instituteforenergyresearch.org/renewable/wind/levelized-cost-of-new-generating-technologies/
275
https://www.google.com/search?q=at+the+maximum+point+what+%25+of+franch+elec+was+nuclear&rlz=1C1EKKP_enUS821US822&oq=at+the+maximum+point+what+%25+of+franch+elec+was+nuclear&aqs=chrome..69i57.26397j0j7&sourceid=chrome&ie=UTF-8
276 http://clipart-library.com/clipart/6cp5X6gxi.htm
277 https://www.world-nuclear.org/information-library/country-profiles/countries-a-f/france.aspx
278 Nuclear Power in France | French Nuclear Energy - World .... https://www.world-nuclear.org/information-library/country-profiles/countries-a-f/france.aspx
279 www.world-nuclear.org/information-library/country-profiles/countries-a-f/france.aspx
280 Advantage and Disadvantages of Thorium Reactors – Pros and Cons. Source; https://www.nuclear-power.net/nuclear-power-plant/reactor-types/thorium-reactor/advantage-and-disadvantages-of-thorium-reactors-pros-and-cons/
281 https://www.forbes.com/sites/jamesconca/2019/03/12/our-military-wants-small-nukes-to-reduce-convoy-casualties/#2150a45cba2b

282 https://publicdomainvectors.org/en/free-clipart/Clown-sketch/61100.html
283 http://www.nonsensibleshoes.com/2009/08/law-of-unintended-consequences-banning.html
284 Malaria - SlideShare. https://www.slideshare.net/doctorrao/malaria-1478424
285 Source https://www.ncbi.nlm.nih.gov/pmc/articles/PMC2821864/ , on article "Conis E. Debating the health effects of DDT: Thomas Jukes, Charles Wurster, and the fate of an environmental pollutant". Public Health Rep. 2010;125(2):337–342. doi:10.1177/003335491012500224.
286 http://arkansasfrogsandtoads.org/true-frogs-ranidae/green-frog/

287 https://americanliterature.com/author/mark-twain/short-story/some-learned-fables-for-good-old-boys-and-girls
288 https://townhall.com/political-cartoons/2019/03/16/164134
289 Green New Deal: AOC is behind it but what will it do for .... https://www.usatoday.com/story/news/politics/2019/02/07/green-new-deal-what-and-what-does-mean-climate-change/2589524002/ Green New Deal: AOC is behind it but what will it do for https://www.usatoday.com/story/news/politics/2019/02/07/green-new-deal-what-and-what-does-mean-climate-change/2589524002/
290 https://www.usatoday.com/story/news/politics/2019/02/07/green-new-deal-what-and-what-does-mean-climate-change/2589524002/
291 https://www.usatoday.com/story/news/politics/2019/02/07/green-new-deal-what-and-what-does-mean-climate-change/2589524002
292 Media and Climate Change Observatory Monthly Summary: The .... https://scholar.colorado.edu/cgi/viewcontent.cgi?article=1026&context=mecco_summaries
293 https://search.yahoo.com/search?fr=mcafee&type=E211US105G10&p=Bernie+sanders+pushes+eugenics+of+rd+world+birth+control
294 WSJ writer slams Ocasio-Cortez's Green New Deal, says it .... https://www.foxnews.com/politics/wsj-writer-slams-ocasio-cortezs-green-new-deal-says-it-looks-like-dem-parody-bill-written-by-gop
295 Interesting, when I queried twitter, message came up saying they understand the request but refuse to fill it? Nice-savenes pas? https://www.bizpacreview.com/2019/02/08/i-was-laughing-so-hard-i-nearly-cried-kimberley-strassel-brutally-breaks-down-aocs-green-plan-722039
296 https://www.foxnews.com/politics/biden-unveils-wide-ranging-climate-change-plan-that-uses-green-new-deal-as-crucial-framework
297 https://www.nytimes.com/2018/10/07/climate/ipcc-climate-report-2040.html
298 Dr. Robert Carter. Source; https://wattsupwiththat.com/2016/01/19/dr-robert-carter-scientist-climate-skeptic-pioneer-friend-r-i-p/
299 https://www.publicdomainpictures.net/en/view-image.php?image=144746&picture=chicken-cartoon
300 https://en.wikipedia.org/wiki/Alex_Epstein_(American_writer)
301 Talks at Google | The Moral Case for Fossil Fuels. https://talksat.withgoogle.com/talk/the-moral-case-for-fossil-fuels
302 https://www.authorhour.co/alex-epstein-moral-case-fossil-fuels/
303 From the book, the Moral Case for Fossil Fuels. https://industrialprogress.com/mcffdata/#7s8d6f87 The air pollution data can be used as is from the EPA data set. Original source: U.S. EPA National Emissions Inventory (NEI) Air Pollutant Emissions Trends Data
304 From the book, the Moral Case for Fossil Fuels. https://i1.wp.com/industrialprogress.com/wp-content/uploads/2018/07/Figure-1.7-color.jpg Original source Sources: BP Statistical Review of World Energy, Historical data workbook, World Bank, World Development Indicators (WDI)
305 According to Thomas Homer-Dixon, wind turbines never recoup the energy it takes to build them. https://www.snopes.com/fact-check/wind-idiot-power/
306 https://en.wikipedia.org/wiki/Bj%c3%b8rn_Lomborg#The_Skeptical_Environmentalist#7s8d6f87#7s8d6f87

307 Bjørn Lomborg - Wikipedia. https://en.wikipedia.org/wiki/Bj%C3%B8rn_Lomborg
308 Hans Kopp - donauschwaben-usa.org. http://donauschwaben-usa.org/kopp_hans.htm

309
310 https://www.lomborg.com/skeptical-environmentalist
311 Photo, courtesy https://www.etsy.com/listing/26647109/fly-fishing-print-original-etching

313 Green New Deal resolution "would bring about mass death" in the United States if put into action. https://newspunch.com/greenpeace-aoc-green-deal-death/
314 https://en.wikipedia.org/wiki/Patrick_Moore_(consultant)#Greenpeace
315 https://wattsupwiththat.wordpress.com/2017/03/03/dr-patrick-moore-was-right-greenpeace-is-full-of-shit/#7s8d6f87#7s8d6f87
316 https://nypost.com/2019/10/23/devine-eco-madness-may-be-reason-for-disastrous-boeing-737-max-safety-issues/#7s8d6f87
317 World Food Day, A Journey To Hunger, 2015 http://venturesafrica.com/world-food-day-2015-africas-journey-to-hunger-eradication/
318 Why are Japanese people living so long? Can we learn any lessons from them? https://www.agewatch.net/secrets-of-longevity/japanese-longevity/
319 https://cchistory322exhibitspring2012.wordpress.com/marie-antoinette/marie-today/
320 https://www.investors.com/politics/editorials/climate-change-global-warming-earth-cooling-media-bia
321 https://emergenteconomics.com/2014/02/24/21-things-they-never-tell-you-about-poor-countries/
322 https://emergenteconomics.com/2014/02/24/21-things-they-never-tell-you-about-poor-countries/
323 Adam T Betz | Centre College - Academia.edu. https://centre.academia.edu/AdamBetz
324 For an interesting historical discussion which makes a compelling case that preventive war justifications and strategic thinking was common among U.S. leaders in World War II, the Cold War, and in the face of the North Korean threat during the Clinton Administration, see Trachtenberg (2007).
325 https://images.search.yahoo.com/yhs/search?p=secret+laboratory+failures+cartoon+drawings&fr=yhs-itm-001&hspart=itm&hsimp=yhs-001&imgurl=https%3A%2F%2Fi.ytimg.com%2Fvi%2FZ0nHUIcshM0%2Fmaxresdefault.jpg#id=49&iurl=https%3A%2F%2Fmedia4.giphy.com%2Fmedia%2FfpdJtLKzju38A%2F200_s.gif&action=click
326 ETHICS, EQUITY AND THE ECONOMICS OF CLIMATE CHANGE PAPER 1 .... https://www.cambridge.org/core/journals/economics-and-philosophy/article/ethics-equity-and-the-economics-of-climate-change-paper-1-science-and-philosophy/DF44EB8C4427F6036DFA8E68CFC41711
327 greatly reduces the cost of the defense while waiting https://www.coursehero.com/file/p3itr8k/greatly-reduces-the-cost-of-the-defense-while-waiting-doesnt-mean-avoiding-war/

328 Whistleblower sues Duke, claims doctored data helped win $200 million in grants; https://www.sciencemag.org/news/2016/09/whistleblower-sues-duke-claims-doctored-data-helped-win-200-million-grants
329 https://www.vox.com/2016/3/24/11299102/scientific-retractions-are-on-the-rise This article comes at a particularly important point as Google has just settled with the Justice Dept on a $150 million fine. They are also being put under the microscope for possibly manipulating the 2020 elections.
330 https://www.csmonitor.com/Science/2012/1002/Fraud-in-scientific-research-It-happens-and-cases-are-on-the-rise
331 https://creation.com/science-fraud-epidemic
332 https://www.theguardian.com/science/2012/sep/13/scientific-research-fraud-bad-practice
333 https://clipartix.com/frankenstein-clipart-image-32727/
334 http://www.henry4school.fr/Sciences/big-brother.htm
335 "Who Controls the Past Controls the Future" Quote Meaning. https://www.thoughtco.com/what-does-that-quote-mean-archaeology-172300
336 https://www.thoughtco.com/what-does-that-quote-mean-archaeology-172300#7s8d6f87 False positives: fraud and misconduct are threatening ....

337 The History of Archaeology Part 1 - The First Archaeologists. https://www.thoughtco.com/the-first-archaeologists-167134
338 Session 18 May 2019 | Page 33 | Cassiopaea Forum. https://cassiopaea.org/forum/threads/session-18-may-2019.47219/page-33
339 Ethics in a Tangled Web: The New Censorship: How did https://kipcurrierethics.blogspot.com/2016/06/the-new-censorship-how-did-google.html
340 https://www.usnews.com/opinion/articles/2016-06-22/google-is-the-worlds-biggest-censor-and-its-power-must-be-regulated. Also see related note 7 above.
341 Google Is the World's Biggest Censor and Its Power Must Be https://www.usnews.com/opinion/articles/2016-06-22/google-is-the-worlds-biggest-censor-and-its-power-must-be-regulated
342 https://www.thegwpf.org/green-tyranny/ Green Economics Research Papers - Academia.edu. http://www.academia.edu/Documents/in/Green_Economics
343 Green Tyranny - Encounter Books. https://www.encounterbooks.com/books/green-tyranny/
344 Rupert Darwall - Encounter Books. https://www.encounterbooks.com/authors/rupert-darwall/
345 To Guard Your Heart Properly Know What It Is - NewCREEations. https://newcreeations.org/guard-your-heart-properly/
346 Matthew 6 - NIV Bible - "Be careful not to practice your https://www.biblestudytools.com/matthew/6.html
347 Matthew 7:15-20 "Beware of false prophets, who come to you https://www.bible.com/bible/114/MAT.7.15-20.nkjv
348 https://stopthesethings.com/2018/12/19/collateral-damage-poor-biggest-victims-of-britains-insane-climate-energy-policies/#7s8d6f87
349 https://www.thegwpf.org/content/uploads/2018/11/10years-CCA.pdf
350 History'smostexpensivevirtuesignal. https://www.thegwpf.org/content/uploads/2018/11/10years-CCA.pdf

351 Rupert Darwall - Encounter Books. https://www.encounterbooks.com/authors/rupert-darwall/
352 https://www.encounterbooks.com/authors/rupert-darwall/
353 "BashudaivaKutumbakkam"- The entire world is our home and .... http://fem.sumdu.edu.ua/images/2019/pdf/aaeoa_00019.pdf
354 Green Economics Research Papers - Academia.edu. http://www.academia.edu/Documents/in/Green_Economics
355 Received: February 20, 2019, | Published: March 07, 2019
Copyright© 2019 Bhandari. This is an open access article distributed under the terms of the Creative Commons Attribution License, which permits unrestricted use, distribution, and reproduction in any medium, provided the original author and source are credited
356 Medani Bhandari | Akamai University - Academia.edu. https://akamaiuniversity.academia.edu/MBhandari
357 http://obamacartoon.blogspot.com/2013/12/naked-chicks-with-guns.html
358 https://worldtop20.org/worlds-best-education-system-ranking-japans-investment-in-education-takes-it-to-the-top
359 https://www.theguardian.com/news/datablog/2010/dec/07/world-education-rankings-maths-science-reading
360 https://www.goodreads.com/author/show/3164882.Mehmet_Murat_ildan
361 https://video.search.yahoo.com/search/video?fr=mcafee&p=wsedish+student+speach+on+climate+change+at+the+UN#id=7&vid=7bc9b8955028748d6ef3cf2422cdefbe&action=click
362 http://anewdomain.net/ted-rall-most-public-school-kids-are-poor-news/
363 https://www.breitbart.com/politics/2019/03/09/teachers-urged-to-include-social-and-emotional-learning-that-created-white-privilege-into-classrooms
364 Teachers Urged to Include 'Social and Emotional Learning .... https://www.educationviews.org/teachers-urged-to-include-social-and-emotional-learning-in-classrooms/
365 https://www.boredpanda.com/satirical-illustrations-pawel-kuczynski/?utm_source=search.yahoo&utm_medium=referral&utm_campaign=organic

366 News - Emotional Learning Will Be the Downfall of Society .... https://www.heartland.org/news-opinion/news/emotional-learning-will-be-the-downfall-of-society
367 Emotional Learning Will Be the Downfall of Society. https://townhall.com/columnists/teresamull/2018/03/10/emotional-learning-will-be-the-downfall-of-society-n2458912
368 https://www.bibliotecapleyades.net/sociopolitica/sociopol_globaleducation33.htm
369 An Education Horror Show - WSJ. https://www.wsj.com/articles/an-education-horror-show-11562532467
370 COLUMN: Views on a variety of topics in the spotlight .... https://www.independenttribune.com/news/column-views-on-a-variety-of-topics-in-the-spotlight/article_b335eb0c-a4c6-11e9-a534-27327c00d0c5.html
371 https://www.publicschoolreview.com/blog/what-are-the-biggest-problems-facing-the-public-school-system
372 https://fineartamerica.com/art/knight

373 Manufacturing consensus: the early history of the IPCC January 3, 2018 by curryja https://judithcurry.com/2018/01/03/manufacturing-consensus-the-early-history-of-the-ipcc/

374 Putting the scientific cart before the data horse. https://curryja.files.wordpress.com/2018/06/slide061.png

375 STATEMENT TO THE SUBCOMMITTEE ON SPACE, SCIENCEAND https://curryja.files.wordpress.com/2015/12/curry-senate-testimony-2015.pdf

376 'Uncertain' Science: Judith Curry's Take On Climate Change", August 22, 2013. Heard on All Things Considered by RICHARD HARRIS https://www.npr.org/2013/08/22/213894792/uncertain-science-judith-currys-take-on-climate-change

377 https://www.the-scientist.com/news-opinion/qa-debate-over-climate-panel-bias-42198

378 https://www.eia.gov/tools/faqs/faq.php?id=427&t=3

379 https://www.eia.gov/tools/faqs/faq.php?id=427&t=3#7s8d6f87

380 https://www.americanthinker.com/articles/2007/02/the_ipcc_should_leave_science.html

381 https://apnews.com/bd45c372caf118ec99964ea547880cd0

382 Is a 1989 'U.N. Predicts Disaster if Global Warming Not https://www.truthorfiction.com/is-a-1989-u-n-predicts-disaster-if-global-warming-not-checked-article-authentic/

383 U.N. Predicts Disaster if Global Warming Not Checked. https://apnews.com/bd45c372caf118ec99964ea547880cd0

384 NASA confirms – Sea levels FALLING across the planet October 12, 2017 by Robert

385 https://townhall.com/columnists/pauldriessen/2018/10/13/the-ipccs-latest-climate-hysteria-n2528023

386 https://www.americanthinker.com/blog/2018/11/nyt_reporter_demands_we_become_hysterical_over_climate_change.html

387 https://www.climaterealityproject.org/blog/climate-change-explained-10-cartoons#7s8d6f87

388 https://www.inquirer.com/news/nation-world/un-chief-predicts-total-disaster-if-warming-not-stopped-20190508.html

389 NASA Sees Climate Cooling Trend Thanks To Low Sun Activity Published on October 4, 2018. Written by James Murphy https://principia-scientific.org/nasa-sees-climate-cooling-trend-thanks-to-low-sun-activity/

390 https://www.iceagenow.info/the-ipccs-latest-climate-hysteria/

391 https://www.cartoonstock.com/directory/p/public_punishments.asp

392 https://www.vox.com/2019/9/23/20879924/greta-thunberg-climate-action-summit-2019-un

393 http://straighttalkmd.com/michael-e-mann-explains-hockey-stick-graph/

394 National Review chart, source https://www.climate-skeptic.com/ US AVERAGE TEMPERATURE TRENDS IN CONTEXT, FEBRUARY 4, 2016 3 COMMENTS Cross-posted from Coyoteblog.

395 https://www.economicsjunkie.com/the-golbal-warming-catastrophe-in-charts/ On Don Easterbrook's Updated Projection. Bob Tisdale / February 6, 2014 https://wattsupwiththat.com/2014/02/06/on-don-easterbrooks-updated-projection/#7s8d6f87

396 https://www.sciencealert.com/scientists-say-it-could-already-be-game-over-for-climate-change
397 https://carboncycle.princeton.edu/research
398 https://clipground.com/galileo-image-clipart.html
399 https://www.breitbart.com/politics/2016/01/15/climate-alarmists-invent-new-excuse-the-satellites-are-lying/
400 https://climatesense-norpag.blogspot.com/2017/02/the-coming-cooling-usefully-accurate_17.html
401 https://climatesense-norpag.blogspot.com/2017/02/the-coming-cooling-usefully-accurate_17.html
402 https://nextgrandminimum.com/2018/11/22/professor-valentina-zharkova-breaks-her-silence-and-confirms-super-grand-solar-minimum/ MINIMUMTO EXAMINE THE SOCIAL AND ECONOMIC IMPACTS OF THE NEXT GRAND SOLAR MINIMUM – SEE ABOUT Professor Valentina Zharkova Confirms "Super" Grand Solar Minimum [Edited}
November 22, 2018Russ Steele
403 Surprising Summer Chill Baffles Global Warming Alarmists ....
https://wattsupwiththat.com/2019/06/28/surprising-summer-chill-baffles-global-warming-alarmists/
404 http://fraterbarrabbas.blogspot.com/2012/09/why-do-i-practice-magick.html
405 Reproduction of frontispiece by Robert Taylor Pritchett from the first Murrayillustrated edition, 1890: HMS Beagle in the Straits of Magellan at Monte Sarmientoin Chile.[1] source; https://en.wikipedia.org/wiki/The_Voyage_of_the_Beagle#7s8d6f87
406 https://en.wikipedia.org/wiki/The_Voyage_of_the_Beagle
407 http://cinema-crazed.com/blog/wp-content/uploads/2018/04/Supermanvs.jpg
408 https://www.publicdomainpictures.net/en/view-image.php?image=47921&picture=happy-sun-face-cartoon
409 https://inhabitat.com/us-vehicle-emissions-hit-record-low-as-fuel-economy-climbs-to-record-high/
410 https://www.higherperspectives.com/evil-person-2492720300.html
411 https://www.art.com/products/p15063687057-sa-i6855783/barbara-smaller-which-of-tonight-s-specials-is-the-most-sanctimonious-new-yorker-cartoon.htm#7s8d6f87
412 http://1.bp.blogspot.com/-AC5oLuqvVQ0/TkNhOocVvZI/AAAAAAACTyI/1Og8tHY58w8/s1600/Famous_Fictional_Characters_04.jpg#7s8d6f87
413 https://timesexaminer.com/science/3425-global-warming-skepticism-for-busy-people
414 https://www.goodreads.com/book/show/41815703-global-warming-skepticism-for-busy-people
415 https://www.nature.com/articles/s41586-019-1666-5
416 https://www.mayo.edu/research/clinical-trials/cls-20467334
417 https://www.worldbank.org/en/news/feature/2012/05/17/india-agriculture-issues-priorities
418 https://www.scientificamerican.com/article/africa-needs-fossil-fuels-to-end-energy-apartheid/#7s8d6f87
419 https://www.mckinsey.com/industries/electric-power-and-natural-gas/our-insights/powering-africa
420 https://www.nj.com/hudson/voices/2010/12/menendez_writes_to_santa_of_hi.html

421 https://www.canadiangeographic.ca/article/truth-about-polar-bears An in-depth look at the complicated, contradictory and controversial science behind the sound bites. By Zac Unger December 1, 2012 in "Canadian Geographic" a magazine of The Royal Canadian Geographical Society
422 https://www.goodfreephotos.com/public-domain-images/chemist-in-lab-vector-clipart.png.php
423 Where Are The Corpses? | Watts Up With That?. https://wattsupwiththat.com/2010/01/04/where-are-the-corpses/
424 https://clipartion.com/wp-content/uploads/2016/04/family-car-clipart-free.jpg
425 https://theheartthrills.files.wordpress.com/2013/08/jiminy-cricket1.jpg

426 https://boeing.mediaroom.com/2011-08-30-Boeing-Launches-737-New-Engine-Family-with-Commitments-for-496-Airplanes-from-Five-Airlines
427 https://clipartion.com/free-clipart-29276/
428 https://c1.staticflickr.com/7/6190/6128984041_c77b82d380_b.jpg
429 Climate change ethics Research Papers - Academia.edu. http://www.academia.edu/Documents/in/Climate_change_ethics
430 https://www.clker.com/cliparts/P/r/y/u/E/R/army-tank-hi.png
431 Article by Adam Betz, making the case for a preventive environmental war. https://www.academia.edu/38869429/Preventive_Environmental_War
432 https://www.pinterest.com/pin/497507090079543950/?lp=true
433 https://www.mrctv.org/blog/ca-govt-push-solar-panels-leaves-residents-stranded-when-power-company-shuts-down-during-fire#7s8d6f87
434 http://www.clker.com/clipart-clown-4.html
435 http://www.clker.com/clipart-2403.html
436 https://r.search.yahoo.com/_ylt=AwrExdxKk7ldMUAAQc6WnlIQ;_ylu=X3oDMTBtdXBkbHJyBHNlYwNmcC1hdHRyaWIEc2xrA3J1cmw-/RV=2/RE=1572471754/RO=11/RU=http%3a%2f%2fwww.pd4pic.com%2fold-drawing-people-man-guy-rich-person-cartoon.html/RK=2/RS=Erwc6MTjwl4y4K8rQUFo0YDDXwc-
437 http://www.clker.com/cliparts/a/0/2/9/13031727432114504058joker037mpsc8-md.png
438 https://www.denverpost.com/2016/10/03/cartoons-of-the-day-congress-overrides-obamas-veto-of-911-bill/
439 https://intellectualfroglegs.com/eminent-domain-and-donald-trump-hates-puppies/
440 https://cdn.pixabay.com/photo/2013/07/13/10/49/group-157841_640.png

441 https://climatechangedispatch.com/nasa-sees-climate-cooling-trend-thanks-to-low-sun-activity/
442 NASA Sees Climate Cooling Trend Thanks to Low Sun Activity. https://www.thenewamerican.com/tech/environment/item/30214-nasa-sees-climate-cooling-trend-thanks-to-low-sun-activity
443 Did global warming stop in 1998? | NOAA Climate.gov. https://www.climate.gov/news-features/climate-qa/did-global-warming-stop-1998
444 https://www.economist.com/science-and-technology/2014/03/06/who-pressed-the-pause-button
445 http://blogs.discovermagazine.com/imageo/2018/03/12/what-science-says-about-role-of-CO2-in-climate-change/#.XK6I5phKg2w

446 https://arxiv.org/pdf/1403.5728.pdf
447 The next Grand Solar Minimum, Cosmic Rays and Earth https://abruptearthchanges.com/2018/01/14/climate-change-grand-solar-minimum-and-cosmic-rays/
448 Implications of the Current Anamalous Sunspot Minimum for .... https://www.youtube.com/watch?v=13a0vfzLW9Y
449 https://arxiv.org/pdf/1403.5728.pdf
450 On the relationship between cosmic rays, solar activity https://arxiv.org/pdf/1403.5728.pdf
451 Astrophysicists link volcanic eruptions and Grand Solar .... https://www.xyz.net.au/astrophysicists-link-volcanic-eruptions-grand-solar-minimum/
452 THE HOCKEY SCHTICK: Cosmic Rays "Off the Chart". https://hockeyschtick.blogspot.com/2010/01/cosmic-rays-off-chart.html
453 https://www.pinterest.com/pin/320529698462697224/
454 https://andthentheresphysics.wordpress.com/
455 https://ak4.picdn.net/shutterstock/videos/11095424/thumb/1.jpg
456 Many Americans Say Made-Up News Is a Critical Problem That https://www.journalism.org/2019/06/05/many-americans-say-made-up-news-is-a-critical-problem-that-needs-to-be-fixed/
457 THE HOCKEY SCHTICK: Cosmic Rays "Off the Chart". https://hockeyschtick.blogspot.com/2010/01/cosmic-rays-off-chart.html

458 Top 10 Climate Change Predictions Gone Spectacularly Wrong.Top 10 Climate Change Predictions Gone Wrong. https://thefederalistpapers.org/us/top-10-climate-change-predictions-gone-spectacularly-wrong. By Analytical Economist. Published January 16, 2016 at 10:50am
459 https://www.thenewamerican.com/tech/environment/item/30214-nasa-sees-climate-cooling-trend-thanks-to-low-sun-activity
460 https://www.readingeagle.com/voices/article/nasa-says-air-pollution-getting-better
461 https://www.thenewamerican.com/tech/environment/item/30214-nasa-sees-climate-cooling-trend-thanks-to-low-sun-activity
462 NASA reporting polar ice growing. https://video.search.yahoo.com/search/video;_ylt=AwrJ7JcL5.ZdIPwA5BNXNyoA;_ylu=X3oDMTByMDgyYjJiBGNvbG8DYmYxBHBvcwMyBHZ0aWQDBHNlYwNzYw--?p=nasa+says+polar+ice+growing&fr=mcafee
463 http://www.minerva.unito.it/E/Climate/CopenhagenCartoons.htm
464 25 Famous Predictions That Were Proven To Be Horribly Wrong. https://list25.com/25-famous-predictions-that-were-proven-to-be-horribly-wrong/
465 Climate Alarmists Have Been Wrong About Virtually Everything. https://www.thenewamerican.com/tech/environment/item/22289-climate-alarmists-have-been-wrong-about-virtually-everything
466 https://climatecrocks.com/2014/01/13/newsweek-science-writer-looks-back-on-infamous-1975-ice-age-piece/

Made in the USA
Columbia, SC
30 April 2020

95230236R00236